Raising the White Flag

CIVIL WAR AMERICA

Peter S. Carmichael, Caroline E. Janney,
and Aaron Sheehan-Dean, editors

This landmark series interprets broadly the history and culture
of the Civil War era through the long nineteenth century and
beyond. Drawing on diverse approaches and methods, the
series publishes historical works that explore all aspects of
the war, biographies of leading commanders, and tactical and
campaign studies, along with select editions of primary sources.
Together, these books shed new light on an era that remains
central to our understanding of American and world history.

Raising the White Flag

How Surrender Defined the American Civil War

DAVID SILKENAT

THE UNIVERSITY OF NORTH CAROLINA PRESS

Chapel Hill

Designed by Jamison Cockerham
Set in Arno, Dead Mans Hand, Cutright, IM Fell English, and Scala Sans
by codeMantra, Inc.

The University of North Carolina Press has been a member
of the Green Press Initiative since 2003.

Cover and pp. i, iii, and ix: Julian Scott, *Surrender of a Confederate Soldier*, 1873, oil
on canvas, Smithsonian American Art Museum, Gift of Mrs. Nan Altmayer, 2012.23.
Image courtesy of Smithsonian American Art Museum/Wikimedia Commons

LIBRARY OF CONGRESS CATALOGING-IN-PUBLICATION DATA
Names: Silkenat, David, author.
Title: Raising the white flag : how surrender defined the
American Civil War / by David Silkenat.
Other titles: Civil War America (Series)
Description: Chapel Hill : University of North Carolina Press, [2019] | Series:
Civil War America | Includes bibliographical references and index.
Identifiers: LCCN 2018031110 | ISBN 9781469649726 (cloth : alk. paper) |
ISBN 9781469672519 (pbk : alk. paper) | ISBN 9781469649733 (ebook)
Subjects: LCSH: United States—History—Civil War, 1861–1865. | Capitulations,
Military—United States—History—19th century. | Capitulations, Military—
Confederate States of America—History. | Capitulations, Military—Social aspects.
Classification: LCC E468.9 .S56 2019 | DDC 973.7—dc23 LC
record available at https://lccn.loc.gov/2018031110

Contents

Illustrations

Raising the White Flag

FIGURE 1. Currier & Ives, "Surrender of General Lee at Appomattox, C.H. Va. April 9th 1865" (Library of Congress, Prints & Photographs Division, LC-DIG-pga-09914)

INTRODUCTION

Shortly after Confederate general Robert E. Lee's surrender to Union general Ulysses S. Grant at Appomattox Courthouse, Virginia, New York printmakers Currier & Ives produced one of the first artistic representations of the scene. Issuing the lithograph in several different versions, in both color and black and white, Currier & Ives depicted the event as many would have envisioned it: the two men alone, seated across the table from each other, Lee writing the terms of the surrender, his sword resting between them on the table, while Grant waits for Lee to finish, his hand outstretched. Unfortunately, the illustrators got nearly everything in their depiction wrong. Lee and Grant sat at separate tables, and the décor bears little resemblance to that in the McLean parlor, which, unlike the image, did not feature olive branch wallpaper. Lee had an aide with him, while Grant had more than a dozen members of his staff present. Grant wrote the original terms of surrender, to which Lee only made minor modifications.[1]

Despite the image's gross inaccuracies, it captured something of surrender's paradoxical nature. The two men appear as equals in the picture, mirroring each other at the table. Yet it was their radical inequality that prompted the meeting at Appomattox Courthouse. Lee's army was surrounded, broken, and outnumbered. His men, some of whom had not eaten in days, could barely march. The image demonstrates none of these inequalities; indeed, if one did not know which man was the victor and which the vanquished, it would be impossible to tell from the image. In this respect, the Currier & Ives lithograph found itself in good company. Artistic depictions of Civil War surrender, those made both during and after the conflict, often created a visual equivalency between those surrendering and those accepting the surrender. They relied on the viewer to provide the subtext.

Surrenders present anomalous moments in times of war, a hiatus from bloodshed and death in favor of negotiation and compromise. They require both warring parties to consider alternatives to fighting and to recognize the humanity in their enemy. They require warring generals to sit across a table from each other, manifesting a kind of interpersonal equality at the exact moment when their armies occupy decidedly unequal positions. In surrenders, the disorder and chaos of the battlefield transform into careful and deliberative conversations that will bring an end to the carnage. They require a cautious and at times paradoxical negotiation between enemies. A combatant may be forced to surrender, but to do so, his surrender must also be accepted: both parties need to consent for a surrender to take place. Unlike war, which only requires an aggressor to begin, surrender must have both the victor and the defeated agree not to fight.[2]

The American Civil War began with a surrender and ended with a series of surrenders, most famously at Appomattox Courthouse in Virginia, but also at Bennett Place, North Carolina, at Citronelle, Alabama, and at Jacksonport, Arkansas, among other sites. Between Fort Sumter and Appomattox Courthouse, both Union and Confederate forces surrendered on dozens of occasions. Some of these surrenders are well known: Fort Donelson, Harpers Ferry, and Vicksburg among them. Many others, such as the Union surrender at San Augustin Springs in the New Mexico Territory in 1861 or the Confederate surrender on Roanoke Island in 1862, linger in relative obscurity. In the largest of these surrenders, soldiers numbering in the thousands laid down their arms. While the surrender of entire armies, such as at Vicksburg or Appomattox Courthouse, presented surrender in its most formal scale, in nearly every Civil War battle, soldiers found themselves in a position where choosing not to fight appeared to be their only option. At its smallest scale, individual soldiers, often because of injury or surprise, often surrendered. In between these extremes, Civil War soldiers surrendered at every level of military organization.

One of every four Civil War soldiers surrendered at some point during the conflict, making it one of the most common military experiences. Although the statistics are woefully incomplete, more than 673,000 soldiers surrendered during the American Civil War, including at least 211,000 Union and 462,000 Confederate soldiers. Formal surrenders, such as Vicksburg, Appomattox Courthouse, or Bennett Place, account for approximately half of this figure. Battlefield surrenders, when individual soldiers threw down their weapons and raised their hands in surrender, make up the remainder. To put these figures in context, the number of soldiers who surrendered during the Civil War is approximately equal to the number of soldiers killed. If death shaped the Civil War, so too did surrender.[3]

In no other American war did surrender happen so frequently. Indeed, surrender's ubiquity during the Civil War seems at odds with a national sensibility that abhors surrender. In recent history, Americans of a variety of backgrounds repudiated surrender, labeling it as un-American. During the Cuban Missile Crisis in October 1962, President John F. Kennedy addressed the nation on live television, declaring, "The cost of freedom is always high, but Americans have always paid it. And one path we shall never choose, and that is the path of surrender, or submission." Nearly every major (and minor) American political figure since has reiterated this sentiment, including Richard Nixon, Ronald Reagan, George W. Bush, and Barack Obama. At the 2004 Republican National Convention John McCain told a cheering audience, "We're Americans, and we'll never surrender." One would be hard pressed to find a clearer distillation of and mantra for contemporary American identity, one that not only shapes our military and political life but also permeates our culture. In movies, video games, and music lyrics, the heroic figure is the one who fights against overwhelming odds. As Bruce Springsteen noted, "No retreat, baby, no surrender."[4]

Against this background, the Civil War presents a startling contrast. Americans, Northerners and Southerners alike, frequently surrendered, usually without stigma. Indeed, Maj. Robert Anderson became a celebrated national hero for his surrender at Fort Sumter, and Robert E. Lee's stature only grew after Appomattox Courthouse. This book seeks to make sense of the anomalous place of surrender during the Civil War and to understand how Americans during the Civil War era understood surrender. It argues that American ideas about surrender at the beginning of the Civil War grew out of inherited notions that surrender helped to distinguish civilized warfare from barbarism. Although one could honorably surrender, dishonor and humiliation always loomed in the periphery and could be avoided only through carefully evaluating whom one surrendered to and whom one allowed to surrender and under what conditions. This initial conception of surrender, present at the time of Fort Sumter, evolved over the course of the Civil War. Demands for "unconditional" surrender, the enlistment of black men into the Union Army, the proliferation of guerilla warfare, and what some historians have termed "hard" warfare all challenged the meaning of surrender in the minds of soldiers, civilians, and politicians. In the final phase of the war, when Confederate defeat became inevitable, surrender became the route to peace, albeit a difficult and perilous one. In the 150 years since the war's end, Southerners and Northerners alike have struggled about how best to remember and commemorate surrenders. Unlike battlefields, where coherent patterns of commemoration decorated the landscape, surrender sites have demonstrated the difficulties Americans have had in making sense of surrender.

A few caveats: First, I do not intend this book to be an exhaustive treatment of every surrender during the Civil War. Upon embarking on this project, I quickly realized that surrender's ubiquity made an encyclopedic approach unfeasible. Instead, I seek to explain how Civil War era Americans understood surrender and how their attitudes evolved over the course of the conflict. Second, in an effort to create reasonable bounds for this project and retain some thematic continuity, I have chosen not to examine the surrender of civilians or the surrender of cities, such as New Orleans, Savannah, Charleston, or Raleigh, by civilian authorities. I have also, for the most part, neglected the issue of surrender at sea, as the dynamics of naval warfare introduce a range of complex issues not present in surrenders on land. These are important topics that I hope other historians will tackle. Third, while the names, dates, and places in this book situate it as a work of military history, much of my approach in writing it draws on social and cultural history. I have made no effort to second-guess any soldier's or general's decision to surrender. Instead, I have been much more interested in how he came to that decision and how the broader community made sense of it. Looking at the Civil War from the perspective of men who surrendered opens new vistas onto familiar topics, providing fresh insights into such diverse issues as the plight of prisoners of war, Confederate guerillas, Southern Unionists, and African American soldiers; the culture of honor; the experience of combat; and the laws of war. These connections reveal that surrender profoundly shaped both the character and the outcome of the Civil War.

1

TREATED WITH THE GREATEST CIVILITY

Winfield Scott, Robert Anderson, and the Path to Fort Sumter

On the eve of the Civil War, no American understood surrender as deeply as Gen. Winfield Scott. Nearly seventy-five years old at the time of Abraham Lincoln's inauguration, Scott had served under every president since Thomas Jefferson, rising in rank to the commanding general of the U.S. Army, a post he held for nearly twenty years. In his youth, he had struck a formidable figure on horseback. At six feet, five inches tall, Scott towered over most of his contemporaries. His attention to military discipline and his fondness for ornate dress uniforms had earned him the sobriquet of "Old Fuss and Feathers." Born in Dinwiddie County, Virginia, in 1786, only a few years after Charles Cornwallis's surrender to Washington at Yorktown, Scott had grown up listening to stories about the Revolution. From an early age, he modeled himself on Washington, whom he lauded for his "calm dignity, wise statesmanship, and moral weight of character."[1] As a young man, Scott read Parson Weems's and David Ramsay's biographies of Washington, which praised his "generous and noble" treatment of the surrendered British. Both biographers included illustrations of General Cornwallis proffering his sword in surrender, although neither volume depicts the scene accurately. Both illustrations suggest that Cornwallis himself rather than a subordinate handed over the sword (in reality Cornwallis missed the ceremony, claiming illness), while the Weems volume incorrectly has Washington rather than Gen. Benjamin Lincoln accepting it. For Scott, these sanitized and patriotic images of Yorktown represented surrender as it ought to be: organized, civilized, and humane.[2]

Many Americans of Scott's generation shared this interpretation of what surrender should look like. It was this version of Yorktown that John Trumbull highlighted in his painting *The Surrender of Lord Cornwallis*. Commissioned by President James Madison as part of a series of four to hang in the Capitol rotunda, the painting depicted the orderly surrender of British troops to American and French forces. Immediately adjacent to it stood Trumbull's painting of the other great Revolutionary War surrender, *The Surrender of General Burgoyne*, after the Battle of Saratoga. Both paintings reflected a civilized ideal in which the victors magnanimously and graciously accepts their foe's surrender, requiring neither submission nor humiliation.[3] Congressmen who later shaped the course of the Civil War would have passed these enormous images daily.

Whatever romantic ideas Winfield Scott had about surrender probably vanished early in his military career. After a brief service in a Petersburg cavalry company after the *Leopard-Chesapeake* affair in 1807, the following year Scott received a commission to captain a light artillery company and was rapidly promoted at the onset of the War of 1812. For Scott and many of his contemporaries, the disastrous attempt to invade Canada at the war's commencement demonstrated the need to reform the nation's military, including how it addressed surrender. Scott recoiled in horror at Gen. William Hull's surrender of Detroit in August 1812. Hull, an aged Revolutionary War veteran, surrendered his force of some 2,000 soldiers to British general Isaac Brock without firing a shot. Brock had artfully deceived Hull into thinking that he had a much larger force under his command, ordering his troops to light individual rather than communal campfires. His Native American ally Tecumseh added to the deception by marching his men repeatedly through an opening in the woods near Fort Detroit. Brock's letter to Hull demanding his surrender not only played up Brock's illusory numerical superiority but also contrasted his civilized offer of surrender with the threat of a massacre at the hands of Native Americans: "The force at my disposal authorizes me to require of you the immediate surrender of Fort Detroit. It is far from my intention to join in a war of extermination, but you must be aware, that the numerous body of Indians who have attached themselves to my troops, will be beyond control the moment the contest commences." In the aftermath of the surrender, General Hull was court-martialed for treason and "cowardice at and in the neighborhood of Detroit," found guilty, and sentenced to death. Although President Madison commuted his sentence in consideration of "Hull's revolutionary services and his advanced age," Hull's surrender received widespread condemnation. Winfield Scott observed that "the disgrace of Hull's recent surrender was deeply felt by all Americans."[4]

In Scott's retelling of events, the dishonor of Hull's surrender pushed American forces, Scott's included, to attack at Queenstown Heights. Crossing the swiftly flowing Niagara River before daybreak to assault the elevated British position, the American soldiers, a combination of local militia and newly recruited regulars, came under heavy fire. Many of them retreated back across the river, leaving their compatriots stranded on the Canadian side. Although an initial assault on the heights resulted in the taking of a British redoubt, reinforcements under General Brock, the victor at Detroit, turned the tide of the battle in favor of the British. Taking command when higher-ranking officers had become wounded, killed, or incapacitated, Lt. Col. Winfield Scott found himself pinned down by British regulars, Canadian militia, and Mohawk and Delaware Indians. A nineteenth-century biographer described Scott's demeanor when he found himself outnumbered in enemy territory: "Scott took his position on the ground they then occupied, resolved to abide the shock, and think of surrender only when battle was impossible." He attempted to rally his soldiers by comparing their bravery to Hull's dishonorable and cowardly surrender. "He mounted a log in front of his much-diminished band: 'The enemy's balls,' said he, 'begin to thin our ranks. His numbers are overwhelming. In a moment the shock must come, and there is no retreat. We are in the beginning of a national war. Hull's surrender is to be redeemed. Let us then die, arms in hand. Our country demands the sacrifice. The example will not be lost. The blood of the slain will make heroes of the living. Those who follow will avenge our fall and their country's wrongs. Who dare to stand?' 'All!' was the answering cry."[5] Despite his bold words, Scott himself later reflected that their position was untenable and the battle unwinnable. "A surrender was inevitable," he wrote. "There was no time to lose." Scott personally carried the white flag of truce to the British commander to surrender himself and his soldiers. Unlike the dishonorable surrender of General Hull, Scott claimed his own "surrender was made on terms honorable to all parties."

Scott's decision to surrender was shaped in part by his desire not to be at the mercy of Mohawk Indians. Scott, like most of his contemporaries, believed that Native Americans did not abide by the rules of civilized warfare that bound American and British soldiers. In his memoir, Scott described the Mohawks as "savages, who were under but little control" by British officers. Before volunteering himself to offer surrender, Scott had sent two soldiers bearing a "flag of truce," but neither had made it to the British commander, failures Scott implied resulted from the Mohawks' refusal to respect the flag of truce. Scott decided to surrender in person in part because he believed that since he was "uncommonly tall and in a splendid uniform, it was thought his chance of being respected by the savages" would be better than that of other soldiers.

Apparently, the Mohawks were less than impressed by Scott's regal bearing, as the surrender party was fired on, only to be rescued by British soldiers.[6]

After surrendering, Scott and his men spent five weeks as prisoners of war. Scott praised his captors for their humanity and hospitality, noting that "the Queenstown prisoners experienced much courtesy from other British commanders." Although generally well treated by his captors, Scott believed that in several episodes, the British did not respect the rights due to prisoners of war. After the surrender, Scott and his men were imprisoned in an inn at Newark, where they were confronted by two Mohawks who desired to "to see *the tall American*." Ostensibly, they had come to see if either of them had managed to shoot Scott, whose height and uniform made him immediately recognizable. Alone with Scott, the two Mohawks began their inspection; one of them "seized the prisoner rudely by the arm and attempted to turn him round to examine his back." When Scott threw his attacker against the wall, the two Mohawks grabbed their "knives and hatchets," exclaiming, "We kill you now!" Scott briefly stood off against his assailants until British soldiers, attracted by the commotion, intervened.

Scott again questioned the British commitment to the fair treatment of prisoners of war near the end of his captivity shortly before his parole. Relocated to Quebec, while Scott and his men prepared to be repatriated to Boston, the British commander ordered his soldiers "to retain, as traitors, every prisoner, who, judging by speech or other evidence, might appear to have been born a British subject." Hearing "a commotion on deck," Scott hurried up to find that twenty of his soldiers had been thus identified for trial by the British. Enraged, Scott confronted the British commissioners, telling the identified soldiers that "the United States' Government would not fail to look to their safety, and in case of their punishment, as was threatened, to retaliate amply." Upon his return to Washington, Scott filed a complaint with the War Department on behalf of the "American prisoners of war surrendered at Queenstown," which prompted Congress to pass retaliatory legislation. In both episodes, Scott believed that in surrendering and becoming a prisoner of war, a soldier ought to have the expectation of fair treatment by his captors. Civilized, modern warfare demanded nothing less.[7]

Although Winfield Scott emerged from the War of 1812 as a national hero, he never forgot his experience surrendering at Queenstown Heights and as a prisoner of war. In the summer of 1815, Scott traveled to Europe, eager to witness Napoleonic armies firsthand. He hoped that he would be able to observe how "extensive armies" performed on the battlefield. Unfortunately for Scott, he arrived in Britain shortly after Napoleon's defeat at Waterloo. He spent more

Scott, Anderson, and the Path to Fort Sumter

than a month in the chaos of postwar France, where he met with both French and Coalition military officers and translated a couple of Napoleon's military manuals into English.[8] Upon his return, Scott received a commission to revise army regulations to bring them into line with modern military thought. He completed his task in 1821, and Scott's *General Regulations for the Army* incorporated his ideas about the proper place of surrender in civilized warfare.[9] Authorized by Congress and Secretary of War John C. Calhoun, the *General Regulations* reflected both the received wisdom of how war ought to be fought, building on European theorists such as Emer de Vattel, and Scott's experience on the battlefield. As historian John Marszalek has noted, Scott's reading and experience "told him that war should be reasonable, [and] that it should be waged according to civilized rules."[10] Regarding prisoners of war, Scott's dictate was clear: "Prisoners taken from the enemy, from the moment that they yield themselves, and as long as they obey the necessary orders given them, are under the safeguard of the national faith and honour. They will be treated at all times with every indulgence not inconsistent with their safe-keeping, and with good order among them." Scott's code directed that the U.S. Army treat prisoners of war with respect, even if the enemy did not, noting that "it is expected that the American army will always be slow to retaliate on the unarmed, acts of rigour or cruelty committed by the enemy, in the charitable hope of recalling the latter to a sense of justice and humanity by a magnanimous forbearance." Wounded prisoners were to be treated identically to American soldiers. A similar magnanimous spirit extended to soldiers participating in truce negotiations, with Scott requiring that they be "treated with the greatest civility by all persons belonging to the army." Intriguingly, Scott did not specify any particular protocols for surrender, and indeed the word "surrender" does not appear anywhere in 355 pages of regulations. Its absence is striking, given the specificity elsewhere in the code, which included, among other topics, detailed recipes and procedures for polishing uniform leather, down to the preferred kind of wax to be used and approved alternatives if necessity compelled. Officers and soldiers, who would have relied on the code for all manner of minutiae about proper behavior and procedure, would have been left in the dark about when, if ever, it was appropriate to surrender and how surrenders ought to be conducted.[11]

The absence of "surrender" in Scott's *General Regulations* reflected an antipathy within the army toward openly discussing surrender. Nowhere was this more true than at the U.S. Military Academy at West Point. Established in 1802, West Point modeled its curriculum on the French École Polytechnique, stressing professionalism (verging at times on elitism), engineering, and honor.

Very little of what cadets learned at West Point touched on strategic questions, including the propriety and mechanics of surrender. With a curriculum overwhelmingly devoted to mathematics and engineering, cadets received only eight class periods of instruction devoted to military strategy during their final semester. Although cadets learned very little that would have prepared them for the strategic reality of surrender, West Point's culture inculcated a certain formality in its students that would later manifest itself in the larger Civil War surrender ceremonies. West Point's most influential instructor, Dennis Hart Mahan, believed that that the institution's primary objective was to "rear soldiers worthy of the Republic." For the hundreds of cadets who passed through his classroom in the decades prior to the Civil War, Mahan's insistence that an officer's dignity and honor reflected upon the national virtue left a lasting impression. Like Winfield Scott, Mahan believed that war ought to be fought according to civilized and orderly principles; modern war was the antithesis of barbarism. Feared and respected by his students (Sherman had nightmares about arriving in his class unprepared), Mahan's lessons shaped not only the tactics employed on the battlefield but also how soldiers conducted themselves during a surrender.[12]

Although Army officers did not train in the art of surrender, they recognized its power as a tool of war, especially against Native Americans, whose relationship with surrender reflected the connection between surrender and civilized war. Thomas Jefferson argued that since Native Americans gave no quarter, they should be offered none. In the Declaration of Independence, Jefferson noted that the only "known rule" of war among the "merciless Indian savages" was "an undistinguished destruction of all ages, sexes and condition." Following contemporary European thought, Jefferson concluded that since Native Americans stood outside the recognized community of civilized nations, there was no moral or legal obligation to allow them to surrender.[13] Yet, while under no obligation to accept Native Americans' surrender, American military leaders believed that they could use surrender to pacify hostile Native Americans. In the Indian Wars that followed the War of 1812, the army adopted an unofficial policy that favored inducing recalcitrant Native Americans to surrender rather than continue to fight. Seen within the context of the humanitarian ethos of Indian removal, forcing Native Americans to surrender became part of the "civilizing" process. Surrendering demonstrated simultaneously their submission to the Federal power and their acceptance of American cultural hegemony. For Andrew Jackson, surrendering demonstrated their

Scott, Anderson, and the Path to Fort Sumter

intent to "cast off their savage habits and become an interesting, civilized, and Christian community."[14] Surrender had the potential to convert Native Americans from enemies into obedient subjects. Surrender's transformative power manifested itself most clearly in the reinvention of Sauk leader Black Hawk, who had built a Native coalition in the Old Northwest, including Sauk, Fox, Kickapoo, Potawatomi, and Ho-Chunk, committed to remaining in their traditional homeland. In May 1832, after local militia and an initial foray by the Regular Army had failed to successfully engage Black Hawk, President Jackson ordered Gen. Winfield Scott to lead an overwhelming expedition. Before Scott and his men arrived, however, Black Hawk's forces were overwhelmed in a series of battles, culminating in a disastrous defeat at the Battle of Bad Axe. Shortly thereafter, on August 27, 1832, Black Hawk surrendered to American forces at Prairie du Chien, Wisconsin. In a widely reprinted surrender speech, Black Hawk lamented, "I am much grieved, for I expected, if I did not defeat you, to hold out much longer, and give you more trouble before I surrendered." Expressing virtues that would have endeared him to American audiences, Black Hawk claimed that his surrender did not undermine his manhood or honor, arguing that as a prisoner, "he can stand torture, and is not afraid of death. He is no coward."[15]

Black Hawk's surrender almost immediately transformed him in the eyes of white Americans from a hated and feared enemy to the heroic embodiment of the noble savage. Taken into captivity by Col. Zachary Taylor, Black Hawk was escorted to Jefferson Barracks near St. Louis by Lts. Jefferson Davis and Robert Anderson. Under orders from President Andrew Jackson, Black Hawk was brought east, where he was greeted by large crowds eager to see the captive Indian. In 1833, released after a brief imprisonment and only a year after his surrender, Black Hawk published (with the aid of a translator) his autobiography and toured New York, Baltimore, and Philadelphia.[16]

Although Black Hawk's surrender indicated that Native Americans could surrender honorably (at least in the eyes of the white adversaries), many army officers concluded that Native Americans could not be trusted to abide by the terms of surrender. During the Second Seminole War (1835–42), Winfield Scott complained that the rules of civilized warfare did not seem to apply in Florida, where the swamps and Native Americans' guerilla tactics seemed the antithesis of the Napoleonic warfare he admired. In March 1837, Gen. Thomas Jesup signed an agreement with Seminole leaders in which they agreed to surrender and to be removed to Indian Territory. Not all Seminoles, however, agreed that the leaders who signed the "Capitulation" had the authority to surrender their land or compel others to emigrate. On June 2, 1837, two Seminoles who rejected the surrender agreement, Osceola and Sam Jones (also known as Abiaca), led 200 men on a nighttime raid to liberate 700 Seminoles in a detention camp where they were awaiting removal. Although both Osceola and Sam Jones would have challenged this interpretation, Jesup concluded that the Seminoles had violated the terms of the surrender and therefore could not be trusted to abide by the laws of war. Later that year, Jesup seized Osceola under a flag of truce near St. Augustine, in clear violation of long-established military protocols. Holding Osceola as a prisoner until his death, Jesup defended his action by drawing upon two contradictory arguments. First, he claimed that since Native Americans did not fight according to the rules of civilized warfare, he was under no obligation to respect a flag of truce. Second, he argued that the March "Capitulation" was still in effect and that Osceola's use of the white flag signaled his intention to surrender. Although Jesup was roundly criticized in the press for his conduct in Osceola's capture, many white Americans shared his belief that the civilized rules of warfare, including the tenets of surrender, did not extend to nonwhites.[17]

The belief that nonwhites could not be trusted in surrender included Mexicans. During the Texas War of Independence, questions over the ethics of surrender shaped three of its defining events: the Battle of the Alamo, the Goliad massacre, and the Battle of San Jacinto. An 1835 Mexican congressional degree labeled the Texan revolutionaries as pirates liable to execution, a measure that Texians (white American settlers in Texas) believed signaled President Santa Anna's intention to not fight according to the laws of civilized warfare. Shortly after laying siege to the former Catholic mission of the Alamo, Santa Anna demanded its immediate and unconditional surrender. Commanding a force ten times larger than the Alamo's garrison, Santa Anna knew that, barring reinforcements, his victory was only a matter of time. After receiving Santa Anna's ultimatum, Col. William Barret Travis, the fort's commander, wrote a public letter asking for reinforcements. "The enemy has demanded a surrender at discretion, otherwise, the garrison are to be put to the sword." Unwilling to comply, Travis implored readers "in the name of Liberty, of patriotism & everything dear to the American character, to come to our aid," as "I shall never surrender or retreat." Travis signaled his refusal of Santa Anna's demand by firing a cannon at the Mexican troops. Just prior to Santa Anna's final assault on the Alamo on March 6, 1836, Travis attempted to rally his garrison, telling a group of Tejanos, *"¡No rendirse, muchachos!"* ("Don't surrender, boys!"). When the fighting became desperate, many of the Alamo's defenders attempted to surrender, waving white kerchiefs or socks as makeshift flags, only to be massacred by Mexican soldiers. A half-dozen Texians did manage to surrender to Santa Anna's men (including Davy Crockett, in some accounts), only to be summarily executed.[18]

Less than a month later, on March 26, 1836, Mexican soldiers under orders from Santa Anna executed more than 400 captive Texian soldiers at Goliad who had surrendered believing that they would be repatriated to the United States. The defeat at the Alamo and the Goliad massacre galvanized the revolutionary movement, prompting Texas president Sam Houston to launch an attack on Santa Anna's army. At the Battle of San Jacinto on April 21, 1836, Texian soldiers under Sam Houston decisively routed Santa Anna's men, with "Remember the Alamo!" and "Remember Goliad!" as their rallying cries. Many Texian soldiers believed that properly remembering the Alamo and Goliad required not only defeating Santa Anna's men but also denying them the opportunity to surrender. Texian descriptions of San Jacinto described it not as a battle but as a massacre. "It was nothing but a slaughter," noted one. Texians shot or clubbed many surrendering Mexican soldiers, including those who were wounded. Moses Bryan, Stephen Austin's nephew, described the battlefield as "the most awful slaughter I ever saw."[19]

The belief that Mexicans would not fight according to the rules of civilized warfare continued during the Mexican War. Although both Mexicans and Americans accused the enemy of atrocities, the pervasive racism of American soldiers dictated that Mexicans could not be trusted to abide by the unwritten laws of war. One Ohio soldier described Mexicans as "a treacherous race," noting that his fellow soldiers "are in favor of prosecuting the war . . . upon different principles, and plunder, and ravage, and give them a taste of war in all its horrors, and see if that will bring them to a sense of their folly in contending with the United States."[20] Therefore, while Americans sought to make Mexicans surrender, thereby demonstrating American superiority, they were loath to submit to Mexican demands to surrender. At Monterrey, the conflict's first major battle, Gen. Zachary Taylor compelled the Mexican forces to surrender on September 24, 1846, after three intense days of urban combat. Although Taylor received criticism for the lenient terms he offered to the surrendering Mexican garrison, allowing them to evacuate the city and keep their weapons, many of his soldiers praised his magnanimity. Appointed by Taylor to negotiate the details of the surrender, Mississippi colonel and future Confederate president Jefferson Davis wrote to his brother that "they were whipped, and we could afford to be generous."[21]

Five months later, Taylor found himself on the other end of surrender negotiations. On February 22, 1847, Santa Anna demanded Taylor's surrender at Buena Vista, informing him that "you . . . cannot in any human probability avoid suffering a rout and being cut to pieces." Pledging to treat surrendered soldiers "with consideration belonging to the Mexican character," Santa Anna told Taylor that the offer of surrender provided the only option to "save you from a catastrophe." Outnumbered by a factor of four, Taylor responded with anger and outrage. "Tell him to go to hell," Taylor instructed an aide. The aide, translating his words into Spanish, moderated his tone, informing Santa Anna that he had received his offer "to surrender my forces at discretion" and that he would "decline acceding to your request." Through the artful use of artillery and a bold charge led by Col. Jefferson Davis, Taylor managed to transform a perilous situation at Buena Vista into one of the great American victories of the war.[22]

A month later at Veracruz, Gen. Winfield Scott hoped to pressure Mexican forces into surrendering and thereby avoid significant causalities. Landing more than 12,000 soldiers south of the city, Scott methodically encircled Veracruz, dragging artillery from warships across deep sand into position. On March 22, 1847, Scott issued an ultimatum to surrender, which the Mexican garrison, hoping for relief from Mexico City, refused. Scott probably expected them to refuse: the offer and decline were part of the civil ritual of a siege, and in Scott's words, "All sieges are much alike."[23] Firing 463,000 pounds of shot and shell over the next four days, Scott pounded the garrison into submission and its surrender on March 27, 1847. Although Scott received some criticism for the destruction that the bombardment produced, he argued that he had engaged in warfare in its most civilized form: he had only attacked after formally demanding that the Mexicans surrender, and in accepting their eventual surrender he produced a victory with comparatively few casualties on either side. Impressed with his own achievement, Scott noted in his *Memoirs* that "the economy of life, by means of head-work, ... was never more conspicuous than on this occasion." He had taken Mexico's "principal port of foreign commerce; five thousand prisoners, with a greater number of small arms; four hundred pieces of ordinance and large stores of ammunition" in only a few days with minimal casualties.[24] Although each of them would draw their own lessons about siege warfare and surrender from what they witnessed at Veracruz, Scott's command included many officers who would participate in significant surrenders during the Civil War, including Robert E. Lee, Pierre G. T. Beauregard, Ulysses S. Grant, Robert Anderson, and Thomas (not yet Stonewall) Jackson.

Antebellum Americans had a panoply of associations for surrender that extended beyond its military meanings. Evangelical preachers told the faithful that salvation depended on repentance and the unconditional surrender to God's will.[25] In the political realm, the idea of surrender was often negatively associated with compromise by those who disparaged political compromise as immoral. Once seen as the epitome of political skill (the Constitutional Compromise, the Missouri Compromise, the Compromise of 1850), the idea of compromise came increasingly under attack in the decades prior to the Civil War as political radicalization over slavery made compromise untenable.[26] Radical abolitionists rejected any compromise on the grounds that one could not compromise on moral questions. At its inaugural meeting in 1833, the American Anti-Slavery Society resolved to reject any form of compensated emancipation because "it would be a surrender of the great fundamental principle that man cannot hold property in man."[27] The declaration's primary author, William Lloyd Garrison, consistently rejected surrendering on any element in the national debate over slavery. In 1854 Garrison declared, "The abolitionism which I advocate is as absolute as the law of God, and as unyielding as his throne. It admits of no compromise." According to Garrison, the slave system was a product of compromise: "How has the slave system grown to its present enormous dimensions? Through compromise. How is it to be exterminated? Only by an uncompromising spirit."[28] Ralph Waldo Emerson affirmed this connection between antebellum political compromise on slavery and surrender in an April 1862 essay, noting, "We cannot but remember that there have been days in American history, when, if the Free States had done their duty, Slavery had been blocked by an immovable barrier, and our recent calamities forever precluded. The Free States yielded, and every compromise was surrender, and invited new demands."[29] For Emerson, as for Garrison, no good could come from compromising with a moral evil.

Slavery's defenders shared abolitionists' rejection of compromise. In a speech before the U.S. Senate in 1837 defending slavery as a "positive good," South Carolinian John C. Calhoun claimed, "We of the South will not, cannot, surrender our institutions."[30] Calhoun reiterated his vociferous objection to surrender through compromise during the debate over what was to become the Compromise of 1850. Too sick to deliver the words himself, Calhoun had his Senate colleague James M. Mason proclaim that the South "has no compromise to offer but the Constitution, and no concession or surrender to make. She has already surrendered so much that she has little left to surrender."[31] Slaveholders like Calhoun hated surrender in part because they saw it as a form of submission. A key component of the Southern ideology of mastery dictated that the relationship between slave owners and slaves rested upon the complete submission of the slave to his or her owner's will. An 1830 North

Carolina Supreme Court decision posited that "the power of the master must be absolute, to render the submission of the slave perfect."[32] For a white man to submit to another, metaphorically at least, made him into a slave.[33] Fire-eaters and Southern radicals therefore decried surrender, as they loathed any form of submission, because of their insistence on independence and mastery.

Surrender also had gendered connotations. Under the legal doctrine of coverture, an antebellum woman surrendered her property and legal identity to her husband, experiencing what one scholar has referred to as a "civil death." This gendered subordination was particularly pronounced in the South, where, as Stephanie McCurry and Peter Bardaglio have observed, the legal subordination of women in marriage was modeled on the subordination of slaves. Unlike slaves, however, Southern white women voluntarily surrendered to their husbands, a choice that symbolized their acceptance of Southern gendered and social paradigms. Based on these associations, surrendering became coded feminine, while accepting the surrender and submission of another adopted masculine connotations.[34]

On the eve of the Civil War, therefore, surrender held distinct and con- tradictory connotations. Within the military context, surrender represented a hallmark of modern civilized warfare, a tool that allowed combatants to avoid unnecessary bloodshed and that carried certain expectations about the treat- ment of prisoners. Within the political and cultural realms, however, surrender increasingly evoked connotations of weakness, subordination, dishonor, and cowardice. Surrender ought not only be avoided, but disdained. John Brown's 1859 raid on Harpers Ferry demonstrated the fatal intersection of the cultural and military conceptions of surrender. Although Brown was uncompromising in his hatred of slavery and militant in his commitment to its abolition, his raid ended not with his death, but with his surrender. Surrounded in the engine house first by local militia and then by U.S. Marines under the command of Col. Robert E. Lee, Brown steadfastly refused to surrender, although some of his men and the captives they held urged him to do so. After midnight on October 18, Lee drafted a message for the men inside the engine house, inform- ing them that "if they will peacefully surrender themselves . . . they shall be kept in safety to await the orders of the President." Lee pointed out that their position was surrounded and that an attack on the engine house would more than likely result in their deaths. "Knowing the character of the leader of the in- surgents," Lee noted afterward, "I did not expect it [the demand to surrender] would be accepted," but he felt obligated to try, hoping to secure the safe release of Brown's hostages. On the following morning, the third day of the raid, Lee

Scott, Anderson, and the Path to Fort Sumter

sent his aide and future cavalry commander J. E. B. Stuart under a flag of truce to deliver the message to Brown. Knowing that "he could expect no leniency," Brown refused, arguing that he "would sell his life as dearly as possible." After an initial attempt to penetrate the blockaded doors with sledgehammers failed, voices inside started to yell their desire to surrender, voices that included some of Brown's men and their hostages. It is unclear whether Lee and Stuart heard the "long and loud calls of 'surrender'" against the din; Brown later supposed that they did not. When the marines finally succeeded in gaining entrance, using a heavy ladder as a battering ram, they confronted fire from some of Brown's men, while others "cried for quarter and laid down their arms." Of those inside, Brown himself seemed the most committed to dying rather than surrendering, only submitting to unconsciousness when he was stabbed and beaten by one of the assaulting marines.

Badly wounded in the attack, Brown became a prisoner largely involuntarily. Yet, in his subsequent interrogations, Brown maintained that he had surrendered, although he asserted that he only "consented to surrender for the benefit of others, and not for my own benefit." Brown complained that the Virginians were not adhering to the unwritten laws of surrender, which dictated that prisoners should be unharmed. Brown claimed that his son Watson had been "murdered" under "a flag of truce" and that he himself received multiple bayonet wounds after his surrender. Brown's rejection of surrender prior to his capture and his embrace of its protections afterward reveal a central tension at the heart of Americans' attitudes toward surrender on the eve of the Civil War. Even John Brown, a man who had no desire to compromise with an immoral institution, who saw no hope within the political process, and who knew that surrender would undoubtedly result in his execution, believed that surrender entitled him and his men to certain protections and rights.[35]

Historians have recounted the story of the secession crisis many times. Its major events and themes present themselves like stations of the cross: Lincoln's election, the subsequent secession of South Carolina and other Lower South states that became the Confederacy, efforts to negotiate a peaceful resolution to the crisis, Lincoln's inauguration, the looming showdown at Fort Sumter, the eventual attack on and surrender of the fort, Lincoln's call for troops, and the secession of the Upper South.[36] Throughout the crisis, surrender, both as an idea and as a military phenomenon, played a significant role in how Americans made sense of the changing political landscape. Refusing to surrender became a mantra for political leaders on both sides of the conflict. However, the secession crisis culminated in one of the Civil War's most significant surrenders at Fort Sumter, a surrender that both sides ultimately wanted, orchestrated, and benefited from, and a surrender that created a template for the dozens of surrenders to come later. This contradiction between rhetorically rejecting surrender and embracing it (under certain conditions) on the battlefield reveals Americans' complex relationship with surrender on the eve of the country's greatest conflict.

The rhetorical aversion to surrender and compromise intensified during the secession crisis after Abraham Lincoln's election. In urging secession, fire-eaters decried any compromise with the incoming administration as a form of subservient surrender. By mid-November 1860, Senator Robert Toombs told the Georgia legislature that any compromise on slavery was tantamount to "surrender," claiming that "the day you do this base, unmanly deed, you embrace political degradation and death." Indeed, the idea that Georgia must refuse to surrender its political rights ran throughout Toombs's speech. "We are said to be a happy and prosperous people," Toombs informed them. "We have been, because we have hitherto maintained our ancient rights and liberties—we will be until we surrender them."[37]

Watching their Southern colleagues abandon Washington, the abolitionist wing of the Republican Party roundly rejected any concession to bring them back into the fold, equating compromise with a disgraceful surrender. Vermont senator Justin Morrill noted that he could see "no compromise short of an entire surrender of our convictions of right and wrong, and I do not propose to make that surrender." Massachusetts senator Henry Wilson condemned the proposed Crittenden Compromise (and indeed any compromise over slavery to forestall secession) as "a surrender" of the nation's most sacred values. Charles Francis Adams also rejected compromise, arguing that Southerners would be satisfied with "nothing short of a surrender of everything gained by the election," while Horace Greeley described it as "a wasted and absolute surrender of our sacred principles." Conversely, those Republicans who advocated compromise bracketed their position by claiming that it would not surrender the party's central tenets. New York journalist Thurlow Weed claimed that compromise would amount to "concession, not surrender."[38]

President-elect Abraham Lincoln joined the chorus of Republicans equating compromise with surrender. "We have just carried an election on principles fairly stated to the people," Lincoln wrote to a political confidant a month after his election. "Now we are told in advance, the government shall be broken up, unless we surrender to those we have beaten. . . . If we surrender, it is the end of us." Historians have traditionally criticized Lincoln's inaction as president-elect, although recent scholarship has done much to rehabilitate his conduct during the secession winter, recognizing that his behind-the-scenes machinations proved more effective and strategically aware than often assumed. In his correspondence and public address, President-elect Lincoln repeatedly drew upon the language of surrender to express his unwillingness to negotiate away his party's central tenets. In an early draft of his inaugural address, Lincoln argued that it would be a betrayal of the "bond of faith between public and public servant" for him to compromise on fundamental principles, thereby "surrendering to those who tried and failed to defeat him at the polls." No one, even his political opponents, would "tolerate his own candidate in such surrender" of fundamental principles, as "such surrender would not be merely the ruin of a man, or a party; but, as a precedent, would be the ruin of the government itself."[39]

The developing situation in Charleston dominated the final months of James Buchanan's and the first month of Lincoln's presidency. The birthplace of secession and home to the greatest concentration of fire-eaters in the South, Charleston hosted four Federal forts and an armory. Intended to be fully staffed only in times of invasion, the forts had a combined garrison of less than a full company of soldiers. At the time of Lincoln's election, Charleston's main garrison resided at Fort Moultrie, while the other three forts (Sumter, Johnson, and Castle Pinckney) remained either unmanned or hosting only a skeleton crew. The most impressive of the forts guarding Charleston, Sumter sat on a reinforced sandbar in the middle of the harbor. Although construction on Sumter had begun in 1829, the fort remained unfinished in 1861, with only half of its intended complement of cannons.

Less than two weeks after Lincoln's election, with rumors of secession rife in Washington, Maj. Robert Anderson was appointed to command the Federal garrison in Charleston. Selected for the post by Buchanan's secretary of war, John B. Floyd (who would soon resign to join the Confederacy), and Lt. Gen. Winfield Scott, the army's highest-ranking officer, Anderson drew upon a lifetime of experience when he assumed command in Charleston. The son of a Revolutionary soldier who had fought alongside George Washington and witnessed the surrender at Yorktown, Anderson grew up on a Kentucky plantation near Louisville.[40] After graduating from West Point in 1825, he fought in the Black Hawk, Seminole, and Mexican Wars. Despite, or maybe because of, his experience in combat, Anderson abhorred war, especially when war caused needless bloodshed. During his military career, he developed a particularly close relationship with Winfield Scott, serving on his staff for many years. In their correspondence, Anderson referred to Scott as "my best friend" and "my most kind friend"; when Anderson married, Scott gave away the bride. Although the two men could not be more dissimilar in appearance or in temperament—Scott's enormous height (and in later years girth) and ostentatious personality were counterbalanced by Anderson's slender, almost diminutive frame and quiet demeanor—they shared common values about the proper conduct of a military officer. Like Scott, Anderson believed that war ought to be fought by professionals according to well-proscribed rules. Nowhere was this more true than during the siege and eventual surrender of Vera Cruz, where Anderson fought under Scott. In letters to his wife, Anderson noted that Scott had artfully arranged artillery around the city, such that they "must soon compel the City to surrender." He noted approvingly that Scott only began his bombardment after his initial demand for surrender was refused and hoped that Vera Cruz's defenders would quickly realize "the inutility of longer delaying the surrender." He hoped "to see this war *civilized*, to witness interchange of civilities between the forces."[41]

In selecting Anderson, Floyd and Scott hoped to not add kindling to the fire. No one could challenge Anderson's expertise or professionalism. As an artillery officer, he had not only seen combat but had written the army's artillery manual and taught the subject at West Point for several years, instructing future Civil War generals William Tecumseh Sherman, Braxton Bragg, and (notably for his tenure in Charleston) P. G. T. Beauregard. Furthermore, he was by birth and inclination a Southerner, and his wife came from a prominent Georgia slaveholding family; so his appointment was unlikely to alienate the local populace, who would likely have balked had a Northerner been appointed.[42] Apolitical by choice and nature, Anderson had never dabbled in politics or even voted, holding that an army officer ought not become involved in partisan disputes. Although Anderson believed in the political right to own slaves and blamed the current political crisis on meddling Northerners, he compartmentalized these sentiments when it came to his professional life as a soldier.

Anderson visited his mentor's New York City officer prior to taking up his post in Charleston. Age had not looked kindly on Winfield Scott. The "Grand Old Man of the Army" suffered from rheumatism, gout, vertigo, and dropsy, which left him unable, as Scott latter admitted, "to mount a horse or walk more than a few paces at a time." A lifetime of indulgence had ballooned his weight to over 300 pounds. Although he still donned his ornate uniform, he now paired it with a large knit afghan and slippers, as shoes hurt his feet.

Scott, Anderson, and the Path to Fort Sumter

Scott could offer little meaningful guidance to his protégé. Although he held the highest-ranking post in the army, Scott had not been regularly consulted by either President Buchanan or Secretary of War Floyd. Scott and Anderson agreed that the situation in Charleston was perilous and that Anderson should proceed cautiously.[43]

Arriving in Charleston on November 21, Anderson quickly assessed Fort Moultrie's vulnerability. Located on a promontory of Sullivan's Island, Moultrie had protected the northern mouth of Charleston harbor since the Revolution. Anderson found the once proud fort had suffered a precipitous decline since his father had been stationed there eighty years earlier: its brick walls crumbled at the touch, and low walls had been buffeted by sand so that errant cattle could walk into the fort unhindered. Even if the sand were removed, Anderson could see that its undersized garrison—sixty-five men, not including an eight-man band—could not defend the fort from a landside attack. Moultrie's indefensibility only increased a month after Anderson's arrival, when on December 20, 1860, South Carolina seceded from the Union. By Christmas, thousands of young men, eager to demonstrate their martial spirit, had flocked to Charleston and formed militia companies, some of which had taken to patrolling outside Moultrie. According to Abner Doubleday, a New Yorker and abolitionist who was Moultrie's second-highest-ranking officer, the scuttlebutt around the city was that more than 2,000 riflemen had been detailed to occupy houses near Moultrie, where they could easily fire into the fort.[44] Recognizing Moultrie's inherent weakness, Anderson ordered the garrison to relocate from Moultrie to Sumter on December 26, 1860.

Anderson's clandestine removal of the garrison to Fort Sumter caused a firestorm of controversy in both Washington and Charleston. Dr. Samuel Wylie Crawford recorded in his diary that Charlestonians expressed "Great indignation at Maj. Anderson's course, called a traitor—hanging too good for him &c." Informed of the development by Mississippi senator Jefferson Davis, who had not yet resigned his post, President Buchanan was both surprised and horrified by the move, which he believed Anderson had undertaken without orders. When pressed by Secretary of War Floyd to justify his action, Anderson articulated a concise defense: he believed that an attack on Fort Moultrie was imminent, "that if attacked my men must have been sacrificed" as "the garrison would never have surrendered without a fight."[45]

Persuaded, albeit reluctantly, that Anderson acted within the confines of his mandate and alarmed by the provocative seizures of Fort Moultrie, Castle Pinckney, and the arsenal, Buchanan ordered reinforcements and supplies sent to Anderson at Fort Sumter. Leaving from New York shortly after the

New Year, the *Star of the West*, a hired civilian steamship, carried 200 soldiers, munitions, coal, and rations, enough to sustain Sumter for months. As it approached Charleston harbor on January 9, it came under fire from Citadel cadets manning a newly constructed battery on Morris Island and quickly returned to safe waters, as the men in Fort Sumter looked on. Although some of the garrison's officers, including Doubleday, thought they should respond to the provocation, Anderson decided on restraint. They should wait on further guidance from Washington before taking any action. To act hastily now would only invite an escalation that would lead to civil war. Anderson maintained his composure when newly elected South Carolina governor Francis Pickens subsequently demanded his immediate surrender of the fort. A unanimous vote of Anderson's officers rejected the demand, asserting their commitment *"not to surrender our trust."* In his reply letter, Anderson noted his "honor to acknowledge the receipt of your demand for surrender" but that "the demand is one [with] which I cannot comply." Anderson argued that ownership of the fort was a political question, not a military one. "I cannot do what belongs to the Government to do," Anderson claimed. "The demand must be made upon them." He asked the governor that "prior to the resort to arms," he be allowed to forward the demand to Washington for consultation.[46]

Pickens acquiesced to Anderson's request, brokering a de facto ceasefire until Anderson's delegate, an ailing Lt. Theodore Talbot, returned from Washington. This truce effectively provided cover to parties on all sides. Relieved that he did not face immediate attack and did not have to surrender his command, Anderson bought himself time to reinforce his position and await orders from Washington. Pickens could use the time to improve Charleston's batteries and train its enthusiastic but untutored crews, while referencing the truce when stalling those who called for an immediate attack on Sumter. Arguing that he could not respond to the demand without consulting Congress, Buchanan also saw an advantage in the de facto truce: if it lasted long enough, he would be out of office before a difficult decision had to be made.

Not everyone embraced the news that the Sumter crisis had been put on the back burner, allowed to simmer rather than boil over. On the day that the delegation from Sumter reached Washington, Jefferson Davis wrote a concerned letter to Governor Pickens. Although his home state of Mississippi had adopted an ordinance of secession on January 9, Davis had not yet received official confirmation and would not resign his Senate seat until January 21. Recovering from "a serious and sudden case of neuralgia," Davis wrote from his sickbed, imploring Pickens to fortify Charleston quickly. Like most in Washington, Davis had heard conflicting and incomplete reports about

Scott, Anderson, and the Path to Fort Sumter

developments in Charleston. What worried Davis was that the situation appeared to be evolving into a siege of Sumter that would result in the garrison's surrender due to starvation. Although such an outcome would produce the desired result—the fort in Southern hands—it would do so with a significant political cost. Davis warned Pickens that "to shut them up with a view to starve them into submission would create a sympathetic action much greater than any which could be obtained on the present issue." Davis correctly diagnosed that there were several routes to Sumter's surrender: voluntary capitulation, starvation, or bombardment. Of these, Davis preferred the first option, although he thought it unlikely. "The temper of Black Republicans," Davis told Pickens, "is not to give us our rights in the Union, or allow us to go peaceably out of it." Consequently, Davis noted, "we are probably soon to be involved in that fiercest of human strife, a civil war."[47]

In the weeks that followed, South Carolina and, later, Confederate officials fortified Charleston harbor to prevent further Federal resupply efforts and prepare for the eventual attack on Fort Sumter. A dozen new batteries were erected, their guns trained at Fort Sumter. Most distressing to the men inside was a battery on Cummings Point, only 1,600 yards away. Pointed directly at the point where the fort's walls were thinnest, its guns were protected by "strong timber, plated with railroad iron, and partially covered with sand." Viewing its construction with dismay, Abner Doubleday knew that "when finished" the battery would be "almost impregnable."[48] Equally concerning was the construction of a "floating battery," essentially an armed barge, which could be towed into position were the fort to be attacked. To prevent a Federal reinvestment of Sumter by deep-keeled naval vessels, Confederate officials sank hulks in the shipping channels. The establishment of the Confederacy in February 1861 brought some order to the haphazard but enthusiastic militarization of Charleston. Appointed by President Jefferson Davis as his country's first brigadier general, Pierre Gustave Toutant Beauregard took command of Confederate Charleston on March 3. A stellar student at West Point, graduating second in his class, Beauregard had developed a particularly close relationship with his artillery instructor, Robert Anderson. Both men subsequently served under Winfield Scott in the Mexican War, where Beauregard quickly developed a reputation for personal bravery and engineering genius. When he arrived in Charleston, Beauregard quickly set to recalibrating the city's batteries, drawing in no small measure from Robert Anderson's West Point lectures.[49]

As only a former pupil and teacher could, Beauregard and Anderson held each other in enormous mutual respect. Shortly after Beauregard's arrival, Anderson wrote to Washington that Beauregard's appointment "insures, I think, in a great measure the exercise of skill and sound judgment in all operations of the South Carolinians in this harbor." Beauregard demonstrated a similar deference to his former teacher, noting in a letter to the Confederate secretary of war in Montgomery that Anderson, "with whom I am personally well acquainted . . . is, in my opinion, a most gallant officer, incapable of any act that might tarnish his reputation as a soldier." As a sign of his respect and admiration, Beauregard sent a case of claret and several boxes of cigars to Fort Sumter, knowing Anderson's appetite and appreciation for both. Mindful of the inferences that might be drawn from such a gift, Anderson promptly returned them unopened but expressed his sincere thanks to Beauregard for the gesture. Only days before he gave the order to fire on Sumter, Beauregard was able to write that "nothing shall be wanting on my part to preserve the friendly relations and impressions which have existed between us for so many years."[50]

Despite their mutual admiration, both men knew that with each passing day, Beauregard's position became stronger and Anderson's became weaker. As Abner Doubleday frequently described it, Fort Sumter had become a prison. By the end of January, they had run out of fuel, followed by "sugar, soap, and candles." One officer noted that "the men could count on their fingers the number of days between them and starvation." Conflicting messages from Washington, sent through official and unofficial channels, offered little guidance. As far as Anderson could make sense of the cryptic instructions, the garrison was not to take any action that might be perceived as hostile or aggressive, but at the same time it should not surrender the fort without provocation.[51]

Sumter's garrison hoped that a change in administration would bring clarity to their situation. In his inaugural address, Lincoln pledged to "hold, occupy, and possess the property and places belonging to the government," a reference all listeners immediately knew referred to the island fort in Charleston harbor. No sooner had Lincoln taken the oath of office and pledged to "hold, occupy, and possess" Sumter than he received a letter from Anderson that the situation there was more dire than Lincoln knew. (According to Lincoln's recollections several months later, this letter was handed to him immediately after his inauguration, although it appears more likely that he received it the following morning.) Lincoln promptly forwarded Anderson's message to Winfield Scott, who informed Lincoln that the time for reinforcing Sumter had passed. Denouncing Buchanan's inaction, Scott claimed that the fort could have been successfully reinforced only weeks earlier, but that was no longer the case.

Scott, Anderson, and the Path to Fort Sumter

Mounting a proper relief expedition would take months to plan and execute, Scott informed Lincoln, by which time the fort would be either starved out or fired upon. "I now see no alternative but a surrender," Scott concluded.

The following day another letter arrived from Anderson providing more details about his situation: the garrison had just twenty-eight days' worth of provisions remaining, after which he would have no alternative but to surrender. In the days that followed, Lincoln received conflicting advice. Francis P. Blair Sr., patriarch of the Republican Party's founding family, rebuked the new president in the White House, saying, "The surrender of Fort Sumter, [is] virtually a surrender of the Union." Most Republicans, however, deferred to Scott's judgment that reinforcing Fort Sumter was untenable. With Secretary of State William Seward taking the lead, Lincoln's cabinet counseled a conciliatory stance toward "the disaffected States" that included evacuating Sumter. Many of them left a cabinet meeting on March 15 convinced they had made a decision to surrender the fort. Holding Lincoln in little regard, Scott assumed that the president would similarly accede to his experience and began drafting plans for Sumter's evacuation.[52]

Lincoln could not bring himself to order Sumter's evacuation. While he recognized that the fort had limited military value and effectively reinforcing the fort would prove practically impossible, Lincoln understood the tremendous symbolic power that the fort held. Surrendering the fort would undermine his political legitimacy while enhancing the legitimacy of the nascent Confederacy. Although some advisors counseled that abandoning Sumter might prevent the secession of the Upper South, Lincoln found this supposition unpersuasive. Furthermore, Lincoln understood that surrendering Fort Sumter would undermine his constitutional stance on secession. From the time of his election and throughout his presidency, Lincoln maintained that the federal union was perpetual and therefore states did not have a constitutional right to secede. As president-elect, Lincoln dismissed secession, claiming that "the right of a State to secede is not an open or debatable question," a sentiment he would reiterate in his inaugural address. If secession was unconstitutional, then the Confederacy was equally illegitimate. To this end, Lincoln went to great pains never to present the Confederacy as anything other than a lawless rebellion within the United States. He worried that surrendering Fort Sumter could be interpreted as the federal government recognizing and thereby legitimizing the Confederacy.[53]

Unwilling to surrender Sumter until all possible avenues for its reinforcement had been considered, Lincoln entertained a proposal from Gustavus Fox, a former navy captain who for months had been lobbying military and political officials to consider clandestinely aiding the Sumter garrison. Introduced to Lincoln by his brother-in-law, Postmaster General Montgomery Blair (son of Frank Blair Sr.), Fox believed he could covertly navigate small civilian vessels—he proposed New York tugboats—past the rebel batteries to resupply and reinforce Fort Sumter. Intrigued, Lincoln ordered Fox to visit Fort Sumter to assess the plan's viability. Allowed passage to the island by Confederates' permissive visitation policy, Fox met briefly with Anderson. Having surveyed the harbor, Fox promptly returned to Washington, reporting to Lincoln that he had no doubt about his plan's success. Anderson, on the other hand, quickly wrote the War Department that he thought the plan preposterous and doomed to failure. Faced with the conflicting reports, Lincoln mulled over the possibilities.

By the end of the month, the political tide had begun to turn in favor of maintaining Sumter. On March 28, just prior to Lincoln's first state dinner, Scott recommended the abandonment of not only Fort Sumter but also Fort Pickens, a fortification near Pensacola under no immediate military threat. Scott argued that abandoning Fort Sumter would not be enough to keep the Upper South, including his home state of Virginia, from seceding. Only by surrendering Pickens as well, Scott claimed, could Lincoln win over those slave states still within the Union. Lincoln received the recommendation with "a cold shock": while there had been extensive conversations about Fort Sumter, this was the first that he had heard about the possibility of also surrendering Fort Pickens. More significantly, Lincoln immediately recognized that Scott's recommendation was based on his political judgment rather than military necessity. In a rare display of anger, Lincoln lashed out at Scott for overstepping his bounds. Dissatisfied with Scott's haughty condescension, Lincoln said that if "General Scott could not carry out his views, some other person might." Lincoln had begun to question not only Scott's judgment but also his loyalty. In the months since his election, Lincoln had witnessed dozens of Southern-born army officers act out of loyalty to their region rather than the nation. To this end, Lincoln had come to no longer trust the reports that Kentucky-born Major Anderson had been sending to Washington. "Anderson had played us false," Lincoln told Scott. Having been lectured by the president, Scott stormed out of the White House just as the first dinner guests arrived.[54]

Lincoln asked his cabinet to remain behind after the dinner, and then he informed them of Scott's recommendation to abandon both Fort Sumter and Fort Pickens. According to Montgomery Blair, Scott's recommendation strengthened Lincoln's resolve to hold on to the forts. Lincoln ordered Fox "to be ready to sail as early as the 6th of April." Over the following week, preparations began for secret reinforcements to both Fort Pickens and Fort Sumter.

Scott, Anderson, and the Path to Fort Sumter

On April 6, Lincoln made the most important decisions regarding Fort Sumter: he would attempt to resupply the garrison with rations but would not reinforce it with additional soldiers, and he would inform South Carolina authorities of his intention to do so. Lincoln's decisions fundamentally altered the nature of Fox's plan. The expedition was no longer a covert mission to strengthen the garrison but an overt effort to supply the existing garrison. In a message to South Carolina governor Pickens, Lincoln wrote that he should "expect an attempt to be made to supply Fort Sumter with provisions only" and that "no effort to throw in men, arms, or ammunition will be made without notice." This strategy would allow him to maintain two pledges he had made in his inaugural address: that he would "hold, occupy, and possess" Federal property and that "beyond what may be necessary for these objects, there will be no invasion." Lincoln knew that the most likely outcome of this mission was that Confederate forces in Charleston would fire at either Fort Sumter or the supply ships. He also knew that forcing the Confederates to act as aggressors, to fire the first shot, would provide a tremendous moral justification for robust military action against the rebellion. Yet Lincoln's decision to modify the Sumter mission on April 6 also doomed the mission to failure and the garrison to fall. As Adam Goodheart has recently described it, the new mission was "not merely destined to fail . . . but designed to do so." Three days later, Fox's flotilla left New York bound for Charleston, virtually guaranteeing the surrender of Fort Sumter.

Lincoln's insistence on a strategy that would prompt Sumter's surrender seems at odds with his aversion to surrender that he had demonstrated after his election and in his first month in office. However, Lincoln's plan to surrender Sumter differed significantly from that espoused by Winfield Scott and others. Whereas Scott advocated unilaterally surrendering the fort, Lincoln's plan enlisted the Confederates as unwilling accomplices in its surrender. While the military result would be the same—the fort would be in Confederate hands—the political ramifications would be very different. Voluntarily surrendering the fort would only demonstrate weakness, while surrendering it after a Confederate attack would allow the Lincoln administration to maintain what Russell McClintock has called the "elusive balance of firmness and magnanimity." Forcing the Confederates to act as the aggressor, Lincoln hoped, would make the fort's surrender a powerful tool to foster Northern solidarity.[55]

In the months since his arrival in Charleston, Robert Anderson had quietly won the respect of his men. Although he continued to have heated debates on the morality and politics of slavery with some of his offers (particularly Abner Doubleday), Anderson's demonstrated professionalism, dedication, and commitment to the Union slowly persuaded the Sumter garrison that they could trust him. Even when they disagreed with some of his decisions, notably his refusal to aid the *Star of the West*, the garrison recognized that Anderson would not unnecessarily put them in harm's way and that he would not give up the fort unless absolutely necessary. An artillery officer at Sumter noted that Anderson's "actions clearly indicated that he would not surrender on demand."[56]

While Anderson had cultivated the admiration of the men under his command, he had largely lost faith in the Lincoln administration. Although he had written daily reports on the garrison's deteriorating situation, he had not received clear guidance from Washington about how he should proceed, or at least nothing that he considered a coherent order to follow. On April 5, Anderson wrote in his ninety-fourth report since arriving in Charleston that "I cannot think that the Government would abandon, without instructions and without advice, a command which had tried to do all its duty to our country." In a rare display of emotion, Anderson implored that he be supplied with some guidance. "After thirty odd years of service I do not wish it to be said that I have treasonably abandoned a post and turned over to unauthorized persons public property entrusted to my change," he wrote. "I am entitled to this act of justice at the hands of my Government, and I feel confident that I shall not be disappointed." The following day, in report number ninety-five, Anderson again implored Washington to provide him with guidance. "Our flag runs an hourly risk of being insulted, and my hands are tied by my orders," he wrote. "God grant that neither I nor any other officer of our Army may be again placed in a position of such mortification and humiliation."[57]

Carrying Lincoln's message informing Pickens about the president's intention to resupply Sumter, Robert Chew arrived in Charleston on April 8. A State Department clerk, Chew must have been glad to be escorted into the city by (recently promoted) Capt. Theodore Talbot. "Finding that Fort Sumter neither been surrendered, evacuated nor attacked," Chew requested a meeting with Governor Pickens. Chew read Lincoln's brief message to Pickens, then handed him a copy. Reading over Lincoln's words closely, Pickens summoned Beauregard. When asked if he could carry a message back to Washington, Chew curtly replied that he was "not authorized to receive any communication from him in reply." Chew was prohibited from visiting Sumter itself, so he and Talbot left that evening on the next train bound for Washington. Wiring Montgomery for guidance, Beauregard received a quick reply: "Under no circumstances are you to allow provisions to be sent to Fort Sumter."[58]

Beauregard recognized that Lincoln's letter and his orders from Montgomery limited his options and constricted his timeline. Fox's flotilla would be arriving soon, no more than a few days away. Finalizing his preparations for what now appeared to be the inevitable bombardment, Beauregard tried one more attempt to remove the garrison without bloodshed. On April 11, under a flag of truce, a Confederate commission rowed to Fort Sumter to demand Anderson's surrender. The delegation included James Chesnut, a former South Carolina senator, signer of the Confederate Constitution, and now aide to General Beauregard (and husband of diarist Mary Boykin Chesnut); Stephen D. Lee, a former U.S. Army officer and now a captain in the South Carolina militia; and Alexander R. Chisolm, a South Carolina planter and representative of Governor Pickens, who also owned the rowboat and its enslaved crew. Anderson read Beauregard's demand to surrender carefully. Demonstrating respect for his former West Point instructor and mentor, Beauregard claimed that the Confederate government, hoping for "the amicable adjustment of all questions" and "to avert the calamities of war," had heretofore "refrained from making any demand for the surrender of the fort." Lincoln's letter to Pickens informing him of his intention to resupply Sumter had changed the equation, necessitating a demand to surrender. Beauregard offered generous terms: Anderson and his men would be permitted to keep their property (including "company arms") and were granted passage to "any post in the United States which you may select." Furthermore, Beauregard would allow a symbolic balm: during the surrender, Anderson and his men could salute "the flag which you have upheld so long and with so much fortitude, under the most trying circumstances."[59]

While Beauregard's delegation waited for a response, Anderson met with his officers. They had all been expecting a demand to surrender for some time and thought Beauregard's terms generous. "Was ever such terms granted to a band of starving men?" Crawford pondered. As they considered Beauregard's demand, Anderson shared a confidential set of orders he had received from Secretary Floyd in early December, when the garrison still resided at Fort Moultrie. If it struck any of them as odd that Anderson would chose this juncture to show them orders given by a now-disgraced former cabinet member from the last administration, they did not voice it then. Despite their antiquity, Anderson saw them as the clearest orders he had yet received, and having not received any since that countermanded them, he felt bound by their dictates. He may have also hoped that revealing these orders to his officers now would help to justify and explain his choices over the last few months. Floyd's orders provided two competing instructions. First, Anderson was directed "to avoid every act which would needlessly tend to provoke aggression." This explained why Anderson had not ordered his men to retaliate when the *Star of the West* had been fired upon. Second, Anderson should "hold possession of the forts in this harbor, and if attacked you are to defend yourself to the last extremity." Although Anderson might have pointed out the use of the plural "forts" justifying his relocation from Moultrie to Sumter, everyone's attention focused on the order's final dictate: defending themselves "to the last extremity" seemed to preclude the possibility of accepting Beauregard's demand to surrender, especially before any shots were fired. Just before Christmas, however, Floyd made a modification to these orders, which Anderson also shared. Floyd added that the dictum to fight "to the last extremity" should not be interpreted as a suicide mission. "You might infer," Floyd wrote, "that you are required to make a vain and useless sacrifice of your own life and the lives of the men under your command, upon a mere point of honor." On the contrary, Floyd urged Anderson to "excise a sound military discretion" as "it is neither expected nor desired that you should expose your own life or that of your men in a hopeless conflict in defence of these forts." If "attacked by a force so superior that resistance would . . . be a useless waste of life, it will be your duty to yield to necessity, and make the best terms in your power. This will be the conduct of an honorable, brave, and humane officer, and you will be fully justified in such action."[60]

As an articulation of when to surrender, Floyd's words seemed clear. Surrender should not be considered unless the situation had become "hopeless," in which case it would be Anderson's "duty" to prevent "a useless waste of life." Ever cognizant of his honor as an officer, Anderson recognized that they had not yet reached the point in which surrender was required. Although the garrison ran perilously short on food and were outnumbered by a factor of 100, Beauregard had yet to attack the fort. Anderson had good reason to believe that the fort could withstand a bombardment, at least temporarily. With possible relief en route, they had not yet crossed the threshold that would justify surrender. Although no one called it by that name, the "Floyd standard" embodied what both Union and Confederate officers believed in 1861 about the proper paradigm for an honorable surrender. A commander ought not surrender without ample justification, but he would also be failing in his duty were he to allow his men to come to harm unnecessarily.

After less than an hour's discussion, the nine officers unanimously decided to refuse Beauregard's demand. In his written response to his former student, Anderson noted that he could not surrender as "my sense of honor, and my obligations to my Government, prevent my compliance." Walking the

Scott, Anderson, and the Path to Fort Sumter

Confederate delegation to their boat, Anderson made a verbal addendum to his written refusal, noting that he would "await the first shot" before contemplating surrender and that "we shall be starved out in a few days." Five hours later, now in the early hours of April 12, the Confederate delegation returned to Sumter with another message from Beauregard: could Anderson specify the hour in which he would abandon the fort? Conferring with his officers for more than three hours, Anderson answered that they would evacuate on April 15 at noon, provided that they did "not receive prior to that time controlling instructions from my Government or additional supplies." Rejecting Anderson's answers as "manifestly futile," the Confederate delegation informed him that Beauregard would commence a bombardment in an hour.[61]

The bombardment of Fort Sumter began at 4:30 that morning and lasted, according to Anderson's calculations, for thirty-four hours. Probably the most remarkable fact about the bombardment is that despite more than 4,000 rounds fired (more than 80 percent by the Confederates), no one was killed and only a few were wounded. Considering his limited manpower and hoping not to unnecessarily expose his men to fire, Anderson elected to man only Sumter's casement guns rather than the more powerful ones on the parapet. This decision meant that Sumter's small garrison could fire with impunity, with little risk from incoming Confederate fire, but only at a limited number of targets and only with solid shot. As Abner Doubleday discovered to his dismay, even perfectly aimed and executed casement shots proved ineffective against the heavily fortified Confederate batteries, bouncing off like "peas upon a trencher, utterly failing to make an impression."[62] In an effort to conserve ammunition, Anderson ordered his men to proceed slowly and methodically. Confederate artillery proved equally ineffective, pockmarking the fort's exterior but posing little immediate threat to the garrison within. Early that afternoon, the first ships in Fox's flotilla arrived outside the harbor. Heavy seas and storms had delayed their journey south. None of Fox's heralded tugboats had arrived, so they had no way to ferry supplies to Fort Sumter. After they debated trying to navigate their larger warships into Charleston harbor, Fox's officers recognized that without a pilot, amidst an ongoing battle, and in heavy seas, such an attempt would undoubtedly fail. They would wait impotently outside the harbor, watching the bombardment of Sumter, until an opportunity presented itself.

At sunset, heavy rains and wind buffeted Sumter. Anderson ordered his men to cease firing for the night to conserve ammunition. Confederates also retired for the evening, although they maintained a regular mortar fire every fifteen minutes through the night. By the next morning, the weather had cleared, revealing the fort largely intact. Breakfasting on slightly rancid salt pork, the Sumter garrison prepared for a second day. By 8:00 A.M., Confederate artillery had managed to set the officers' quarters aflame by firing furnace-heated solid shot into the fort. Despite the garrison's frantic efforts to extinguish them, the flames spread rapidly, filling the fort with acrid smoke. Fearing an explosion if the fire reached the magazine, Anderson ordered his men to remove as much powder and shell as they could before sealing the magazine's heavy copper door and packing earth around it. "The roaring and crackling of the flames, the dense masses of whirling smoke, the bursting of enemy's shells, . . . the crashing of the shot, and the sound of masonry falling in every direction," Doubleday observed, "made the fort a pandemonium."[63] While the garrison continued to fire its cannons amidst the smoke and debris, Anderson recognized that if they had not yet reached the Floyd standard, they were perilously close to it.

Ultimately, it was not an exploding magazine but a toppled flagpole that proved the critical development in Anderson's decision to surrender. Nearly 100 feet tall, Fort Sumter's flagpole could been seen from all of the Confederate batteries, some of which used it as a target. Struck by a Confederate cannonball, the pole fell with a thunderous crash, albeit one whose impact was drowned out by the incessant cannonade. Seeing the garrison's storm flag on the ground, Sgt. Peter Hart paused in his efforts to extinguish the growing flames long enough to snatch the flag and attach it to a makeshift flagpole on the parapet, exposing himself to considerable Confederate fire in the process. Although the flag was down only momentarily, its brief absence over Sumter set off a cascade of events that culminated in surrender. When Beauregard saw the flag fall, he immediately sent a delegation (this time William Porcher Miles, Roger A. Pryor, and Stephen D. Lee) to the island, ostensibly to see if Anderson required aid "in subduing the flames inside the fort" but also to see if he would take the fallen flag as an opportunity to surrender. Leaving from Charleston harbor, Beauregard's delegation began rowing toward Sumter, but when they noticed the flag's return via Hart's improvised flagpole on the parapet, they started to return to the city.[64]

As the members of Beauregard's delegation rowed toward Sumter, Confederate colonel Louis T. Wigfall scrambled up the island's shore. A pugnacious and argumentative former senator from Texas, Wigfall had arrived in Charleston a couple of weeks earlier and managed to have himself appointed as Beauregard's aide, a largely symbolic gesture as Beauregard's stable of aides now included representatives from most of the seceded states and prominent political factions. Stationed on Cummings Point, Wigfall saw Sumter's fallen flag as an opportunity to insert himself into the historic course of events.

Scott, Anderson, and the Path to Fort Sumter

Commandeering a Confederate private, three slaves, and a skiff most deemed unseaworthy ("small, leaking, and without a rudder"), Wigfall hurried off to Sumter. While two slaves rowed and the third bailed water with a bucket, Wigfall fashioned a flag of truce from a white handkerchief and attached it to his sword. Much to the consternation of Pvt. William Young, who feared their small vessel would capsize, Wigfall insisted on standing up "so that the small flag could be seen."[65]

"Your flag is down," Wigfall argued to the Union garrison, "you are on fire, and you are not firing your guns. General Beauregard wants this to stop." Only one of Wigfall's four observations proved to be accurate. Although flames and smoke still engulfed a significant portion of the fort, an officer pointed out to him that the flag floated again, and while Anderson's guns had slowed, they had not stopped. Most importantly, however, Wigfall had no way of knowing Beauregard's intentions and falsely represented himself as the general's representative, although he had not seen him since the bombardment began. Wigfall told Anderson that he could "have almost any terms." Believing that he had negotiated with Beauregard's deputized representative, Anderson ordered his men to lower the garrison flag and replace it with a white flag of surrender. Wigfall promptly departed to report the agreement to his superiors.[66]

No sooner had Wigfall left than Beauregard's delegation arrived. Having reversed course when they saw the return of the American flag over Sumter, they had changed course again when it was replaced by a white banner. Confused about what message the garrison was trying to communicate and ignorant of Wigfall's recent visit, Beauregard's delegation were surprised that their arrival had not prompted a more engaged reception. Exhausted from months of siege and two days of bombardment, Anderson naturally assumed that the three uniformed men had come to provide aid in extinguishing the fort's fire. He assured them that he had the situation under control and that no assistance was necessary. To Anderson's horror, they told him that neither they nor Wigfall had the authority to accept his surrender. Mortified that he had surrendered to an unsanctioned party, Anderson told them that there had been "a misunderstanding on my part, and I will at once run up my flag and open fire again." Lee, Miles, and Pryor quickly talked Anderson out of resuming hostilities, urging him to "reduce to writing his understanding with Colonel Wigfall," which they would then take to Beauregard for consideration. Before they left, however, a second delegation from the general arrived. Notified of Wigfall's agreement with Anderson, Beauregard wisely sent two aides to ensure that the surrender stuck. By 7:00 P.M. that evening, they had finally agreed to terms: the garrison would leave the following morning, after they had the opportunity to salute the flag.[67]

Although historians have frequently commented on the Wigfall mission, as it is commonly called, as a comedic episode in Sumter's fall, few have noted its broader significance for surrenders in the Civil War. It raised two important questions that would confound Civil War officers over the next four years. First, who should initiate surrender? Anderson's behavior upon Wigfall's arrival indicates that he was willing to surrender. Conditions within the fort had clearly met the threshold established by the Floyd standard. However, Anderson felt it necessary to wait for the enemy's entreaty to surrender rather than simply volunteering to capitulate by raising a white flag. Future Civil War officers would generally follow this model; honor dictated that surrender be offered before it could be accepted. Second, to whom was it acceptable to surrender? Anderson was willing to surrender when he thought Wigfall acted as Beauregard's surrogate and horrified when he discovered that Wigfall had no such mandate. Concluding that his agreement to surrender was therefore invalid, Anderson believed that he needed to resume hostilities. Although Wigfall's authority existed only in his own head, the episode highlights how the status of the party accepting the surrender shaped its outcome. In subsequent battles, many officers concluded that while they could honorably surrender to someone of equal or higher rank, they could not surrender to an officer of lower rank. Therefore, while some aspects of the Wigfall mission were unique to Fort Sumter's surrender, it also raised important theoretical issues that would never be fully resolved.

That evening, Confederate Charleston celebrated its victory with church bells, fireworks, and bonfires, while the Sumter garrison sullenly packed their few belongings for their departure in the morning. When the sun rose on April 14, Charleston's harbor had filled with vessels of every description, their passengers eager to see the garrison's departure and the fort's occupation by Confederate soldiers. At Anderson's insistence, the garrison assembled in the parade ground for a final formal salute to the flag, which had once again been raised over the parapet. Although some Confederates worried that they would fire 34 shots in the salute, one for every state in the Union, including those that had seceded, Anderson ordered his men to prepare for a 100-gun salute. Nearly halfway through the ceremony, a wind-blown cartridge fragment landed on a pile of ammunition, causing an explosion that killed one man instantly, fatally wounded another, and seriously injured several more. Horrified that the garrison had survived the battle without a casualty only to lose two of their number in an accident, Anderson ordered that a 50-shot salute would suffice. The first man killed in the Civil War, Pvt. Daniel Hough, an Irish immigrant, was interred on the parade ground that afternoon, delaying the garrison's departure. Taking the tattered flag with him, Robert Anderson boarded the ferry tasked with carrying them to the Union fleet moored outside the harbor. In the delays caused by the explosion and unscheduled funeral, the tides had shifted, leaving the ferry stuck on a sandbar. Anderson and his men would have to wait until the tide came in the next morning before they could rendezvous with the *Baltic* to begin their journey to New York.[68]

Historians have long recognized the significance of Fort Sumter's surrender in rallying Northern public support for a military response to the Confederacy, in Lincoln's call for 75,000 troops, and in the subsequent secession of the Upper South states of North Carolina, Virginia, Tennessee, and Arkansas. Recently, many historians have lauded Lincoln's handling of the crisis, praising his principled rejection of secession as unconstitutional and his concrete actions that forced the Confederates to take the first shot.[69] Often overlooked, however, is the important role that Fort Sumter played in shaping subsequent Civil War surrenders. Although not without its flaws and horrendous accidents, Sumter would serve as a template of how both Union and Confederate armies should behave during surrender. It created the ritual framework that future surrenders would either replicate or consciously choose to deviate from.

In a curious way, almost everyone emerged from the surrender with their reputations enhanced. Beauregard came away from Sumter as the first Confederate hero and would command the Confederate army to victory at Manassas in July 1861. However, as Chapter 2 will demonstrate, Robert Anderson, Abner Doubleday, and the rest of the garrison would also be labeled as "Fort Sumter Heroes." Their behavior during the siege, battle, and surrender demonstrated that even defeat could be heroic. Furthermore, their conduct would be praised not only in the North but also by many Confederates. One Confederate officer noted that "Major Anderson and his command left the harbor, bearing with them the respect and admiration of the Confederate soldiers. It was conceded that he had done his duty as a soldier holding a most delicate trust."[70] That both Anderson and Beauregard emerged from the surrender with their reputations enhanced indicates how surrender created an unusual parity between victors and vanquished. The same dualism played out in the political sphere: both Lincoln and Davis could claim that they had achieved their primary objective at Charleston.

Almost every contemporary commentator on Fort Sumter noted its transformative effect. By early May, one New York woman observed that "the 'time before Sumter' seems to belong to some dim antiquity. It seems as if we never were alive till now; never had a country till now."[71] If the first shot fired at Fort Sumter signaled the beginning of the Civil War, the fort's surrender thirty-four hours later suggested the kernel of the war's culmination. Just as Beauregard and Anderson left Sumter valorized, so too would Grant and Lee at Appomattox Courthouse, almost exactly four years later. The path between Fort Sumter and Appomattox Courthouse, however, would not be straight or easy.

Scott, Anderson, and the Path to Fort Sumter

HEROES AND COWARDS

Honor and Shame in Early Civil War Surrenders

The Civil War's first two years witnessed a fuller articulation of the relationship between surrender and honor. Maj. Robert Anderson's conduct at Fort Sumter epitomized how one might surrender honorably. Praised for his valor, propriety, and commitment to duty, Anderson served as a model for how to behave in combat and in surrender. Conversely, Union surrenders at San Antonio, San Augustin Springs, and Harpers Ferry and Confederate surrenders at Fort Donelson and Fort Jackson demonstrated the scorn that could befall those who were seen to have surrendered dishonorably. While Anderson became of the Union's earliest heroes, the vitriol levied against David Twiggs, Isaac Lynde, and Dixon Miles for their shameful surrenders indicates the potential peril that officers entertained when they chose to surrender. They were labeled as traitors and cowards, and the scorn heaped on them served as a warning about the boundary between honorable and dishonorable surrender for the remainder of the conflict.

The reception that Anderson and his men received when they arrived in New York reflected the degree to which Fort Sumter epitomized an honorable surrender. If any of them anticipated the celebratory reception that awaited them, they showed no indication of it when they boarded the *Baltic* at sunrise on April 15, 1861. Ferried to the vessel through a crowded mass of ships that had filled Charleston harbor, Abner Doubleday noted that "the bay was alive with floating craft of every description, filled with people from all parts of the South, in their holiday attire." The Confederates' celebratory mood was matched by the Union soldiers' melancholy. Doubleday remembered that when they boarded the *Baltic*, they were "received with great sympathy and feeling by the army and navy officers present."

We do not know what Anderson, Doubleday, and their men thought or said during the four days it took for them to make the journey from Charleston to New York. They undoubtedly reflected on the events of the previous days: the Confederate firing on Fort Sumter, their valiant efforts to defend it against overwhelming odds, and their eventual surrender. They also probably pondered what kind of reception they would receive in New York. Would they be blamed for not holding the fort longer? Anderson appeared to be physically and mentally overwhelmed by the ordeal. Dr. Samuel Wylie Crawford, the fort's surgeon, noted that while all of the men demonstrated some degree of shock in the aftermath of the shelling and surrender, Anderson's "physical as well as mental condition" made him unable to file a report on the surrender. Crawford requested that Gustavus Fox, the *Baltic*'s captain, complete the task. With strong headwinds slowing the voyage, the *Baltic*'s passengers had plenty of time to think about what awaited them.[1]

No one aboard the *Baltic* expected the scene that greeted them when they arrived in New York harbor on April 19, 1861. Just as they left a crowded Charleston harbor filled with vessels eager to see their departure, now they "were received with unbounded enthusiasm." Abner Doubleday recalled that "all the passing steamers saluted us with their steam-whistles and bells, and cheer after cheer went up from the ferry-boats and vessels in the harbor." A caravan of well-wishers escorted them into the harbor. Anderson, looking "careworn and fatigued," joined the other men from Sumter on the deck, observing the spectacle. The flag that had been lowered during the surrender at Sumter now flew from the *Baltic*'s mizzenmast, "almost in rags." The *New York Tribune* described Anderson as a "short, slim, bronzed-faced, and apparently feeble gentleman, whose very appearance give the lie to any doubt of his courage or patriotism. He was too exhausted and too much overcome by his emotions to speak."

To avoid the crowds swarming Battery Park, eager to see Anderson and his men, the *Baltic* anchored in the narrow waterway separating Manhattan and Governor's Island. According to Doubleday, "Several distinguished citizens at once came on board, and Major Anderson was immediately carried off to dine." Whatever expectations Anderson had about his reception in New York, he did not imagine that he would become the toast of the town. Over the next couple of days, Anderson turned away many visitors, spending his time with his wife, whom newspapers reported "has been very much impaired in consequence of the anxiety she has felt for her husband's fate."[2]

Although Anderson received the lion's share of attention, Abner Doubleday wrote that the entire Fort Sumter garrison had become celebrities. Doubleday noted, "Our captivity had deeply touched the hearts of the people, and every day the number of visitors almost amounted to an ovation. The principal city papers, the *Tribune, Times, Herald,* and *Evening Post,* gave us a hearty welcome. For a long time the enthusiasm in New York remained undiminished. It was impossible for us to venture into the main streets without being ridden on the shoulders of men, and torn to pieces by hand-shaking." Among the visitors paying their respects was Rev. Henry Ward Beecher, the noted preacher and abolitionist, who "came down to the fort to meet us, and made a ringing speech, full of fire and patriotism. It seemed as if every one of note called to express his devotion to the cause of the Union, and his sympathy with us, who had been its humble representatives amidst the perils of the first conflict of the war."[3]

The New York City that Anderson, Doubleday, and company arrived in had been transformed over the previous week. The news of Anderson's surrender had reached New York City on April 14, galvanizing a city that had in recent months been a hotbed of anti-Lincoln sentiment. The *New York Herald* correctly predicted that "the gallant Major [Anderson] will no doubt receive a magnificent reception on his arrival to the city." Even before his arrival in the city, a photography store on Broadway advertised carte-de-visite "portraits of Major Anderson" for twenty-five cents. On April 15, diarist George Templeton Strong noted a "change in public feeling marked, and a thing to thank God for. We begin to look like a United North." The city's newspapers, he observed, had almost instantaneously changed their outlook; having denounced Lincoln vociferously since his inauguration, they now supported his call for troops. The lone exception to this, according to Strong, was the *New York Courier & Enquirer,* which "devotes its leading article to a ferocious assault on Major Anderson as a traitor . . . and declares that he has been in collusion with the Charleston people all the time. This is wrong and bad. It is premature, at least."[4]

The *Courier & Enquirer*'s condemnation of Anderson is worth noting, if only for its singularity and the responses it generated from its competitors. "Sumpter [*sic*] has fallen—surrendered, we fear, by a traitor," the newspaper claimed, "and that traitor [is] Major Robert Anderson. This is harsh language; but it is the language of truth demanded by what appears to be the greatest act of treason ever perpetrated in this or any other country." Comparing Anderson to Benedict Arnold, the *Courier & Enquirer* argued that "Anderson arranged with Beauregard for the surrender of Sumter before it was assaulted; that the defence was but a sham, and that it was deemed important the surrender should take place before relief could be afforded by the government." Rather than surrender, the newspaper argued, Anderson should have fought until "his walls [were] breached and three-fourths of his command slaughtered," rather than "ignominiously surrender[ing] his post, and virtually proclaim[ing] himself a traitor to his country, and false to his honor, and his God." According to the newspaper, surrendering with honor was impossible, claiming that even if "every man of his command [had been] either killed or wounded, his duty would have been to have told those who survived to get under cover" and continue the fight. The newspaper called for Anderson to be court-martialed for treason, his surrender a "great national disgrace." The only possible conclusion, the newspaper argued, was that Anderson "ignobly, disgracefully and treacherously surrendered."

The other New York newspapers lambasted the *Courier & Enquirer* for its treatment of Anderson. The *Herald* described the piece as "the most remarkable, uncalled for and unjust editorial." In response, the *Herald* argued that

> Major Anderson has proved himself a brave and faithful officer.
> Mr. Lincoln seems to be satisfied with his conduct, and the President
> is, perhaps, better qualified to form a correct judgment in this case
> than even our Wall street contemporary. . . . That Major Anderson is a
> humane man, and wished, as far as possible, to avoid the shedding of
> the blood of our Southern brethren, is probable; but we cannot believe
> that he has undergone in the service of the United States all his labors
> and privations since December last, and all the hardships and dangers
> of a bombardment of thirty hours, merely to prove himself a traitor.
> Let him and his officers and men be heard before he is condemned.[5]

Other New York newspapers joined in the *Herald*'s condemnation of the editorial, claiming that it was unreasonable to expect an officer to sacrifice his men on a point of honor and that no evidence, other than Anderson's Southern birth, suggested that he was less than loyal to the Union.

On April 17, two days before the *Baltic* arrived, prominent New Yorkers, Democrats and Republicans alike, met at the Chamber of Commerce to organize a "monster meeting" on April 20 to honor the heroes of Fort Sumter and to demonstrate the city's loyalty to the Union. They decided to hold the rally in Union Square, a locale whose symbolic name was not lost on the organizers. On the morning of the Union Square rally, the *New York Times* observed, "This will doubtless be the largest public meeting ever held in this City, or indeed on this continent. For once the people of New-York are entirely united, and in promoting the objects for which this meeting is held, they will speak with one voice."[6]

Early Civil War Surrenders

The Union Square rally would have been appropriate for a victorious general. More than 100,000 New Yorkers (the *New York Times* reported the crowd as "the entire population of the city") flooded the park and the surrounding streets. The *Times* noted that "Broadway from Fourteenth-street almost to the Battery was a surging mass of human beings all the afternoon. The stores were closed, and everywhere, on house-tops and mastheads, and on men's hats and next their hearts, and even in ladies bonnets were the Stars and Stripes. . . . Union-square was a red, white and blue wonder. Countless little flags were hung from windows or waved by ladies and children who looked forth from them." Much of the crowd arrived in the park before daybreak, eager to catch a glimpse of Anderson and his men. When Robert Anderson appeared, it was "the signal for an outburst of applause seldom, if ever, equaled. The mass of human beings seemed to recognize at once the object of attention, and it was with the greatest difficulty that the Police made way for him through the enthusiastic crowd." As Anderson made his way to the podium, the enormous crowd swelled and roared, as "the eager populace pressed closer and closer to view the hero of the first battle in the pending war." Unused to such attention and in poor health, Anderson appeared "nervous and agitated as he never was in the face of the enemy." To thunderous applause, he "acknowledged the homage" with a meager wave. In the hours that followed, Anderson was praised by a series of orators as a "gallant commander," "the Hero of Fort Sumter," who had survived "the smoke and flame." Anderson himself remained silent throughout the event, politely recognizing the crowd's deafening applause whenever his name was mentioned. Over the next few weeks, Anderson was mobbed by well-wishers wherever he went. Schoolchildren from an orphanage assembled outside the house where Anderson temporarily resided, ready to serenade him with patriotic songs whenever he emerged. Newly organized military companies paraded in front, hoping to catch a glimpse of Anderson. It is difficult to ascertain what Robert Anderson thought about the public laudations he received in the weeks after his surrender. In poor health and physically exhausted after the siege and bombardment of Fort Sumter, Anderson remained almost entirely silent in the celebrations that greeted him in New York and in the weeks afterwards.[7]

Robert Anderson's surrender at Fort Sumter became the prototype of the honorable surrender during the Civil War. The *New York Herald* identified several elements that made Anderson's surrender heroic. First, he fought valiantly until he concluded that both continuing to fight and retreating were untenable, such that "there can be no doubt that Major Anderson did all that man could do." With the fort on fire, "the brave soldiers in Sumter behaved as heroes." Second, Anderson negotiated the terms of the surrender so as not to disgrace either himself or his soldiers. He did not surrender his sword or his flag, taking both of them with him when he abandoned the fort for New York. Third, he maintained a dignified and cool demeanor throughout the battle, never succumbing to fear or passion, ever the professional soldier.[8] Indeed, Anderson's public standing improved dramatically after the surrender. On May 1, 1861, President Lincoln wrote to Anderson that he wished to express the "approbation and gratitude I considered due you and your command from this Government," and he asked Anderson to visit him in Washington so that he could "personally testify my appreciation of your services and fidelity." Anderson was promoted to the rank of brigadier general and commissioned to raise regiments in Kentucky and in western Virginia. In the days after his arrival in New York, Anderson was bombarded with letters and gifts from well-wishers. His name and image became a common feature on patriotic envelopes, including one labeling him as the "Hero of Sumpter" [sic] and another bearing his likeness next to a depiction of the fortress flying an over-sized American flag.[9]

Praise for Anderson was not restricted to the North. The *Charleston Courier* praised "the gallant Anderson." The *Richmond Daily Examiner* observed that "the straightened circumstances in which its garrison was placed, reflects the highest honour and credit on the gallant Major in command and the noble band of heroes that so faithfully served under him. . . . The force at the disposal of Major Anderson was totally inadequate to the protracted and proper defense of the work. . . . Taking all the facts together, it does not appear possible that a more gallant defense could have been made. The anxiety of the officers and the men must also be borne in mind."[10]

The praise that Anderson received from both Northerners and Southerners alike suggests that, in early 1861, Americans broadly shared a conception of honorable surrender. A series of disastrous surrenders in 1861 and 1862 indicates that the Union and Confederate public also employed similar rubrics when judging surrender dishonorable. While the public's attention was focused on the developing crisis at Fort Sumter, more than 1,000 miles away another Union fortification surrendered to Confederate pressure. Although now largely forgotten, Gen. David E. Twiggs's dishonorable surrender at San Antonio in February 1861 served as the mirror image of Anderson's heroic surrender at Fort Sumter.[11]

A native Georgian, Twiggs had served in the U.S. Army for forty-eight years and, after Winfield Scott, was its highest-ranking officer. During his lengthy career, Twiggs had fought under Andrew Jackson against the Seminole and under both Scott and Taylor in the Mexican War. In 1857, he had been tapped to head the Department of Texas, one of the prewar army's most important appointments, commanding nineteen posts and more than 2,600 soldiers, some 15 percent of the Regular Army, and was tasked with protecting the border with Mexico and hostile Comanche. Seventy years old, Twiggs had been on sick leave in New Orleans for most of 1860, leaving the department under the command of Col. Robert E. Lee, who had resumed his Texas posting after John Brown's raid. Twiggs returned to Texas on December 16, 1860, only days before South Carolina seceded from the Union and with secession fever gripping the Lower South.

Twiggs was still in very poor health (one observer described him as an "invalid"), and his motivation for returning to his post at this critical moment remains obscure. Upon his return to San Antonio, the headquarters for the Department of Texas, Twiggs told Lee that he expected the Union to be dissolved in a matter of weeks and that he intended to return to his family in New Orleans. Over the next few weeks, Twiggs wrote repeatedly to Washington asking for instructions on how to proceed. He argued that Texas's secession was imminent and that he wished to have some direction about the disposition of his soldiers and Federal property under his supervision. As with Robert Anderson at Fort Sumter, Twiggs's calls for guidance generated only silence from Washington. In late December, he wrote that "there can be no doubt that many of the Southern States, and Texas among the number, will cease to be members of the Union, I respectfully ask instructions, or some intimation, as to the disposition of the United States property, such as arms, ammunition, and transportation. It appears to me some steps should be taken very soon." A week later, he followed up with an almost identical letter, noting that "there is no time to lose." When he finally received a response, nearly a month after his first letter, the contents were cryptic at best. General Scott informed him that since the situation "contained a political element," he could offer no specific orders without the direction of President Buchanan, who, he lamented, refused to provide guidance. In closing, Scott noted he could not "tender you any special advice, but leaves the administration of your command in your own hands."

Left in the lurch, Twiggs watched the political developments in Texas with apprehension. In his response to Scott, he said that "I am placed in a most embarrassing situation. I am a Southern man, and all these States will secede. What is left will not be the 'United States,' and I know not what is to become [of] the troops now in this department." He argued that resisting secession would be both improper and impractical. He noted that "as soon as I know Georgia has separated from the Union I must, of course, follow her." With this in mind, Twiggs asked be relieved of his command by March 4, the date of Lincoln's inauguration. Upon receiving Twiggs's request, Scott immediately ordered that he be relieved of command and replaced by Col. Carlos Waite, a New Yorker and staunch Unionist.

Slow communications between Texas and Washington undoubtedly con-tributed to confusion and anxiety in both locations. Although Scott ordered Twiggs's dismissal on January 28, Twiggs did not receive it in San Antonio until February 15, and Waite did not receive his instructions to relieve Twiggs until several days after that. Stationed at Camp Verde, some ninety miles from San Antonio on the road to El Paso, Waite's primary responsibility, as far as he knew, was managing the eighty-odd camels stationed there. Part of a project initiated under Secretary of War Jefferson Davis in 1855, the camels had proved to be more of a burden than an asset. Although they adapted easily to the desert environment of west Texas, the camels frightened the army's horses and mules. Soldiers complained that they smelled horrible.

While letters between Washington and San Antonio moved at a glacial pace, political and military developments in Texas accelerated. In mid-January, secessionists in the Texas legislature called for a convention on January 28. Even before the convention met, rumors suggested that armed mobs planned to seize government stores. Unionist governor Sam Houston made overtures to Twiggs that in the event of Texas's secession, Twiggs should consider surren-dering Federal property to him rather than to the secessionist legislature. The Secession Convention voted on February 1 in favor of secession, pending the results of a statewide referendum on February 23. In the meantime, the conven-tion authorized a Committee of Public Safety to orchestrate the state's defense and negotiate the immediate surrender of Federal property. The committee immediately sent commissioners to negotiate with Twiggs for his surrender and appointed Benjamin McCulloch to raise a cavalry regiment to pressure Twiggs if negotiations did not progress.

Born in Tennessee, Ben McCulloch had followed Davy Crockett to Texas, arriving shortly after Crockett's death at the Alamo. A veteran of the Texas War for Independence under Sam Houston and the Mexican War under Zachary Taylor, McCulloch had gone to California during the Gold Rush and served as sheriff of Sacramento and as President Buchanan's personal envoy to Brigham Young in 1859. A newspaper claimed that McCulloch had "killed more bear than Davy Crockett and fought more Indians than Daniel Boone."[12] In early February 1861, McCulloch quietly began to assemble a cavalry regiment to assault the Alamo if necessary.

Initially, Twiggs and the commissioners from the Committee of Public Safety agreed on a number of fundamental issues. By February 11, after only three days of talks, they had agreed to surrender all Federal property on March 2, the date that Texas's secession ordinance would take effect. Twiggs told the commissioners that he was "strongly in favor of Southern rights," assured them that he had no intention of firing on American citizens, and showed them copies of his letters to Washington to that effect. He also intimated that he had been offered a military commission from Georgia but had turned it down due to ill health. From this, the commissioners concluded that he was "no doubt, a good Southern man," possessing the proper "hatred to Black Republicanism" as any secessionist.

Negotiations broke down, however, when Twiggs refused to budge on the disposition of his soldiers' arms. Twiggs insisted that he would never surrender unless his soldiers were allowed to keep their arms, while the Texans demanded that the surrender include laying down all weapons, small arms included. When Twiggs refused to put into writing a statement of "what he was willing to do," the Texas commissioners sent for Benjamin McCulloch to "bring as large a force as he may deem necessary, and as soon as possible, to San Antonio." On February 15, Twiggs received word from Washington that he was to be relieved of his command upon the arrival of Colonel Waite. He also heard reports that McCulloch's force of more than 600 men (and possibly as many as 2,000) was approaching San Antonio. Although Twiggs had more than 2,600 men under his command, only 160 of those were in San Antonio, stationed mainly at the Alamo. Left a ruin after its fall to Santa Anna in 1836, the former Catholic mission had been repaired but functioned more as a supply depot than a fortification intended to sustain a siege.

In the predawn light of February 16, 1861, McCulloch led his Texas volunteers into San Antonio, where they occupied the buildings surrounding the Alamo. McCulloch had learned the night before that Waite had been ordered to relieve Twiggs, and his decision to march on San Antonio reflected the belief that Waite was far less likely to surrender. Surrounded and outnumbered, General Twiggs received an order from Colonel McCulloch "to deliver up all military posts and public property held by or under your control"; he threatened to attack if Twiggs did not surrender in the next six hours. Although Twiggs almost immediately gave his verbal consent to "give up everything," negotiations again stalled over whether Federal soldiers would be allowed to keep their weapons.

The two main eyewitness sources for Twiggs's surrender offer conflicting interpretations of what transpired in the parade ground in front of the Alamo. Caroline Darrow, the wife of a government clerk, claimed the whole affair amounted to a charade and that Twiggs and McCulloch had effectively conspired to stage the surrender. A young teacher who had taken up the secessionist cause as a cavalryman in McCulloch's regiment offered a very different assessment. Standing only a few steps away, he overheard Twiggs tell McCulloch that "you have treated me most shamefully, ruining my reputation as a military man and now I am too old to reestablish it. . . . If an old woman with a broomstick in hand had come . . . demanding his surrender, he would have yielded without a word of protest." What infuriated Twiggs about McCulloch's behavior was that he had come "without papers, without any notice" and had "assembled a mob and forced me to terms." The former teacher noted sympathetically that "in his humiliation [Twiggs] wept like a child."[13]

Over the next two days, with McCulloch's army swelling to 1,100 men, the terms of surrender were agreed upon, with the Texas commissioners relenting to Twiggs's demand that his men keep their weapons and Twiggs agreeing that his soldiers would leave via the coast as the Texas commissioners insisted. Twiggs ordered all Federal troops in Texas to evacuate their posts and march to Indianola, taking rations and small arms with them, while the Texas commissioners sent a circular letter urging Texans to allow the surrendered soldiers safe passage. On February 18, the same day as Jefferson Davis's inauguration, Twiggs formally surrendered all Federal property in Texas to McCulloch. Relieved of his command, Twiggs promptly returned to his family in New Orleans, where he was "received with public honors."[14]

When Colonel Waite arrived in San Antonio on February 19, the day after the surrender, he attempted to rescind the surrender order, claiming that Twiggs did not have the proper authority to surrender the entire department, given his impending replacement. He quickly realized that any concerted effort to retract the surrender order would be unlikely to succeed. Several Federal officers refused to accept Twiggs's order to surrender and march to the coast, although all these efforts were short lived. At Fort Brown, near Brownville, Federal soldiers ignored the order as illegal and held on to their position. A Philadelphia newspaper account contrasted the commanding officer, "Captain

Hill," with the treasonous Twiggs and compared him favorably to another officer then holding a fort against Confederate encroachment: "Captain Hill now occupies a position of honor and patriotism similar to that distinguishing Major Robert Anderson at Fort Sumter."[15] Although some resisted, many more officers and soldiers resigned from Federal service and enlisted in Texas units. The surrender presented both a symbolic and a material victory for the Texas secessionists. Twiggs's department encompassed 19 forts and property valued at $1.3 million, including 44 cannons, 1,900 long arms, 400 pistols, 5,500 pounds of gunpowder, and several magazines full of ammunition, plus more than 300 wagons, 1,450 mules, and 80 camels.

The most significant barrier to the orderly surrender across Texas came from Texan officers who refused to allow Federal soldiers safe passage. By the beginning of April, half of the Federal soldiers who had not resigned to join Texas units had left from Indianola, bound to either New York or garrison duty in Key West, leaving some 1,200 soldiers still en route or waiting in Indianola for passage, mostly from the 8th Infantry, which had been stationed in west Texas to protect the border with Mexico and confront hostile Comanche. When the shelling of Fort Sumter began, Confederate officials in Montgomery declared that since war had begun, all U.S. troops within Texas should be held as prisoners of war. Earl Van Dorn, who had assumed command from McCulloch, immediately arrested the remaining Federal soldiers, including Colonel Waite.

In one of the largely forgotten coincidences of the war, Col. Robert E. Lee arrived in San Antonio in the early afternoon of February 16, the day McCulloch invested the city. When Twiggs resumed command in San Antonio in December 1860, Lee had returned to his regiment at Fort Mason, nearly 150 miles by stagecoach northwest of San Antonio. On February 4, he received an order from Scott to report to Washington by April 1 for reassignment. When he arrived in San Antonio, Lee was immediately accosted by men wearing strips of red flannel sewed onto their shoulders, identifying them as members of McCulloch's militia. In the crowd, Lee recognized a friend's wife, who told him that "General Twiggs surrendered everything to the State this morning, and we are all prisoners of war." According to her recollection, Lee heard the news with "astonishment . . . his lips trembling and his eyes full of tears," asking rhetorically, "Has it come so soon to this?" Changing into civilian clothes, Lee made a brief visit to Twiggs's headquarters before returning to his hotel, where guests heard him pacing and talking to himself, perhaps in prayer, late into the night.[16]

During the week he spent in San Antonio, Lee met with Charles Anderson, Robert Anderson's younger brother, who had moved to Texas hoping that the climate would improve his health. According to Anderson, Lee affirmed his loyalty to the United States, although his duty to "Virginia ought to take precedence over that which is due the Federal government. . . . If Virginia stands by the old Union, so will I." Indignantly, Lee told Anderson that a "lawless trio" had demanded that "unless he would then and there engage to resign his commission in the United States Army, and to take one under the confederate authority," they would seize his personal property. Asking for Anderson's help in protecting and shipping his effects, Lee expressed his disgust at the ruffians' behavior. In his forty years of military service, "to be thus maltreated by such a committee was beyond his patience to endure." Having secured Anderson's assistance, Lee slipped out of San Antonio, arriving in Confederate New Orleans on February 25 and his home in Alexandria on March 1.[17]

Lee never explicitly articulated his thoughts on Twiggs's surrender, either in the days that followed or in the years to come. If Lee met with Twiggs during that week in San Antonio, he left no record of it. Given his statements at the time, it seems unlikely that Lee approved of Twiggs's decision to surrender, though he probably sympathized with the old general's competing loyalties. Other soldiers were less circumspect in their comments. One officer proclaimed that it was "the most disgraceful surrender the world has ever known" and that Twiggs formed a "notorious trio" with Benedict Arnold and Judas Iscariot. Writing to his brother Robert, still ensconced at Fort Sumter, Charles Anderson pronounced Twiggs's surrender "treason, pure and simple."[18]

When news of Twiggs's surrender reached the east coast, Northern newspapers from across the political spectrum condemned his actions. Most concluded that Twiggs had colluded with Confederate forces. The *Independent* argued that "the treachery of Gen. Twiggs—whose name throughout the North has been almost universally coupled with that of Benedict Arnold—is meeting with great applause in the South. On his arrival in New Orleans, he received an enthusiastic welcome—but it was old the enthusiasm of traitors for a prince of traitors. Arnold's correspondence with Sir Henry Clinton was not more dastardly than Twiggs's pre-concert with Jefferson Davis." The *Philadelphia Inquirer* pronounced "General Twiggs a Traitor," claiming that "the nation has received a fresh shock in the defection of General Twiggs, who has chosen to abandon the flag that he has carried in triumph over a score of battle-fields in order to link his fortunes with the mad reign of secession. It is difficult to fathom the motives of a brave soldier who flights away the honorable fame of a lifetime for the sake of giving his adherence to a rebel organization controlled and guided by traitors and plunderers." *Freedom's Champion*, a Republican paper from Atchison, Kansas, claimed that "if there is any more disgraceful punishment than that of the gallows, it should be meted out to the villain and traitor, Twiggs."[19] If Twiggs had any defenders in the North, they remained silent. In the South, Twiggs received praise for his patriotism. Louisiana's secessionist governor Thomas Moore reported proudly that Twiggs was "welcomed to New Orleans with civic and military honors worthy of his bravery, his talents, and his long and very distinguished services." In March 1861, the legislature of Twiggs's native state of Georgia passed a resolution praising his "duty and patriotism" and "recogniz[ing] in him a brave and honorable soldier."[20]

In response to the public outcry, the outgoing Buchanan administration ordered Twiggs "dismissed from the Army of the United States for his treachery to the flag of his country in having surrendered" to Texas secessionists.[21] Twiggs apparently did not take his dismissal lightly, subsequently "threatening President BUCHANAN with the severest chastisement, because he branded him a traitor."[22] It came as no surprise when in May 1861 Twiggs assumed a sinecure as a major general in the Confederate Army, tasked with defending New Orleans. In very poor health, Twiggs did not hold the post for long before resigning a few months later and succumbing to his maladies in July 1862.

Twiggs's surrender at the Alamo and Anderson's surrender at Fort Sumter present an interesting study in contrasts. Both men were career soldiers, were born in the South, and held political views hostile to the incoming Lincoln administration. Both men pleaded in vain for guidance from Washington and ended up surrendering their commands to an overwhelmingly superior secessionist force. Yet while Anderson became the Union's first hero, Twiggs became a pariah, branded as a traitor. The fundamental difference between them, at least in the view of the Northern public, was their conduct prior to, during, and after their surrenders. While Anderson refused to surrender until all other options had been exhausted and stayed with his garrison in their return to New York, Twiggs had surrendered before a shot had been fired and abandoned his men to rejoin his family in New Orleans. Even before the fall of Fort Sumter, "the difference between Major ANDERSON and Gen TWIGGS," the *New York Times* reported, was apparent to "every man, woman and child." When rumors circulated that Lincoln intended to appoint Anderson to the post Twiggs vacated, the newspaper opined that Anderson deserved "the highest rewards in the gift of a grateful country," thereby helping "to restore dignity and public respect to the position which TWIGGS has disgraced."[23]

If Twiggs received condemnation as a traitor, Maj. Isaac Lynde was branded a coward for his surrender at San Augustin Springs on July 27, 1861. Unlike Anderson and Twiggs, no one ever doubted Lynde's loyalty and commitment to the Union. A Vermont native, Lynde had served in the army for thirty-four years in a variety of frontier postings. By June 1861, the army's presence in New Mexico proved to be only a shadow of what it had been a year earlier. Army regulars had been recalled to the east after Fort Sumter, and efforts to replace them with locally recruited volunteers had yielded few results. Many Federal officers had resigned in early 1861. The department's commander, Col. E. R. S. Canby, had only assumed the post in mid-May, when his predecessor joined the Confederacy. On June 16, Canby ordered Major Lynde to abandon Fort McLane, near Santa Rita, and relocate to Fort Fillmore, some eighty-five miles to the south, near Mesilla. Canby hoped that Lynde's presence would strengthen Fort Fillmore against a possible Confederate invasion of New Mexico and curb the disloyal element rumored to be present among the officers.

Upon his arrival at Fillmore, Lynde found much that disturbed him. Secessionist sentiment appeared strong in the local populace and among the garrison. Morale generally was low, as some of the soldiers had not been paid in over a year. Worse yet, the fort seemed almost totally indefensible in the face of a Confederate attack. A U-shaped fort with its open end facing the Rio Grande, Fillmore had been designed for defense against Native Americans on horseback, not a force armed with artillery. Its adobe walls could be punctured easily by even the lightest cannonball. "The fort was so placed as to be indefensible against artillery," Lynde wrote, "being commanded on three sides by sand hills with easy range of a six-pounder." Worse yet, although the fort had been intended primarily as a cavalry outpost, most of Fillmore's horses had been stolen by local secessionists, and Apache raiders had absconded with most of its livestock.[24]

Charged with occupying abandoned or vulnerable forts along the Texas frontier, Confederate lieutenant colonel John Baylor led approximately 300 men into New Mexico on July 23, with Fort Fillmore his initial target. Informed of Baylor's presence and intentions by a Confederate deserter, Lynde decided to take the offensive. Marching on Mesilla, Lynde initially demanded Baylor's surrender, which Baylor promptly refused. Commanding about 380 men, Lynde attempted to invest the town, but the late hour and heavy sands caused him to abort the mission and return to Fillmore. The following day Lynde attempted

Early Civil War Surrenders

to reinforce the fort, ordering his men to dig trenches and pile sandbags, but hearing reports that Baylor had received reinforcements, including artillery, convinced him that Fillmore had become indefensible. "Other officers, with myself," Lynde reported, "became convinced that we must eventually be compelled to surrender if we remained in the fort." At 10:00 P.M. on March 26, Lynde ordered the men to prepare to evacuate. Because of the paucity of draft animals, soldiers were instructed to take only what they could carry (five days' rations and a blanket) and to destroy everything else to prevent it from falling into Confederate hands. Lynde hoped to relocate his force to Fort Stanton, approximately 150 miles to the northeast. His objective for "the first day's march would be 20 miles to Saint Augustine Springs, where there would be abundance of water." Hoping to evade detection by Confederates, they left at 1:00 A.M.[25]

The march proved to be much more difficult than Lynde anticipated. The route to San Augustin Springs, actually closer to thirty miles than the twenty miles Lynde expected, took the garrison into the high desert, almost entirely devoid of water or shade. They marched primarily uphill, including five miles up the Organ Mountains. The presence of approximately 100 women and children, family members of the garrison, coupled with the shortage of horses or mules slowed their progress. Their greatest obstacle proved to be the desert heat. "Until daylight the command advanced without difficulty," Lynde wrote, "but when the sun arose the day became intensely hot, and soon after the men and teams began to show signs of fatigue." By sunrise, most of the soldiers found their canteens empty, and some were suffering from hangovers and dehydration, having consumed the garrison's medicinal whiskey supply the previous evening. "As early as nine o'clock," one junior officer remembered, "the extreme heat of the sun, made doubly hot reflected from the sand and want of water, caused many of the men to fall out of the ranks, exhausted, to seek the shade of the bushes, which were so small as to cover their heads." Six miles short of the Springs, they reached the pass over the Organ Mountains, Lynde reported, and "here the men and teams suffered severely with the intense heat and want of water, many men falling and unable to proceed." By noon, the vanguard of Lynde's command had reached San Augustin Springs, although many soldiers tailed miles behind. Historian Megan Kate Nelson has estimated that nearly one of every five men under Lynde's command perished that day from dehydration and heatstroke, an extraordinary death rate even by Civil War standards. Lynde himself was not spared from the heat. On more than one occasion, Lynde found himself "so much exhausted from fatigue and excessive heat that I could sit on my horse no longer, and had to stop to dismount . . . suffering from such intense pain in my head as to be almost blind." His bizarre behavior and sometimes contradictory orders indicate that Lynde had entered a heat-induced stupor.[26]

With most of his men barely able to walk and scattered along six miles of dusty road, Lynde received a report that they were being pursued by "eight companies of mounted men, supported by artillery and a large force of infantry." Unable to effectively rally his remaining men, Lynde wrote, "I considered our case hopeless; that it was worse than useless to resist; that honor did not demand the sacrifice of blood after the terrible suffering that our troops had already undergone." Seeing no other option, Lynde signaled his intention to surrender. After a short parley with officers from Baylor's cavalry, Lynde surrendered his entire command. At least on paper, Lynde surrendered to a force only a third the size of his own. According to Baylor's report, with which other sources essentially agree, "Major Lynd's command was composed of eight companies of infantry and four of cavalry, with four pieces of artillery, the whole numbering nearly 700 men. My own force at the surrender was less than 200."[27]

When they learned of the surrender, many of Lynde's officers immediately protested the decision. Horrified that they had been "voluntarily surrendered without striking a blow," Capt. Alfred Gibbs argued that "nearly every officer protested earnestly, and even violently, against this base surrender; but Major Lynde said: 'I am commander of these forces, and I take upon my shoulders the responsibility of my action in the matter.'" According to his account, "The altercation by Major Lynde's subordinates became so violent" that Baylor nearly had to intercede between them. Gibbs's account was confirmed by a Confederate soldier who noted that "When Lynd[e]'s soldiers found that they had to surrender to a mob of ragged Texans, they were ready to mutiny."[28]

The decisive factor in Lynde's surrender was not his cowardice but the environmental pressures of the desert.[29] The soldiers involved in the surrender, however, sought to pin their misfortune on human agency rather than the environmental conditions. Most concluded that Lynde had agreed to a deeply dishonorable surrender, although they differed about the degree to which Lynde himself was culpable. Most believed that Lynde bore sole responsibility for their misfortune. Dr. James C. McKee, the fort's surgeon, described Lynde as "the old imbecile" who demonstrated "marked incompetence and cowardice." Outraged at the surrender, he asked rhetorically in his memoirs if "there ever [was] such a suicidal, cowardly, pusillanimous surrender as that in all [of] history?" The entire garrison, the surgeon argued, had become "victims of [Lynde's] cowardice and imbecility." Capt. F. J. Crilly noted that "many of the officers at the time and all of the men ascribed the surrender of the troops to the treachery on the part of Major Lynde." Crilly himself believed that the surrender was not a product of cowardice or treachery but "the actions of a man superannuated and unfit for active command." While Crilly sought to minimize Lynde's culpability, other soldiers placed the blame elsewhere. "Lynde's surrender was, as I believe, consequential upon whiskey," one soldier noted, claiming that a significant portion of the garrison had imbibed the evening before the march. He added that a secondary factor was "the tampering of the loyalty of the men by the officers who have joined the Rebels."[30]

Although the surrender brought temporary relief to their suffering, for most of the Fort Fillmore garrison, their trek through the desert had only just begun. Baylor ordered his men to provide food and water to the weakened Union soldiers, but he believed that he had neither the resources to maintain them as prisoners nor the ability to guard them if he came under a Union attack. Except for a handful who refused the parole or joined the Confederacy, Baylor elected to parole the Union soldiers, essentially releasing them on their honor not to fight again until properly exchanged, giving them fifty antiquated carbines to protect themselves against Indians as they marched across the Jornada del Muerto (Day's Journey of the Dead Man) to Fort Craig. Before they arrived, however, several officers, Gibbs foremost among them, placed Lynde under arrest for dereliction of duty.[31]

A week after the surrender, Canby forwarded Lynde's report to Washington, failing to disguise his feelings in the accompanying cover letter: "The report is in all respects unsatisfactory, and subsequent rumors, not yet confirmed, give a still more unfavorable complexion." Alfred Gibbs, who had been present at the surrender, urged Canby to pursue "charges against Major Lynde, under the fifty-second and ninety-ninth Articles of War" and subsequently requested a formal court of inquiry to "report on the facts and circumstances connected with a bearing upon the surrender of Major Lynde's command." Gibbs hoped that such a formal inquiry would not only pin the blame on Lynde but also absolve the other officers of any responsibility.[32]

With coverage of Bull Run and its aftermath dominating the newspapers in late July and early August 1861, the San Augustin Springs surrender did not receive the media attention that Twiggs's surrender six months earlier had. Those newspapers that did cover the story uniformly attributed the surrender to Lynde's cowardice. Short on particulars about the situation in New Mexico, newspaper coverage focused on two main elements: Lynde had surrendered to a smaller Confederate force and had done so without firing a shot. The only reasonable conclusion that could be drawn from these two facts, they argued, was that Lynde was an abject coward, if not a traitor.

According to the *New York Times*, "Major LYNDE, without firing a gun, and without making a show of resistance, surrendered his whole force into the hands of the enemy. Whether cowardice, bribery or treachery prompted the deed, we are at a loss to determine." A month later, the paper reported that Lynde had arrived at Hannibal, Missouri, "under arrest . . . [but] not ironed, as he deserved to have been." Expressing pity for the men under Lynde's command, the *Ohio State Journal* argued that "these soldiers, of all ranks, are furious at this villainous act of their commander, who has thus disgraced them forever. . . . It makes the blood of every true man tingle in his veins to think of this villainous commander." The newspaper noted that Lynde had been brought to St. Louis for trial, though "whether the charge of treason can be successfully maintained is of little uncertainty." Nonetheless, the newspaper assured its readers that "his cowardice and incompetency will certainly dismiss him from service."[33]

On December 4, a congressional resolution directed the secretary of war to investigate why Lynde "surrendered a largely superior force of United States troops under his command to an inferior force of Texas troops without firing a gun or making any resistance whatever; and whereas it is charged and believed that said surrender was the result of treason or cowardice," to explain "what measures have been or ought to be taken to expose and punish such of the officers now on parole as were guilty of treason or cowardice in that surrender, and relieve from suspicion such as were free from blame."[34] In response, Secretary of War Simon Cameron issued a report that noted "by direction of the President of the United States" and "by command of General McClellan," Lynde had been "dropped from the rolls of the Army" after a preliminary investigation revealed that "no other officer of the command was in any way involved in the suspicion of complicity in the offense" and that the totality of the blame rested on Lynde's shoulders.

Although the Lincoln administration considered the case closed with Lynde's dismissal, few of those directly involved in the surrender found this resolution satisfactory. Lynde himself believed that he had been wrongly blamed for circumstances beyond his control and fruitlessly demanded a court-martial to exonerate him. To this end, he traveled to Washington for an audience with the president, but Lincoln refused to see him. Many of the soldiers under Lynde's command were also displeased with this resolution. Writing to Gen. George McClellan in December 1861, Gibbs urged him to authorize a court of inquiry, as "blame if not disgrace will be imputed to Major Lynde's subordinates unless some steps are taken" to clear their names.[35]

Early Civil War Surrenders

Alfred Gibbs's concern that Lynde's dishonor would extend to the men under his command reveals an intriguing dimension to how surrender could taint not only those who activity consented to it but also those involuntarily surrendered. Unless positive evidence to the contrary conclusively demonstrated his innocence, he believed that his military career and honor would be tainted by Lynde's decision. This fear proved unfounded in Gibbs's case: subsequent to his exchange in August 1862, he received multiple promotions and served with distinction in a number of battles, especially during the 1864 Overland Campaign. Yet the idea that soldiers could be tainted by their commanding officer's decision to surrender was not without foundation, as the Union garrison at Harpers Ferry would discover after their surrender in September 1862.

Infamous as the site of John Brown's 1859 raid, the town of Harpers Ferry changed hands a half-dozen times in the first two years of the Civil War. Confederates seized the town in April 1861, although not before a Union sympathizer set fire to the armory buildings and fled to Pennsylvania. After the town's monthlong occupation, during which Col. Thomas J. Jackson salvaged material from the armory and organized regiments of Virginia militia, Gen. Joseph Johnston deemed the site indefensible and ordered it abandoned in favor of Winchester. Union forces under Gen. Robert Patterson occupied the town shortly thereafter, only to have it reclaimed a month later by Confederate cavalry under Capt. Turner Ashby in August 1861. Over the next six months, control over Harpers Ferry alternated four more times, revealing that both Union and Confederate leadership believed that the location had strategic value, but not enough to warrant occupying and defending it. Although these repeated occupations produced fairly little bloodshed, they had a decisive effect on the town itself. One Union soldier noted in early 1862 that Harpers Ferry no longer resembled a town but "a complete wreck." Novelist Nathaniel Hawthorne, visiting as a reporter for the *Atlantic Monthly*, noted its "inexpressible forlornness resulting from the devastations of war and its occupation by both armies alternatively."[36]

The Union made more concerted efforts to hold the site after Gen. Nathaniel Banks occupied Harpers Ferry in February 1862. Gen. Rufus Saxton effectively defended the site from attack by Gen. Thomas (now Stonewall) Jackson in late May of that year, indicating the Union's intentions to hold the town permanently. As the pressing needs of the front line necessitated that the most competent officers and experienced soldiers be sent elsewhere, the

Harpers Ferry garrison consisted disproportionately of green recruits and in-effectual officers. Few of the more than 6,000 Union soldiers based at Harpers Ferry at the dawn of September 1862 had seen combat; privates in the 111th and 126th New York Volunteers had only mustered in late August 1862. The garrison's commander, Col. Dixon Miles, did not think much of these new recruits: the officers were inexperienced and naive, and the men had "never had a gun in their hands until the boxes were opened and the muskets issued to them yesterday."[37]

An 1824 West Point graduate (although a very poor student), Miles had a long but largely undistinguished military career, including service in the Sem-inole and Mexican Wars and myriad frontier garrison assignments. Miles was an alcoholic, and his most distinguished accomplishment during nearly forty years in uniform is that he managed to avoid disciplinary action for incompe-tence and dereliction of duty. Recalled from a posting at Fort Leavenworth, Kansas, in 1861 to assist in the defense of Washington, Miles was accused of drunkenness at Bull Run. A military board of inquiry confirmed the accusation, as witnesses testified to his visible inebriation: "If I have ever seen an intoxi-cated person," one Michigan officer noted, "I think he was one." Although the board concluded that Miles had been intoxicated, it found insufficient grounds for a court-martial. Miles received the appointment in March 1862 to command the garrison in Harpers Ferry, where most believed he would see no action.[38]

Largely overshadowed by Antietam, Stonewall Jackson's siege of Harpers Ferry formed a critical part of Lee's 1862 Maryland Campaign. Crossing the Po-tomac starting on September 4, Lee sent Jackson with three divisions to seize Harpers Ferry. Lee hoped that the site would not only provide needed supplies but also strengthen his supply routes and secure a possible avenue of retreat. Recognizing the possible threat to Harpers Ferry, Miles received instructions to "be energetic and active, and defend all places to the last extremity. There must be no abandoning of a post, and shoot the first man that thinks of it." The garrison nearly doubled in size with soldiers evacuated from Winchester and Martinsburg, under the command of Gen. Julius White. A personal friend of Abraham Lincoln, White had resigned from a patronage appointment as the customs collector for the Port of Chicago after Bull Run to raise an Illinois regiment. Promoted for his bravery at the Battle of Pea Ridge, White had only recently been transferred to garrison duty when Lee's invasion of Maryland began. Although White held higher rank, he deferred command because of Miles's "familiarity with the topography of the vicinity."[39]

Although Miles may have had greater familiarity with the area, his plan to defend Harpers Ferry did not reflect it. Located on the promontory where the Shenandoah joins the Potomac, the town of Harpers Ferry is dwarfed by Loudoun Heights, across the Shenandoah in Virginia, and by the smaller Maryland Heights across the Potomac. Ignoring the counsel of subordinates, who recommended securing both of these sites, Miles arranged his primary defenses along Bolivar Heights, the low range of hills west of the town, and delegated command of the small force on Maryland Heights to Col. Thomas H. Ford. A forty-seven-year-old Mexican War veteran, attorney, and abolitionist, Ford had served as Ohio's lieutenant governor under Salmon Chase. Although a competent officer, Ford was in no position to command troops in the field: he had only recently returned from sixty days' leave after having a fistula removed from his buttocks and was unable to ride a horse or run.[40]

On September 12, 1862, the same day that the last of White's regiments arrived, Jackson's troops began their investiture of Harpers Ferry, seizing the undefended Loudoun Heights and methodically assaulting the Federal position on Maryland Heights. The following day, Joseph Kershaw's South Carolina and William Barksdale's Mississippi brigades easily routed the scattered Union defenses, including the greenhorn recruits from the 126th New York Volunteers, who ran in "a shameful panic and flight." By nightfall, Jackson had surrounded Harpers Ferry on three sides, leaving no avenue of escape for the 13,000-strong Union garrison. That evening, Miles tasked a small cavalry squad to break out of siege to "try to reach somebody that had ever heard of the United States Army, or any general of the United States Army, or anybody that knew anything about the United States Army, and report the condition of Harper's Ferry." Miles believed he could hold out for forty-eight hours, "but if he was not relieved in that time he would have to surrender the place."[41]

Jackson's men spent the morning of September 14 positioning the artillery on Maryland and Loudoun Heights and preparing for an infantry battle on Bolivar Heights. The bombardment began shortly after 1:00 P.M. A newspaper reporter embedded with Miles wrote that "shell followed shot, and shot followed shell in quick secession, each nearer than the last." Col. William H. Trimble of the 60th Ohio claimed that there was "not a place where you could lay the palm of your hand and say it was safe." Although the Union garrison attempted to return fire, the elevated Confederate artillery positions proved out of range or nearly impossible to hit. In the process, the garrison used up nearly all of their ammunition by nightfall. That evening, Ohio private Lewis Hull noted in his diary, "A general feeling of depression observable in all the men. All seem to think that we will have to surrender or be cut to pieces." When the fog lifted early the next morning, the Confederate bombardment resumed.

Nearly 20,000 strong, Jackson's infantry on Bolivar Height appeared poised to assault the Union line.[42]

Recognizing the futility of their situation, Dixon Miles and Julius White met with their brigade commanders to assess their options. Ohio colonel William H. Trimble articulated the clearest assessment of their situation: there was "nothing left for us but to surrender or see our men slaughtered." Furthermore, Trimble added, continuing to fight for even an hour with such inexperienced troops would result in "such a destruction of human life," and they would be held "morally responsible to the country for permitting" their men to die unnecessarily. In his testimony before the military board afterward, Trimble maintained that the decision to surrender was not one he made lightly. If there had been any chance that they could survive long enough to be reinforced, he told the board, "I would not have consented to surrender if all the men in the universe had asked me to do it." After some brief discussion, they unanimously decided that surrender was their only option.[43]

With White tasked with negotiating terms of surrender, the other Union officers rode out along Bolivar Heights, waving white handkerchiefs as tokens of surrender. The Confederate bombardment slowed but did not cease, presumably because low visibility prevented artillery officers from ascertaining the surrendering officers' intentions. In the confusion, fragments from an exploding artillery shell hit Col. Dixon Miles and "tore the flesh entirely from his left calf." Bleeding profusely, Miles lived long enough to be carried to his bed, thank his officers for the efforts, and blame McClellan for not sending reinforcements. Before expiring the next day, Miles told his aide that he believed "he had done his duty; he was an old soldier and willing to die."[44]

With Miles's death, the garrison's command passed to Julius White, who then had the unfortunate responsibility of negotiating the surrender. According to one of Jackson's aides, White rode out to meet Jackson "mounted on a handsome black horse" and "handsomely uniformed, with an untarnished sabre, immaculate gloves and boots." In a scene that would later echo in Lee's surrender to Grant in 1865, White "must have been somewhat astonished to find in General Jackson the worst dressed, worst mounted, most faded and dingy looking general he had ever seen anyone surrender to." In their brief meeting, White asked for terms, to which Jackson replied that "the surrender must be unconditional." Without other options, White agreed. Under Jackson's guidance, Gen. A. P. Hill arranged the terms: officers would keep their sidearms and baggage, and each regiment would be allocated two wagons for personal possessions. To expedite his reunion with Lee's branch of the army, Jackson decided to immediately parole the entire Union garrison.[45]

Early Civil War Surrenders

Many of the soldiers at Harpers Ferry expressed outrage and regret at the news that Miles had surrendered. One soldier recalled that "the indignation of Union men and officers at the surrender was terrible—some sobbed like children, some swore, some were angry beyond words." Another noted that "I have never seen ten thousand men all terribly angry in my life but this once." This sense of betrayal seemed most pronounced in the soldiers who had yet to fire a shot during the siege and among those who had only recently enlisted. To surrender in their inaugural experience in combat, they worried, suggested that they lacked the masculine discipline to face combat bravely. Even if the decision to surrender rested with their commanding officers, the enlisted men felt deeply dishonored. "Our disaster was greater than in actual numbers [of casualties]," wrote one soldier. "It consisted of the lasting shame of the surrender, and the demoralization of our men."[46]

Harpers Ferry proved to be the Union's largest surrender in the Civil War. Not only did Jackson manage to secure the surrender of 12,000 Union prisoners, but he also captured 13,000 small arms, 200 wagonloads of supplies, and 73 artillery pieces. The breadth of this achievement after only a four-day siege with minimal casualties has led historian James I. Robertson to conclude that Harpers Ferry was "the most complete victory in the history of the Southern Confederacy." It also proved to be the most embarrassing Union surrender in the entire conflict. Its capitulation prompted outrage and recriminations across the North. Typical of the newspaper coverage, the *New York Herald* expressed outrage at the "disgraceful, costly and humiliating surrender of Harper's Ferry." Unlike the surrenders at San Antonio and San Augustin Springs, where blame was quickly attributed to David Twiggs and Isaac Lynde, respectively, the surrender at Harpers Ferry produced multiple culprits.[47]

The outcry after the surrender of Harpers Ferry produced one of the largest and most intense military investigations of the war. Chaired by Gen. David Hunter, the commission heard testimony from forty-four witness between October 4 and October 30. In its report, issued on November 4, 1862, the commission distributed the blame among various parties but argued that Col. Dixon Miles deserved the lion's share. The investigators attempted to treat Miles judiciously, recognizing that "an officer who cannot appear before any earthly tribunal to answer or explain charges gravely affecting his character, who has met his death at the hands of the enemy, even upon the spot he disgracefully surrendered, is entitled to the tenderest care and most careful investigation. These this Commission has accorded Colonel Miles, and, in giving an opinion, only repeats what runs through our nine hundred pages of evidence, strangely unanimous upon the fact that Colonel Miles' incapacity, amounting to almost imbecility, led to the shameful surrender of this important post." The commission not only blamed Miles for the surrender of Harpers Ferry but also argued that he had some culpability in the horrendous death toll at Antietam. Had Miles not surrendered so quickly, they argued, Jackson would have been delayed in reuniting with Lee; 1,000 lives lost at Harpers Ferry might have prevented 2,000 deaths at Antietam. The commission also sanctioned Col. Thomas H. Ford for his conduct during the attack on Maryland Heights, concluding that the collapse of the Union defenses there arose in part from Ford's ineptitude, and that he "abandoned his position without sufficient cause" drew attention to "the disgraceful behavior" of the 126th New York for their conduct on Maryland Heights.[48] Due to a recent change in Federal policy, the 12,000 paroled soldiers from Harpers Ferry were not sent home but to parole camps, initially in Annapolis, but then in Chicago, where they would stay until exchanged for an equal number of Confederate prisoners.

Located on the South Side of Chicago, Camp Douglas served multiple roles during the Civil War, variously as a training camp, a prisoner of war camp, and a parole camp. When the Harpers Ferry parolees arrived, the camp still held some Confederate prisoners awaiting parole, mainly from the surrender of Fort Donelson. Separated by a partition, the two sets of inmates suffered under similar conditions. In their two-month stint at Camp Douglas, more than forty Union soldiers died and many more suffered from illness caused by poor sanitation, maggot-ridden meat, and overcrowding. Adding to the discontent were persistent rumors that Secretary of War Edwin Stanton intended to send them to Minnesota to fight in the Dakota War, an assignment many of the soldiers felt violated the terms of their parole. Many of the soldiers reported on the demoralizing effect of the parole camp, prompting many soldiers to desert and others to set fires. After a fire destroyed the barracks of two Vermont companies, one officer reported that "there is a bubbling at the bottom and considerable excitement." Less than a week later, a general riot broke out in Camp Douglas, requiring the camp's superintendent to bring in reinforcements to pacify the unruly parolees. For many of the Harpers Ferry parolees, the most lasting memory of their tenure at Camp Douglas was the verbal abuse they received from newly recruited Illinois soldiers, who mocked them as "Harper's Ferry Cowards." Finding the jeering as "more than flesh and blood could bear," the parolees took "the redress of their wrongs into their own hands, hands which had strong sinews and hard knuckles, as the taunting Illinois boys found to their cost." Although the epithet of "Harper's Ferry Cowards" largely ceased after the soldiers redeemed themselves at Gettysburg, many of them felt that the stigma of their surrender at Harpers Ferry remained for years afterward. The taint of cowardice was not easily erased, even for veterans.[49]

Between February and April 1862, the Confederacy also suffered from a string of costly surrenders. In eastern North Carolina, the Union invasion under Gen. Ambrose Burnside overwhelmed Confederate defenders, prompting the surrender of Roanoke Island (February 8) and Fort Macon (April 26). In Tennessee, Union forces under Flag Officer Andrew Foote and Gen. Ulysses S. Grant forced the surrender of Fort Henry (February 6) and Fort Donelson (February 16). Near Savannah, Fort Pulaski surrendered (April 11) after a devastating artillery bombardment from nearby Tybee Island. In Louisiana, the garrison at Fort Jackson near New Orleans capitulated to a substantially larger Union force (April 28). In most of these cases, surrender appeared to be justified using the paradigm established at Fort Sumter: facing inevitable defeat and disaster, after sustaining heavy fire, surrender was preferable to a suicidal and fruitless defense. After the fall of Fort Macon, for instance, the *Charleston Mercury* pronounced that its "defense, though of brief duration, was gallant and honorable . . . and the surrender was certainly as free from humiliation as any surrender may be." Yet the cumulative effective of so many surrenders in such a short time frame suggested an uncertain commitment to the Confederate cause. Confederate pundits argued that the frequency that rebels raised the white flag demonstrated a weakness in Confederate nationalism.[50]

Only at Fort Donelson did Confederate commanders suffer the level of public opprobrium that befell their Union counterparts at San Antonio, San Augustin Springs, and Harpers Ferry. The Union siege of Fort Donelson began immediately after Gen. Ulysses S. Grant and Flag Officer Andrew Foote had taken Fort Henry on February 6. Only eleven miles apart, the twin forts had been designed to anchor Confederate defenses on the Tennessee River. Although similar in construction, the low-lying Fort Henry had effectively been defeated by the elements before Grant arrived. Heavy rains had swollen the Tennessee River, flooding parts of the fort in two feet of water and rendering some of the cannons and much of the powder useless. Believing that Henry had a garrison of approximately 10,000, Grant called for a bombardment by Foote's ironclad gunboats with a simultaneous assault from land, anticipating that the siege would last at least a couple of days before the rebels capitulated. However, on the day of the attack, the capture of Fort Henry had proved less challenging than anticipated. Muddy roads slowed Grant's men, so Foote's ironclads began their bombardment at the appointed hour alone. After less than three hours of shelling, Gen. Lloyd Tilghman ordered the Confederate flag lowered from the parapet, raising a white flag in its stead. By that time, only Grant's advance guard had arrived on the site. Still marching along the muddy roads, many of the Union soldiers were initially confused when the echoing sounds of the cannonade stopped prematurely. "We were tramping along in the mud, when a messenger passed along the line announcing the capture of the fort by the gunboats," noted one Illinois soldier. "Some of us cheered, but others were silent and really felt sore at the sailors for their taking the fort before we had a chance to help them." Grant himself arrived an hour after Foote had accepted Tilghman's surrender. He discovered that only 100 men remained from the original garrison of 2,800, Tilghman having ordered the indefensible fort evacuated the previous evening. The swift victory pleased Grant, relieved that he did not have to engage in a lengthy siege. Having taken Fort Henry, he reported to Halleck that "I shall take and destroy Fort Donelson."[51]

The attack on Fort Donelson proved much more difficult. Situated on high ground eighty feet above the Cumberland River, Donelson was both better situated and better defended that Fort Henry. In addition to an impressive array of artillery that effectively defended the fort from approach by water, the garrison numbered over 16,000. Most of the Confederates at Donelson were recent arrivals. The fort's commanding officer, Gen. John B. Floyd, had arrived on February 13, bringing with him a brigade of reinforcements. A former Virginia governor and U.S. secretary of war, Floyd had only been reassigned to the western theater after demonstrating mild ineffectiveness under Robert E. Lee in Virginia. Floyd assumed control of the fort from Gen. Gideon Pillow, who himself had arrived on February 9. Like Floyd, Pillow owed his position primarily to his political connections rather than his military acumen, a shortcoming Pillow managed to demonstrate on more than one occasion during the first year of the war. Despite the relative incompetence of Floyd and Pillow (who distrusted each other), the Confederate command did contain a couple of agile military minds. One was Gen. Simon Buckner, a West Point graduate (who later taught at the academy) and Mexican War veteran. The other was Lt. Col. Nathan Bedford Forrest. Enlisting as a private in 1861, Forrest had rapidly risen in the ranks and had cultivated an unusual devotion among his men. Like the other Confederate commanders, Forrest had only recently reached Fort Donelson, arriving on February 10 with 800 cavalry.

Grant's army marched from Fort Henry toward Donelson on February 12, investing the fort on two sides. Probing assaults over the next two days revealed that the Confederate fort would not fall easily. A blizzard on February 13 covered both armies in three inches of snow as temperatures dropped well below freezing. Confederate artillery effectively repulsed Foote's fleet from the river on February 14. Despite these initial successes, the rebels worried that Union reinforcements would prompt a lengthy siege that would cause their men to either freeze or starve. On the morning of February 15, the Confederates attempted to fight their way out of the fort. Although they were initially successful in opening a corridor on the Union right flank, Grant effectively closed the door that afternoon, retaking the positions the rebels had held that morning. By sundown, the Confederates were again ensconced within Fort Donelson, casting recriminations for the failure of that morning's breakout.

Late in the evening of February 15, Confederate commanders and their staffs met to discuss surrendering the fort. Although only the third-highest-ranking officer, Simon Buckner had the most military experience and offered the initial assessment, laying out a pessimistic analysis of their situation. He knew that many of the Confederate troops had become demoralized by long exposure in poor weather. Buckner argued that if Grant attacked in the morning (and Buckner was convinced that he would), the fort would fall within thirty minutes. Fighting their way out of the fort would also be disastrous, he argued, estimating that only one in four Confederates would survive such a breakout unscathed. The only option remaining was to surrender.

Buckner's superiors Floyd and Pillow quickly agreed with his assessment.[52] Although both thought the fort had to surrender, neither man wanted to take responsibility for the surrender itself. As Buchanan's secretary of war during the secession crisis, Floyd had relocated war materiel south, which was subsequently seized by Confederates. Fearing prosecution, Floyd argued that he could not be allowed to be taken prisoner, telling the room, "Gentlemen, I cannot surrender. You know my position with the Federals. It wouldn't do; it wouldn't do." Pillow likewise refused to be taken prisoner, believing his political prominence would make his capture a liability for the Confederacy. "I am determined that I will never surrender the command nor will I ever surrender myself a prisoner," Pillow argued; "I will die first." With Floyd and Pillow absolving themselves of responsibility for the fort, command passed to Buckner, who reluctantly agreed to surrender the fort and its garrison. Disgusted with Floyd and Pillow for their abnegation of responsibility, Buckner told Floyd, "Surrender here is as bitter to me as it is to you or anyone else. I feel, however, that it necessary here. At the same time I must for my own honor and sense of duty not separate myself from my own command. Their fortune is my fortune."

Irate at the discussion of surrender, Forrest would have none of it. "I had not come out for the purpose of surrendering my command," he announced to the room. He would lead any men who were willing to fight their way out the fort. Receiving Pillow's blessing, Forrest began to organize his breakout, saying, "All who wanted to go could follow me, and those who wished to stay and take the consequences might remain in camp." Confusion reigned in the hours between the conclusion of the officers meeting at 2:00 A.M. and sunrise. While Buckner prepared a written offer of surrender, rumors quickly spread among the soldiers, many of whom expressed shock, disbelief, and disappointment in the decision. Floyd and Pillow hurried to flee: Pillow took a moonlit raft across the Cumberland, and Floyd escaped at daybreak via a crowded steamboat with two regiments of Virginia infantry. At first light, Forrest escaped Fort Donelson with approximately 500 men from his own command and assorted soldiers from other regiments who thought flight more honorable than surrender. Riding through icy Lick Creek, they made their way toward Nashville unmolested by Union soldiers.[53]

Many of the Confederate soldiers at Fort Donelson expressed surprise and horror that they had been surrendered. Maj. Nathaniel Cheairs called Donelson "the most disgraceful, unnecessary, and uncalled for surrender" of the entire war. When he first heard that his commanding officers intended to surrender, Cheairs could not sustain his incredulity, noting, "Going to Surrender after whipping Grant as we had done, I don't believe it." Nonetheless, Cheairs found himself tasked as a messenger to deliver Buckner's offer of surrender to Grant. He cut a strip of canvas from his tent and fastened it to a hickory pole to serve as a flag of truce. He selected a bugler from the regimental band to accompany him, and the two men wondered "what call should be made [on the bugle] for a Surrender," as "None of us know any particular call to make as it was our first experience of a Surrender."[54]

Buckner's offer conformed to fairly standard language for surrender in the nineteenth century. In a concisely worded statement, Buckner recognized the "circumstances governing the present situation of affairs" and asked for the appointment of commissioners "to agree upon terms of capitulation of the forces and post under my command." To allow the commissioners time to do their work, he proposed an armistice until noon. The practice of appointing commissioners (usually inferior officers) to negotiate the finer points of the surrender was a fairly conventional element in formal surrenders during the eighteenth and early nineteenth centuries: the surrender at Yorktown had been orchestrated through the use of commissioners, as had most of the surrenders in the Napoleonic Wars. Many historians have postulated that Buckner hoped to negotiate favorable terms based on his past friendship with Grant. They had attended West Point together and served alongside each other in the Mexican War. In 1854, Buckner had loaned a penniless Grant money to pay for a hotel room in New York.

If Buckner's offer to surrender was entirely conventional, Grant's response was not. Equally concise, Grant wrote, "SIR: Yours of this date, proposing armistice and appointment of commissioners to settle terms of capitulation, is just received. No terms except unconditional and immediate surrender can be accepted. I propose to move immediately upon your works." Grant's demand for unconditional surrender stood outside established norms of how most military thinkers thought of surrender. Usually only employed against enemies deemed barbaric or outside the community of civilized nations, demands for unconditional surrender had almost entirely disappeared from European battlefields by the eighteenth century.[55] Within the context of the Civil War, Grant's demand was unprecedented. Earlier surrenders had always functioned under the pretext that they had been the product of a negotiation between equals in which the victorious party offered some concession to their foe. This fiction had been a feature even in those surrenders, like Fort Sumter, where the besieged party had been almost entirely overpowered and could offer no meaningful resistance.

Grant never explained why he believed unconditional surrender was necessary. His private and professional letters from the time offer no elucidation, and in his *Memoirs*, Grant simply reprinted the correspondence between Buckner and himself without commentary or analysis. Some evidence suggests that the idea for unconditional surrender did not originate with Grant. Bearing Buckner's surrender offer, Major Cheairs was escorted through the Union lines by Gen. Charles F. Smith. Smith had been Grant's (and Buckner's) instructor at West Point, and since 1861 he had served Grant as both mentor and confidant. Cheairs noted that when he delivered the message, Smith "& Grant held a private consultation and wrote out some dispatches for me to take to Buckner." Asked his opinion of Buckner's offer, Smith tersely quipped, "No terms to the damned rebels." Taking Smith's counsel, Grant translated his sentiment into a more politic but no less biting reply. His threat "to move immediately upon your works" was no bluff; at the same time that he sent Cheairs back with his reply, Grant ordered his subordinates to prepare for an attack upon the fortification, suggesting that Grant was unsure if Buckner would agree with his demand. Although most of the attention has been given to Grant's demand that the surrender be unconditional, his demand that the surrender be immediate might have been the more important tactical decision he made that morning.

Grant undoubtedly had been informed that Confederate soldiers were evacu-ating Fort Donelson that morning, as Pillow, Floyd, and Forrest did not appear to be making any particular effort to disguise their movements. Grant may have suspected that an armistice until noon would have provided cover for additional Confederate evacuations.[56]

Reading Grant's reply, Buckner expressed shock and dismay. Disbelieving Grant's heterodox demand, Buckner felt that he had no choice but to "accept the ungenerous and unchivalrous terms which you propose." If Grant's initial message suggested incivility and implied harshness, his subsequent behavior manifested generosity and forbearance. With Buckner's agreement in hand, Grant and his aides rode to meet with the Confederate general in the Dover Hotel, the same building that had hosted the contentious rebel meeting the previous evening. What must have begun as a very uncomfortable meeting quickly evolved into a more amicable discussion. According to one of Grant's aides, over some "vile Confederate coffee . . . the two enemies of an hour be-fore, smoking pacifically, discussed the surrender." Reminiscing about their experiences in Mexico, the two old friends exchanged mutual compliments about their recent military performance. After discussing the absence of Floyd and Pillow, about which both men shared a laugh, the discussion turned to the number of men surrendered. With the recent nighttime departures, Buckner could only estimate that they numbered between 12,000 and 15,000. Although he did not know how many men he had under his command, Buckner did know that many of them were hungry, and Grant offered rations on par with those his own men received. At Buckner's request, Grant allowed Confeder-ate officers to keep their sidearms and body servants, although other African Americans would be liberated to work "for the benefit of the Government." Buckner also asked permission for a Confederate detail to go outside his lines to bury the dead. Grant allowed this, although he recognized that "many got beyond our pickets unobserved and went on. The most of the men who went in that way no doubt thought they had had war enough, and left with the inten-tion of remaining out of the army. Some came to me and asked permission to go, saying that they were tired of the war and would not be caught in the ranks again, and I bade them go." The only person who appeared uncomfortable at the meeting was Gen. Charles F. Smith, who refused Buckner's offer of coffee and cornbread.[57]

Grant's insistence on unconditional surrender was not the only unorth-odox element of the surrender at Fort Donelson. Never comfortable with ex-cessive formality or ceremony, Grant eschewed any of the pomp that usually accompanied surrender. Shortly after his meeting with Buckner, Grant was questioned by Dr. John H. Brinton, a member of his staff, about "how soon, or when, the enemy would be paraded and the formalities of surrender gone through with, such as the lowering of the standard and the stacking of the guns, and the delivery of the Confederate commander's sword." Grant replied, "There will be nothing of the kind." There was no need for a ceremony, as "the surrender is now a fact. We have the fort, the men, the guns. Why should we go through vain forms and mortify and injure the spirit of brave men, who, after all, are our own countrymen?" Brinton left the conversation mystified, as "all this seemed very strange to me whose mind was filled with the pageantry of European warfare." Although he was disappointed to miss the spectacle, he was impressed with Grant's generosity in victory, as "it showed the kind of man Grant was." This aversion to embarrassing the defeated foe remained a constant element of Grant's thinking on the propriety of surrender. At Vicksburg, Grant also eschewed a formal surrender ceremony, and although more formalities attended the surrender at Appomattox Courthouse, Grant absented himself from these, refusing to take an active role in ceremonies that might embarrass the defeated foe. At all three surrenders, Grant refused to demand the rebel general's sword and actively dissuaded his own troops from flaunting their triumph with excessive celebration.[58]

For all his apparent generosity, Grant understood that unconditional surrender carried with it enormous, if not unlimited, power over the defeated enemy. The clearest articulation of this came a few days after the surrender when Grant was escorting Buckner and the other Confederate prisoners to Cairo. En route, Buckner complained that his men were being mistreated, with Union soldiers appropriating their blankets and confiscating officers' sidearms. "This compels me to say things which I hoped to avoid speaking of, because I wanted to save your feelings," Grant told Buckner. "Your men have committed the grossest outrages. I know you can not approve of them, and I suppose you could scarcely prevent them." During the surrender, a Confederate officer "growing angry" had shot a Union officer "in the back." Rebel "soldiers have stripped my dead, and left them naked on the field, while in your possession. They have taken every blanket from prisoners," among other crimes. Furthermore, "The weather is cold, and my troops need these blankets. By the laws of war they are entitled to them; for in an unconditional surrender, every thing belongs to the victors." He promised that the prisoners would be well treated, receiving the same rations as his own soldiers, and that their captivity in Union prisons would be humane, unlike those experienced by Union soldiers in

Confederate prisons. According to one of his aides, "Grant's staff had never heard him speak so vehemently on any subject." Buckner was stunned into silence and sat mutely for a few minutes before excusing himself.[59]

By situating "unconditional surrender" within the "laws of war," Grant articulated the legal and moral imperatives incumbent upon both the victor and the vanquished. The victor could, if he so chose, deprive the surrendered party of all their material possessions. The only limitations to this power were the obligations under the laws of war to treat captured soldiers humanely. To be sure, at this point in the conflict, the "laws of war" were more an amorphous concept than a text to be consulted: both the Dix-Hill cartel and the Lieber Code lay in the future. Nevertheless, Grant understood the enormous power he possessed when accepting an unconditional surrender, and he chose to exercise that power judiciously.

Soldiers on both sides responded predictably to the news of the surrender. Many rebels saw the surrender as unnecessary and disgraceful. One soldier noted that "in this surrender, we have lost the chivalry and flower of our whole army." Many of the surrendered garrison greeted the news by getting drunk and throwing their weapons into the Cumberland River in disgust, preferring that their weapons lie in a watery grave than be handed over to the Union. Alexander Jackson Campbell of the 48th Tennessee spoke for many in the garrison when he observed that they "felt an outrage had been committed in surrendering them." Union soldiers, by contrast, were relieved that the surrender meant that they would not have to assault Fort Donelson. "We all expected a great slaughter," wrote an Ohio officer, relieved that the fort had fallen without causalities on either side. An Illinois soldier remembered the cheering that went up when Grant's men learned of the Confederate surrender. "Did we shout? Well, if we didn't use our lungs then, we never did."[60]

The surrender of Fort Donelson was a decisive moment in the military careers of many of its participants. After the surrender of Fort Donelson, both Pillow and Floyd were relieved of their command, and neither held a prominent command again. Gideon Pillow briefly reassumed command of the 3rd Division of the Army of Central Kentucky before Jefferson Davis removed him for "grave errors in judgment in the military operations which resulted in the surrender of the army." He was later reinstated, serving under Braxton Bragg, but after being accused of cowardice at Stones River, he was reassigned to supervising conscription for the Army of Tennessee. Jefferson Davis also relieved John B. Floyd of his command. The former Virginia governor briefly took command of his native state's Home Guard, but he died of ill health in 1863.

Saddled with the burden of conducting the surrender, Simon Buckner fared better than Floyd or Pillow. Imprisoned for five months in Boston harbor, much of it in solitary confinement, Buckner was exchanged in September 1862 and immediately promoted to major general. In the first action of his new command, Buckner forced the Union garrison at Munfordville, Kentucky, to surrender. Performing admirably at Perryville and Chickamauga, Buckner was again promoted to lieutenant general, serving as Edmund Kirby Smith's chief of staff until the war's conclusion. After the war, Buckner had a successful political career, including a term as governor of Kentucky.[61]

While some deemed the Confederate surrender at Fort Donelson dishonorable because of the behavior of two of its commanders, the surrender three months later at Fort Jackson became infamous for the dishonorable behavior of its soldiers. Alongside its twin, Fort St. Philip, Fort Jackson guarded the approach to New Orleans. Its garrison mutinied after two weeks of bombardment from Union gunboats under Admiral David Farragut and his foster brother Commander David Dixon Porter and immediately surrendered the fort, easing the subsequent Federal occupation of the city. No sources document the mutiny from the perspective of the mutineers, so their precise motivations remain unclear. Union officials attributed the mutiny to the effectiveness of naval artillery and the fear of an anticipated infantry invasion under Gen. Benjamin Butler. Confederates claimed that the garrison, many of whom were immigrants, mutinied because they were less than fully committed to the Confederate cause.[62]

In the official inquiry into the fall of New Orleans, Fort Jackson's commander, Lt. Col. Edward Higgins, attempted to salvage his own reputation. He argued that the mutineers had effectively repulsed officers' efforts to bring them into line and appeared poised to bring about "a general massacre of the officers, and a disgraceful surrender of the fort." Higgins negotiated with the mutineers to "prevent this disgraceful blot upon our country" and was able to engineer "an honorable surrender." Noting that he did not want to "dwell any longer on this humiliating and unhappy affair" in which the mutineers "basely dishonored their country," Higgins did not articulate why he believed a capitulation conducted by the mutineers amounted to "a disgraceful surrender," while an identical action undertaken by officers was "an honorable surrender," though he suggests that honor requires surrender to be conducted with "the passion of the men in check." There could be no honor without mastery over both subordinates and emotions.[63]

The Fort Jackson mutiny raised difficult questions about the relationship between surrender and Confederate nationalism. If the garrison did not believe enough in the Confederate cause or their officers to prolong their defense, what did this say about the depth and sincerity of Southern commitment one year after Fort Sumter? The mutiny could have been written off as the act of a handful of misguided individuals had it not taken place in the wake of the rash of surrenders during the previous three months, prompting a robust debate in the Confederate press about the merits of the white flag. On February 21, 1862, the *Richmond Daily Examiner* published a letter from an anonymous officer concerning "the late reverses at Fort Henry and Roanoke Island, which may be grating to ears polite, but is rendered necessary by the condition of the country." The letter was published alongside news that Fort Donelson had surrendered, although the text suggests it was written several days earlier. The letter writer argued, "It is high time that these surrenders should cease—for, considering the character of the war in its consequences to us, they have been truly amazing." Both surrenders, he claimed, were entirely unnecessary, unmanly, dishonorable, and detrimental to the war effort. At Fort Henry, "a *brigadier-general*, unwounded, having a garrison almost intact, lowers his flag over a dozen guns of the largest calibre, and with a hackneyed compliment yields up his bloodless sword." Lloyd Tilghman's bloodless surrender represented an affront to the honor of Confederate men everywhere: "How withering and humiliating to our Southern manhood." With Tilghman then imprisoned at Fort Warren, the anonymous officer opined whether after his exchange (which would not come until August 1862) he was morally fit to return to "rolls of the Southern army as an officer." He found the surrender at Roanoke Island equally humiliating, noting that the "Roanoke affair is perfectly incomprehensible," as the Confederate soldiers there had also surrendered "with no blood on their bayonets" and after only a handful of casualties. For the letter writer, these recent surrenders suggested that the celebrated Confederate martial bravery had abated. Heretofore, newspapers were "filled with extravagant laudations of our valor; the annals of Greece and Rome offer no parallel; whole regiments were defeated by companies, and we yielded only to death." The surrenders at Fort Henry and at Roanoke Island, he argued, revealed that the tide had turned and that the "whole army had better surrender at once, for it will eventually come to it."[64]

The *Richmond Daily Examiner* letter was widely reprinted in Northern newspapers, including such diverse outlets as the *New York Times, Frank Leslie's Illustrated Weekly,* and the *Christian Recorder,* an African American newspaper based in Philadelphia. In its reprinting of the letter, the *Weekly Vincennes Western Sun* cheekily wondered "what this writer thinks of the surrender of Buckner with 15,000 unharmed men at Fort Donelson." The *Burlington (Iowa)*

Weekly Hawk-Eye suggested that the letter indicated that Southern "people are getting disheartened at their successive defeats. . . . If the tide of battle does not soon turn in favor of the South, the country may witness the unusual spectacle of a rebellion within a rebellion." On March 11, 1862, Senator John S. Carlile quoted extensively from the *Richmond Examiner* letter on the floor of the Senate. He argued that the letter revealed that most Confederate soldiers had only a lukewarm commitment to the cause. The recent surrenders at Roanoke, Fort Henry, and Fort Donelson, he claimed, indicated declining morale among Confederate soldiers. "If the rebel force had been animated by the spirit that inaugurated this rebellion," he argued, "it would never have surrendered as it did."[65]

Subsequent Confederate surrenders in March and April prompted more critical letters in Southern newspapers. After the surrender of Fort Jackson and the fall of New Orleans, the *Richmond Dispatch* ran a letter under the heading "No More Surrenders." The surrender not only had dishonored the Confederate military but had placed Southern ladies "under the tyrannical yoke of our Northern oppressors, subject to the despotism of such bipeds as Butler and consorts." The only option remaining, the letter argued, was to renounce surrender as a tool of war and adopt Patrick Henry's invocation to "give me liberty or give me death." Henry's dictum, the letter argued, "should always be present to the mind of every soldier on the battle-field."[66]

The sentiment that Confederate forces surrendered too frequently did not abate. In November 1863, the *Richmond Enquirer* complained that although "the people and the army of the Confederate States have been so much complimented upon the prowess and gallantry of their arms, . . . they have lost sight of the fact that more surrenders have been made by their armies than by armies of any other nation. What nation in three years of war ever lowered their flag eleven times in surrender?" Generally known for greater restraint than the *Examiner* or the *Dispatch*, the *Enquirer* editorial enumerated an incomplete list that included the recent disasters at Vicksburg, Port Hudson, and Cumberland Gap. The dishonor of these surrenders had been exacerbated by an absence of accountability: "There has not been an instance of punishment in this long list of disasters; but on the contrary, promotion has in some cases followed swift upon the surrender." The frequency with which Confederate forces surrendered mattered, the newspaper argued, because European powers would not take the Confederacy seriously if it continued to "exhibit more surrenders than ever befell the arms of any other nation." The quest for foreign recognition, which the Confederate government had vigorously pursued since secession, had failed in part because "foreign nations see [Confederate] surrenders so complacently made."

The *Enquirer* made clear that it did not intend to cast aspersions on the valor of Confederate officers and soldiers. It noted that many of the surrenders featured "instances of great gallantry." Soldiers had fought bravely, and officers often had good justification for concluding that surrender provided the best and only option available. Yet the cumulative effect of these surrenders was to undermine not only the individual honor of Confederate generals but also the Confederacy's national honor. As a new republic, the Confederacy's international reputation remained inchoate. "We do not mean to intimate that all of these surrenders were equally disgraceful," the newspaper concluded, "but we do say that not one of them conferred any honor upon the arms of the Confederate States."[67] The ongoing debate concerning the propriety of surrender reflected the growing sentiment that the Confederation national project was being undercut by low morale, inept leadership, and officers lacking sufficient grit. Unlike Northerners, who tended to pin the blame for a dishonorable surrender on an individual scapegoat, Confederates saw the potential for surrender, even if conducted on an honorable basis, to dishonor the entire nation and jeopardize their quest for independence.

INSTINCTIVELY MY HANDS WENT UP

Soldiers, Agency, and Surrender on the Battlefield

Commanding officers had the luxury of time to assess the merits of surrender. For soldiers in the heat of battle, however, the decisions about whether to surrender or to accept the surrender of an enemy had to be made instantaneously. The confusion, noise, and danger of the battlefield complicated the dynamics of consent. Official records and modern historians often use the term "captured" to describe soldiers held as prisoners of war after a battle, a usage that obscures a dynamic process of transformation from an active soldier to a prisoner of war, effectively equating soldiers with captured battle flags, cannons, railroad depots, or hilltops. Unlike inanimate objects or geographic locations, however, soldiers had to throw down their guns, raise their hands or a white flag, and yell, "I surrender!" before being taken prisoner. Surrender also required the enemy soldier to accept the surrender, transitioning instantaneously from combatant to captor. Made in the heat of battle, with weapons aloft, amidst the confusing roar of gunfire and blinding smoke, these fraught decisions reflected how the desires of soldiers to fight bravely and honorably competed with their desire for self-preservation. Looking at surrender from the ground level offers a perspective very different from that occupied by commanding officers contemplating surrender. While officers usually had time to consider the merits of surrender and could negotiate for terms to their advantage, soldiers had none of those luxuries. For soldiers, the decision to surrender presented an almost unconscious choice. Surprised by the sudden appearance of rebels, a Wisconsin soldier in Arkansas recalled that "instantly and almost instinctively my hands went up in token of surrender."[1]

Although soldiers rarely had the opportunity to deliberate and reflect during combat, the ability to surrender presented one of the few autonomous choices they felt empowered to make on the battlefield. The command structure of both Union and Confederate armies dictated that the primary responsibility of enlisted men was to follow orders. They were ordered when, where, and how fast to march. They were ordered when to fire, reload, and charge; when to wheel; when to reform from column to file; and when to retreat. A popular drill manual used to train both Confederate and Union recruits distinguished between officers and common soldiers as those "who command" and "those who obey."[2] Soldiers who failed to obey could be harshly, at times draconically, punished. Within the confines of severely limited autonomy, a soldier's ability to surrender presented the most visible manifestation of his agency.[3] To be sure, some soldiers did not consent to be captured, such as those so badly injured as to be unable to resist, and existing records make it impossible to distinguish between those who actively surrendered and those who were taken prisoner while incapacitated. However, the evidence suggests that the majority of soldiers who ended up listed in muster rolls and official records as captured, outside the large formal surrenders orchestrated by their commanders, did so by choosing to surrender. If the ability to surrender demonstrated one aspect of a common soldier's agency, so too did his ability to accept or demand an enemy soldier's surrender.

Throughout the Civil War, soldiers made the complex dynamic of surrender a ubiquitous feature on the battlefield. In every battle, individual soldiers found themselves in a position where surrendering seemed to be the best, if not the only, option. Soldiers who served longer than a year had a one in six chance of being called on to surrender, and even greater chances of accepting the surrender of an enemy soldier.[4] For more than 300,000 Union and Confederate soldiers, the decision to surrender presented the most decisive choice they would make, one with immediate consequences for their life or death. This chapter endeavors to uncover how, when, and why Union and Confederate soldiers surrendered.

Few enlisted soldiers understood the complexity of surrender at the ground level as well as James Blackburn. Born in Tennessee in 1837, Blackburn moved with his family in 1856 to Texas, where he taught school. In February 1861, he joined Col. Ben McCulloch's forces in west Texas and had been within earshot when McCulloch accepted Twiggs's surrender at the Alamo. Fighting in the 8th Texas Calvary, commonly called Terry's Texas Rangers, Blackburn was present at or near many significant surrenders over the course of the war. In February 1862, he helped to shuttle supplies out of Fort Donelson prior to its surrender. In the summer of 1862, he fought under Nathan Bedford Forrest and was present when Forrest demanded the surrender of Murfreesboro. In April

1865, he was with General Johnston in North Carolina but attempted to flee to Texas rather than surrender with Johnston at Bennett Place. He had hoped to rendezvous with General Kirby Smith in Texas to continue the fight, only to find that Kirby Smith had also surrendered. In his memoirs, however, Blackburn did not dwell on these large surrenders, but on the numerous occasions on the battlefield when he had to choose whether to surrender and whether to accept an enemy's surrender.[5]

In the aftermath of Shiloh, Blackburn participated in a rear-guard action as Confederates retreated toward Corinth. With Union forces in close pursuit, Forrest's cavalry sought to delay them long enough for the main body of Confederate soldiers to make their escape. Charging headlong into the advancing Union skirmishers, 200 cavalrymen "went like a cyclone." They waited until they were nearly upon their enemy before firing their shotguns, creating a scene of "destruction and confusion." Blackburn remembered that under such circumstances, "every man seemed to act upon his own judgment. . . . We were all generals and colonels." Although the skirmish ended, as Blackburn described it, "in a twinkling of an eye," the chaos of combat pushed some Union soldiers to offer to surrender. Not all were accepted.

Blackburn participated in one of these attempted surrenders. "In our pursuit of the flying enemy," Blackburn recalled,

> as I rushed by a stump of a tree, . . . I became suddenly aware of a bayonet near my body in the hands of a red faced Dutchman, and I could not tell whether he made a thrust at me and missed me or whether he intended to use it on me if I bothered him. I turned upon him, fully intending to kill him, but when I leveled my pistol at him, he dropped his bayonetted gun upon the ground and with the greatest terror depicted in his face, said, "I surrender." In an instance I forgave him and let him live. I think surrender was the only English word he could speak, neither could he understand a word I said. I said, "take that gun up and break it against the stump" and when I found he didn't know what to do and stood trembling I pointed to the gun and made signs to take hold of it and motions to strike. I got him to understand me, he broke the breech off and I motioned him to our rear and went off at a lively gait.[6]

Blackburn's decision not to kill the Union soldier came in a moment. Indeed, in the fury of battle, Blackburn had to suppress his desire to fire, as he aimed "fully intending to kill him." Only when the soldier dropped his weapon and expressed his desire to surrender did Blackburn reconsider his intention to kill him. Blackburn makes it clear, however, that the soldier's intention to surrender did not guarantee that Blackburn must accept it, noting, "In an instance I forgave him and let him live." Although the regulations of both armies and common practice dictated that surrendering soldiers were prisoners of war and therefore entitled to humane treatment, Blackburn evidently believed that within the midst of combat, he was not compelled to accept the soldier's surrender.

Blackburn's supposition that the word "surrender" was "the only English word" the German American soldier knew is also revealing. It suggests that soldiers believed that requests to surrender would be taken seriously. In this situation, the German American soldier had to make an instantaneous decision about whether to strike Blackburn with his bayonet or to throw down his weapon and offer to surrender. In a dangerous mental gamble, he concluded that he was more likely to live if he attempted to surrender than if he struck an armed cavalry soldier on horseback. He evidently had thought about the likelihood of needing to surrender enough that he was able to utter the words in a moment of high stress and anxiety.[7]

Alongside his story of accepting a German American soldier's surrender, Blackburn described how another soldier in his regiment made a very different decision during the same battle. Blackburn described Ed Kaylor as "a good soldier, never showing any fear about him." During the cavalry charge, Kaylor "came upon a captain who had vainly tried to rally his men as they ran to the rear." With his soldiers chaotically fleeing behind him, the Union captain "fired on Kaylor as he rode towards him. They exchanged three shots each; Kaylor slowly advancing upon him. When Kaylor closed in upon him he threw up his hands and offered to surrender." Unlike Blackburn, Kaylor did not accept the Union captain's offer to surrender. According to Blackburn, Kaylor yelled, "'Oh H-ll you are too late' and fired another shot, killing him instantly."[8]

Describing the attempted surrenders in consecutive paragraphs in his reminiscences, Blackburn silently contrasts them without comment. Given the size of the battlefield and the length of this particular engagement, the two events could not have taken place more than a few minutes apart and more than a hundred yards distant. Blackburn offered no explicit judgment about the merits of his or Kaylor's actions. If he thought that Kaylor should have accepted the surrender and spared the Union captain's life, he did not record it in his reminiscences. He does, however, hint at some of the elements that may have pushed Kaylor to fire, while Blackburn decided to accept the proffered surrender. First, he describes the encounter between Kaylor and the Union captain as a "pistol duel" and a "game." In firing at each other with comparable weapons and with an equal number of shots, Kaylor and the Union captain were, to Blackburn's eyes, engaging in an individual duel, with the rest of the skirmish in the background. As all Southern white men knew, duels were fought according to rules, and the Union captain had violated those rules by attempting to surrender. Second, Kaylor seemed to enjoy the act of killing the surrendering Union captain. Blackburn observed that it made him "smile so sweetly." When Blackburn asked him about it later, Kaylor reported that he did not know he was smiling but that "he surely did enjoy that scrap immensely." Some Civil War soldiers developed a lust for bloodshed. The hatred that many soldiers developed for the enemy may have driven some soldiers to kill rather than accept an offer of surrender.[9]

As Blackburn noted, accepting an offer to surrender entailed an element of forgiveness, a term loaded with religious connotations. Not all soldiers were willing to extend such grace to a hated enemy. One Confederate soldier, after the Seven Days, wrote in his diary, "May God avenge us of our infernal enemies—and if I ever forgive them it is more than I Expect. 'Forgive your Enemies' is the Divine precept—a hard one to obey—How can one forgive such enemies as we are contending against?" His anger reflected not only his pain from losing friends and comrades in battle but also his hatred of the captured Union soldiers he had been assigned to guard.[10]

Refusing to accept an enemy's offer of surrender was the exception rather than the rule. While there was always a chance that an offer to surrender would be refused, Civil War soldiers believed, with some justification, that if they threw down their rifles, their surrender would be accepted. In this respect, Civil War soldiers proved unusual, as studies of combat in the Napoleonic Wars, the Franco-Prussian War, and the World Wars indicate that only half of all offers to surrender in those conflicts were accepted, and soldiers were generally loath to surrender, knowing that there was a fair probability that their would-be captors would kill them.[11] Most Civil War soldiers did not have this fear; they expected that offers to surrender would be honored. African Americans and Southern Unionists proved the notable exceptions to this paradigm, as Confederates did not consider either group legitimate soldiers and therefore denied them the sanctuary provided by surrender.

Although quick to brand officers who formally surrendered unnecessarily as cowards, soldiers almost never criticized a fellow soldier (on either side) for surrendering himself on the battlefield. Surrendering in combat required a dangerous proximity to the enemy, a proximity that shirkers and cowards avoided. Indeed, many Civil War soldiers recognized that the soldiers most likely to find themselves in a situation to surrender tended to be brave and unfortunate rather than cowardly. As James McPherson has observed, Civil War soldiers often worried that their courage would fail them in battle, and many soldiers feared being labeled cowards more than they did dying in battle. This fear sometimes manifested itself in soldiers taking unnecessary risks. Soldiers who advanced too quickly or retreated too slowly often found themselves isolated and surrounded. Confederate Gart Johnson had often prayed during the war that "I might never be wounded," but "I never gave much thought to be captured—at least not enough to make it an object of prayer." In a September 1864 skirmish near Harpers Ferry, Johnson "didn't hear the command [to retreat] and stayed at the front too long." Surrounded, Johnson recognized that "the alternative was surrender or die. I chose the former, and threw my sword as far as I could send it."[12]

As Johnson's case indicates, one's position and role on the battlefield factored significantly into which soldiers surrendered. Civil War armies tended to fight in close formations, soldiers marching "shoulder to shoulder" and fighting at "the touch of the elbow." Tactical manuals emphasized the importance of unit cohesion, limiting individual autonomy. Only when the chaos of battlefield fractured the neat lines did individual soldiers find themselves with the isolation and the agency to surrender. No matter how well drilled or disciplined the troops, most Civil War battles reached a point in which the forces of entropy overcame the power of regulation. A New York soldier noted, "Disintegration begins with the first shot. To the book-soldier all order seems destroyed, months of drill apparently going for nothing in a few minutes."[13] The more chaotic a battle became, the more often soldiers found themselves cut off from their regiment, and the more likely they found themselves in a position to surrender.

Hasty retreats created the most chaotic environments on a battlefield and produced a significant number of surrenders. As Joseph Glatthaar has noted, almost every regiment retreated at some point during the Civil War. Although orderly retreats did take place, most became panicked and anarchic, if only for a moment. Illinois soldier Samuel Boggs described chaos when he was forced to surrender at Chickamauga: "The Rebels made a desperate charge; there was a crashing roar; the air seemed full of bullets, dust and Rebel yells. Men went down on all sides of me; we were in a hand-to-hand encounter; some of our men had saved themselves by timely flight, but our retreat was cut off; it was either surrender, or foolishly throw our lives away."[14]

The primary weapon of the Civil War soldier, the rifle musket, often conspired against him, compelling his surrender. In recent years, historians have reevaluated how significant a technological innovation the rifle musket represented. As historian Earl Hess has persuasively argued, although the rifle musket in theory had a longer range than its smoothbore predecessor, few soldiers were skilled enough to take advantage of it. For all its supposed superiority over the smoothbore musket, the rifle musket remained a difficult weapon to use. Loading a rifle required a complex nine-step process. The oft-invoked statistic that veteran soldiers could fire three shots per minute probably proved more accurate on the parade ground than on the battlefield, where soldiers rarely fired more than once every two minutes. Once discharged, the rifle proved as much a burden as an asset until reloaded. Although the unloaded rifle could function as a serviceable club or, with a bayonet attached, as a spear, soldiers knew that such secondary functions would prove suicidal against an enemy with a loaded weapon. A Union soldier at Chickamauga surrendered when a Confederate pointed "his gun point blank at my breast." He noted in his memoir that at the moment he surrendered, "I had loaded my gun but not capped it," effectively rendering it useless. He acutely understood the likely outcome were he not to surrender immediately: "There was a good Enfield rifle pointing at me, not ten feet away, in that gun was an ounce ball, behind that ball was sufficient powder to blow it a mile, on the gun was a water-proof cap, warranted to explode every time, and behind the whole was a Johnny who understood the combination to a nicety." Seeing that the Confederate clearly "had the drop on me," he handed over his loaded but uncapped rifle in surrender. Rifles could also turn against their owners. After two dozen shots, rifles often became jammed with powder residue and required cleaning before they could be fired again. Rifles often misfired, usually from damp or defective ammunition or improper loading. On occasion, soldiers surrendered because they were out of ammunition. A surrounded Yankee scout at Shiloh answered the question "Will you surrender?" with "I have discharged my last bullet."[15]

Soldiers whose role on the battlefield required them to fight independently or in small groups surrendered at a very high rate. Skirmishers, pickets, and sharpshooters all functioned with greater autonomy than soldiers fighting in closed formation and consequently found themselves in surrender scenarios much more frequently. As historian Earl Hess has observed, the expanded use of skirmishers presented one of the Civil War's most important tactical innovations. Deployed in open formations in advance of the main battle line, skirmishers provided valuable information about the enemy and served as the first line of attack and defense. An Ohio soldier observed that skillful skirmishing required "excellent judgment, coolness, and true bravery," all traits that demonstrated skirmishers' agency. Because of their proximity to the enemy, skirmishers often took and became prisoners. Similarly, soldiers assigned to picket duty found themselves particularly vulnerable to capture. One Union picket isolated "between two hostile armies . . . felt some apprehensions for my safety, and though I was a soldier, I must frankly confess I feared the rifles of the Confederate sharp-shooters." A Confederate raid overtook him, and "the fight was unequal, and I was overpowered and taken prisoner."[16]

Rice C. Bull, a New Yorker with Sherman's army, drew more than his fair share of picket and skirmish duty and discovered that his proximity to the enemy entailed numerous calls and demands for surrender. Once on a light skirmish line, Bull found himself facing a much larger Confederate advance. Beating a quick retreat, Bull noted that "we skirmishers were loaded with our full equipment," which "made it harder for us to retreat than for them to follow." With the pursuing Confederates "calling on us to surrender," Bull ran as fast as he could, "every man for himself." He escaped on that occasion, but a few weeks later, Bull had the opportunity to return the favor. On early morning picket duty, Bull participated in a daring advance, capturing "their entire picket line of nearly two hundred men" by sneaking up on their rifle pits. Caught unaware, the Confederate pickets, some of whom were sleeping on duty, "surrendered at once without making any resistance." Even more so than pickets or skirmishers, sharpshooters tended to work alone, which granted them extraordinary agency and rendered them vulnerable to surrender. One Confederate observed that sharpshooters had an unusual amount of autonomy, as they "were exempt from the usual soldier's routine . . . and that every man acted on his own free will when there was anything doing, without restraint, subject only to orders from the division commander or Longstreet himself." Louis Leon, a Confederate sharpshooter, witnessed the ease with which sharpshooters could take and be taken prisoner at the Wilderness. Far removed from the main Confederate force, within the space of a few minutes Leon saw a fellow sharpshooter take an unsuspecting Union officer prisoner, just before Leon himself was overwhelmed by Union soldiers who forced his surrender.[17]

Couriers also frequently found themselves alone and surrounded by enemy soldiers. At Chickamauga, Illinois courier Henry Eby rode in the twilight to where he thought his division was located, only to find himself in the midst of rebel soldiers from Mississippi and Louisiana, who evidently mistook him for a fellow Confederate. While he plotted how to "make my escape from inside the enemy's lines," two Confederates saw his blue Union uniform in the dusk light and ordered him to "surrender, here, get off your horse," pointing the muzzles of their rifles at his face.[18]

Surrender on the Battlefield

John Hadley's prison narrative reveals something of the frequency with which couriers, scouts, and skirmishers could take and be taken prisoners. A courier in the 5th Corps, Hadley spent the morning of May 5, 1864, in the saddle, delivering orders to reorient the division's skirmishers in an effort to identify the location of Lee's army. Hadley complained that "interlacing trees and tangled underbrush" made effective scouting almost impossible; at times he had to dismount his horse to navigate the foliage, and it was "wholly out of the question to see twenty feet in advance." Ferrying orders and reports as the battle began, Hadley encountered a lone soldier at some remove from the skirmish line. Initially supposing him to be a Union skulker, Hadley quickly discovered that he was a Confederate sharpshooter. Leveling his sidearm faster than the Confederate could shoulder his rifle, Hadley "dropped my revolver on his breast with a demand for surrender." The rebel sharpshooter quickly dropped his rifle, and Hadley began to escort him to the rear.

Although he had bettered the rebel in this encounter, Hadley recognized the peril in his situation. "All manner of doubts and fears crowded upon me," he wrote. "I could not see fifty feet in any direction, except along the path. My distinct words with the stranger, my horse, [and] my uniform were all tell-tales, and I thought I could hear as many rebels in the bushes as there were leaves upon the trees." Having accepted the Confederate's surrender, Hadley could not ride faster than the rebel could walk. His prisoner evidently sensed Hadley's unease, as he "manifested great nervousness, as if he thought I would shoot him, and every few steps would look back at me with an appealing eye." When Hadley reassured him that he had no intention of harming him, the rebel informed Hadley that they had earlier that morning captured a Union courier, whom Hadley quickly identified as a good friend.

Reaching a Union skirmish line, Hadley turned over his prisoner and rode out to reconnect with the extended Federal line. With the battle now fully engaged, Hadley became disoriented, as "the roll of muskets was incessant" and "smoke was hovering in clouds among the trees." The noise spooked his horse, which became "as wild as a ranger." Riding at full speed when his horse was hit, Hadley flew through the air and slammed into a tree, and his horse landed on him. Union soldiers freed the unconscious Hadley from under his horse but, retreating frantically, left him on "the field as mortally wounded." Not long afterward, those same Union soldiers who had liberated him from his horse returned to the site as prisoners, having surrendered themselves. They placed Hadley's body on a blanket and carried him to a Confederate field hospital. He awoke the next morning to discover he was a prisoner.[19]

Cavalrymen also participated in a disproportionate number of surrenders, both taking and being taken prisoners. Their speed and maneuverability enabled them to attack with precision, forcing isolated soldiers to surrender, and then return to the safety of their own lines. Skilled cavalry commanders recognized their capacity to harass and force the surrender of unsuspecting enemy soldiers. As a form of psychological warfare, their sudden and unexpected appearance could intimidate enemy soldiers into surrendering. Cavalry raids, such as those led by J. E. B. Stuart, John Hunt Morgan, or Judson Kilpatrick, often took hundreds of prisoners, as concentrated cavalry units temporarily overwhelmed thinly spread infantry. The ability of the cavalry to penetrate enemy lines, however, also made it vulnerable to capture. In July 1863, Lt. G. E. Sabre of the 2nd Rhode Island Cavalry rode with two dozen men to scout behind rebel lines near Port Hudson. Encountering a whole legion of Confederate cavalry, Sabre's scouting party was "attacked on all sides, and after a desperate conflict against overwhelming odds, I gave what are termed in military parlance 'stampeding orders.'" While some escaped, most of the Union cavalrymen, include Sabre, were forced to surrender.[20]

The sensory overload on a Civil War battlefield conspired to make surrender difficult. Surrender on the battlefield usually required both parties to see and hear each other. Soldiers often reported that they rarely saw the enemy clearly, their vision obscured by rifle and cannon smoke. At the Battle of Peach Tree Creek, one Union soldier noted, "The clouds of smoke from the muskets of both sides . . . poured down on us to hide everything but the flash of the enemy's guns." The incessant noise of the battlefield left many soldiers temporarily deaf. A soldier at Shiloh noted that "his sense of hearing is well-nigh overcome by the deafening uproar going on around him. The incessant and terrible clash of musketry, the roar of cannon, the continual zip, zip of the bullets as they hiss by him, interspersed with the agonizing screams of the wounded or the death-shrieks of comrades falling in dying convulsions right in the face of the living."[21] Only when soldiers got close to the enemy could these factors be overcome. A soldier only threw down his arms in surrender if he were sure that the enemy could see him clearly; he would only demand surrender when he knew that his yell could be heard over the cacophony. Even under ideal conditions, communicating an offer to surrender could be difficult. Surrounded during one of the initial charges at Missionary Ridge in November 1863, an Iowa soldier waved a newspaper "in token of my surrender." The attacking Confederates evidently

Surrender on the Battlefield

"didn't read the Ledger" and fired upon him. Only when he ran toward one of the rebel lines did the Confederates accept his surrender.[22] To overcome the ambient noise of combat, demands for surrender had to be yelled. Such full-throated demands had the added effect of intimidating the target and venting the yelling soldier's anger and aggression prior to accepting his role as captor. A Confederate became a prisoner when a Union cavalryman "presented his loaded carbine, demanded my surrender with unrepeatable violence of language that suggested bloodshed."[23]

Surrendered soldiers were quickly stripped of their weapons. Recognizing that surrendered firearms would be used by the enemy, many soldiers took pains to render them inoperable, tossing away a revolver's cylinder or smashing a rifle against a tree to bend its barrel. Most soldiers, however, allowed themselves to be disarmed without incident, recognizing that refusing to comply with their captors' demands might prove fatal. The most significant exception to this occurred when an officer was called upon to surrender his sword to a soldier of lower rank. When a Confederate adjutant demanded his sword near Jonesville, Virginia, a Union major rebuffed him, declaring, "I will never surrender to my inferior in rank!" Although it momentarily looked like the Union officer would be shot for refusing to surrender, the Confederate fetched a higher officer, who relieved the Union officer of his sword.[24] The frequency with which this episode replayed itself throughout the war suggests that soldiers and officers alike recognized the established decorum for surrender and the mutual obligations that potential captors and prisoners held.

Upon surrendering, soldiers expected to be stripped of not only their weapons but also their personal effects. Although regulations for both armies obligated soldiers to respect prisoners' personal property, these regulations were rarely enforced. Expecting to be searched, surrendering soldiers attempted to hide keepsakes, jewelry, and money from their captors. Captured in the Wilderness Campaign in 1864, George Crosby of the 1st Vermont Cavalry expressed a typical sentiment about losing keepsakes. "I found myself in the midst of a squad of Rebel cavalry," he wrote in his diary. After surrendering his carbine, Crosby was accosted by "two ruf[f]ians of the 12th VA Cavalry"; one of them "took my hat, the other took my pocket book out of my pocket. In short they took everything that I had except this Diary and its contents which they did not find, it being in my breast pocket. I asked them to let me have some keepsakes of no value to them that were in my pocket book but [they] would give me nothing." Taken prisoner at the Battle of Cedar Creek in 1864, one Union soldier noted that his Confederate captors had the prisoners stand "up in line, and certain non-commissioned officers, delegated for the purpose, 'went through' each individual of the line with a thoroughness and precision that indicated previous practice."[25]

Recognizing that Union soldiers were often better equipped, Confederates often forced captured Union soldiers to "trade" with them. "I swap[p]ed canteens with a prisoner," noted one Georgia soldier. "Their things are of much better quality than ours and our soldiers are quite eager to get them." Another soldier noted, "Thanks to the Yank I captured the other day, I have a very good pair of blue pantaloons. The poor rascal begged very hard for his pants, but as mine were in a very dilapidated condition I considered it my duty to trade with him." After a Union cavalryman surrendered near Port Hudson, "a drove of rebel soldiers fell upon me like a pack of rapacious and ravenous wolves. After unceremoniously depriving me of my hat, boots, and blankets, they made me disgorge the contents of my pockets, and finally 'swapped' clothes."[26]

By comparison, Union soldiers rarely looted the belongings of captured rebel soldiers, although this was probably due to the inferior quality of Confederate goods rather than more pronounced convictions about robbing prisoners. A Confederate soldier captured at Antietam noted that he and his fellow prisoners had little worth stealing, as "fully one-third of the prisoners there collected had neither shirt nor drawers, but wore a dilapidated uniform over the bare skin. Blankets or oilcloth not a man of us owned, our sole wealth consisting of a smutty haversack which contain for rations perhaps a few green apples."[27]

Soldiers had mixed and complicated emotional reactions to being taken prisoner. An Illinois soldier said, "I cannot describe the state of my mind just then, but guess I felt like the boy, after getting a good whipping which he did not deserve, very despondent." For some soldiers, surrendering in the midst of battle put them into a fugue. Called on to surrender at Shiloh, an Ohio soldier entered a trance, as "I seemed to lose all thought of home, wife, friends, earth, or heaven." Similarly, an Ohio soldier taken prisoner in 1861 recalled that after his surrender, "what we had undergone had so blunted and benumbed our feelings that we were unable to realize the full extent of our calamity." Soldiers indicated that upon surrendering, the battle around them seemed to pause and fade into the background. This cognitive detachment from their environment reflected the alienating process at work as they transitioned from soldiers to prisoners.[28]

The surrendering process created unusual venues for conversations between Confederate and Union soldiers. "I had a talk with a Johnny among a number of prisoners laying around there," one Union soldier wrote in his diary.

"He wanted something from me as a relic, such as a comb, a penknife, or anything so as it would come from a yankee." Despite their precarious situation, some prisoners boldly proclaimed their devotion to their national cause as they understood it. The liberality and boldness with which they expressed these sentiments indicates that they believed their captors would respect the sanctity of prisoner status, no matter how inflammatory the prisoner's rhetoric. Taken prisoner at Peachtree Creek near Atlanta, Confederate James Nisbet impressed his captors with his nonchalance. Asked why he manifested no fear, Nisbet noted that "I have captured thousands of your men, since the war commenced, and always treated them right." He expected that his Union captors would behave in a similar fashion. For Nisbet, surrenders were familiar environments, even if he was usually on the other end of the surrender. These interactions between prisoners and captors allowed some soldiers to look beyond the demonized caricature they had created of the enemy. Before battle, Confederate and Union soldiers alike tended to vilify their foes, branding them as uncivilized and savage. In the process of surrendering, some soldiers recognized the humanity in their enemy, which forced them to reconsider prejudices and oft-repeated slurs.[29]

Recently surrendered soldiers often vividly recalled the unexpected kindness of their captors. Taken ill several days earlier, Isaac Johnston could not keep up with the rest of his unit during a retreat at Chickamauga and surrendered to the advancing Confederates. He later regretted not learning the names of the two officers who accepted his surrender, as "they treated me with marked kindness, as brave men ever treat a conquered foe." A Connecticut cavalryman captured in July 1863 observed that his "treatment by my immediate captors was gentlemanly in the extreme."[30] These laudatory comments about their treatment on the battlefield often contrasted sharply with their later treatment by prison guards, who rarely recognized their humanity. On the battlefield, soldiers recognized their common peril and the vicissitudes of fortune; accepting a surrender today did not forestall being forced to surrender tomorrow.

The fate of surrendered prisoners often remained mysterious for some time after their capture. Unless someone witnessed a surrender firsthand, fellow soldiers and family members found themselves in the dark. Writing to his brother, Confederate David Henkel noted four men from his regiment had recently been captured. "They were sent out on a scout," Henkel wrote, "and I suppose venture[d] too far." The circumstances of their capture remained unclear, although he heard conflicting rumors that "they were captured beyond Winchester near or at Woods factory. There have been so many different rumors about them—one scarcely knew what to believe. One day reports would be they were captured and another day they were not—but I believe it is now confirmed." Oftentimes when individual soldiers surrendered, they were listed in regimental records as "missing" or "unknown," nebulous categories for soldiers who had not returned from battle. As historian Drew Faust has illustrated, such amorphous designations terrorized soldiers' families, who did not know if their loved one was dead, wounded, or captured. Many families were relieved to receive a letter from an imprisoned soldier. Adding to their anxiety, newspapers often misreported battlefield casualties. Matthew Jack Davis of the 19th Mississippi noted that "I had been reported killed on the day I was captured. I read my own obituary."[31]

Throughout the war, soldiers heard rumors about conditions in enemy prisons. Starting in 1861, prison narratives published in both the North and the South documented the horrors of captivity. As an 1864 Sanitary Commission report indicated, these accounts were not accepted wholesale: "One class have accepted them as true; another have felt them to be exaggerated; still another have pronounced them wholly false, fictions purposely made and scattered abroad to inflame the people against their enemies."[32] If the dynamics of the battlefield occasionally gave soldiers the agency to surrender, their expectations of their fate after they surrendered shaped how often they decided to lay down their arms. If they anticipated a lengthy tenure in a prisoner of war camp, physical abuse, or worse, soldiers became apprehensive about surrendering, even when the alternative was imminent defeat or death. Conversely, if they anticipated that they might be quickly paroled or receive otherwise humane treatment, surrender became a more appealing option. Over the course of the war, these expectations varied widely, significantly influencing soldiers' dispositions to surrender. The expectations of soldiers about their fates after surrender fell into four distinct phases.

Characterized by a great deal of uncertainly, the first phrase lasted until July 1862. Before Bull Run, few soldiers thought about the possibility of surrendering or being captured by the enemy. Soldiers enlisted with romantic ideas about honor in battle, tempered perhaps with a fear of maiming injury or death. When William Crossley joined the 2nd Rhode Island Volunteers six weeks before Bull Run, he envisioned the heroism and horror of battle but not the possibility that he would end up a prisoner of war. "From the day of my enlistment to the morning of this notorious battle," he wrote in his diary, "I had never heard the word [prisoner of war] mentioned, nor had I even thought of it. . . . With all this gabble about war and its alluring entertainments not

Surrender on the Battlefield

a solitary word about 'Prisoner of war.' So you see, it was not merely a surprise to us, a little something just out of the ordinary, but it was a shock, and not an every day feeble and sickly shock either, but a vigorous paralyzing and spine-chilling shock, that we couldn't shake off for days or weeks after we were captured."[33] An Ohio soldier captured at Carnifex Ferry expressed an almost identical sentiment: "This was one of the exigencies of war which few, if any of us, had counted on. Most of us had realized that we were liable to be sick, wounded, or killed, but had not dreamed of the possibility of being captured: but here we were at the very beginning of our term of service in the hands of the rebels, deprived of arms, accouterments, and liberty itself."[34]

Although few soldiers gave serious thought to surrender, questions about the treatment of prisoners of war did circulate prior to Bull Run. In early June 1861, the *Charleston Mercury* worried that the Union had decided that Confederate soldiers fell outside the protections of the laws of war and would be executed if captured. "We fear the military authorities of the Confederate States do not duly estimate the enemy with whom they have to deal. They call us rebels and pirates, and seem to think that the usual rules of civilized warfare can be dispensed with in their relations towards us. If we yield at all to these views of our enemies, the existing war will be one of the most bloody the annals of the world will record. Retaliation will fall into the hands of individuals. There will be no surrenders—and no prisoners."[35] The *Mercury's* association between surrender and civilization speaks to the anxiety that some had about the nature of the impending conflict. Would it be a civilized war in which soldiers would be allowed to surrender, or would it become a savage conflict in which soldiers fought without restraint?

Confederate and Union officers alike expressed uncertainty about how they ought to treat surrendered soldiers. As late as July 12, 1861, army quartermaster general Montgomery Meigs complained to Secretary of War Simon Cameron that the War Department had made no formal plans to house and care for prisoners of war. He observed that "in the conflict now commenced it is to be expect that the United States will have to take care of large numbers of prisoners of war." Meigs's warning proved prescient; the following day the War Department received a letter from Gen. George McClellan that he had accepted the surrender of nearly 1,000 Confederates near Beverly, Virginia. He wrote that he had accepted their "surrender agreeing to treat them with the kindness due prisoners of war," but that he did not know what he should do with them, claiming that "the question is an embarrassing one." He urged Washington to send "me immediate instructions by telegraph as to the disposition to be made of officers and men taken prisoners of war."[36] On the same day, in a letter to his wife, McClellan noted that "the prisoners are beyond measure astonished at my humanity towards them." The Confederate prisoners' astonishment reflected the uncertainty and dread that befell some of the earliest surrenders in the war.[37]

The issue of prisoners of war came to the forefront after the Battle of Bull Run on July 21, 1861. The battle culminated in a rout by Confederates in which they took more than 1,000 Union soldiers prisoner, a number that reflected green soldiers' willingness to put themselves at the mercy of their enemy. For young men who had never seen combat before, many of whom had enlisted for a scant ninety days' service, the prospect of surrendering themselves probably did not occur to them prior to the battle. Similarly, Confederate soldiers probably did not put much thought into taking prisoners. The experience of a young Confederate artillerist reflected the uncertainty surrounding surrender at Bull Run. During the Union retreat, Louisianan C. C. Bier noted a lone Union soldier riding toward him on horseback. Taking aim with his revolver, Bier was surprised when the Union soldier waved a white handkerchief. When Bier pledged not to harm him, the young New York officer allowed himself to be taken prisoner. The New Yorker begged Bier to release him, promising to resign his commission and return home. Bier released him and "told him to go back to his friends, saying that one prisoner more or less did not make much difference."[38]

The prisoners taken at Bull Run included one of the first Union combat heroes. Col. Michael Corcoran had immigrated from Ireland in 1849. An officer in the prewar New York militia, in 1860 Corcoran had refused to march in a parade honoring the visiting Prince of Wales and was facing court-martial when the Civil War began. The charges were dropped, and Corcoran led the 69th New York, an Irish regiment, at Bull Run. According to Corcoran's published account, they fought with the bravery of veterans, charging Confederate positions with little regard for their own safety. Pinned under his dead horse, Corcoran surrendered when Confederates took the field late in the afternoon.[39]

Initially imprisoned in Richmond, Corcoran befriended the other notable prisoner of war taken at Bull Run, Congressman Alfred Ely. Ely had come to the battlefield to visit with soldiers from the 13th New York Volunteers, most of whom came from his district. Ely had not intended to get anywhere near actual combat, but the "striking of a rifle-ball near where I was standing admonished me of the danger of my position." Ely took refuge behind a large tree, immobilized "from fear of being shot if I moved." Thus ensconced, Ely waited until accosted by rebel soldiers, who seized him and told him that he was now a prisoner. Shortly after his capture, Ely was menaced at gunpoint by a Confederate

Surrender on the Battlefield

officer, who threatened to "blow out your brains on the spot," before being rescued by another rebel officer, who rebuked his colleague, saying, "You must not shoot that pistol, he is our prisoner."

Ely marched with other prisoners of war from the battlefield to the Confederate headquarters, some seven miles along "the dustiest road that it was ever my fortune to travel." There he spent the night with what he estimated to be 1,000 prisoners. Without shelter, the captured soldiers were exposed to the driving rain that night, lying in the mud on the "bare ground." Because of his position, Ely slept in the "officers' quarters," which he described as a "miserable old barn." The next morning, Ely got a better view of the men who had been captured. He noted that "having been taken from different regiments on the field, they were mostly strangers to each other, and silence prevailed." From what he could see, Ely believed that he was the "only prisoner in civilian dress." From Manassas, the captured prisoners were taken by train to Richmond. En route they worried that they "would be met by an uncontrollable mob . . . and our lives endangered." Their fears proved unwarranted, as they arrived without incident and marched from the rail station in Richmond to a disused tobacco warehouse.

No sooner had the Bull Run prisoners arrived in Richmond than Alfred Ely began plotting for their release. With Michael Corcoran's assistance, Ely prepared a petition requesting that President Lincoln take "immediate steps" to free them. Although he signed Ely's petition, Corcoran adopted a more stoic attitude toward his imprisonment, claiming that "if the good of my adopted country demanded that I should languish in fetters, [I] welcome the heaviest fetters that could be forged." Despite his resolute bearing, Corcoran expressed surprise and sorrow at the length of his imprisonment, as "I had expected that before this I would have been exchanged, according to the usages of war."[40]

When it reached Washington, Ely's petition fell on deaf ears. Fearing that exchanging prisoners would legitimize the nascent Confederate government, the Lincoln administration rejected the idea. As David Herbert Donald has observed, Lincoln maintained throughout the Civil War that secession was unconstitutional, and therefore the Confederacy did not exist as an independent nation but as an illegal insurrection. Particularly in the conflict's first year, Lincoln went to extraordinary lengths to avoid using language or taking actions that would legitimize the Confederacy in the eyes of the world.[41]

Lincoln's intransigence on the Confederacy's legal status complicated the issue of prisoner exchange in other ways. In April 1861, Jefferson Davis had authorized the use of privateers. Lincoln quickly condemned the move, claiming that since the letters of marque came from an illegitimate government, crews acting under them would be charged with piracy, a crime punishable by execution. In early June, the Union navy seized three privateers, the *Savannah*, the *Jefferson Davis*, and the *Petrel*, near Charleston and imprisoned their crews. When their trials began in October 1861, Confederate officials responded with outrage. In retaliation, the Confederate War Department declared that Union officers, including Michael Corcoran, would suffer the same fate as the privateers. Although the crisis abated when Lincoln reclassified the privateers as prisoners of war in February 1862, it hung over the issue of prisoner exchange throughout the war's first year.[42]

Soldiers captured in 1861 had enormous uncertainty about their fate. Among the Union prisoners in Richmond, "no question is so often discussed and none upon which there is such a variety of opinions as that which so directly affects us prisoners. . . . Every heart beats anxiously to hear of the least movement on the part of our government which tends to either an exchange or parole." The prisoners debated among themselves the merits and legality of prisoner exchange. Despite their uncertain situation, "we cannot but feel hopeful when we realize the great principle involved in our release. No soldier can go into battle with confidence if the prospect of a long imprisonment is before him."[43]

While the Lincoln administration was loath to engage in prisoner exchange for fear of the political and constitutional ramifications, it had little interest in holding Confederate prisoners of war. Throughout the summer and fall of 1861, Lincoln authorized the release hundreds of Confederate prisoners on "oath not to engage in arms against the United States."[44] More importantly, the Lincoln administration allowed, if not tacitly encouraged, local Union commanders to exchange prisoners. Between September 1861 and July 1862, hundreds of Union and Confederate prisoners, many of whom spent only days in captivity, were exchanged as a product of these agreements. Local exchanges were particularly common in Missouri. On September 3, 1861, Union colonel W. H. L. Wallace orchestrated the exchange of four prisoners with Confederate general Gideon Pillow. Although Wallace asserted that the exchange "shall not in any sense be regarded as a precedent," that initial exchange resulted in a series of local agreements that grew progressively larger over coming months. Despite their willingness to exchange, Union officers were adamant that the exchange did not amount to formal recognition of the Confederacy. "In regard to the exchange of prisoners," Ulysses S. Grant wrote to Confederate general Leonidas Polk in October 1861, "I recognize no Southern Confederacy." Despite this political misgiving, Grant and Polk were able to agree to exchange prisoners on several occasions. Even among Union generals in Missouri, little uniformity existed concerning the propriety of prisoner exchange. Some Union commanders refused to exchange prisoners categorically. "To exchange prisoners," wrote Gen. Charles F. Smith, Grant's mentor at West Point, "would imply the United States government admitted the existing civil war to be one between independent nations. This I cannot admit and must therefore decline." While many Union officials expressed disdain at the idea of prisoner exchange, the Confederate government actively encouraged its generals to exchange prisoners whenever possible. Like their Union counterparts, Confederate officials had little interest or capacity to hold prisoners, which they saw as an unnecessary cost and burden. Moreover, Confederate officials believed that prisoner exchange would help to provide incremental evidence of their national legitimacy and might contribute to foreign recognition. In November 1861, Acting Secretary of War Judah Benjamin urged Confederate generals to "exchange your prisoners on the best equal terms you can get."[45]

Like surrender negotiations, these early prisoner exchange discussions presented anomalous moments in the context of war. They required Union and Confederate offers to meet under a flag of truce, usually in the aftermath of battle, to discuss how to most humanely dispose of surrendered soldiers. While these irregular prisoner exchanges were most common in Missouri, Union and Confederate commanders reached similar ad hoc arrangements in Virginia, where Gen. Benjamin Huger and Gen. John E. Wool negotiated a series of exchanges in December 1861.[46] What emerged by the end of 1861 was a piecemeal policy in which the fate of surrendered soldiers largely depended on the disposition of local commanders. Some soldiers were almost immediately exchanged or, in some cases, simply released. Others were paroled once they had taken an oath to never fight again. Those less fortunate found themselves confined to a prison with no clear expectation of release.

Accounts of prison camps during 1861 and early 1862 indicate that these facilities, while often unsanitary and deeply unpleasant, bore little similarity to the venues they would later become. Letters written from Camp Chase, near Columbus, Ohio, indicate that Confederate prisoners felt adequately cared for. Part of the force surrendered at Fort Donelson, William Coleman wrote to his mother that the prisoners lived in "comfortable houses large enough to entertain twelve or fifteen persons. . . . The houses are comfortably built & streets regularly laid. . . . Our rations are issued to us of the same quantity & quality as they give their own soldiers, perhaps a little better. With the rations & what delicacies we have we live in fine style." He added that "the authorities here are very kind indeed & try to make us comfortable." A prisoner who surrendered at Island No. 10 wrote to his brother that "I am as well situated as I could expect under the circumstances. We are furnished with common rations of soldiers."[47] While Federal officials undoubtedly censored these prison letters, little evidence suggests any systematic mistreatment of Confederate prisoners of war during this early phase.

Early Confederate prisons received little praise from their inmates but also bore little resemblance to the chronically overcrowded venues they would become in the war's final years. Housed in repurposed tobacco warehouses in Richmond, in a converted cotton factory in Salisbury, or in slave prisons in Atlanta, Charleston, Montgomery, or New Orleans, Union prisoners rarely praised their living conditions. Nonetheless, they generally had adequate protection from the elements, tolerable if unsatisfying rations, and reasonable medical care. While unpleasant accounts of prison life appeared in both Union and Confederate newspapers, they were unlikely to dissuade many soldiers from surrendering themselves if the choice was between surrender or death.

Public pressure mounted to replace this informal and patchwork system. In the aftermath of Bull Run, the *New York News*, a Democrat paper, called for prisoner exchange on humanitarian grounds, arguing, "Let us have war, if war we must have, conducted according to civilized usages—not a savage struggle."[48] The longer Union soldiers remained in Richmond prisons, the more vocally the press criticized the Lincoln administration for failing to exchange them. In November 1861, *Harper's Weekly* complained that "it is hard for men going into battle to think that if captured, they cannot be exchanged."[49] This public pressure culminated in a congressional joint resolution in December 1861 urging President Lincoln to "inaugurate systematic measures for the exchange of prisoners in the present rebellion." That same month, Henry Halleck, who in addition to his role as major general in command of the Department of Missouri was the Union's foremost authority on international law, advised McClellan that "after full consideration of the subject I am of the opinion that prisoners ought to be exchanged. The exchange is a mere military convention," not political recognition of the enemy as a legitimate entity. "The exchange of prisoners of war is only a part of the ordinary *commercia belli*."

Despite the public pressure, a congressional resolution, and Halleck's council, Lincoln still needed convincing that establishing routine prisoner exchange did not imply formal recognition of the Confederacy as a nation. On December 10, 1861, Lincoln and his cabinet received a New York delegation advocating for "an exchange of prisoners, with special reference to the case of Col. Corcoran." The cabinet split over the political and diplomatic implications of authorizing prisoner exchange, debating furiously while Lincoln listened attentively. By the end of January 1862, the president and his cabinet came to the conclusion that they should pursue a robust system of prisoner exchanges, recognizing their obligation "to take measures for the relief of the brave men who having imperiled their lives in the military service of the Government are now prisoners and captives."[50]

After lengthy and contentious negotiations, on July 22, 1862, Confederate and Union officials agreed to a formalized exchange arrangement known as the Dix-Hill cartel. Named after its chief negotiators, Union general John A. Dix and Confederate general D. H. Hill, the cartel built on the exchange regime used during the War of 1812. The Dix-Hill cartel established a two-stage process for prisoner exchange. Under the agreement, all prisoners had to be paroled within ten days of capture (including all those held at the time of the agreement) at Aiken's Landing, Virginia, for the eastern theater and Vicksburg, Mississippi, for the western theater. Paroled prisoners would be honor-bound not to resume fighting until they had been exchanged for an equivalent number of prisoners from the other side. The agreement created a point system for exchange depending on rank, with noncommissioned officers worth twice as much as enlisted men, second lieutenants valued at three times as much, and up to sixty enlisted men for a commanding general. Commissioners of exchange would keep lists of paroled prisoners, reconciling the exchanges on a regular basis.[51]

The piecemeal development of the prisoner exchange system mirrored the Union's stuttering approach to the status of runaway slaves. In both cases, local commanders were initially left to their own devices to formulate solutions as the situation presented itself, with commanding officers in different locales often arriving at radically different conclusions about how to approach the problem of runaway slaves and prisoners of war. Indeed, many of the same figures who helped to formulate Union policy on runaway slaves also played a significant role in negotiating the terms for prisoner exchange early in the war, including Benjamin Butler, John C. Frémont, and Henry Halleck. Abraham Lincoln presented his initial proposal for the Emancipation Proclamation to his cabinet on the same day (July 22, 1862) the Dix-Hill cartel was finalized.[52]

The prisoner exchange accord could not have happened at a more fortuitous time. Intense campaigning in early 1862 had swelled both Union and Confederate prisons beyond capacity. Fort Donelson's surrender in February resulted in 12,000 Confederate soldiers entering Union prisons, an influx they were hardly prepared or equipped to handle. Approximately 7,000 rebels who surrendered at Island No. 10 joined them less than two months later. At Shiloh, 4,000 soldiers, three-quarters of them Union, surrendered. Union soldiers captured during the Peninsula Campaign and Jackson's Valley Campaign added more than 8,000 men to Richmond's prison population. The difficulty in transporting and housing Confederate prisoners led some Union commanders to simply parole them on the battlefield. For example, in coastal North Carolina, Ambrose Burnside paroled more than 3,000 soldiers who surrendered at Roanoke Island, New Bern, and Fort Macon.[53]

In its early months, the Dix-Hill cartel demonstrated remarkable efficiency. Within weeks, Union and Confederate prisons alike emptied as their prisoners were released on parole. In July 1862, when the cartel was ratified, Union prisons held 20,500 Confederates. After one month of exchanges, one-third of those prisoners were paroled. By year's end, only 1,286 remained imprisoned. William Hoffman, the Union commissary-general of prisons, ordered the remaining Confederate prisoners of war consolidated at Alton Penitentiary, Camp Chase, and Johnson's Island, closing the remaining camps. Confederate prisons also emptied. At the end of August 1862, the last Union prisoner left Salisbury Prison in North Carolina. Over the next few months, outlying Confederate prisons at Macon, Lynchburg, Charleston, Mobile, Atlanta, and Tuscaloosa closed, leaving only the Richmond prisons open.[54]

The rapid parole of surrendered soldiers became one of the distinctive and controversial features of the Dix-Hill cartel. Pledging on their honor not to resume military careers until exchanged, individual soldiers took their responsibility to uphold the system seriously. Paroled soldiers often refused to engage in labor they believed violated the terms of their parole. For instance, soldiers in the 9th Michigan who had surrendered at Murfreesboro in July 1862 and had been subsequently paroled refused to assist in building fortifications at Nashville because they had not yet been exchanged. Similarly, Union soldiers who had surrendered at Harpers Ferry in September 1862 refused to be sent to Minnesota to fight in the Dakota War, arguing that any military service, even against a different enemy, would be a violation of their parole. While some soldiers may have been eager to face the enemy and tempted to violate the terms of their parole, the evidence suggests that almost none did during the height of the Dix-Hill cartel. Soldiers who violated their parole oath faced execution if recaptured before properly exchanged. That only a handful of soldiers, Union and Confederate alike, faced accusations of parole violation in 1862 indicates how seriously they took their oaths as a reflection of personal honor.[55]

Parole violation cases tended to arise from paroles issued prior to the Dix-Hill cartel, when the mechanisms of parole and exchange remained inchoate. Of these, the best known is that of Confederate colonel Ebenezer Magoffin, the younger brother of Kentucky governor Beriah Magoffin. Unlike his brother, who attempted to negotiate a pro-slavery neutrality, the younger Magoffin had been an early advocate of secession and enthusiastically joined the Confederate cause. He received an officer's commission in the spring of 1861, fought at the battle of Carthage, and recruited a Confederate regiment. In late August 1861, Gen. Ulysses Grant sent a Union regiment to capture the "principal rebels or secessionists" between Jefferson City and Lexington, Missouri, with Magoffin prominently on the list. On September 1, the regiment encountered rebels in Georgetown, exchanging fire and discovering that Magoffin was among them. After a search of the town, they found Magoffin, armed with a revolver, hidden in a hotel garret and persuaded him to surrender. Once the town was pacified, witnesses identified Magoffin as the assailant who had shot and killed a Union officer earlier that day. Questioned by an Illinois officer, Magoffin denied any affiliation with "either the Missouri State Guard or the Southern Confederacy." If he was not a Confederate soldier, the Union officer replied, then he did not deserve any protections under the laws of war but was "guilty of assassinating U.S. troops." Magoffin was taken to Lexington as a prisoner, but he was liberated when Confederate general Sterling Price overwhelmed the Federal garrison, using hemp bales as shields to advance unharmed on the garrison and compel their surrender. Promoted by Price, Magoffin resumed his recruiting duties. In early December, he received word that his wife, at their home in Union-held territory, had fallen deathly ill. Through a friendly Union officer, Magoffin received what he considered a safeguard but the officer maintained was a parole to spend ten days with his wife. Nine days later, on December 19, Gen. John Pope overwhelmed a Confederate force at Blackwater Creek, Missouri, and compelled their surrender, discovering Magoffin among the 684 Confederates prisoners.

At Halleck's direction, a military commission charged Magoffin with violating his parole and "wantonly and maliciously killing" a Union officer at Georgetown. Denying that the military tribunal had jurisdiction, Magoffin argued that he had shot the Union officer in self-defense and as a legitimate act of war. The charge of violating his parole proved more complicated. In his defense, Magoffin seemed more worried about his "honor . . . as a gentleman and a soldier" than the possibility of his execution. Claiming that he lived by "the most romantic standard of honor," Magoffin maintained that he had never agreed to a parole and that a guilty verdict required that the violation be intentional. Moreover, he argued that while he had been among the Confederates surrendered at Blackwater Creek, he was neither armed nor acting as "an aider, abettor, or combatant."

Acquitted of the murder charge, Magoffin was found guilty of violating his parole and sentenced to be shot. After his brother's conviction, Governor

Beriah Magoffin rallied Kentucky Democrats to protest the decision. Judge Advocate General John F. Lee, the Union Army's highest-ranking lawyer, also expressed misgivings about the military commission's jurisdiction and about the harshness of Magoffin's sentence. Sensitive to the possible political ramifications, on March 25, 1862, Lincoln ordered the sentence suspended until a review panel could consider the matter. Before the panel could meet to discuss the verdict's merits, Magoffin and nearly three dozen other prisoners tunneled out of Alton Prison and escaped.[56]

The complexity of Magoffin's hearing, involving three surrenders (Georgetown, Lexington, and Blackwater Creek), tense jurisdictional issues, and lengthy debates about the difference between a safeguard and a parole, suggests that it was an aberration, motivated more by politics than the enforcement of a military parole. However, in the discussion of parole violations in the commission hearings and in the machinations that followed Magoffin's conviction, all participants admitted that parole violations were exceedingly rare. In his report, Judge Advocate General Lee argued that there was no American case law on parole violations and that legal theorists, including Halleck, had never defined an appropriate punishment.

A more straightforward case of parole violation emerged a year later concerning Union soldiers who had been surrendered at Lexington, the same battle that freed Ebenezer Magoffin from his initial captivity. As part of the surrender negotiations at Lexington, Confederate general Sterling Price agreed to immediately parole all 3,000 enlisted Union soldiers, contingent on a verbal pledge not to take up arms until formally exchanged, "under penalty of death if so taken." Negotiations a month later between Price and Frémont resulted in the exchange of most of the paroled Union soldiers. Believing themselves "regularly exchanged and entirely released from their oath," the Lexington parolees returned to military service. Some of them were later captured at Shiloh and "recognized [by Confederates] as having been previously taken at Lexington and were heavily ironed and sentenced to be executed." The Confederates informed them that they had not been included in the exchange and therefore were in violation of their parole. Confederates executed several Union prisoners, including bludgeoning one to death, and released the remainder, telling them to inform their officers that they would be shot if captured again. Returning to the Federal encampment at Corinth, they recounted their experience and discovered after a subsequent investigation, to their horror, that many of them "had not been exchanged as had been represented to us by our officers, and had been and were still serving in the field in the face of the enemy in direct violation of our oath." Unwilling to have them

Surrender on the Battlefield

so exposed, Grant sent the surviving Lexington parolees to St. Louis, where they were discharged.[57]

Both of these cases concerned paroles issued prior to the Dix-Hill cartel, when significant uncertainty and irregularity pervaded parole and exchange agreements. With both Ebenezer Magoffin and the Lexington parolees, the alleged violations appear to have been inadvertent rather than intentional, indicating that soldiers on both sides took their pledges remarkably seriously. Once the formal exchange regime took effect and standardized terms of parole, Union and Confederate officials expected soldiers to respect and live up to them. Not until the Dix-Hill cartel began to fall apart in 1863 did accusations of parole violations resume.

For most of the exchange regime's life, more Union soldiers surrendered than Confederates. Therefore, while Confederate prisoners were routinely exchanged and returned to military service, Union soldiers often had an extended period on parole before they could be paired with an equivalent Confederate soldier for exchange. Initially, many paroled Union prisoners simply went home. Captured at Second Bull Run on August 30, 1862, just a week after the cartel was negotiated, Union soldier William Cline received his parole the next day and immediately returned to his wife and four children in Waverly, Ohio. Except for a brief period when he traveled to Columbus to be paid for his military service, Cline remained with his family until the end of March 1863. From his diary, it is unclear whether Cline ever received instructions to report to a parole camp or simply ignored them. When Cline eventually did report, he was court-martialed for his absence, found "giltey and Docked three month[s']" pay. Considering the possible sentences for desertion, the punishment he received indicates that Maj. Samuel Hurst, who presided over his court-martial, felt sympathy for Cline. His trial concluded, Cline immediately returned to active duty.[58]

Few soldiers benefited more from the Dix-Hill cartel's provisions than Confederate Alexander Hunter. From Alexandria, Virginia (where he was Robert E. Lee's neighbor), Hunter enlisted after Fort Sumter and fought at Bull Run, Yorktown, and Seven Pines, among other battles. At the Battle of Frazier's Farm, near the end of the Seven Days, Hunter's regiment found itself outnumbered and broke into a chaotic retreat. "Officers and men broke and scattered," he later recalled, "for each individual was acting under his own orders— general, colonel, captain and private all combined in his own consciousness. The timid were striking for the rear, the cautious were snugly ensconced in the ditches awaiting developments; the reckless and the bulldogs ramming home their cartridges with unrelenting ardor." It is unclear which of these categories

Hunter placed himself in, but when the Union line approached to within ten feet, Hunter and his ditchmates yelled, "Billy Yank, we surrender!" Escorting Hunter to the rear, one of the Union soldiers noticed blood on his trousers and asked if he was injured. A quick self-inspection revealed that he was unharmed, the blood from "some unfortunate, splashed over me." Marched to Harrison's Landing that evening, Hunter received rations of "crackers, coffee, sugar and meat of good quality and fair quantity." He noted that "some of the 'Billy Yanks' showed us most disinterested kindness by sharing with us their hot coffee and doing all in their power to alleviate our woes." Boarding a steamboat the next day, Hunter and the other prisoners received blankets and full rations for their journey north.

When he surrendered himself on June 30, 1862, Hunter had no way of knowing how long his captivity would last. Imprisoned at Fort Warren, in Boston harbor, Hunter had little to complain about: "Certainly no prisoners of war had ever been treated so luxuriously before. . . . Breakfast consisted of coffee—*real*, not ground rye or corn,—fresh loaf bread, mess-beef, hominy, broiled ham and eggs *ad libitum*." Three weeks of such fare transformed "the hungry, gaunt crowd" that had surrendered into "well-dressed, lazy men sauntering about the fort." The finalization of the Dix-Hill cartel ended Hunter's brief imprisonment. The agreement called for the immediate parole of all prisoners held by either side. After less than a month in captivity, Hunter and his fellow prisoners would be returning to the Army of Northern Virginia. Dreading the return of meager Confederate rations and camp life, Hunter noted, "Well, of course we were glad to go, and yet sorry." In later years, Hunter recalled that "the Federal Government had treated us royally" and that "our captivity was but a summer jaunt North, an ocean voyage and several weeks guest at a watering-place, where we were treated more as honored guests than as prisoners of war."

After a brief furlough, Hunter rejoined his regiment, sharing stories of his captivity with other Confederate soldiers. He returned in time to fight at Second Manassas and participate in Lee's march into Maryland. On the extreme Confederate right at Antietam, not far from the Burnside Bridge, Hunter's undersized regiment took heavy casualties. Only one of two men from his regiment taken prisoner when their position was overrun, Hunter was grateful that he survived the battle unharmed. Before marching them to the rear, their Federal captors allowed the two rebel soldiers to survey the field for the bodies of their fallen comrades. Hunter's second captivity proved even shorter than his first. He was paroled two days after Antietam, along with "the whole battalion of prisoners, numbering five hundred and fifty officers and men."

They received news of their parole with "delight," as they would be "sent home instead of being forwarded North and confined in prisons. Full rations were given to us." Instructed to "remain at their homes until notified by the proper Southern official that they had been exchanged," Hunter and his fellow prisoners were escorted to the Potomac, where they waded across into Confederate territory. After a few weeks, Hunter was exchanged and returned to service, participating in the defense of Fredericksburg.[59] In eighty days, Hunter had surrendered twice. His quick return to arms after each episode indicated not only the efficiency of the Dix-Hill cartel but also the mild treatment he received from his Union captors.

Despite the relatively benign experience of prisoners of war under the Dix-Hill cartel, few were eager to repeat it. One recently exchanged Confederate soldier noted in May 1863 that "I had much rather miss such a chance than fall into their hands again unless I feel there is no other choice than between capture and death. Of course then I would surrender everytime."[60] His final caveat reflected a broadly held belief among both Confederate and Union soldiers during the heyday of the exchange regime: one should not surrender unless confronted with the choice between "capture and death," in which case, surrender seemed like the only reasonable option.

The generosity of the Dix-Hill cartel gave both Union and Confederate soldiers ample incentive to surrender. Indeed, some worried that its terms would prove an inducement to surrender unnecessarily. One Union soldier complained that the liberal parole policy encouraged malingering soldiers to surrender in order to obtain a "little rest from soldiering." All they needed to do, he claimed, was engage in "straggling in the vicinity of the enemy" and allow themselves to be captured. After parole, they could "visit home, and sojourn awhile where [there] were pleasanter pastures than at the front." Some Union government officials agreed that the parole system induced soldiers to surrender. Secretary of War Edwin Stanton opined in September 1862 that "there is reason to fear that many voluntarily surrender for the sake of getting home." Especially after the large Union surrenders at Harpers Ferry and at Munfordville, Stanton received letters from concerned citizens that the parole system was undermining the Union war effort. One writer complained that he "had seen enough of paroled prisoners and heard enough of them talk to know that unless the paroling system is abandoned we will be beaten by the number of paroled prisoners we shall have. It is an inducement not only for cowards, but for men discontented with their officers, or even homesick to surrender." The letter writer recommended abandoning the Dix-Hill agreement, as it would "force upon the South the necessity of feeding or releasing our soldiers, and if our men understood positively that they are to be prisoners in the South if taken they would strike with more energy and desperation."[61]

In an effort to dissuade soldiers from surrendering unnecessarily, the Union established parole camps at Annapolis, Columbus, and St. Louis to house Union soldiers who had been paroled but not yet exchanged. These parole camps proved deeply unpopular with both the Northern public and soldiers. Subjected to overcrowding, epidemic disease, and poor food, Union soldiers complained about being held prisoner by their own government. One Union officer wrote home from a parole camp, "Thank Heaven you have never had the experience of a 'Paroled Camp,' and may you never! . . . The men feel unanimously that we have no right to ask a thing of them, while the line officers hold that doing guard duty and police work is violation of their parole, as well as drilling. If the Government will only let us go home, we will take care of ourselves till our exchange."[62] When the "Harpers Ferry Cowards" rioted at Camp Douglas in October 1862, it reflected the frustration that paroled soldiers felt in being held captive by their own government.

The debate over the status of surrendered soldiers that produced the Dix-Hill cartel also contributed to the Civil War's most coherent codification of the unwritten laws of war, officially General Order No. 100, but popularly known as the Lieber Code. Its author, German American legal philosopher Francis Lieber, in an August 1861 *New York Times* editorial, had critiqued the Federal reluctance to exchange prisoners after Bull Run. He argued that "the exchange of prisoners involves no question of acknowledgement of right, but a simple recognition of fact and reality." Lieber sent a copy of the editorial to his friend Senator Charles Sumner, confessing his "desire to write a little book on the Law and Usages of War."[63] Lieber followed his editorial with a series of public lectures at Columbia College that would form the basis of the Lieber Code. He lauded the introduction of regular prisoner exchanges in 1862, viewing it as a hallmark of a more civilized style of warfare. However, he condemned parole of surrendered soldiers, arguing that a parole oath not to fight until exchange violated a soldier's primary oath to fight for his country. Like other critics of the Dix-Hill parole system, Lieber believed that it "put a fearful premium on cowardice." In December 1862, he received an appointment to a five-member commission tasked with crafting a codified "set of rules and definitions providing for the most urgent issues, occurring under the law and usages of war." Drafted primarily by Lieber, with substantial editorial help from commission

Surrender on the Battlefield

chair Henry Halleck, the resulting codification received Lincoln's blessing. The president issued the document as General Order No. 100 on April 24, 1863.[64]

The rights of surrendering and surrendered soldiers formed the heart of Lieber's code. It decreed that all soldiers taken "by individual surrender" or who had "thrown away their arms and ask for quarter" were "entitled to the privileges of a prisoner of war." Among those rights was protection against "any intentional infliction of any suffering, or disgrace, by cruel imprisonment, want of food, by mutilation, death, or any other barbarity." In its efforts to codify the unwritten laws of war, the Lieber Code inscribed the long-assumed right to individual surrender into military jurisprudence, claiming that "it is against the usage of modern war to resolve, in hatred and revenge, to give no quarter. No body of troops has the right" to refuse to accept an individual soldier's surrender.

The Lieber Code added greater clarity to the Union's stance on Confederate guerillas. Lieber had long railed against guerillas as contrary to the laws of war, and recent scholarship has demonstrated that guerilla warfare was more widespread than previously thought. Starting in 1861, most Union officials considered guerilla warfare as a profound violation of the unwritten laws of war, and therefore participants were ineligible for the protections afforded to prisoners of war. Prior to the Lieber Code and without clear guidance from Washington, Union commanders adopted a patchwork of policies concerning surrendering Confederate guerillas. In August 1861, John. C. Frémont proclaimed martial law in Missouri, decreeing that captured guerillas would be court-martialed and executed. His replacement, Gen. Henry Halleck, upended that policy, ordering that captured guerillas in Missouri should be tried by military tribunals, though not by court-martial. He argued that since guerillas were not "duly enrolled in the service of an acknowledged enemy," they had no right to prisoner of war status. In 1862, Gen. Samuel Curtis prohibited his soldiers from accepting the surrender of Confederate guerillas, ordering that no bushwhacker in Arkansas should be taken alive.[65] By the end of 1862, Union officers had created a confusing patchwork of policies, often inconsistently applied.

Federal policy under the Lieber Code lumped all men fighting out of uniform ("divesting themselves of the character or appearance of soldiers") as guerillas and therefore "not entitled to the privileges of prisoners of war" but subject to summary execution "as highway robbers or pirates." While the newly standardized Federal policy treated all irregular fighters as guerillas, Confederates tended to disaggregate irregular soldiers, depending on the degree of oversight from the Confederate government. At one end of the spectrum were Partisan Rangers, irregulars fully sanctioned by the Confederate government. At the other end were guerilla bands who operated completely outside Confederate supervision and answered only to themselves. Between those extremes were a morass of irregular fighters, sometimes labeling themselves Home Guard, state militia, light cavalry, or bushwhackers. Although they employed similar tactics and fought out of uniform, Confederate guerillas took these fine gradations between different classes of irregular fighters seriously. In particular, Partisan Rangers saw themselves as legitimate Confederate soldiers and therefore felt entitled to the same protection as prisoners of war as other surrendered rebel soldiers. Confederate officials shared this sentiment, arguing that the Union had no right to decide who was a legitimate Confederate soldier. If the Union followed through on its promise to execute Confederate guerillas, they threatened to retaliate by executing an equal number of captured Union soldiers.[66]

The Lincoln administration feared a harsh policy on Confederate guerillas would prompt retaliation against captured Union soldiers and engender escalating levels of violence. Finding themselves outside the protection afforded to prisoners of war, Confederate guerillas fought with increasing desperation. Notorious for their brutality in the war's final years, Quantrill's raiders originally saw themselves as legitimate soldiers, enlisting as Home Guard, with William Clarke Quantrill receiving a commission under the 1862 Partisan Ranger Act. As legitimate soldiers fighting under the laws of war, Quantrill's men regularly paroled captured Union soldiers in 1861 and early 1862, expecting that they would receive comparable treatment were they to surrender. Once outlawed, however, Quantrill's tactics took a decidedly barbaric turn, embracing the notion that if they could not surrender, the laws of civilized warfare no longer applied to them. Confederate guerillas also responded by threatening to engage in retaliation by executing Union prisoners. When Gen. Don Carlos Buell ordered the execution of four of guerilla John Hunt Morgan's men as outlaws, Morgan threatened to execute thirty-six Union prisoners, pushing Buell to recant the execution order. Although the Lieber Code intended to curtail guerilla warfare by denying guerillas the right to surrender, it may have intensified its brutality. A Missouri resident noted in 1864 "murder, arson of daily occurrence. Fights rendered horrible by their ferocity. No quarter given, no mercy shown. It is horrible."[67]

At the same time that the Lieber Code placed guerillas firmly outside the protections of the laws of war, it asserted that African Americans were entitled to the full panoply of rights afforded to soldiers, as "the law of nations knows no distinction of color." From the earliest appearances of African Americans in uniform, Confederates denied that they could be legitimate soldiers entitled to surrender and treatment as prisoners of war. Viewing black men in arms as tantamount to slaves in rebellion, Confederates responded with outrage when Union officials in Louisiana and South Carolina began enlisting African Americans in 1862. In November 1862, Confederates captured six black soldiers on Saint Catherine's Island in Georgia. The local commander noted that "they are slaves with arms in hand against their masters and wearing the abolition uniform," and he recommended that "some swift and terrible punishment should be inflicted that their fellows may be deterred from following their example." Confederate Secretary of War James Seddon agreed, recommending that one of the black soldiers "be executed as an example."[68] This incident prefaced the creation of broader Confederate policy that black troops would not be afforded prisoner of war status. In April 1863, the Confederate Congress concluded that arming African Americans would "bring on a servile war" inconsistent with the principles of civilized warfare, and therefore surrendered black soldiers would be returned to slavery and white officers leading black soldiers would be "deemed as inciting servile insurrection, and shall if captured be put to death."[69]

Some Confederate generals hoped to sidestep the issue of black prisoners of war by simply refusing to accept the surrender of black soldiers. After Henry McCulloch took black prisoners at Milliken's Bend, he received the condemnation of his superior officer, Gen. Edmund Kirby Smith. "I have been unofficially informed that some of your troops have captured negroes in arms," Kirby Smith wrote McCulloch; "I hope this may not be so." Instead, he counseled a policy of "giving no quarter to armed negroes and their officers. In this way we may be relieved from a disagreed dilemma." Confederate Secretary of War James Seddon eventually overruled Kirby Smith, claiming that black soldiers were "deluded victims" who "should be received and treated with mercy and returned to their owners." Seddon did not object to the execution of some black soldiers, as "a few examples might perhaps be made," but he argued that "to refuse them quarter would only make them, against their tendencies, fight desperately."[70] Like many Confederates, Seddon incorrectly assumed that black soldiers would surrender at the first sight of danger. Convinced that African Americans were naturally docile, subservient, and cowardly, many military professionals in both the North and the South did not anticipate that they would make good soldiers. As events on the battlefield would reveal, these assumptions proved categorically incorrect.

Although official Confederate policy called for captured black Union soldiers to be returned to slavery, the realities of black surrender on the battlefield proved to be somewhat different. Enraged by the presence of black men in uniform, many Confederates refused to take prisoners. Reports from the Battle of Milliken's Bend in June 1863, the first significant engagement for black soldiers, indicate that rebel soldiers shouted "no quarter," fighting under the "black flag." Before the Battle of Olustee in February 1864, a Confederate officer instructed his men that the enemy were "negroes from Georgia and South Carolina, who have come to steal, pillage, run over the state and murder, kill, and rape our wives, daughters and sweethearts. Let's teach them a lesson. I shall not take any negro prisoners in this fight." Reports of Confederates refusing to accept the surrender of black soldiers or executing black prisoners after the battles at Port Hudson (May 27, 1863), Goodrich's Landing (June 29, 1863), and Battery Wagner (July 18, 1863) indicate that many rebel soldiers had no intention to take black prisoners. Only recently exchanged himself after four months imprisoned in St. Louis, a Texas officer noted the brutality with which Confederate soldiers engaged with black troops. "I never saw so many dead negroes in my life," he wrote. "We took no prisoners, except the white officers, fourteen in number; these were lined up and shot after the negroes were finished." Having executed the prisoners, the rebel soldiers tossed their bodies, including some "hardly dead," into the Ouchita River. As historian Dudley Cornish observed, "For many [white] Southerners, it was psychologically impossible to see a black man bearing arms as anything but an incipient slave uprising complete with arson, murder, pillage, and rapine."[71]

Confederate policy and practice effectively made it impossible for black soldiers to surrender. They knew that under the best conditions, surrender would result in their reenslavement by being dragooned into building Confederate fortifications or returned to their prior owners. Joseph T. Wilson, who would fight with the 2nd Louisiana Native Guard and the 54th Massachusetts, observed that when confronted with black troops, Confederate soldiers believed that "honor forbade them to ask or give quarter. This fact was known to all." In 1863, a white officer of the 2nd Louisiana Native Guard wrote that his men "fight like bloodhounds, and never surrender." In July 1863, the *Charleston Daily Courier* explained the paucity of black prisoners by noting that those few who did surrender "believe they are to be hung, and gave as a reason for fighting as well as they did, that they would rather die of [a] bullet than [a] rope."[72]

Some black soldiers and their white officers concluded that if Confederates would not accept their surrender, they were under no obligation to respect the surrenders of rebel soldiers. "We are outlawed, and therefore not bound by the rules of regular warfare," observed Col. James Montgomery, commander of the 2nd South Carolina (African Descent), one of the earliest

Surrender on the Battlefield

black regiments. To be sure, many black soldiers and white officers rejected the idea that Confederate policy absolved them of their obligations under the laws of war. Critical of Montgomery's stance, the 54th Massachusetts's Col. Robert Gould Shaw noted "my own distaste for this barbarous sort of warfare, I am not sure that it will not harm very much the reputation of black troops and of those connected with them." Nonetheless, numerous references suggest that black soldiers, largely in retaliation for Confederate policy, felt no obligation to take rebel prisoners. A soldier in the 2nd Maine Cavalry noted that black soldiers refused to take prisoners, claiming that "it did not make eny differance [*sic*] to them about the Rebs surrendering." He added that officers had difficulty stopping black soldiers from "killing all the prisoners."[73]

At the end of July 1863, Lincoln reinforced the Lieber Code's stance on black soldiers. In General Order No. 252, Lincoln proclaimed, "To sell or enslave any captured person on account of his color and for no offense against the laws of war is a relapse into barbarism and a crime against the civilization of the age." He ordered that "for every soldier of the United States killed in violation of the laws of war a rebel soldier shall be executed, and for every one enslaved by the enemy or sold into slavery a rebel soldier shall be placed at hard labor . . . until the other shall be released and receive the treatment due to a prisoner of war." Despite his harsh rhetoric, Lincoln was loath to actually execute Confederate prisoners. When pressed by Frederick Douglass to adopt a policy of retaliation, Lincoln demurred, claiming that "once begun, I do not know where such a measure would stop."[74]

Although the Lincoln administration did not follow through on the pledge to retaliate against Confederate prisoners for the treatment of black soldiers, the issue of black prisoners proved fatal to the Dix-Hill exchange regime. Its demise came gradually, as Union officials issued repeated ultimatums demanding equal treatment for surrendered black soldiers. On May 25, 1863, Union officials stopped the exchange of officers, and by August 1863, the exchange of enlisted men had effectively ground to a halt. Although periodic exchanges of prisoners, usually the sick or wounded, continued until Ulysses S. Grant halted all exchanges in April 1864, they amounted to only a small fraction of the total number of soldiers taken into captivity during that period. In an early September 1863 letter, James C. Bates of the 9th Texas Cavalry explained how the introduction of black soldiers affected the prisoner exchange regime and the willingness of soldiers to surrender. Bates noted that exchange commissioners had come to an impasse, "and I think it hardly probable they will come to any understanding." According to Bates, "The difficulty is . . . that Lincoln insists on *negroes* being recognized and treated as, prisoners of war, and that when captured they shall be exchanged for white men. This will never be submitted to by the confederate authorities & the exchange of prisoners will therefore be at an end." Bates concluded that without the promise of exchange, soldiers would not surrender, and "it will not be long before no prisoners are taken." For his part, Bates saw no reason to take black prisoners, claiming that "the only course . . . is to take every Negro found in arms, and every man connected with them, into some thicket or swamp and hang them as soon as captured. This course we have heretofore pursued and our men will continue to do so."[75]

Few soldiers understood the consequences of the cartel's demise as well as Alexander Hunter. After his second stint as a prisoner of war and a convalescent in a Confederate hospital, Hunter used his connection to General Lee to secure a transfer to a cavalry regiment. After Gettysburg, Hunter's regiment, the Black Horse Cavalry, was tasked with raiding Union lines and taking prisoners. "The design of our detail," Hunter wrote, was "to get within the enemy's line on foot and lurk near their camp," capture unsuspecting cavalrymen, and return to Confederate lines with their prisoners and horses. "It would seem at first sight almost impossible for one man to convey several prisoners alone through a dangerous country and by circuitous routes over fifty odd miles . . . yet it was done frequently, and but few escaped." While they managed to capture "thousands of prisoners" in the months immediately after Gettysburg, the subsequent winter proved very different. "Few prisoners were taken that winter," Hunter wrote. "The Yankees had learned caution."

Hunter should have taken the lesson of caution to heart. On January 1864, he rode out on a solo scouting mission, intent upon capturing Union horses. Encountering a Union patrol, Hunter attempted to take shelter in a nearby church. He had nearly escaped capture when "my confounded, infernal horse gave a long, loud neigh." Scrambling up a ladder into the church loft, Hunter listened to the Union cavalrymen search for him. Deducing his hiding location, the Union soldiers threatened to burn down the church unless he surrendered. Acquiescing, Hunter threw down his revolvers and descended the ladder. His capture marked the third time that Hunter had surrendered. Compared with his earlier experiences, this surrender would prove markedly different. The provost marshal accused him of being a guerilla and told him that he "deserved to be shot" and that "every Rebel found with arms ought to be hanged." Exposed to bitter cold and wind, Hunter and the other prisoners struggled without blankets, shelter, or fire; only by pacing all night did they keep themselves from freezing. All around the prisoners' pen, Hunter could see Union soldiers well fed and sheltered: "Billy Yank was comfortable in body and stuffed to the throat with the good things of life." Sent to Old Capitol Prison, Hunter found the conditions better than he expected, as "the rooms were large, well venti-lated, very well heated by open grates at each end," and "the fare was ample and wholesome, much better indeed than Dixie could afford to give her troops." Despite the relative comfort, Hunter quickly grew despondent, as "it was not a hopeful outlook that the future gave. That all exchange of prisoners was ended was patent to all. . . . It was a bitter thing to look forward to, that of being caged like so many wild beasts." Hunter recognized that the indeterminate prison terms fundamentally changed the paradigm of surrender. "For Northerner or Southerner," Hunter wrote, "the dragging out of a prison life was grievous enough to bear. . . . Many held death a preferable fate."[76]

BETTER TO BE A
PRISONER THAN A CORPSE

Surrender at the Battle of Gettysburg

Sometimes described as the bloodiest battle ever to take place on the North American continent, the Battle of Gettysburg saw nearly 8,000 soldiers lose their lives. Photographer Timothy O'Sullivan titled his famous image of scattered corpses "A Harvest of Death," a harvest of "honored dead" that Lincoln claimed "shall not have died in vain." Yet for all the emphasis on Gettysburg as a site of mass death, the battlefield saw more soldiers surrender than killed. Approximately 5,800 of Lee's soldiers were listed as prisoners or missing, 20 percent more than the 4,700 Confederate soldiers killed. Union soldiers surrendered in almost equal numbers, with 5,365 listed as captured at the battle's conclusion. Those choosing to surrender included mostly enlisted men, but also many officers, including four generals and at least thirty other officers at the rank of captain or above.[1]

This chapter examines the Battle of Gettysburg from the perspective of the men who surrendered and the men who accepted or demanded those surrenders. It illustrates how the surrender of individual soldiers permeated Civil War battles. From the earliest shots on July 1, 1863, until the collapse of Pickett's Charge on July 3, 1863 (and indeed during Lee's retreat into Virginia), Union and Confederate soldiers alike found themselves in a position where they believed that surrendering themselves appeared to be the best option. These surrenders took place at every point on the battlefield and at every stage of the fight. This idiosyncratic retelling does not pretend to offer a comprehensive analysis of the battle as a whole. However, viewed from the perspective of surrender, many of the battlefield's storied figures and locations remain at the forefront.

Gettysburg occurred at a critical moment in how soldiers understood surrender. Almost all of the soldiers who fought at Gettysburg had experienced combat before, as nearly 90 percent of the Army of the Potomac and 94 percent of the Army of Northern Virginia had "seen the elephant."[2] Many of the soldiers had experience with surrender, either surrendering themselves or accepting the surrender of the enemy. Among them were several of the "Fort Sumter Heroes," including Capt. Abner Doubleday and surgeon Samuel Wylie Crawford, both now Union generals, and Lt. Norman J. Hall, who would go on to play a central role in Pickett's Charge. Also among the men who fought at Gettysburg were members of the Harper's Ferry Brigade, commonly ridiculed as the "Harper's Ferry Cowards," who had only recently returned to active service in the Army of the Potomac.[3] These men brought their experiences with surrender with them to the battlefield, experiences that shaped their willingness to both surrender and accept an enemy's surrender.

Some of the men who fought at Gettysburg had only recently surrendered, but because of the efficiency of the Dix-Hill cartel, they had quickly returned to combat. Maj. Charles C. Blacknall of the 23rd North Carolina had surrendered at Chancellorsville, two months prior to Gettysburg. According to a letter he wrote home while in Union captivity, at Chancellorsville Blacknall had charged and occupied an "enemy redoubt with four hundred men," only to find that "my position was flanked & surrounded by a large force & I was under the necessity of surrendering." Attempting to reassure his family, he noted in his letter that although he had been "slightly disabled" in the battle, he was "now quite comfortable. Have been treated with kindness & consideration by the Federal Officers." Critically, he "expected to be exchanged soon." Held in the Old Capitol Prison, Blacknall was indeed paroled on May 18, less than two weeks after his surrender. Reporting to a Confederate parole camp, he hoped that he would not be immediately exchanged so that he could "run out home [for] a day or two." Unfortunately for Blacknall, he was promptly exchanged; he returned to his regiment before the end of May and helped to lead a Confederate advance at Gettysburg on the afternoon of July 1.[4]

For soldiers like Charles Blacknall, their experience of surrender, brief detention, parole, and exchange suggested that being captured on the battlefield proved to be only a minor hindrance to their military service. Blacknall undoubtedly discussed his experience with some of his fellow soldiers, and even those who did not hear his story directly might have interpreted his brief tenure as a prisoner of war as an indicator of surrender's viability. Examples like Blacknall's would shape how the soldiers who fought at Gettysburg evaluated their options when they found themselves in a position when surrender seemed like the only option. However, the Dix-Hill cartel, never entirely stable, would prove unreliable. Now almost a year old, the agreement for exchanging captured soldiers had begun to show considerable strain and indeed was on the verge of collapsing entirely. Many of the soldiers who went into Gettysburg assuming that they would be quickly paroled if they surrendered discovered, to their horror, how fragile the exchange regime was.

THE FIRST DAY: JULY 1, 1863

Neither Robert E. Lee nor George Meade, the newly appointed Union commander, had chosen Gettysburg as the site that would become the largest and most important battle of the Civil War. The battle's location derived primarily from an accidental intersection at the fringes of both armies. Once the first shots were fired, both Confederate and Union forces rushed reinforcements, arriving in uneven waves throughout the day. The chaotic fighting that ensued often pitted unevenly matched forces against each other, situations in which surrender seemed the best option. Much of the fighting that morning took place on either side of the Chambersburg Pike, sometimes referred to as the Cashtown Pike, one of the major approaches to the town of Gettysburg from the west. Confederate general Henry Heth ordered the two leading brigades to begin marching along the pike at five in the morning. Joe Davis, the Confederate president's ambitious nephew, commanded a newly formed brigade of Mississippians and North Carolinians north of the pike. South of the pike, James J. Archer led a brigade of soldiers from Alabama and Tennessee. Neither man had the full confidence of the soldiers he commanded. Joe Davis owed his post to nepotism and had little experience leading men in battle. James Archer, an Old Army officer, had a reputation for bravery but never had the affection of his troops. One of his soldiers remembered that "the make up of Gen. Archer was enigmatical. His exterior was rough and unattractive, small of stature and angular of feature, his temper was irascible, and so cold was his manner."[5]

Significantly outnumbered, dismounted Union cavalry under John Buford effectively slowed the Confederate advance along the pike, allowing John F. Reynolds to bring in reinforcements in the form of the Union 1st Corps, forming a defensive line along McPherson's Ridge. Reynolds ordered the Iron Brigade, soldiers from Wisconsin, Michigan, and Indiana famous for their distinctive black hats and their bravery on the battlefield, to defend the area south of the Chambersburg Pike, an eighteen-acre woodlot belonging to farmer John Herbst, which effectively shielded their position from the advancing Confederate forces. The other defining feature of the landscape was a deep railroad cut just north of the Chambersburg Pike. Running parallel to the pike, the unfinished railroad bed sliced into McPherson's Ridge, creating a steep-banked

Surrender at the Battle of Gettysburg

fissure. Both Herbst's Woods and the railroad cut would feature centrally in surrenders later that morning.

Reynolds had just managed to position a brigade of New York and Pennsylvania regiments across the Chambersburg Pike and on either side of the railroad cut when Confederates under Archer and Davis attacked. As Archer's forces south of the pike entered Herbst's Woods, Reynolds rallied the Iron Brigade: "Forward, men! Forward for God's sake, and drive those fellows out of the woods." Almost immediately thereafter, Reynolds was fatally shot. Upon Reynolds's death, command passed to his senior division commander and old West Point classmate, Abner Doubleday, hero of Fort Sumter.

Through the smoke and trees, Archer's men saw that their opponents were not local militia, as many of them surmised, but the Army of the Potomac. According to Doubleday, Archer's Confederates recognized the Iron Brigade's distinctive headwear and "were heard to exclaim: 'There are those d—d black-hatted fellows again! 'Taint no militia. It's the Army of the Potomac.'"[6] After a brief firefight, charging Michigan and Indiana regiments managed to flank Archer's brigade to the south, causing the Confederates to break ranks and retreat. Those in the front of Archer's brigade, however, had no choice but to surrender. One Confederate claimed that in an instant, "the bluecoats soon covered the hillside in our front, ordering us to surrender." Alabaman William Bird claimed, "It seemed to me there was 20,000 Yanks down in among us hollowing surrender. I had just discharged my gun at them just before they got us, and of course I had to surrender." Facing armed Union soldiers demanding his surrender, a lieutenant found himself unsure about how to respond. "Bird," he said, "what in the hell shall I do?" Sensing the futility of their situation, Bird responded simply: "I don't see what you can do, but surrender." Sensing the wisdom in his subordinate's advice, the lieutenant threw down his sword. Eventually, he was not the only Confederate officer in Archer's Brigade who did understand the proper decorum for surrendering. Another officer attempted to surrender by offering his sword point first to a Union lieutenant, who rebuffed him: "Surrender, that is no way to surrender." He knocked the Confederate officer's sword from his hand, adding, "If you surrender, order your men to cease firing, pick up your sabre and order your men to go to the rear as prisoners."[7]

Other Confederates surrendered as they attempted to retreat, including Gen. James Archer. Patrick Maloney, "a brave patriotic, and fervent young Irishman" with the 2nd Wisconsin (who was killed later that day), spotted Archer among those bolting across Willoughby Run. Hoping to avoid the dishonor of surrendering his sword, Archer attempted to break it on the ground, only to find that the "beautiful steel-scabbard sword" resisted his efforts. "Very much exhausted with fatigue," Archer acquiesced to surrender after being subdued by Maloney and other Union soldiers, but he refused to turn over his sword to an enlisted man. Instead, Archer proffered his sword to Maloney's captain, Charles C. Dow, but Dow refused: "Keep your sword, General, and go to the rear; one sword is all I need on this line." As Archer tramped to the east of Herbst's Woods, where Union soldiers were corralling captured Confederates, he was accosted by Lt. Dennis Dailey, who demanded Archer's sword. Despite Archer's protests that Dow had permitted him to keep his sword, Dailey insisted, discarding his own sword in favor of Archer's more ornate one. Archer also encountered Abner Doubleday, whom he had served alongside during the Mexican War. Evidently hoping to cheer up his despondent former comrade, Doubleday greeted Archer: "Good morning, Archer! How are you? I am glad to see you!" For his part, Archer would have none of it, telling Doubleday, "Well, I am not glad to see you by a damn sight."[8] Although Archer only reluctantly surrendered, many of the soldiers taken with him believed that surrender was the only feasible option. One noted that "General Archer was near me, and was captured with me and quite a number of others besides us. The only alternative was to surrender or retreat for miles under a raking artillery fire in a clear open country without any protection." All told, approximately 800 soldiers under Archer's command surrendered at Herbst's Woods.[9]

Almost simultaneously with Archer's surrender south of the Chambersburg Pike, a series of surrenders took place on the northern end of the Union line, as an unfinished railroad cut just north of the Chambersburg Pike became the site of both Union and Confederate surrenders. The New York and Pennsylvania regiments under the command of Lysander Cutler had just scrambled into position when they were assaulted by Joe Davis's brigade; indeed, much of the 76th New York and 56th Pennsylvania had not yet reached McPherson's Ridge when they were fired upon by Confederate skirmishers concealed in a nearby wheat field. Already exhausted from more than three miles of double-quick marching, the Union soldiers north of the Chambersburg Pike found themselves vastly outnumbered. The only Union regiment north of the Chambersburg Pike in position, the 147th New York faced three larger Confederate regiments (2nd and 42nd Mississippi and 55th North Carolina), which threatened to flank them, forcing the Union soldiers to lie prone in the juvenile wheat to avoid the crossfire.

According to Capt. James Coey, their choices were clear: "It was surrender and save further loss or fight and fall back." Sustaining heavy losses, the 147th New York retreated, seeking shelter within the confines of the railroad cut. New Yorker Francis Pease later recalled that the cut provided an excellent temporary protection from gunfire, especially for soldiers who had been wounded, as the "Rebel balls whistled over the ravine like hail." The respite proved only momentary, as "soon the Rebels came up each side of the bank in large numbers, and we had to throw down our arms and surrender ourselves to them as their prisoners." Along with sixty other men from his regiment, Pease marched two miles to the rear of the Confederate lines.[10]

Confederate control over McPherson's Ridge north of the Chambersburg Pike did not last long. With Archer's Confederates south of the pike in full retreat or surrendered, Abner Doubleday ordered the northernmost Union regiments to "Go like hell!" to the assistance of Cutler's men. Foremost among those going to Cutler's rescue was the 6th Wisconsin's Lt. Col. Rufus Dawes. Firing from the fence rail that lined the road, Dawes's soldiers forced the Confederates to seek shelter, and many of them "ran to the railroad cut," where they proceeded to "pour [gunfire] upon us from their cover in the cut." With the Confederates ensconced in the cut, Dawes's men were "now receiving a fearfully destructive fire from the hidden enemy." Not all of the Confederates sheltering in the railroad cut were as impressed with its merits as a defensive position. A soldier with the 42nd Mississippi claimed that "the cut was too deep to fire over" and the soldiers within the cut were packed in "too thick to either fight or escape." While the railroad cut effectively protected the Confederates from Union fire, it would ultimately prove to be a trap.

Unable to dislodge the sheltering Confederates from his location, Dawes ordered his men to charge the fifty or so yards to the railroad cut. Joined by two other Union regiments, Dawes's men advanced, sustaining heavy losses from Confederate fire, before they reached the lip of the railroad cut. They pointed their rifles down upon the enemy, and Dawes heard a "general cry from our men of: 'Thrown down your muskets! Down with your muskets!'" Dawes found himself "face to face with hundreds of rebels, whom I looked down upon in the railroad cut, which was, where I stood, four feet deep." Dawes shouted, "Where is the colonel of this regiment?" When a Confederate officer (Maj. John Blair) identified himself, Dawes offered an ultimatum: "Surrender, or I will fire." Wordlessly, his Confederate opposite handed Dawes his sword in surrender, and his men "threw down their muskets." In retrospect, Dawes wished that he had had the presence of mind to have refused when the Confederate officer had proffered his sword, as it would have been a "handsome thing to say, 'Keep your sword, sir.'" However, as he was "new to such occasions," he accepted the sword, and "when six other officers came up and handed me their swords, I took them also," leaving him with an "awkward bundle in my arms."

Reflecting on the event years later, Dawes remarked at how quickly his soldiers transitioned from attackers intent upon killing their enemy to captors charged with the protection of prisoners. He was impressed by "the coolness, self-possession, and discipline which held back our men from pouring in a general volley saved a hundred lives of the enemy, and as my mind goes back to the fearful excitement of the moment, I marvel at it." Even after sustaining heavy losses charging on the railroad cut, Dawes's men concluded that the Confederate soldiers would surrender rather than attempt to fight their way out of the cut. Despite the noise, confusion, and adrenalin of battle, Dawes managed take at least 232 Confederates prisoner.

Dawes's account of the Confederate surrender at the railroad suggests that a single Confederate officer was responsible for the surrender. From the perspective of the men within the cut, however, this wasn't necessarily the case. Confederate soldiers from three different regiments surrendered at the railroad cut, and according to Maj. John Blair, the officer whom Dawes describes as offering to surrender, "all the men were jumbled together without regiment or company," in large part leaderless, "for the want of officers." Just as the initial call for surrender came not from Dawes but from his men who arrived at the lip of the cut before him, the decision to surrender was largely made by the Confederate soldiers before Blair handed Dawes his sword; indeed, many of the Confederates had by that point already dropped their weapons. At the same time, some Confederate soldiers refused to surrender. Not more than thirty yards from Blair and Dawes, Confederate and Union soldiers fought over the 2nd Mississippi's regimental flag, a bloody fracas that left more than a dozen men killed or wounded. The collective decisions of Confederate troops to surrender rather than try to fight their way out of the railroad cut and the collective decisions of Union troops to demand and accept their surrenders reflected soldiers' peculiar kind of agency on the battlefield.[11]

The story of the first afternoon at Gettysburg can be told largely as the arrival of successive waves of Confederate and Union reinforcements. By noon, the remainder of the Union 1st Corps had arrived to reinforce Doubleday, as had the vanguard of O. O. Howard's 11th Corps. Recognizing the severity of the situation, Howard called for additional reinforcements from the 3rd and 12th corps. Meanwhile, Henry Heth had managed to bring up his two remaining divisions from the west. They were joined by Dorsey Pender's division, more than 6,000 strong, giving the Confederates in excess of 10,000 soldiers entering the fray's western front. From the north, Robert Rodes's five divisions and Richard Ewell's two divisions arrived in a piecemeal manner in the early afternoon, giving the Confederates a considerable, if temporary, numerical advantage.

Arriving with little knowledge of the current state of combat, the local geography, or the location of the enemy, these largely uncoordinated waves of reinforcements often found themselves thrust unprepared into battle. These unexpected engagements between Union and Confederate soldiers created the circumstances both for deadly assaults by an unseen opponent and for soldiers to surrender after suddenly encountering a numerically superior enemy. For example, early in the afternoon, Alfred Iverson's North Carolina brigade marched directly into a volley of Union gunfire, "a sheet of flame and smoke," from several regiments of Pennsylvania and New York soldiers hidden behind a low fieldstone wall. A soldier with the 88th Pennsylvania noted, "The rebels suffered so much that they finally manifested a disposition to surrender, many of them throwing up their hats and in other ways indicating that they had had more than enough, and were willing to be taken back into the Union." Indeed, while some Confederate soldiers who had survived the barrage beat a hasty retreat across an open field that exposed them to Union gunfire, others "rose singly and in groups, and came running towards us, holding their hands in tokens of surrender." Many of Iverson's men who surrendered were wounded, including the recently exchanged Charles Blacknall, who had been shot in the jaw but still had the presence of mind to drop his weapon and hold up his hands in surrender. Although the Confederates were unarmed, not all the Union soldiers positioned behind the stone wall immediately accepted their surrender, as "our officers . . . were suspicious as to their sincerity, many thinking it a trap." Ordered to charge, the "regiment sprang over the wall with a shout, followed by most of the brigade, and charging the rebs, ran over their line of battle, receiving the surrender of hundreds of prisoners and capturing the flags of the 23rd North Carolina and an Alabama regiment." Although estimates vary widely, more than 300 men surrendered from Iverson's force.[12]

By midafternoon, the Confederate advantage north and west of the town had become evident. The arrival of Jubal Early's division around 3:00 P.M. overwhelmed Union defenders northeast of the town along the Heidlersburg Road, and a resumed assault by Rodes's and Pender's troops pushed what was left of the 1st Corps back to the Lutheran Theological Seminary. By 4:00 P.M., O. O. Howard, who had assumed control of Union forces until Meade could arrive, ordered a general retreat to Cemetery Hill, which had been reinforced with artillery. Since Cemetery Hill was located south of the town, Union soldiers would have to retreat through the town itself to reach safety. The panicked and disorganized retreat through the streets created ample opportunity for isolated Union soldiers, fleeing blindly down alleyways and through gardens, to be forced to surrender. As one Union soldier noted, once they were within the town itself, "every man commenced to look after himself without further orders."[13]

News of the order to retreat spread unevenly to the besieged Union troops in the field. Most of those who received the order early safely relocated to Cemetery Hill. However, in cases where the order had been delayed or never received, Union soldiers found themselves isolated and overwhelmed by the advancing Confederates, leaving them with few options but to run or surrender. Among the last of the Union forces to retreat in the confused fighting to end the first day was the artillery brigade of the 1st Corps, commanded by Col. Charles S. Wainwright. Ordered earlier in the afternoon to hold Seminary Ridge, Wainwright's soldiers found themselves without protection, for as Wainwright later remembered, "our infantry had all gone from around me." Fearful of inciting a panic that would cause his men to abandon their cannons, Wainwright ordered a slow retreat toward the town. Able to see the approaching Confederate soldiers, Wainwright concluded that he "had very little hope for getting them all off, for the rebs were close upon us." With the nearest Confederate regiment within fifty yards, Wainwright attempted to conceal his sense of dread from the soldiers under his command. "As I sat on the hill watching my pieces file past and cautioning each one not to trot," Wainwright observed, "there was not a doubt in my mind but that I should go to Richmond. Each minute I expected to hear the order to surrender."[14]

Wainwright managed to avoid surrendering during the retreat, but not all Union soldiers were as fortunate. Captured in the retreat from Seminary Ridge, Asa Hardman had earlier that day had the "satisfaction of seeing General Archer with 800 of command captured" and "the majority of General Davis's Mississippi brigade surrounded in the railroad cut and compelled to surrender." By the afternoon, however, the tide of the battle had turned. Hardman noted that "our hard pressed line would be compelled by overwhelming numbers to retire from Seminary Ridge." Overwhelmed by Confederate soldiers, Hardman later recalled that "the men were almost instantly surrounded, standing in a vortex of fire from both flanks and rear, with their cartridge boxes empty." At first, Hardman's commanding officer "encouraged them to fight with the naked bayonet, hoping to cut his way out." Quickly realizing that continuing to fight would be suicidal, he raised a "white handkerchief and waved it in token of surrender," resulting in an immediate ceasefire. In the noise and the confusion, however, not all of the Union soldiers realized that they were surrendering. Among them was a wounded sergeant who had "not seen the colonel's signal" and continued to fire on the advancing Confederate soldiers. In response, the Confederates "opened fire again with tremendous effect," killing many of the men alongside Hardman, some of whom had already dropped their weapons to surrender. The commanding Union officer hurried into a nearby house, seized a large white tablecloth, and attempted to surrender a second time. This larger "token of surrender," Hardman noted with relief, "the Rebels acknowledged and quit firing." While most of the unwounded men who surrendered alongside Hardman were marched to the rear, the Confederates left Hardman and six other healthy soldiers to tend to their wounded comrades. They spent the next couple of days "doing the best we could for the wounded . . . provide temporary shelter, remove their bloody garments, bathe their wounds, and see that they had plenty of water." Later, a Confederate officer "took our names and regiments and informed us that we had been paroled for the purpose of tending to the Yankee wounded, and if found serving in the ranks again before we were [ex]changed, we would at once be shot."[15]

A similar scenario played out north of the town, as the disorganized retreat gave advancing Confederates ample opportunity to compel Union soldiers to surrender. Among the first to surrender were those tasked to protect the retreat. Ordered by General Robinson to "hold . . . as long as there was a single man left" to facilitate the retreat of the rest of the regiment, "every man" in the 16th Maine "knew that the movement meant death or capture." Spreading out to intercept as much of the quickly advancing Confederate force as possible, the 16th Maine "fought like hell." Flanked and overwhelmed, nearly all of the 16th Maine, more than 100 men, surrendered, but not before tearing the regimental flag to pieces to prevent it from falling into Confederate hands. Similarly, Charles Tilden, who had protested their assignment as suicidal, tried to break his sword by jabbing it into the ground to avoid surrendering it, but like James Archer's, Tilden's effort failed.[16] A similar fate befell the brigade under Charles Coster, whom Howard had sent in as reinforcements to cover the retreat. An officer with the 154th New York noted that his men "stood, firm as the Pyramids, fighting with the desperation of a forlorn hope, a murderous fire all the time raking them in front and flank. The enemy was gradually closing in upon us, and to remain longer was certain capture." Although a "few in the confusion escaped," he observed, the vast majority of his regiment "were either killed, wounded or captured."[17]

Maps of Gettysburg offer the misleading impression that the town possessed a clear grid pattern that would allow armies to pass quickly through it. However, as Rufus Dawes noted when his regiment retreated through the town from Seminary Ridge, "the streets were jammed with crowds of retreating soldiers, and with ambulances, artillery, and wagons."[18] In addition to its main thoroughfares, however, the town also possessed a labyrinthine warren of alleys, many of which dead-ended. For soldiers unfamiliar with the town (and most were), these alleyways proved to be an irresistible lure during the retreat; unlike the thoroughfares, which exposed retreating soldiers to rifle and cannon fire, narrow alleyways offered the promise of a sheltered shortcut through the town. Among those seduced was Samuel Boone of the 88th Pennsylvania. Earlier in the afternoon, Boone's regiment had been instrumental in taking more than 200 North Carolinians' surrender. Separated from his regiment, Boone recalled running "along alleys and bystreets until I reached the southern suburbs, where after crossing one fence of a lane, I fell into the lane, too exhausted to cross the other fence." After "a short breathing spell," Boone squeezed through a missing plank in a board fence and crossed a garden, only to find that "when I stuck my head beyond the corner of the house, I stood face to face with one of the most desperate soldiers in the Rebel Army—a 'Louisiana Tiger.' He was so close to me that he was obliged to jump away from me in order to level his piece at me." Such individual face-to-face encounters were relatively rare in the Civil War, and consequently, "for an instant, we both stood transfixed, neither of us knowing if we were the victor or the vanquished. It took but a minute for him to decide, as I had my sword sheathed, and was unprepared to meet him. With his finger on the trigger and with the black muzzle of his gun pointed at my breast, ready to send me into eternity in an instant, he very excitedly ordered 'Surrender.' I was at his mercy. Throwing my right hand up I also excitedly said 'You've got the best of me.'"[19]

Many soldiers retreating through Gettysburg's streets did not have Samuel Boone's luck. J. Warren Jackson of the 8th Louisiana described that chaos of the Federal retreat: "We shot them down, bayoneted them & captured more prisoners than we had men. . . . We ran them thro town & caught hundreds of them in the houses & cellars." To avoid capture, many Union soldiers attempted to conceal themselves in the town. According to Rufus Dawes, who earlier in the day had accepted the Confederate surrender at the railroad cut, "the cellars were crowded with men, sound in body, but craven in spirit, who had gone there to surrender." Prussian-born Union general Alexander Schimmelpfennig, who hid in a culvert during retreat on July 1, subsequently bunkered down in a shed for several days while Confederates occupied the town.[20]

Other Union soldiers barricaded themselves in buildings, hoping to be liberated when reinforcements arrived. Soldiers from the 45th New York sheltered in the Eagle Hotel opposite Christ Lutheran Church on Chambersburg Street. After fortifying the hotel and neighboring buildings, they rebuffed "repeated

Surrender at the Battle of Gettysburg

demands to surrender." Once the sun had set, however, the soldiers within saw no evidence that they were going to be rescued. After a parley, the Confederates agreed to allow Capt. Francis Irsch safe passage to "see the hopelessness" of their situation. Escorted through the town and to the base of Cemetery Hill, he saw that the entire town was "full of the enemy," with "no Federals in sight, excepting such as having taken refuge in cellars and houses were brought out as prisoners." When he returned to his men, Irsch ordered them to surrender.[21]

Surrendering Union soldiers slowed the Confederate advance through the town, giving other Union troops time to retreat to Cemetery Hill. Virginia chaplain J. Marshall Meredith found that his brigade's advance in the town delayed the "long and large force of Federal prisoners marching back on the Cashtown road westward." Although his soldiers wanted to continue the attack toward Cemetery Hill, Dorsey Pender had to instruct the 1st South Carolina "to halt, and go back and take the prisoners out." Several Union soldiers who surrendered late that afternoon could not find a Confederate interested in escorting them to the prisoner corral north of the town. Unsupervised, some dutifully walked there alone, while others took the opportunity to escape.[22]

Incomplete records make calculating the number of soldiers who surrendered on the first day of Gettysburg impossible. However, the available evidence allows for some gross estimations: more than 3,000 Union soldiers surrendered, most of them in the retreat that afternoon, while Confederate losses were even more significant, with more than 5,000 soldiers surrendering.[23] To put these figures into context, approximately one of every eight Union and Confederate soldiers engaged that day surrendered.

Surrendered prisoners provided valuable information about the enemy's strength, location, and disposition. Captain of the all-German 26th Wisconsin regiment, Bernhard Domschcke claimed that Confederate officers "pumped me for information: the strength of our forces, the direction of our approach, whether the entire Army of Potomac had arrived, who had replaced the former commanding general, [Joseph] Hooker, and so forth." Recognizing the value of this information, Domschcke refused to answer, and "the curiosity of these worthy gentlemen went unsatisfied."[24] Although persistent in their questioning, both Union and Confederate captors at Gettysburg stopped short of torturing soldiers for information. Most prisoners willingly disclosed their name and unit affiliation. Properly compiled, this information could be used to ascertain which enemy regiments had arrived on the battlefield, potentially valuable information in devising strategies for the remainder of the battle. Before fighting resumed on July 2, George Sharpe of the Bureau of Military Information reported to Meade that "prisoners have been taken today, and last evening, from every brigade in Lee's Army excepting the four brigades of Pickett[']s Division." Sharpe met with Meade again later that evening and informed him that prisoners had been taken from 100 Confederate regiments, allowing Meade to conclude which regiments had fought and which had been held in reserve.[25]

THE SECOND DAY: JULY 2, 1863

The first significant engagement of Gettysburg's second day did not occur until midafternoon, as both Union and Confederate forces awaited reinforcements. Attempting to flank Union forces to the south, Gen. John Bell Hood personally led the advance toward a pair of hills known as the Round Tops. Ensconced in a warren of large boulders known as the Devil's Den, the 4th New York Independent Battery fired an artillery barrage that wounded Hood and several other Confederate officers. With the division effectively leaderless, the Texas and Alabama soldiers "became broken and confused and the men exhausted." Despite their heavy losses and lack of coordination, once the Confederates reached the Union battery, they overwhelmed its defenders. Confederates, "leaping to and fro from boulder to boulder," took "between 140 and 200 prisoners." The Devil's Den's labyrinthine structure, further obscured by the smoke of cannon and rifle fire, facilitated face-to-face encounters between attacking Confederates and defending Union soldiers, creating ample opportunity for demands of surrender. A soldier with the 3rd Arkansas noted, "Each side wanted the protection of those rocks, one in particular. It was very large, about four or five feet high. I saw smoke coming from behind that one and made a run for it, swerving to the right, with my gun ready. I cried, 'Hands up,' they dropped their guns and came out from behind the rock. There were six of them. One said, 'Young man, where is your troops?' I told them I was it, and showed them to the rear."[26]

Having taken the Devil's Den, the Confederates sought to dislodge Union defenders occupying the smaller of the pair of hills in front of them. Hastily occupied by four regiments under Col. Strong Vincent, Little Round Top formed the southernmost end of the Army of the Potomac. On the far left of Vincent's line stood the 20th Maine, commanded by Joshua Lawrence Chamberlain, who prior to the war had been a professor of rhetoric at Bowdoin College. Ordered by Vincent to "hold this ground at all costs," Chamberlain and his men repelled repeated Confederate advances. Nearly out of ammunition, Chamberlain ordered an unexpected bayonet charge from Little Round Top. One soldier observed that "the rebel front line amazed at the sudden movement, thinking we had been reinforced." The exhausted Confederate soldiers began to "throw down their arms and cry out 'don't fire! We surrender,' the rest fled in wild confusion."[27]

Pursuing the fleeing Confederates down the hill and into the saddle that separated Little Round Top from Big Round Top, the 20th Maine accepted hundreds of Confederate surrenders while simultaneously ruthlessly attacking those who attempted to escape. Capt. Ellis Spear recalled that "painful as the necessity was, we were obliged to shoot them. I mean those who were trying to scale the fence & escape without asking leave. The rest, who dropped their guns & showed signs of repentance, we magnanimously spared, and accepted their apologies."[28] The juxtaposition of the merciful acceptance of disarmed soldiers' surrender and the merciless pursuit of their retreating compatriots reflected how quickly Civil War soldiers had to make instantaneous choices about the merits of accepting surrender. Having begun the bayonet charge with the intent of killing their enemy, Chamberlain's men repeatedly made hasty decisions to spare a Confederate soldier's life by accepting his surrender, only to resume the attack moments later. Describing the collapsing Confederate line, Col. William Livermore noted, "Some threw down their arms and ran, but many rose up, begging to be spared. We did not stop but told them to go to the rear, and we went after the whipped and frightened rebels, taking them by scores."[29]

The chaotic Confederate retreat from Little Round Top destroyed whatever command structure and unit cohesiveness remained, allowing soldiers wide discretion whether to run, fight, or surrender. John W. Stevens, a soldier in Hood's Brigade, described the confusion of the retreat: "The balls are whizzing so thick around us that it looks like a man could hold out a hat and catch it full. . . . [The enemy] were not over 25 or 30 paces from us and the balls were flying as thick as hail (apparently.) This thing continued until we had fired some 10 or 12 rounds—the roar of artillery and the din of small arms was so deafening that we could not hear each other in an ordinary tone of command." Only dimly aware of the location of his comrades amidst the smoke and noise, Stevens ran. Although "it had never occurred to me that there was any danger of being captured," Stevens felt "a slap on my back with a sword and an order to throw down my gun and behave myself." The demand, Stevens later recalled, "came like a sudden clap of thunder." Once he had a chance to compose himself, Stevens "looked around [and saw] the woods behind me were full of Yankees. My own fragment of our company were already disarmed and a guard around them. Realizing the fact that I was a prisoner, I took out an old knife and cut my cartridge box off."[30]

For many of the Confederates surrendering at Little Round Top, the opportunity to lay down one's weapon and rest came as a welcome relief. Decimus et Ultimas Barziza (his unusual name was the product of parents who concluded that ten children was enough) surrendered after being wounded and separated from his unit. Barziza had arrived at Gettysburg at 2:00 A.M. on the morning of July 2 after a twenty-four-hour march. Footsore and exhausted, Captain Barziza received orders that his men would lead the charge on Little Round Top. Advancing from the Devil's Den, they found themselves bombarded from the heights as "shells and grape shot, canister and Minnie balls, came hurtling through our ranks, busting, screaming, whistling." Continuing to advance, Barziza and his men charged up the base of Little Round Top, where the "trees were literally barked, and thousands of bullets flew up to atoms against the hard rocks." Wounded in the assault, Barziza could not retreat with the rest of his unit when the Confederate line faltered. At first, he "tried to feign dead," but when the ruse was discovered, he had no choice but to surrender.[31] Like Barziza, many of the Confederates surrendering at Little Round Top had been wounded in the assault. Shot through the lung and bleeding profusely, Lt. Col. Michael Bulger refused to tender his weapon to a Union captain, claiming that he would "never surrender my sword to an officer of lower rank," professing that he would rather die than surrender dishonorably. The captain, "so amused at the old Colonel's high notions of military etiquette," fetched his colonel to accept Bugler's surrender.

In later years, some of the Confederate survivors who managed to retreat from Little Round Top claimed that they never considered surrendering. Alabama colonel William Oates claimed that he narrowly escaped being taken prisoner despite being "overcome with heat and exhaustion." Oates could not countenance surrender, as "I dreaded prison more than death." Many of the men under Oates's command, however, made a different calculation, deciding surrender was preferable to death. It is unclear how many Confederate soldiers surrendered when Chamberlain's soldiers charged down Little Round Top. Chamberlain himself counted 368 Confederate prisoners (and other Union sources estimated that more than 400 surrendered), while some Confederates claimed that as few as 218 were taken.[32]

Northwest of Little Round Top, the other half of James Longstreet's corps under Lafayette McLaws engaged with Federal soldiers at the Peach Orchard and the Wheatfield. Unlike earlier sites of surrender on the Gettysburg battlefield, the relatively open terrain here should have made surrender difficult. The noise of the cannons would have made hearing demands and offers of surrender almost impossible. Nevertheless, over the course of the late after-noon and early evening, hundreds of Union and Confederate soldiers surren-dered there. The initial Confederate attack on the Peach Orchard caused a Union rout, with those Federal soldiers who could not escape surrendering. According to McLaws, his men "gallantly . . . swept the enemy before them, away from the Peach orchard," with the surrendering "enemy running towards our lines." In the chaos, skirmishers from the 57th Pennsylvania took shelter in the Sherfy Farm. "Amid the noise and the confusion," the message to retreat did not reach them. Capt. Alanson Nelson attempted to alert them, running frantically from building to building on the outskirts of the orchard. Leaving the last structure, he saw that "the enemy was in the yard in large force not fifty feet away. They saw me as soon as I did them, and ordered me to surrender." Outnumbered and at close range, Nelson had to make an instantaneous deci-sion. More than most soldiers, Nelson feared capture, writing, "I had always said I would never be taken prisoner as long as I could fight or run. There was nothing I dreaded so much as to be taken prisoner." Driven by his fear of cap-ture, Nelson "took the chance" to run. Under heavy fire, he somehow managed to avoid being shot, later claiming that "either their aim was poor, or else I outran their shots for they never touched me." Despite his efforts, not all of the 57th's soldiers managed to escape from the Sherfy farm and were "summoned to surrender by the rebels."[33]

Confederates took 200 prisoners at the Peach Orchard, including Brig. Gen. Charles Graham, the highest-ranking Union officer to surrender at Gettysburg. Graham surrendered only after sustaining multiple injuries. "I had twice been wounded, had a horse shot out from under me, and my sword shot out of my hand," he later recalled. "Although exhausted by the loss of blood," Graham had obtained another horse, which was promptly felled by five rebel bullets. "Unable to rise," he wrote, "I remained on the ground until . . . I surrendered."[34]

Some of the most confused fighting on Gettysburg's second day took place at the Wheatfield, just east of the Peach Orchard. Over the course of the late afternoon and early evening, possession of the Wheatfield changed hands at least six times, as Confederate and Union reinforcements arrived. Repeated efforts to dislodge the enemy prompted headlong charges that quickly brought soldiers into close proximity. One charge by a regiment of the Irish Brigade into a woodlot bordering the Wheatfield resulted in Confederate and Union soldiers standing within arm's reach of one another. According to Col. St. Clair Mulholland,

Here took place a rather extraordinary scene. Our men and their opponents were mingled together. In charging we had literally run right in among them. Firing instantly ceased, and we found there were as many of the enemy as there were of ourselves. Officers and men of both sides looked for a time at each other utterly bewildered; the fighting had stopped, yet the Confederate soldiers stood there facing us, still retaining their arms and showing now disposition to surrender. At this moment I called out, "Confederate troops, lay down your arms and go to the rear!" This ended a scene that was becoming embarrassing. The order was promptly obeyed and a large number of what I think were men of Kershaw's Brigade became our prisoners.[35]

The "bewilderment" that the Union and Confederate soldiers experienced reveals something about how they understood surrender functioning on the battlefield. Rather than engage in close-quarters or hand-to-hand combat with the enemy, which would have resulted in heavy causalities, soldiers on both sides concluded that when enemy soldiers came in such close contact, surrender was the inevitable result. The only question here, given their relative parity, was which side would end up surrendering. In this respect, the soldiers' behavior reflected the high-water mark for battlefield surrenders. In later battles, after the Dix-Hill cartel had collapsed, soldiers in similar situations were more likely to fight than surrender.

Although Mulholland's men managed to take a significant number of prisoners, their captivity did not last long, as Confederate reinforcements liberated their surrendered comrades and drove the Union soldiers back across the Wheatfield. Attempting to carry a wounded officer to safety, George Whipple fell behind the rest of his regiment and became overrun by advancing Confederates. "Surrender you d—m Yankee," they yelled at him. Whipple acquiesced but requested a moment to attend to his dying captain, "but the bayonet was close to my back, with awful threats to put it through me if I refused." Recognizing the futility of his situation, Whipple obeyed the order to "Go to the rear you d—d Yankee son of a b—h."[36]

Hearing the fight from the vantage point of Ziegler's grove on Cemetery Ridge, soldiers in the Harper's Ferry Brigade feared that they would not be allowed to fight, as the stigma of their surrender had tainted them to the point where no general would send them into action. Labeled the "Harper's Ferry Cowards" during their parole at Camp Douglas, they had only recently returned to the Army of the Potomac after six months on garrison duty in Washington, D.C. On July 2, they were the last brigade of the 2nd Corps to arrive on Cemetery Ridge, assigned to guard the baggage train the previous day. Ridiculed by their fellow soldiers as "band-box soldiers" unfit for combat, the men of the Harper's Ferry Brigade hoped that they could redeem their lost honor at Gettysburg. "All we ask of our countrymen is justice," one officer wrote; "we should not bear the odium of a result for which we were not responsible."[37]

When a 300-yard gap opened in the Union line, Gen. Winfield Scott Hancock ordered Gen. Alexander Hays "to send one of your best Brigades over there." Turning to Col. George Willard, who had recently assumed command of the Harper's Ferry Brigade, Hays told him, "Take your Brigade over there and knock Hell out of the rebs." Although no one would have considered the Harper's Ferry Brigade among the "best" under his command, Hays believed that in their zeal to reclaim their lost honor, they would fight. Attaching bayonets, they charged into the fray, yelling "Remember Harper's Ferry!"

Entering the Wheatfield around sundown, the soldiers of the Harper's Ferry Brigade quickly recognized their adversary as Barksdale's Mississippi Brigade, the same soldiers to whom they had surrendered less than a year earlier. One chronicler of the brigade's exploits that evening observed, "The venom of that old taunt, 'Harper's Ferry cowards!' which had so long burned in their veins . . . now excited them to fury. . . . Nothing could restrain them, nothing could resist them. . . . Such was the excitement caused by the cry that had electrified them, that it seemed as if they eagerly poured out their heart's blood to wash away that old stain upon their honor." In their zeal to redeem themselves, the Harper's Ferry Brigade took heavy casualties, including Colonel Willard, but also managed to repel the Confederate attack. The ferocity of their assault intimidated the Mississippians, many of whom "in craven fear fell on their faces and threw up their hands in token of surrender." After months of ridicule and shame, the soldiers of the Harper's Ferry Brigade felt enormous pride in accepting the surrender.[38]

Fighting at the Wheatfield continued well after sundown. In the twilight, soldiers easily became disoriented and detached from their units. In one of the last charges of the day, E. H. Sutton of the 24th Georgia surrendered when the Pennsylvania Reserves overran his position. After he dropped his weapon and carriage box, Sutton started toward the rear with the other prisoners from his regiment. He was taken unsuspecting when "a burly Irishman presented his gun at my breast and was pulling the trigger, cursing me." The gun was knocked aside by another Union soldier, who saved Sutton's life and reprimanded him to "go forward and fight those who had not surrendered."[39] As the fighting on the Wheatfield died down, a lone Confederate soldier, evidently disoriented, came wandering "unattended" toward Union lines. Amused by this "ludicrous" situation, the Union soldiers yelled, "Hello, Johnny! . . . You aren't going to capture us all alone, are you?" Even after the bloody fighting that afternoon and evening, the Union soldiers were willing to spare the isolated Confederate soldier, allowing him to drop his weapon and offer to surrender himself.[40]

Most of the surrenders on Gettysburg's second day took place in the southern half of the battlefield, near the Devil's Den, Little Round Top, the Peach Orchard, and the Wheatfield. There soldiers often surrendered in small groups, entering captivity alongside their comrades. On other parts of the battlefield, soldiers frequently surrendered alone. Positioned north of the Peach Orchard along the Emmitsburg Road, not far from the Codori farm, Massachusetts private Roland Bowen had often thought about how a soldier ought to conduct himself in battle. Facing a Confederate charge at Gettysburg, the men of the 15th Massachusetts "poured one continual storm of lead on them, but they heeded not." Amid the onslaught, Bowen noticed that the regiment to their left had begun to break and that "it was only too evident that in thirty seconds everything would be lost." Three options presented themselves: retreat, surrender, or fight. A voice in his head told Bowen that "nothing but cowards run" and that "I looked upon it as a disgrace to run." A neighboring soldier evidently reached a different conclusion, proclaiming that he would "never be a prisoner, never," running to safety behind Union artillery, whereupon the "stampede became general." Bowen stood his ground and "blazed away one last time" before he "threw down my gun and held up both hands, my cap in one and begged that they might spare my life." To his surprise, the attacking Confederates ignored him, as they "spoke not a word to me but passed over and on," as "every reb[']s eye seemed to be fixed on our artillery."

Bowen now found himself alone, behind the enemy, within the range of his own artillery, and unarmed. Presumably, he could have picked up his rifle and resumed fighting, but he concluded that rearming himself would be either improper or imprudent. Fearing that he would be subject to Union grapeshot, Bowen ran as fast as he could for "the rear of Lee's army," now the only direction open to him. Bolting from piles of fence rails to boulders, Bowen discarded any possession that would slow down his flight, looking in vain "for some ravine or hole or place to hide myself from the balls and shell." Eventually he found a Confederate soldier, who he concluded had been shirking and who proved more than happy to escort him into Confederate lines.

"For the first time in my life I was a prisoner," Bowen later recalled, "but I was not alone." That evening he was marshaled along the Hagerstown Road to where it intersected with Willoughby's Run. There "a large number of Prisoners

Surrender at the Battle of Gettysburg

had been collected and a guard stationed around them." Bowen could see men wearing corps insignia from all parts of the Army of the Potomac: "the Sphere, Cross, Maltese Cross, Diamonds, Trefoils, and above all the Crescents." The surrendered men talked into the night, trading stories and information about the ongoing battle. The men who had surrendered on July 1 were particularly keen to discover what had transpired since they had been taken. Eventually Bowen found a handful of men from his regiment. Gathering around a large tree, the men of the 15th Massachusetts concluded that "it were much better to be a *prisoner* than a *corpse*."[41]

THE THIRD DAY: JULY 3, 1863

At the end of the Confederate assault on Cemetery Ridge on July 3, a Mississippi soldier asked a despondent Joe Davis, "General Davis, where is your brigade?" Wordlessly, Davis "pointed his sword up to the skies . . . and walked on."[42] Pickett's Charge (or as some historians now prefer, the Pickett-Pettigrew-Trimble Charge) marked the effective end of Davis's Brigade as a fighting force. He had lost more than half of his men and all of his field officers at Gettysburg. In pointing his sword to the heavens, Davis implied that his missing soldiers had been killed. However, he was mistaken about the fate of his men: most were not dead but in Union captivity. At least 200 soldiers from Davis's Brigade had surrendered at the railroad cut two days previous, and at least an equal number surrendered during Pickett's Charge. From Davis's perspective, the difference was negligible; killed or captured, the men were not available for combat. For the soldiers themselves, however, the difference was monumental.

Few events in the Civil War (or indeed in all of American history) have been immortalized and mythologized like Pickett's Charge. In 1883, it became the subject of artist Paul Philippoteaux's epic Gettysburg cyclorama, a nearly 400-foot version of which is on display at the National Park Service's Visitor Center. For novelist William Faulkner, it was the moment embedded in the mind of "every Southern boy fourteen years old" who daydreamed about "the desperate gamble." In Ronald Maxwell's 1993 film *Gettysburg*, based on Michael Shaara's bestselling novel *The Killer Angels*, the scenes depicting Pickett's Charge lasted longer than the historical charge itself did. However, none of these depictions featured surrender centrally. Yet for many Confederate soldiers (and more than a few Union soldiers), Pickett's Charge ended when they raised their arms in surrender. The Lost Cause mythology that has so shaped how Pickett's Charge has been remembered has effectively erased their experiences.

For all that has been written about Pickett's Charge, much still remains unclear. Historian Carol Reardon has observed that "for a pivotal moment in military history replete with eyewitnesses, consensus on many aspects of the afternoon's events is surprisingly difficult to reach." As Allen Guelzo has recently illustrated, this is particularly true of scholarly estimates of the casualty numbers from Pickett's Charge, which vary considerably. In recent years, historians have calculated that the number of Confederate soldiers killed in Pickett's division (which made up less than half of those who participated in the assault, but for whom the best records survive) ranged anywhere from 232 to 626. Despite this uncertainty, the records indicate that at least twice as many Confederates surrendered as died during the charge.[43]

The Confederate assault began after an hourlong artillery barrage that attempted and failed to destroy Union batteries. Stretched out over a mile-long front, the rebel forces would converge to half that length over the course of the three-quarters-of-a-mile charge. On the Confederate left flank, James J. Pettigrew's division had the shorter distance to cover before reaching Union lines. Facing heavy flanking artillery and musket fire, approximately half of Pettigrew's division advanced beyond the sunken Emmitsburg Road. Those who did faced Alexander Hays's division ensconced behind a low stone wall. Before his promotion, Hays had previously commanded the Harper's Ferry Brigade, which formed the heart of his division and the northern end of the Union line. Decimated from their fight in the Wheatfield the previous afternoon, the thinly spread men of the Harper's Ferry Brigade remained committed to restoring their lost honor and delighted in taking rebel prisoners. Hays reported that rebels who reached Union lines "were throwing away their arms and appealing most piteously for mercy." A captured Confederate officer passing Hays retorted, "If I had known that this is all you have, I would not have surrendered." Among the trophies that the Harper's Ferry Brigade took from surrendering Confederate soldiers was a regimental flag, probably belonging to the 28th North Carolina, which listed HARPERS FERRY among its battle honors. Hays "rode the length of the brigade in his front, trailing the flag on the ground amid the continuous and deafening cheers of the men."[44]

Some of the Confederate soldiers surrendered en masse. The officers of the 11th Mississippi, probably the only regiment from Davis's division to advance past the Emmitsburg Road, found themselves isolated on the battlefield and concluded that pushing farther up the hill toward the Union fence line would prove suicidal. They decided that "the only alternatives were to fight uselessly until annihilated, to surrender, or to try to escape." Recognizing that "withdrawing slowly and in perfect order under the tempest of deadly shot and shell" would prove "a Quixotic affectation," they waved a white flag and signaled their intention to surrender. Sgt. Thomas Geer of the 111th New York instructed them to drop their weapons and progress toward the Union rear. When, out of either anger or ignorance that the rebels had surrendered, a nearby Union soldier aimed his musket at them, Geer knocked the musket away and "with a word of reproach, asked the soldier if he did not see that these men had surrendered."[45]

Trailing behind Pettigrew's division, few of the soldiers under Trimble made it close enough to Union lines to surrender. According to Lt. Burwell Cotton of the 34th North Carolina, as soon as they got within range of Union rifles, "our lines were broken and we commenced retreating. A good many surrendered rather than risk getting out." In a letter to his parents the next morning, Smith Brown of the 126th New York noted that the charge ended when "Rebels laid down their arms & came in." Looking over the men who surrendered from Pettigrew's and Trimble's divisions, Hays was amazed at how many Confederate soldiers put themselves at the mercy of his men. "Of the prisoners which fell into our hands," he noted in his official report, "I regret that no accurate account could be kept but by estimate, which cannot be less than 1,500."[46]

The most intense fighting during Pickett's Charge took place at the Union center in an area immortalized as the Bloody Angle and the Copse of Trees. Here many Confederate soldiers under Gen. George Pickett, mostly fresh troops who had not fought in the two previous days, managed to clear the stone wall and engage Federal troops at close quarters. Mythologized as the "High Water Mark of the Rebellion," the particular arrangement of trees and low stone walls at the Union center provided cover that allowed Union and Confederate soldiers to fight in an intimate proximity uncommon on Civil War battlefields. At times, rebel and Federal troops took temporary shelter behind opposite sides of a stone wall not more than two feet high. In the midst of the melee, many Confederate soldiers elected to surrender, especially those who had discharged their weapons and feared exposing themselves long enough to reload. One Union soldier noted that at the Bloody Angle, "by the side of several who were firing, lying down or kneeling, were others with their hands up, in token of surrender." According to Col. Norman J. Hall, veteran of Fort Sumter, the bloodiest part of the fighting at the Angle ended "after a few minutes of desperate hand to hand fighting," when many of the Confederates "threw down their arms and were taken prisoners of war, while the remainder broke and fled in great disorder."[47]

Confederates' willingness to surrender enabled an officer in the 1st Minnesota to take eleven prisoners single-handedly south of the Copse. According to the *New York Times*, "Corporal [Anson R.] Hayden, of the First Minnesota, was captured—escaped, seized a musket and seized a rare opportunity, and actually made ten rebels surrender. While marching them to General Gibbons' quarters, a rebel behind a tree drew a bead on him with his rifle. Hayden saw him in time to bring his piece to a level and cry out 'Surrender.' The fellow actually threw down his gun and joined the procession, and Hayden came in with eleven captives."[48] The frequency of Confederate surrenders during Pickett's Charge indicates that many rebel soldiers went into the assault believing that allowing themselves to be taken prisoner was preferable to assaulting an ensconced Union line. More than a few Confederate officers and enlisted men expressed the view beforehand that a frontal assault was tantamount to suicide.

Union soldiers also surrendered during Pickett's Charge, especially at the Angle. Reaching the corner of the low stone fence, Wiley Woods of the 1st Tennessee heard soldiers from the 71st Pennsylvania "hollowed out we surrender and no [Confederate] officer said anything. I said crawl over to our side & you shant be hurt." Just a few yards to the south, at least eighteen soldiers from the 69th Pennsylvania also elected to surrender. After laying down their arms, they had to make their way without a guard to Confederate lines across the open battlefield. En route, they encountered the advancing 56th Virginia, crying out, "Don't Shoot! We surrender! Where should we go?"[49]

Confederate surrenders did not stop when the attack on Cemetery Ridge abated. Confederate troops who had advanced closest to Union lines received no official order to retreat from either Lee, Longstreet, or Pickett, but they decided autonomously that further advance was impossible and holding ground was untenable. While most Confederates elected to retreat to the safety of rebel lines, others elected to surrender rather than expose themselves to fire while retreating. One Union chaplain noted, "Hundreds of the charging line prostrated themselves on their back on the Emmettsburg road, and waved their hats and handkerchiefs in token of surrender." Positioned on the northern flank of the Union line, an officer with the 8th Ohio observed that after the Confederate retreat, "the whole plain was covered with unarmed rebels, waving coats, hats, and handkerchiefs in token of a wish to surrender." Included among them were hundreds of wounded soldiers who found themselves unable to make their way to the Confederate rear. Once the retreat became widespread, according to a Connecticut soldier, Union troops, "leaped over the wall and advanced towards the retreating foe," whereupon "rebel wounded and unwounded in large numbers rose up and surrendered themselves."[50]

For decades afterward, the failure of Pickett's Charge loomed large in the Confederate psyche, as Lost Cause proponents attributed blame to Longstreet or Pettigrew, among others.[51] In these recriminations, accusations, and scapegoating, few authors were willing to attribute the charge's failure to the willingness of Confederate soldiers to surrender (and by extension Union soldiers' willingness to accept their surrenders). As a counterfactual, it is worth considering how Pickett's Charge may have unfolded had the option to surrender not been exercised so frequently. At the apex of the rebel advance, at the so-called High Water Mark of the Confederacy, blue- and gray-clad soldiers fought at relative parity. Many of these Confederate soldiers ended up surrendering. Were that option not available, it is within the realm of possibility that Confederate troops would have penetrated the Union line, allowing them to flank and rout the thin Federal defenses, taking and suffering heavy casualties. Unable to hold Cemetery Ridge, Union forces would have been forced to beat a hasty retreat, allowing Confederates to capture supplies and artillery and lodge a significant victory on Union soil. While such counterfactuals properly belong in the realm of fiction rather than history, they suggest that surrenders were not merely incidental to the battle but integral to how the conflict developed and its outcome. Indeed, surrenders factored into so many of the pivotal points at Gettysburg that they fundamentally shaped its character. For all the destruction and carnage that the battle brought about, every soldier that surrendered was a soldier who could have found himself in the grave. Although it may not have been a typical Civil War battle, Gettysburg reveals how the surrenders of individual soldiers and small units permeated the battle. From the time the first shots were fired on July 1, 1863, both Union and Confederate soldiers found themselves in a position where surrender presented the only reasonable option.

THE AFTERMATH

The Battle of Gettysburg is often cited as a turning point in the Civil War. Although the conflict would continue for almost two more years, after Gettysburg (and the surrender of Vicksburg on July 4, 1863), Confederate military efforts never regained the momentum and initiative that had been present beforehand. Gettysburg also marked a turning point in the experiences of surrendering soldiers. While most soldiers came into the battle with the expectation that surrendered soldiers would be briefly imprisoned, paroled, and exchanged. This supposition, which undoubtedly played a role in soldiers' propensity to surrender, proved fundamentally and disastrously wrong. With the collapse of the Dix-Hill cartel, the thousands of soldiers who surrendered at Gettysburg found themselves in long-term detention in overcrowded prison camps with little expectation of release.[52]

Almost immediately after their surrenders, most of the healthy Confederate prisoners were taken away from the battlefield and transported to temporary prisoner of war camps in nearby Pennsylvania towns. From there, they were sent to Fort McHenry in Baltimore and then distributed to more permanent prisoner of war camps. On July 11, President Lincoln received a report than nearly 7,000 prisoners taken during the Gettysburg Campaign had been processed at Fort McHenry.[53] While Union forces could easily shuttle captured rebel soldiers to nearby towns for processing and relocation to more permanent confinement, Union soldiers who surrendered at Gettysburg were congregated at a temporary prison camp located not far from Lee's headquarters. With each passing hour and day, the population of this prison camp increased. Heavily guarded, the prisoners were promised rations, although most reported that they did not receive them. Stripped of whatever foodstuffs they had on their persons when they surrendered, the prisoners grew increasingly hungry and desperate.

Lee recognized that guarding, feeding, and herding more than 6,000 Union prisoners would place a significant burden on a retreating army. Their presence would compound daunting logistical challenges that lay before him as he endeavored to maneuver his army, much of which was sick or wounded, along with lengthy supply trains, over the 175 miles that separated them from Confederate territory. According to the testimony of several Union prisoners, early on the morning of July 3, before Pickett's Charge, Lee passed by the prison camp, close enough that one of them could overhear Lee order their removal to a location farther in the Confederate rear. Marching past a "long line of negro cooks baking corn pone," the prisoners could hear the cannonade that preceded Pickett's Charge. Stopping for the evening, Maj. John W. Fairfax, a member of Longstreet's staff, began to record the prisoners' names in preparation for a parole or battlefield exchange. Gen. Charles Graham, the highest-ranking prisoner, informed Fairfax that no Union soldier would accept a battlefield parole, as it was prohibited by army regulations and the Dix-Hill cartel. Although there was considerable debate and discussion among the surrendered Union soldiers about the merits of the parole, in the end, fewer than 2,000 Union prisoners accepted the offer, far fewer than Lee had hoped.[54]

All of the parties involved recognized that these battlefield paroles did not conform to the dictates of the Dix-Hill cartel. The Union soldiers who accepted the paroles knew that their commanding officers would consider the paroles invalid and therefore return them to active service. They also knew that were they to be taken into Confederate captivity again, they would be considered in violation of their parole and therefore subject to execution. According to one captured Union soldier, they were clear about the consequences of accepting the proffered paroles: "Many of the boys had not had any thing to eat for two days and were willing to do any thing to get out of that. Another says, but our Government won't recognize the parole and will put us in the ranks again, then if 'Bob' catches us he will give us Hell. And so the argument went on, they appeared to be about equally divided." Lee appears to have been aware of their perilous position. On July 7, he wrote to Jefferson Davis, "We captured at Gettysburg about 6,000 prisoners. . . . Fifteen hundred of these prisoners and the wounded were paroled, but I suppose that under the late arrangements these paroles will not be regarded."[55]

Just after sunrise on July 4, through a flag of truce, Lee proposed to Meade an exchange of prisoners "to promote the comfort and convenience of the officers and men captured." Taking more than two hours to compose his response, Meade replied that "it was not in my power to accede to the proposed arrangement."[56] Meade's answer to Lee was not entirely honest. Only a day earlier, the secretary of war had issued General Order No. 207, reminding Union officers that under the Dix-Hill cartel all prisoners had to be sent to the designated exchange sites for parole or exchange; "the only exception allowed is the case of commanders of two opposing armies, who are authorized to exchange prisoners or release them on parole at other points mutually agreed upon." Lee's proposed battlefield exchange clearly fell under this exemption; indeed, on the same day, Grant's terms of surrender at Vicksburg paroled 20,000 Confederate soldiers under its auspices. Although Meade never explicitly explained his decision to refuse Lee's offer, he may have thought that escorting so many Union prisoners would slow Lee's retreat and create opportunities for Union forces to attack before the Confederates returned to rebel soil.

Failing in his negotiations with Meade to engage in an exchange and only marginally successful in getting Union prisoners to accept battlefield paroles, Lee acknowledged that he would have to transport more than 4,000 Union prisoners along with his army. Hoping to expedite his retreat, Lee ordered the most significantly wounded Confederates, nearly 7,000 men, to be left in Gettysburg, where they would be taken into Union captivity. To attend them, Lee ordered a handful of Confederate surgeons to remain behind, physicians that would also be taken prisoner once the rebel army had left.[57] Lee's decision to leave behind wounded soldiers reflected not only the pragmatic need to relieve himself of slow hospital wagons but also his conviction that like other surrendered soldiers, the Confederate wounded would be well treated by their Union captors.

Meade has often been unfairly criticized for not pursuing Lee's army more vigorously. Although he decided not to order a general counterattack with his battered army, Meade did not allow Lee's army to retreat into Confederate territory unmolested. Early on the morning of July 4, he ordered cavalry regiments to "harass and annoy him as much as possible in his retreat."[58] These Union raids against the retreating Confederate column resulted in the liberation of a significant number of prisoners of war and the surrender of thousands of Confederates. Stretching more than a dozen miles, the long Confederate columns provided Union cavalry with easy targets. At the same time, Union cavalry conducting these raids occasionally found themselves outnumbered by Confederates, requiring the cavalrymen to surrender.

To expedite the retreat and lessen the traffic on the roads, Lee divided his army. He ordered Brig. Gen. John Imboden to escort the majority of the Confederate wounded and supply wagons west along the Chambersburg Pike. Lee would command the infantry and artillery along a shorter but more dangerous route south along the Fairfield Road. Almost all of the Union prisoners of war traveled in this latter column, flanked by soldiers from the remnants of Pickett's division. Torrential rains on July 4 slowed both halves of the Army of Northern Virginia, as the roads turned to mud. The first major Union attack took place that evening, as the vanguard of Lee's column passed through Monterey Pass. There Kilpatrick's cavalry attacked, capturing more than 1,300 Confederates and 250 supply wagons. Although Kilpatrick's men suffered very few causalities in the raid, some managed to get themselves captured. John L. Collins of the 8th Pennsylvania Cavalry helped to force the surrender of dozens of rebels in the raid, but after midnight he became separated from his unit. At sunrise, he was accosted by 150 Confederate cavalrymen, who greeted him by "cheerfully" saying, "Good morning, sir! I am sorry to say you are a prisoner." Relieved of his weapons, Collins joined the other Union prisoners. He was not alone. Collins noted that during their march south, "fresh prisoners were added all the time, mostly cavalry."[59]

Among those taken in subsequent days was West Virginian Samuel Wheeler. Like Collins, Wheeler had participated in the raid at Monterey Pass. At a raid the next day at Hagerstown, his squad unexpectedly "met Lee's entire army...lined up for battle; infantry, cavalry and artillery." His commanding officer was immediately shot, telling his men as they lowered him to the ground, "Boys, you may as well surrender." Wheeler did not initially take the dying officer's advice and attempted to ride away when "a large Marylander cavalryman (Rebel) dashed in front of me and ordered me to surrender in no very polite terms." Despite the presence of "thousands of Rebels," Wheeler elected to fire his revolver at his would-be captor, earning a temporary reprieve; but when he emptied his revolver, the Marylander again demanded his surrender, and Wheeler acquiesced. He refused, however, to help the rebel locate the other men in his unit, saying, "I was not surrendering men to him."[60]

In the aftermath of the Monterey Pass raid, Confederate officers again attempted to relieve themselves of their Union prisoners by offering battle-field paroles. Exhausted and malnourished, many prisoners complained about Confederate mistreatment. Some of them had not eaten since surrendering and had resorted to begging for food. One soldier recalled that on July 6, "the rebels renewed negotiations for our parole. They saw how difficult it was to transport so many prisoners, that a strong escort would necessarily be required there-for[e], which they could make use of better elsewhere, and finally they seemed to fear an attack of our army resulting in our escape. They called us together and renewed the Gettysburg proposition. We consulted. Owing to Gen. Halleck's order and noticing their anxiety to get rid of us, we promptly declined their offer." Another soldier remembered the event differently, claiming that "a large number of officers and men agreed to take their paroles." However, before the paroles could be issued, the offer was countermanded by General Longstreet, and they were told that "all would have to go to Richmond."[61]

Not unsurprisingly, the Confederate guards were not overly zealous about the care of their prisoners. An unknown number of Union prisoners managed to escape during the trek. According to one soldier, "Many of the boys took advantage of their marching us through the mountains in the night and ran away. The Rebel guard had not slept any too much during the previous week and did not seem to care wither we ran away or not." Similarly, Bernhard Domschcke noted that "some officer-prisoners took advantage of darkness and confusion, sneaked past the guards, and hid in the forest covered mountains until the Rebel hordes disappeared." Domschcke undoubtedly considered escaping, noting that they "could see that the Rebels craved to be rid of prisoners once and for all." Weighing the risks of running away, he elected to stay a prisoner temporarily. He hoped that Union raids would "flank the retreating enemy and free us" and that "the magnitude of our victory guaranteed short life to the Confederacy and thereby ruled out a long imprisonment for us."[62]

Domschcke's hopes would go unfulfilled. Although Union raids plagued the Confederate retreat, forcing the surrender of nearly 3,000 rebels soldiers, relatively few of the Union prisoners were liberated. After crossing the Potomac at Williamsport on July 13, the prisoners were marched to Staunton and then taken by rail to Richmond. There the officers were confined to Libby Prison and the enlisted men were sent to Belle Isle. Located in the James River adjacent to the Tredegar Iron Works, the Belle Isle prison initially opened in June 1862, only to be closed a few months later when the efficiency of the Dix-Hill cartel left it empty. The camp was briefly reopened after the battles of Fredericksburg (December 1862) and Chancellorsville (May 1863). After Gettysburg, however, and the collapse of the exchange cartel, Belle Isle became the semipermanent home of thousands of Union prisoners.

Treated more fully in Chapter 5, the collapse of the Dix-Hill exchange had profound effects on the soldiers who surrendered at Gettysburg. On July 13, the same day that Union prisoners crossed the Potomac into Virginia, Secretary of War Edwin Stanton ordered the exchange of enlisted men halted "until there is better understanding in relation to the cartel and a more rigid adherence to its stipulations on the part of the rebel authorities." This measure built upon a proclamation on May 25 halting the parole and exchange of officers. The impasse between Union and Confederate officials effectively sentenced prisoners to a lengthy term in increasingly overcrowded prison camps.

Conditions on Belle Isle deteriorated rapidly. Arriving malnourished from inadequate rations and exhausting marching, the Gettysburg prisoners died at a high rate. One prisoner noted that during that summer on Belle Isle, "from fifteen to twenty and twenty-five die every day and are buried just outside the prison with no coffins—nothing but canvas wrapped around them."[63] To minimize the overcrowding at Belle Isle and Libby Prison, Confederate officials decided to parole 800 Gettysburg soldiers and officers in September 1863, including Gen. Charles Graham. The remainder, however, suffered a very difficult winter, such that "when winter began, hunger grew to starvation. We ate dogs, mice, and rats. . . . Every morning we found comrades frozen to death or dead by starvation." Many of the enlisted men were finally paroled in March 1864, but others were sent to the newly opened prison at Andersonville, Georgia. For those Gettysburg prisoners not paroled, their expectations slowly evaporated. One prisoner noted, "All our hopes of being exchanged or paroled have been dissipated one after another, and our captivity is passing with rapid strides from the last green of summer to the sere yellow of autumn; from faint hope to settled despair." One of the Union soldiers taken at Gettysburg, Newell Burch, would have the unfortunate honor of serving the longest tenure in Confederate prison. Captured on the first day of Gettysburg, Burch spent 661 days imprisoned at Belle Isle and Andersonville.[64]

Confederate prisoners also lamented that they would never be paroled or exchanged. Union officials split rebel prisoners, with officers sent to Johnson's Island, located in Lake Erie, near Sandusky, Ohio, and enlisted men sent primarily to Fort Delaware. Of the two groups, the enlisted men had slightly better prospects of release. Although the Dix-Hill cartel had effectively collapsed by late 1863, some paroles were granted, especially for sick prisoners. One Confederate prisoner captured during the first day at Gettysburg "learned that a load of sick prisoners was to be sent South, and I made up my mind to be one of that number." He persuaded the prison's doctors that he was very ill and arrived in Richmond as "gay as a lark and as sound as a dollar." His comrades were not as lucky, as "my friends, who assisted me in fooling the doctors and getting out, had to remain in prison at Fort Delaware until the war was over."[65]

Held at Johnson's Island, Edmund Patterson also lamented a month after his capture that "we still hear nothing definite in regard to an exchange." Like his fellow inmates, Patterson listened skeptically to the persistent rumors that paroles would be renewed. Initially, he accepted the fact that paroles were in abeyance "until our government consents to treat captured negroes as prisoners of war." If treating black soldiers equally was the cost of his freedom, Patterson wrote, "I hope that there may never be another exchange." A year later, however, Patterson's tone had changed. On the anniversary of his surrender, he noted in his diary that "I am almost ready to say let this day be stricken from the calendar and let it be remembered no more forever. . . . Little did I think at that time that long weary months would elapse" before he would be released. He reiterated this sentiment a few weeks later on the anniversary of his arrival on Johnson's Island. "Little did I think at that time," he wrote, "that the Summer of 1864 would find me still a prisoner. It is so hard to be shut up here when our country needs us so much. It would be better, it seems to me, to be killed at once on the battlefield."[66]

Many of Patterson's fellow Johnson's Island prisoners shared his growing despair. One noted that during their first winter after Gettysburg, "when exchange rumors were prevalent and exchange hopes alternately rising and sinking, there appeared a paragraph in nearly all the journals announcing" that a parole was imminent, only to be proven illusory. He kept one of these newspaper announcements in his journal, so that whenever someone confronted him with the most recent rumor of a proposed exchange, he would show him the article to remind him not to get his hopes up. Faced with indefinite confinement, some Johnson's Island prisoners plotted to escape, including Gen. James Archer, who made two attempts. On the first occasion, he ventured onto the frozen ice but had to retreat when the ice cracked; he returned "nearly frozen to icicles." A few days later, he attempted to escape by bribing a sentinel with a gold watch, only to have the guard turn the conspirators over and pocket the watch.

Some of the officers relieved their boredom by engaging in a snowball fight, a novelty for Southern soldiers, many of whom had never seen snow before their captivity. In January 1864, they fought a "great snow battle" that pitted one part of the camp against another. Commanded by Gen. Isaac Trimble, who had had a leg amputated since his capture at Pickett's Charge, the upper blocks fought valiantly but ultimately had to withdraw. The lower blocks not only took the field but also captured "many prisoners" who were subsequently paroled. Like Gettysburg, the snowball fight spread over three days. One participant noted that he was "captured several times," only to be liberated by a regular "exchange of prisoners." Unfortunately for those confined, such exchanges proved substantially more difficult to obtain beyond the bounds of their frozen prison.[67]

5

WORSE THAN MURDER

Ulysses S. Grant, Nathan Bedford Forrest,
and Unconditional Surrender

No two men had more experience with surrender during the Civil War than Ulysses S. Grant and Nathan Bedford Forrest. Between them, they demanded surrender more than a dozen times. Grant famously brought about Confederate surrenders at Fort Donelson in 1862, at Vicksburg in 1863, and at Appomattox Courthouse in 1865. Combined, approximately 70,000 Confederates laid down their arms in these three surrenders. By comparison, Forrest's victories through surrender were smaller and less well known, although more numerous. By his own count, Forrest accepted the surrender of 31,000 Union soldiers over the course of the war.[1]

Despite the frequency and prominence of surrender in their military careers, neither man articulated a coherent theory or doctrine about the role of surrender in warfare. Outside of his after-action reports (many of which may have been written by a subordinate), Forrest left few accounts of his experience during the Civil War. Grant proved a far more prolific writer: not only did he craft a two-volume memoir shortly before his death, but his collected correspondence runs to thirty-one volumes. Although neither Grant nor Forrest elected to write at length about the meaning of surrender, both men clearly thought about its merits and morals. This chapter argues that Grant and Forrest embraced very different ideas about surrender. Grant saw the offer of surrender as a magnanimous gesture, an opportunity to avoid bloodshed, and a route to peace. Forrest, by contrast, saw the demand to surrender as a tactical weapon, a stratagem designed to engender terror. Between them, Forrest and Grant present a stark contrast of how Americans used and thought of surrender during the Civil War.

Grant and Forrest never met. Born less than a year apart (Forrest on July 13, 1821; Grant on April 27, 1822), the two men lived very different lives prior to the Civil War, sharing few common interests or attitudes. Grant was a West Point graduate and Mexican War veteran; Forrest had no military experience before 1861. Forrest made a fortune in slave trading and real estate; Grant demonstrated moderate ineptitude in business during his time away from the military. Grant enjoyed drinking and smoking (to excess on occasion); Forrest abstained from both. Forrest dressed stylishly and ostentatiously in prewar Memphis and maintained an impressive and impeccable uniform when in command; Grant cared little for his personal appearance. Even putting politics aside, if the two men had ever met, it is unlikely they would have found much in common except their mutual love of horses and horsemanship.

The closest they ever came to meeting was during the siege of Fort Donelson in February 1862. Pledging "never to surrender my command," Forrest led a cavalry regiment out of the fort prior to Buckner's surrender. Grant's victory at Fort Donelson was heralded throughout the Union. Speaking prematurely but eager to publish any good news after a series of setbacks in the eastern theater, *Harper's Weekly* claimed that the Confederate surrender at Donelson was "probably the culminating point in the struggle between the United States Government and the malcontents." In an unusually immodest letter to his wife, Grant claimed Donelson was "the greatest victory of the season" and "the largest capture I believe ever made on the continent." More than 15,000 Confederate soldiers surrendered at Fort Donelson, making it the largest surrender in American history to that point, larger than either Saratoga or Yorktown.[2]

In Fort Donelson's aftermath, newspapers began referring to "Unconditional Surrender" Grant, a nickname that remained with him for the rest of the war. After Vicksburg, a popular ballad immortalized this nickname in a song titled "Unconditional Surrender, or The Grant Pill," whose lyrics began, "We were sworn to death or victory for our Union, God defend her; And to only take from rebels unconditional surrender." Although the nickname fit nicely with his initials, in some senses, he may not have deserved it. The idea to demand unconditional surrender at Fort Donelson originated not with Grant but with Gen. Charles Smith. Sixteen months later, Grant initially demanded the unconditional surrender of Pemberton's army at Vicksburg, only to subsequently bow to several of Pemberton's conditions, and at Appomattox, Grant accepted Lee's surrender with several conditions attached. Indeed, throughout the Civil War, Grant embraced a flexible conception of surrender that allowed surrendering Confederates to maintain their honor and dignity. Grant saw surrender as a tool of war that allowed him to minimize the unnecessary loss of life and fulfill his military objectives with celerity.

If anyone at Fort Donelson deserved a sobriquet linking him with unconditional surrender, it was Nathan Bedford Forrest. Over the next two years, Forrest would repeatedly demand (and usually receive) the unconditional surrender of Union forces throughout the western theater. Unlike Grant, Forrest became ferociously and dogmatically attached to the idea of "unconditional surrender." He had seen firsthand the fear that talk of surrender had engendered in men like Pillow and Floyd, clouding their judgment and causing them to behave erratically. He believed that he could use that fear as a tactical weapon to subdue and defeat his enemies. Over time, Forrest developed a conception of unconditional surrender that differed meaningfully from Grant's usage. The difference between Grant's and Forrest's versions of unconditional surrender rested on competing ideas about the laws of war and the limits of civilized violence.

Five months after Fort Donelson, Forrest made his first demand for unconditional surrender. Leaving Chattanooga on July 9, 1862, with two cavalry regiments, Forrest rode to Murfreesboro, the site of an important Union supply depot on the Nashville & Chattanooga Railroad. Attacking before sunrise, Forrest surprised the divided Union garrison. The post's commander, Gen. Thomas Crittenden, had arrived only two days before, "having no instructions, and knowing nothing of the [local] affairs." From his predecessor, Col. Henry Clay Lester, Crittenden learned that due to an inadequate water supply, the post had been divided into three separate camps a few weeks earlier. Despite reassurances that there was no imminent threat from rebel forces, Crittenden worried that the divided post invited attack. In his initial assessment, Crittenden also found the pickets inadequate, "being dissatisfied with its strength and locations." Although Crittenden resolved to improve the situation, Forrest's attack exploited all of the post's weaknesses. First, he "surrounded and captured the pickets . . . without firing a gun." Second, he systematically attacked the Union camps, forcing each of them to surrender in turn.[3] By the end of the day, Forrest had taken more than 800 prisoners while suffering minimal casualties.

The First Battle of Murfreesboro has now largely been forgotten, overlooked in favor of the more famous Second Battle of Murfreesboro, also known as Stones River, that took place several months later. For Nathan Bedford Forrest, however, this first battle demonstrated the tactical value of demanding unconditional surrender. Forrest arrived in Murfreesboro with a force only slightly larger than the Union post defending the town. Conventional wisdom suggested that it would be difficult, if not impossible, for an attacker to dislodge a fortified force without at least a two-to-one advantage, and then only after a lengthy siege. The divided Union post made obtaining this numerical advance possible, but only if they remained separate and unable to call for reinforcements. By demanding unconditional surrender, Forrest employed his cavalry's speed to its fullest advantage. Had he been obligated to fight and defeat each of the Union forces separately, it seems likely that the remaining Union camps would have reorganized and been more able to mount an effective defense. By tactically demanding unconditional surrender, Forrest defeated the Federal soldiers at Murfreesboro in a matter of hours rather than days, while at the same time minimizing his own casualties.

The victory at Murfreesboro also demonstrated to Forrest how the demand for unconditional surrender could instill fear. Forest wrote to the garrison commander, "I demand an unconditional surrender of your force as prisoners of war or I will have every man put to the sword. You are aware of the overpowering force I have at my command, and this demand is made to prevent the effusion of blood."[4] For Forrest, an enemy's refusal to surrender unconditionally meant that he was absolved of any guilt or responsibility for what transpired afterward. Once the demand to surrender had been made and rejected, the standard rules of civilized warfare no longer applied. Forrest used this rhetoric of surrender over and over again. Indeed, many of the same phrases appear almost verbatim in his later demands for surrender.

It is difficult to say how Forrest arrived at this particular doctrine of unconditional surrender. Forrest never attended West Point or served in the Old Army; he was one of the few in either army to reach elevated rank without formal military training or experience. He was not known to have read deeply in military history or strategy or to have placed much credence in military regulations. One of Forrest's soldiers noted that "in his early battles he was so disregardful of the ordinary rules of tactics," including his unorthodox "messages to opposing commanders, his matchless shrewdness in impressing them with the overwhelming superiority of his forces and the necessity for surrender."[5]

One possible explanation for Forrest's understanding of surrender can be traced to his experience as a slave trader and plantation master. Deeply invested in the cult of Southern honor and white racial ideology, Forrest would have seen surrender as akin to submission, a trait associated with slavery. To surrender, therefore, would be to metaphorically assume the position of the slave, and to accept an enemy's surrender would mean to become the slave master. For most white Southerners, the power that owners had over slaves ought to be unqualified: in the words of one Southern jurist, "The power of the master must be absolute, to render the submission of the slave perfect."[6] If the slave/master metaphor formed the intellectual architecture for Forrest's understanding of

Grant, Forrest, and Unconditional Surrender

surrender, the only legitimate form of surrender was unconditional. Refusing to submit to unconditional surrender was tantamount to refusing to submit to a master's dictates. Forrest may have subconsciously seen Union officers who refused to surrender as disobedient slaves that required punishment. Although this explanation of Forrest's understanding of surrender remains speculative, it helps to explain not only his insistence on unconditional surrender but also his fear of surrendering. Forrest refused to surrender at Fort Donelson because doing so would metaphorically transform him into a slave.[7]

Forrest gleefully reported to Braxton Bragg about the success of his raid. "Attacked Murfreesboro 5 A.M. last Sunday morning," he wrote, "captured two brigadier-generals, staff and field officers, and 1,200 men," as well as 500 mules and horses, 60 wagons, and 4 cannons. He also seized nearly $500,000 in stores, burning what he could not carry. He could not hold Murfreesboro after the surrender, owing to the "large number of prisoners to be guarded." He destroyed the railroad depot to prevent it from being used by the enemy. His total casualties for the day, he boasted, were only "16 or 18 killed; 25 or 30 wounded."[8]

Forrest's success at Murfreesboro prompted his promotion to the rank of brigadier general and encouraged his aggressive tactical use of unconditional surrender. On December 10, 1862, Bragg ordered Forrest into west Tennessee. Utilizing his cavalry's speed, Forrest repeatedly surprised small Union outposts, taking thousands of prisoners. On December 18 at Lexington, he routed 1,000 Union infantry and cavalry, capturing 150 Federal soldiers. From Lexington, he rode to Jackson, capturing more than 100 Federal soldiers at Webb's Station. On December 20, he forced the surrender of 400 Union soldiers at Trenton, which he followed up the next day with the surrender of Union City "without firing a gun," capturing about 100 Illinois soldiers. In the space of four days, Forrest had managed to successfully attack four different Union outposts, forcing the unconditional surrender of two of them and taking more than 700 prisoners. To give the illusion that he had reinforcements constantly arriving, Forrest ordered his men to march repeatedly in front of the Union prisoners. Paroled, the men were marched to Columbus and dutifully informed Union officers that Forrest had as many as 20,000 men under his command, nearly six times more than his actual force. This had enormous consequences for the subsequent success of Forrest's strategy of unconditional surrender. From December 1862 onward, Union commanders consistently and grossly overestimated the size of Forrest's command. Fearing annihilation at the hands of a numerically superior foe and believing in shadows, time and time again Union commanders bought into the myth that Forrest had created and succumbed to his demands to surrender.[9]

In these victories, Forrest not only developed his tactical prowess to force Union surrenders but also cultivated intimidation techniques to coerce reluctant Union officers into raising the white flag. For instance, in late March 1863 his cavalry attacked a fortified railroad bridge over the Harpeth River near Nashville. Firing a warning shot, Forrest ordered a subordinate to "take in a flag of truce, and tell them I have them completely surrounded, and if they don't surrender I'll blow hell out of them in five minutes and won't take one of them alive if I have to sacrifice my men in storming their stockade." Capt. Elisha Bassett of Michigan quickly "took in the situation and surrendered."[10]

Union officers protested Forrest's tactics as contrary to the laws of war. At Columbus, Capt. Samuel Logan told Forrest that his "demand to surrender my force" was "utterly contrary to honorable warfare."[11] If anything, such remonstrations only emboldened Forrest, who expanded his use of surgical attacks, using his cavalry's speed and maneuverability in conjunction with terror to compel Union surrenders. Of the surrenders Forrest orchestrated in the winter and spring of 1863, none demonstrated his genius as clearly as that of Col. Abel Streight at Cedar Bluff, Alabama. In March 1863, Gen. William Rosencrans ordered Streight to lead a raid across northern Alabama into Georgia. His brigade consisted of veteran Northern infantry and recently organized Southern Unionist cavalry. Lacking adequate horses, Streight mounted his men on mules, much to the consternation of his men and the mockery of the enemy, who called them the "Jackass Brigade."

The raid appeared ill-fated from the beginning. The mules proved to be an inadequate substitute for horses. Mostly unbroken, aged, or infirm, many of the mules died en route. Poor coordination with other Union units exposed Streight's movements, and poor weather muddied roads and slowed the mule train to a pace hardly faster than walking. Streight's most significant problem, however, was near-constant harassment by Forrest's cavalry. Although he commanded a force only a third the size, Forrest was able to use his superior speed to harry the Union column and offer the illusion of a much larger force. By the time he reached Cedar Bluff, Alabama, on the morning of May 3, Streight found both his men and his mules utterly worn out, such that "men, being unaccustomed to riding, had become so exhausted from fatigue and loss of sleep that it was almost impossible to keep them awake long enough to feed." To make matters worse, much of their ammunition had gotten wet and was rendered useless.

Under a flag of truce, Forrest demanded Streight's surrender later that morning. During the surrender negotiations, Forrest arranged for phony couriers to announce the arrival of nonexistent Confederate units, adding to the

Grant, Forrest, and Unconditional Surrender

ruse that he had Streight outnumbered. Believing that Forrest outnumbered him three to one, Streight quickly consented to surrender. Only after his men had been disarmed did he become aware that Forrest's numbers were illusory and that he had surrendered to a force only a third the size of his own. Several accounts describe Streight's reaction to the revelation. In one, he asked Forrest, "Where is the rest of your command, General?" to which "Forrest smiled grimly and made no reply." In another version, Streight, enraged by the deception, demanded his weapons back, only to have Forrest laugh at him, pat him on the shoulder, and say, "Ah, Colonel, all is fair in love and war you know." Alternatively, a more threatening Forrest rebuked him, saying, "Dry those tears or you'll be drying them in hell."

"I wasn't certain," said Forrest, "when I demanded his surrender, which would have to give in, him or me. But it was just like a game of poker, I called him on a 'pair' to his 'full [house]' trusting to luck. He seemed, at first, to have very little confidence in my hand; but I said 'I give you five minutes to decide. I've followed you and fought you for two weeks, and now I've got you just where I want. I'm tired of sacrificing lives, and I offer you a chance to stop it. If you don't I won't be answerable for the consequences.'" Forrest concluded that Streight had been "fairly bluffed."[12] Forrest's use of a gambling metaphor reflected a lifetime at the card table. If slave trading was Forrest's vocation, gambling was his avocation. Like many Southern men of honor, Forrest gambled with passion and intensity, unafraid to wager with high stakes. Although he was known to bet on racehorses and dice, Forrest preferred five-card stud, a game that places a high premium on shrewdness and bravado. Even with a weak hand, Forrest knew with proper posturing one could bluff to victory. Forrest later described Streight's predicament: "He was in a strange country. His adversary was known to be a desperate man. His command was jaded. What could he do?"[13]

While Forrest gambled to secure a series of small Union surrenders, Ulysses Grant had wagered on a much larger prize. Starting in December 1862, Grant began a grueling campaign that culminated in the siege and surrender of Vicksburg. Located on a high bluff overlooking a bend in the Mississippi River, the city was the only remaining Confederate fortification along the Mississippi; once it was taken, the Union Army would have unfettered control of the country's most important waterway. Jefferson Davis described Vicksburg as "the nail head that holds the South's two halves together." The lengthy campaign culminated in a six-week siege of Vicksburg. After taking Jackson on May 14 and defeating Confederates at Champion Hill and Big Black River Bridge,

Grant's forces had effectively isolated Vicksburg. Although Lt. Gen. John C. Pemberton's garrison of 18,500 soldiers was one of the largest Confederate forces in the western theater, it was dwarfed by Grant's force of 35,000. A native Pennsylvanian, Pemberton had married a Virginian and resigned his U.S. Army commission in 1861 in deference to her and his many years of military posting in the South. Although distrusted for his Northern birth, Pemberton had been rapidly promoted based on his military experience in the Mexican and Third Seminole Wars. Surveying his situation, Pemberton hoped that Vicksburg's natural and man-made defenses would prove sufficient until reinforcements under Joseph Johnston arrived. Even so, the forecast looked grim. On the day Grant's siege began, Confederate captain Gabriel Killgore noted in his diary that "our army is said to be completely demoralized."[14]

After Grant's initial efforts to assault the city on May 18 and May 22 failed, he ordered his men to begin constructing a series of trenches encircling Vicksburg. Hoping that "no more loss of life shall be sustained in the reduction of Vicksburg, and the capture of the Garrison," Grant instructed his subordinates to take "every advantage . . . of the natural inequalities of the ground to gain positions from which to start mines, trenches, or advance batteries." Creeping Union advances and constant shelling of the city quickly ate away at the Confederate resolve. "No news of any relief coming to us," Killgore wrote in his diary, "our case is getting desperate." Ensconced in defensive trenches, there was little he or his men could do. Alternately baking in the Mississippi summer sun and soaking in torrential downpours, they were repeatedly reassigned along the Confederate line as reinforcements. On June 11, Killgore noted that this was the "25th day Since we have been 'Cabined Cribbed and Confined' within these lines exposed to an almost incessant fire both day and night of Shells Shot and Minnie balls." Inadequate stores for a lengthy siege reduced Confederate soldiers to one-quarter rations. It seemed like only a matter of time before Vicksburg surrendered.[15]

Many Confederate soldiers did not wait for Pemberton to surrender, preferring to surrender themselves rather than risk death or injury from Union sharpshooters, mortars, heatstroke, disease, or starvation, all of which were taking their toll on the Confederate garrison. According to one Union soldier, "There is not a day but there is men coming into our lines from Vicksburg. And they all say they are scarce of provisions. They will have to give up soon." Sometimes Confederates deserted their posts en masse, including a Confederate captain who surrendered his whole company, telling his captors that although "his heart is as strong in the Confederacy as ever, . . . he was not going to stay in there to be starved to death." He expected that "the men will desert in a short time if the Commander does not surrender the place." On July 28, Pemberton received an anonymous letter from "Many Soldiers" informing him of the imperative to surrender. Rations had been "cut down to one biscuit and a small bit of bacon per day, not enough, scarcely, to keep soul and body together." Facing the starvation of his soldiers left him with no other options. "If you can't feed us, you had better surrender." Surrender, they informed Pemberton, as "horrible as the idea is," was the only honorable option. Failing to surrender, they warned, could result in only two alternatives: "desertion" or "mutiny."[16]

Recognizing the inevitable and feeling abandoned by Richmond, Pemberton polled his generals on July 1. They shared his pessimistic assessment: while the Confederate garrison had been ground away by the siege, Grant had received reinforcements. With 77,000 men under his command, it was only a matter of time before Union trenches and mines penetrated the Confederate defenses. The only reasonable option left was surrender. On July 3, Pemberton sent a note to Grant requesting an armistice "with a view to arranging terms for the capitulation of Vicksburg." Like Buckner, Pemberton suggested that both generals appoint commissioners to negotiate the terms of the surrender. Hoping to save face and improve his negotiating position, Pemberton argued that he was only surrendering "to save the further effusion of blood, which must otherwise be shed to a frightful extent, feeling myself fully able to maintain my position for a yet indefinite period." Pemberton sent the note with Gen. John Bowen, who had been Grant's neighbor in Missouri before the war.[17]

Receiving Bowen, Grant had anticipated an offer to surrender. Well acquainted with Pemberton, with whom he had served in the Mexican War, Grant knew he was brave but not rash or foolhardy. Deciding to refuse Pemberton's offer, Grant replied, "The useless effusion of blood you propose stopping by this course can be ended at any time you may choose, by an unconditional surrender of the city and garrison." He promised the "men who have shown so much endurance and courage as those now in Vicksburg . . . will be treated with all the respect due to prisoners of war."[18] Sending Bowen back with the reply, Grant added that he would be willing to meet with Pemberton if the Confederate general so wished.

Grant never explained why he felt it necessary to demand Pemberton's unconditional surrender. Unlike at Fort Donelson, time was not a pressing issue, and the terms of a negotiated surrender through commissioners would hardly have been less favorable to the Union. The lesson that Grant learned from Fort Donelson, however, was that the symbolic value of an unconditional surrender significantly outstripped its military value. Even if the difference between a negotiated surrender and an unconditional surrender proved nominal in terms of its effect on the battlefield, the effect on the morale of both the army and the home front would be immeasurable.

Grant's meeting with Pemberton that afternoon came about as a product of miscommunication. Grant had told Bowen that he would be willing to meet with Pemberton at 3:00 P.M. if Pemberton so wished. Bowen evidently informed Pemberton that Grant wished to meet with him. Pemberton arrived late, irritating Grant, who impatiently chewed on his cigar. When the two commanders met, accompanied by staff members, their conversation began with a tense silence, as both generals supposed that the other had initiated the meeting. When this initial awkwardness had passed, Pemberton asked what terms Grant would be willing to offer, to which Grant replied that the only terms were unconditional surrender. Pemberton reminded Grant of their mutual experience in Mexico, noting, "I have been present at the capitulation of two cities in my life, and commissioners were appointed to settle the terms, and I believe it is always customary to appoint them." If Grant "had no terms to propose other than were contained in his letter," Pemberton testily noted, "the conference could terminate and hostilities be resumed immediately." Claiming that he had sufficient supplies to sustain a lengthy siege, Pemberton told Grant, "I can assure you, sir, you will bury many more of your men before you will enter Vicksburg." With the meeting on the verge of breaking up, either Grant or Bowen (with Grant's acquiescence) made a surprising suggestion: two officers from each side "should retire for consultation and suggest such terms as they might think proper." In essence, Grant agreed to Pemberton's original proposal to appoint commissioners. While their aides hammered out the details of the surrender, Pemberton and Grant sat at some distance. Although the content of their conversation could not be overheard, their body language communicated volumes: Pemberton "was laboring under great excitement; while Grant was, as usual, perfectly cool, and sat smoking his cigar and pulling up tufts of grass." Sensing their commanders' impatience, the four-man ad hoc commission quickly hammered out the details of the surrender, including the disposition of personal property, paroles, and rations. A series of letters between Pemberton and Grant finalized the deal sometime after midnight.

In his *Memoirs*, Grant offered an unconvincing explanation for why he opted not to insist on unconditional surrender. Under the Dix-Hill cartel, Vicksburg was one of two sites specified for prisoner parole. Grant argued that if Vicksburg surrendered unconditionally, it could not function as a site for prisoner parole and that the prisoners would therefore have to be transferred to Virginia to be handed over to Confederate authorities: "Had I insisted upon an unconditional surrender there would have been over thirty thousand

Grant, Forrest, and Unconditional Surrender

men to transport to Cairo, very much to the inconvenience of the army on the Mississippi. Thence the prisoners would have had to be transported by rail to Washington or Baltimore; thence again by steamer to Aiken's—all at very great expense." Furthermore, Grant argued that much of the Vicksburg garrison was from the lower Mississippi Valley and would likely return home if paroled.[19]

There are two significant problems with Grant's explanation. First, nothing in the Dix-Hill agreement suggests that if one of the parole sites were to surrender, only one parole site would remain. Article 7 of the agreement specified that "in case the vicissitudes of war shall change the military relations of the places designated . . . so as to render the same inconvenient for the delivery and exchange of prisoners, other places bearing as nearly as may be the present local relations of said places to the lines of said parties shall be by mutual agreement substituted." Second, the Dix-Hill agreement did permit commanding generals, by mutual consent, to exchange or parole prisoners on the battlefield. It was this provision that Gen. Robert E. Lee hoped to employ with George Meade at Gettysburg at precisely the time that Pemberton and Grant were negotiating the terms of surrender at Vicksburg. Grant's correspondence indicates that he was deeply familiar with the precepts of the prisoner exchange protocol, so it is unlikely that he formulated this explanation based on a misunderstanding of the agreement.

Grant's real motivation probably had more to do with his desire to avoid launching a final assault on Vicksburg, an attack that would have resulted in heavy casualties on both sides. While he would have preferred that Pemberton surrender unconditionally, he was unwilling to call his bluff. Recognizing that Pemberton's pride prevented him from submitting to his initial demand of unconditional surrender, Grant decided that he would swallow his own pride rather than allow Pemberton to walk away. More than once, Grant had looked out on the carnage of a battlefield and recalled the lines of Scottish poet Robert Burns: "Man's inhumanity to man / makes countless thousands mourn." Hoping to prevent unnecessary bloodshed, Grant demonstrated compassion in the face of hostility. Grant's pragmatic decision to bend on the question of unconditional surrender reflected his aversion to prolonging the siege unnecessarily. It was not a decision that Nathan Bedford Forrest, dogmatically committed to unconditional surrender, would have made.

Initially, many Vicksburg Confederates expressed grief and disappointment when they learned they had been surrendered. One Louisiana soldier noted that news of the surrender "pierced our hearts. Brave, strong-hearted men bowed their heads and wept like timid children." After fighting for six weeks, he lamented having to "stack our guns and surrender as prisoners."

However, "when we learned that we were to be paroled (put under oath not to fight again until legally exchanged) and not incarcerated in intolerable prisons, it lightened our sorrow and assuaged our grief."[20]

Occupying Vicksburg the following day, the Fourth of July, Grant made every effort to avoid the appearance of a conquering victor. As at Fort Donelson, he attempted to dissuade his soldiers from celebrating excessively. At 10:00 A.M., the Confederate soldiers ceremonially marched out of their fortification and stacked arms, a formality that Pemberton insisted upon. For two hours, "with sad faces the men of each regiment stacked their arms, threw down upon them knapsacks, belts, cartridge-boxes, and cap-pouches, and then tenderly crowned the piles with their faded and riddled colors." According to one observer, the Union soldiers "looked on with soldierly sympathy, never uttering a taunt." Only after the formalities had ended did Grant and his staff enter Vicksburg. Riding alongside Grant, journalist Charles Dana noted that "the Confederate soldiers were generally more contented even than we were. Now they were going home, they said. They had enough of war." Another of Grant's companions noted "in the streets ... Confederates and Yankees mingling indiscriminately, sharing rations, playing euchre, and discussing the war, generally in entire friendliness." Seeing Grant that afternoon, many of the surrendered Confederates were impressed with his composure. One noted that "General Grant's dark face, with its short, black stubby beard, gave me the impression at the time that it was the face of a just but determined man. The moment I saw it I felt that our men would be treated well." Famished after weeks at partial rations, they appreciated the distribution of "Lincoln coffee," bread, and bacon, handed out by Union soldiers as "a peace measure. . . . For this, and other reasons, Grant was praised among the Confederates in a quiet way." If some Confederate soldiers approved of Grant's presence, Pemberton did not share in it. According to Grant's son, who accompanied his father into Vicksburg, Pemberton received him "in a most frigid, cold manner." When Grant asked for a glass of water for relief from the Mississippi summer sun, one of Pemberton's junior officers informed Grant that if he wanted a drink, he could get it himself. When Grant's staff complained about the Confederates' rudeness, Grant dismissed it, saying, "If Pemberton can stand it, under the circumstances I can."[21]

Pemberton later admitted that he timed his offer to surrender with Independence Day, believing "that upon that day I should obtain better terms ... that to gratify their national vanity they would yield then what could not be extorted from them at any other time." In Grant's version of events, Pemberton offered to surrender on July 3, hoping to avoid having the city fall on the Fourth.[22] In either case, neither Pemberton nor Grant could miss the symbolic

Grant, Forrest, and Unconditional Surrender

importance of the American flag flying over Vicksburg on Independence Day. Although overshadowed in the eastern press by the Union victory at Gettysburg, Vicksburg's surrender marked a crucial turning point in the war. It removed a major Confederate army from the field and, along with the surrender of Port Hudson five days later, secured Union control of the Mississippi. Pemberton surrendered not only 30,000 soldiers (2,166 officers and 27,230 enlisted men) but also 172 cannons, 50,000 rifles, and literally hundreds of tons of artillery shells and ammunition, all of which Union armies used in subsequent campaigning. Lincoln praised Grant's "almost inestimable service you have done the country."[23]

Not everyone, however, lavished Grant with praise for his conduct at Vicksburg. Although Grant believed he had followed the exchange regime's protocol to the letter, some in Washington disagreed. Long critical of Grant, General-in-Chief Henry Halleck rebuked him, writing, "I fear your paroling the prisoners at Vicksburg, without actual delivery to a proper agent as required by the seventh article of the cartel, may be construed into an absolute release, and that the men will immediately be placed in the ranks of the enemy."[24] The criticism was unwarranted, as Grant had already delivered the parolees to the Confederate commissioner for exchange in Vicksburg.[25] Furthermore, Grant's supposition that many of the paroled Confederates would desert proved accurate. Instructed to march east to parole camps at Enterprise, Mississippi, and Demopolis, Alabama, many Confederate soldiers simply returned home. Trying to corral what remained of his command, Pemberton wrote to Jefferson Davis that "most of the Mississippi and Missouri troops have already deserted. Very few remain. I have no arms and cannot prevent it." Short on manpower, Confederate officials forced some of the paroled soldiers to return to active duty even though they had not been exchanged. After the Battle of Chickamauga in September 1863, Union officers reported capturing Confederate soldiers "whom Grant paroled at Vicksburg. They spoke freely of the fact that they had been ordered on duty, although not yet exchanged." Although only a handful of Vicksburg parolees fought at Chickamauga, Halleck took the news as evidence that Grant had erred. Reminding Grant of his earlier criticism, Halleck noted that

> the greater part of the prisoners paroled by you at Vicksburg . . . were illegally and improperly declared exchanged, and forced into the ranks to swell the rebel number at Chickamauga. This outrageous act, in violation of the laws of war, of the cartel entered into the by rebel authorities, and of all sense of honor, gives us a useful lesson in regard

to the character of the enemy with whom we are contending. He neither regards the rules of civilized warfare or even his most solemn engagements. You may therefore expect to meet in arms thousands of unexchanged prisoners, released by you or others on parole.[26]

Although Grant defended his decision, he recognized, like Halleck did, that the framework for surrender and parole had shifted significantly in the latter half of 1863. Vicksburg represented the last major surrender to take place under the Dix-Hill cartel before its absolute collapse. It would also be the last major surrender until Appomattox Courthouse.

Promoted to major general and given an independent command in December 1863, Nathan Bedford Forrest now had free rein to deploy his particular brand of intimidation tactics. Among his objectives in 1864 was the capture of Fielding Hurst. A native of east Tennessee, Hurst had been imprisoned in the state penitentiary at the start of the war for his vocal Unionism. Liberated when Union forces occupied Nashville, Hurst formed a Unionist guerilla band. Although this band later became officially incorporated into the Union Army as the 1st West Tennessee Cavalry (subsequently rebranded the 6th Tennessee Cavalry), Hurst operated independently, much to the consternation of Union officers. In retribution, Confederate guerillas targeted Hurst's family, murdering his nephew and assaulting his elderly sister. Hurst captured the five guerillas he believed responsible and executed them, burying their bodies along the road as a signal to guerillas in the region. Arguing that the five executed men were properly under his command, Forrest demanded "the surrender of Col. Fielding Hurst and the officers and men of his command guilty of these murders, to be dealt with by the C.S. authorizes as their offenses require." When Union officials rejected his demand, Forrest declared "Fielding Hurst, and the officers and men of his command, outlaws, and not entitled to be treated as prisoners of war falling into the hands of the forces of the Confederate States." Since Hurst did not surrender, Forrest believed that he had forfeited all privileges afforded by the laws of war. While Forrest pursued Hurst, Hurst was ordered to pursue Forrest. Two days after Forrest branded him an outlaw, Hurst received orders to "hang on and harass" Forrest. Given Forrest's threat to execute Hurst and the men under his command, Hurst's orders included the unusual warning to "not allow yourself to be drawn into any trap or to be surprised."[27]

On March 15, 1864, Forrest rode north with 2,800 men from Tupelo, Mississippi, on a raid into west Tennessee and Kentucky. By March 20, he reached

Grant, Forrest, and Unconditional Surrender

Jackson, Tennessee. After surveying the situation in the region, Forrest split his forces, leading the majority of his troops north into Kentucky while tasking Col. William L. Duckworth with capturing the Federal depot at Union City. The Union City depot was rumored to be not only well supplied but also garrisoned by Tennessee Unionists, whom Forrest held in contempt as traitors to their region. "I am going to send you there to clean them up," Forrest told Duckworth; "if you don't, never come back here."

Duckworth attacked Union City before sunrise on March 24, routing the Federal pickets and surrounding the fort. Outnumbered three to one, the Union garrison repulsed several waves of rebel cavalry charges. Without artillery, Duckworth reasoned that further attempts to assault the fort would prove fruitless. Instead, he decided to use the fear that Forrest engendered in Union officers as a tactic to take the fort. Forging Forrest's signature, Duckworth sent Forrest's now-standard demand for unconditional surrender, promising destruction if refused. Adding to the ruse, Duckworth brought faux cannons made of wood within sight of the fort, had buglers sound artillery calls, and arranged his forces to give the illusion of greater numbers.

Duckworth hoped that the Union commander, Col. Isaac Hawkins, might be intimidated into surrendering. A dedicated Unionist, Hawkins had a long career in west Tennessee politics, including serving as a delegate to the February 1861 Peace Convention. As a member of one the first Union cavalry regiments raised in Tennessee, Hawkins had been among those surrendered to Forrest at Trenton in December 1862. Because of his previous experience as a prisoner, "he was not now held by Forrest's men to be a dangerous or hard-fighting opponent."

Having read the message under a flag of truce, Hawkins asked to confer with Forrest personally to discuss the terms of surrender. He promptly received a message, purportedly from Forrest, claiming that "I am not in the habit of meeting officers inferior to myself in rank under a flag of truce, but I will send Colonel Duckworth, who is your equal in rank, and who is authorized to arrange terms and conditions with you under instructions." Hawkins begged for a few minutes to confer with his officers, which Duckworth granted. Against the advice of his officers, Hawkins decided to surrender unconditionally. He ordered his men to march outside the fort and stack arms. Disgusted, many of the soldiers hid or destroyed their weapons before exiting the fort.

Only after they were relieved of their arms and taken prisoner did the Union soldiers become aware of Duckworth's ruse. To a man, they blamed Hawkins, "denouncing Colonel Hawkins as a coward, in surrendering them without cause." To the rebels' amusement, "the [Union] officers and men cried

like a whipped child," as they "cursed Colonel Hawkins, and said he was a traitor." The Joint Committee on the Conduct of the War also blamed Hawkins
for the debacle at Union City. Investigating the surrender in conjunction with
its inquiry into the Fort Pillow massacre, the committee heard from several of
Hawkins's subordinates, who all claimed that they could have held the fort.
One officer described Hawkins's behavior as "a little cowardly, and surrendered
to an imaginary foe," noting, "I felt so disgusted with him that I never spoke a
word to him after the surrender."

Poorly guarded as they were marched to Trenton, many of the 500 Union
prisoners managed to escape. The remainder suffered through two days of hard
marching to Trenton, where they were paraded in front of the courthouse,
with Confederates "taking boots, hats, coats, blankets, and money from them."
Loaded onto trains, they were sent to the recently opened Confederate prison
at Andersonville, where they arrived "hatless, bootless, and shoeless, without
coats, pants, or blankets." Ill-clad and maltreated by prison guards for being
Southern Unionists, the soldiers of the 7th Tennessee Cavalry suffered one of
the highest death rates of any imprisoned Union regiment. Only one out of
three men surrendered at Union City lived to see the end of the war.[28]

On the day after the Union City surrender, Forrest's main contingent
reached Paducah, Kentucky. In anticipation, civilians fled across the Ohio
River into Illinois, leaving the defense of the town to the Union garrison at
Fort Anderson and two gunboats patrolling the river. Shortly after midday, Forrest's men had surrounded the fort. After an hour of firing into the fort, Forrest
raised a flag of truce and demanded its unconditional surrender, issuing what
by now had become his standard missive: "Having a force amply sufficient to
carry your works and reduce the place, and in order to avoid the unnecessary
effusion of blood, I demand the surrender of the fort and troops, with all public property. If you surrender, you shall be treated as a prisoner of war; but if I
have to storm your works, you may expect no quarter." Having heard about the
debacle at Union City, Col. Stephen Hicks decided to refuse Forrest's demand,
replying that he had "been placed here by my Government to defend this post"
and he "must, therefore, respectfully decline surrendering as you may require."
Infuriated, Forrest's troops assaulted Fort Anderson three times, failing in each
endeavor. Running short on ammunition, Hicks ordered the remaining rounds
equally divided among his troops and ordered them "to fix their bayonets; to
make good use of the ammunition they had, and, when that was exhausted, to
receive the enemy on the point of the bayonet, feeling fully determined never
to surrender while I had a man alive."[29]

Forrest's behavior at Paducah differed from his earlier efforts to coerce Union surrenders in two important respects. First, Forrest did not have "a force amply sufficient to carry your works." Unlike at Murfreesboro or Cedar Bluff, Forrest's ability to carry out his threatened assault was mostly bluff. Although Forrest had significantly more men under his command (more than 3,000) than did Hicks (665), this numerical advantage provided ineffective. As the subsequent battle demonstrated, Forrest could not decisively take Fort Anderson. Second, according to some reports, Forrest used the flag of truce to improve the position of his troops, moving sharpshooters to houses near Fort Anderson. During the ensuing battle, these sharpshooters were able to fire into the fort, killing a number of Union artillerymen, "shooting nearly all of them in the head." This action was in clear violation of the laws of war: both Union and Confederate policy heretofore had treated flags of truce as sacrosanct. Francis Lieber argued that "so sacred is the character of a flag of truce, and so necessary is its sacredness, that . . . its abuse is an especially heinous offense."[30] Forrest had expanded his understanding of the tactical uses of surrender. Demands to surrender could be used not only to intimidate an enemy and prompt a faster and less costly victory but also to deceive an enemy about the strength of one's forces and provide cover for advancing troops. Forrest would carry all of these lessons forward into future conflicts.

Forrest's targeting of Union artillerymen during the attack on Fort Anderson may have had motives beyond simply weakening the fortification's defenses. The fort's artillerymen belonged to the 1st Kentucky Heavy Artillery, African Descent. Later rebranded the 8th U.S. Heavy Artillery, the 271 men in the 1st Kentucky had only recently joined the Union Army, as recruitment of black troops had been delayed in Kentucky until early 1864. The fight at Fort Anderson was their first experience in combat, but despite the efforts of Forrest's sharpshooters, they did not abandon their posts. According to Hicks, "I have been one of those men who never had much confidence in colored troops fighting, but those doubts are now all removed, for they fought as bravely as any troops in the fort." The Battle of Paducah was Forrest's first encounter with African American soldiers. It is impossible to say whether he ordered the sharpshooters to target them because they were artillerymen (a popular target for sharpshooters) or because they were black. However, given subsequent events, it seems likely that Forrest was particularly incensed by their presence.

Unable to dislodge the Federals at Fort Anderson, Forrest sent Hicks a message the next morning, offering to exchange prisoners. He had in his possession, the letter indicated, thirty-five to forty prisoners taken at Paducah (mostly injured soldiers unable to make it to Fort Anderson) and "about five hundred who were captured at Union City." He proposed to "exchange man for man, rank for rank, so far as you may hold Confederate soldiers." Hicks refused Forrest's offer to exchange prisoners, claiming that he did not have the authority to do so, but added that if he did, "I would most cheerfully do it." Crestfallen, Forrest retreated from Paducah. In his official report, Forrest unconvincingly claimed that the battle had been a victory, since he had occupied the town and only abandoned it because of the prevalence of smallpox there. Both Forrest and his men must have felt dejected in their march back to Tennessee after the Battle of Paducah, one of few defeats Forrest suffered. That their defeat came at the hands of black soldiers particularly incensed them, as it demonstrated the falsehood in Confederate claims that African Americans were inherently inferior soldiers. Even worse, the defeat had unmasked Forrest as a liar. He had promised "no quarter" if his demand to surrender were refused, a threat he proved impotent to carry out.[31]

The most infamous, contentious, and well-studied event in Forrest's military career came just seventeen days later at Fort Pillow. Almost all historians now agree that Forrest's soldiers massacred nearly 300 Union soldiers after they attempted to surrender and that they targeted African American soldiers. Much of the recent debate concerning Fort Pillow has focused on the degree of Forrest's culpability in the massacre. Forrest's defenders argue that no direct evidence demonstrates that Forrest ordered his men to kill surrendering Union soldiers. Viewed from the perspective of Forrest's long relationship with and use of surrender, however, it becomes clear that the intended subtext of Forrest's words and actions during the assault on Fort Pillow sanctioned and encouraged his men to take the lives of Union soldiers, particularly black soldiers, who had thrown down their weapons and raised their arms in surrender.

Built with slave labor by Confederates in early 1862, Fort Pillow sat on a high bluff overlooking a bend in the Mississippi River, forty miles north of Memphis. Abandoned by Confederates and occupied by the Union in June 1862 after the fall of New Madrid and Island No. 10, its strategic importance declined significantly, especially after Vicksburg's surrender. By early 1864, Gen. William T. Sherman concluded that Fort Pillow had little military value and ordered the isolated outpost abandoned. Either the local commander in Memphis ignored the orders or they had not yet been carried out at the time of Forrest's attack.

If the fort had so little value, why did Forrest attack it? Forrest provided differing explanations both before and after the battle to justify his actions. On April 4, Forrest noted, "There is a Federal force of 500 or 600 at Fort Pillow,

Grant, Forrest, and Unconditional Surrender

which I shall attend to in a day or two, as they have horses and supplies which we need." His subsequent references to Fort Pillow indicate that his primary target was not the fort or its supplies but the men garrisoning it. In a postwar interview, Forrest derided Fort Pillow's occupants, noting that "the fort was filled with niggers and deserters from our army." Composed of soldiers from the 13th Tennessee Cavalry and elements of the 3rd Light and 6th Heavy Colored Artillery, the Union garrison embodied all that Forrest detested in the Union war effort. Substantiating his own prejudices, Forrest heard rumors that "bands of Federal and negro soldiers made frequent raids through the country," robbing local families and raping white women. Among those clad in the uniform of the 13th Tennessee Cavalry were a handful of "galvanized Yankees," Confederate deserters, several from regiments now under Forrest's command.[32]

Forrest's assault on Fort Pillow on April 12 followed the model he had established in earlier attacks. Starting around 10:00 A.M., Forrest began artillery fire that would batter the fort throughout the morning and early afternoon. Occupying nearby hills, rebel sharpshooters fired into the fort, targeting Union artillerymen, much as they had done two weeks earlier at Paducah. Among those killed was Maj. Lionel Booth, upon whose death the command of the fort passed to Maj. William Bradford. Dismounted Confederate cavalrymen advanced cautiously, occupying outlying barracks. By 3:00 P.M., Forrest decided that the fort had suffered enough damage that it would be willing to surrender. Forrest's demand contained familiar language: he required unconditional surrender, claimed overwhelming military superiority, and concluded with the thinly veiled threat that "I cannot be responsible for the fate your command" were his men to assault the fort. In substance and content, the ultimatum closely resembled Forrest's words in earlier surrenders. The only novel element in the message was its opening sentence: "The conduct of the officers and men garrisoning Fort Pillow has been such as to entitle them to being treated as prisoners of war." Forrest did not articulate what about the Union soldiers' conduct made them worthy of being treated as prisoners of war, or if the offer extended to black soldiers as well as white soldiers. In reply, Bradford asked for an hour to consider the demand, which Forrest denied, informing Bradford that he would assault the fort in twenty minutes if a surrender was not forthcoming.[33]

Recent events at Union City and Paducah weighed on both commanders. Although he would be loath to admit it, Forrest felt ashamed by his failure at Paducah and was eager to remove the stain from his honor. In rejecting Forrest's demand to surrender, Bradford retorted that "there was none of Hawkins's men there, and he would never surrender." He evidently believed that Forrest may not actually be present and Confederate troops were attempting to duplicate the ruse practiced at Union City. Bradford's cryptic reply to the initial demand to surrender, "Negotiations will not produce the desired result," indicates that he thought the Confederates were bluffing. Infuriated and baffled by Bradford's message, Forrest stormed up to the Union officers under the flag of truce. According to Forrest's account, they "had expressed a doubt as to my presence, and had pronounced the demand a trick, I handed them back a note saying: 'I am General Forrest. . . . I demand an answer in plain, unmistakable English. Will he fight or surrender?'"[34]

Both Union and Confederate soldiers used the lull during the flag of truce to taunt and threaten one another. Although some of Forrest's sharpshooters had seen black soldiers at Paducah, for most of the rebels at Fort Pillow, this was the first time they had seen black men in uniform, and "the sight of negro troops stirred the bosoms of our soldiers with courageous madness." Turning Forrest's boast back upon them, black soldiers threatened them "that if we charged their breast works to show no quarter." As was the case at Paducah, Forrest's sharpshooters used the flag of truce as an opportunity to advance to more favorable locations. One Confederate officer recalled later that "while the flag of truce was up," he led "some picked men [who] crawled up close under the guns to be ready in case they refused to surrender."[35]

Receiving no reply, Forrest ordered a furious assault on the fort. Both Union and Confederate testimony afterward indicates that many of the fort's defenders attempted to surrender, only to be killed by the invading Confederate troops. "As soon as the rebels got to the top of the bank there commenced the most horrible slaughter that could possibly be conceived," noted one Minnesota soldier. "Our boys when they saw they were overpowered threw down their arms and held up, some their handkerchief & some their hands in token of surrender, but no sooner were they seen than they were shot down." In a letter to his sisters only a few days after the battle, Confederate Achilles Clark described the scene with what he admitted were inadequate words: "The poor deluded negroes would run up to our men, fall upon their knees and with uplifted hands scream for mercy, but they were ordered to their feet and then shot down. The white men fared but little better. Their fort turned out to be a great slaughter pen—blood, human blood stood about in pools and brains could have been gathered up in any quantity." Throughout the massacre, Confederate troops were reported to have yelled, "No quarter!" "Black flag!" and "Kill the damned niggers; shoot them down!" Many black soldiers fled out the back of the fort and down the steep embankment into the Mississippi, pursued by rebel soldiers who butchered them on the shore. Although black soldiers

Grant, Forrest, and Unconditional Surrender

suffered the brunt of the rebels' inhumanity, many white soldiers suffered a similar fate. One Union soldier reported that he had been shot twice during the battle, "once before he surrendered and once afterwards." He heard a Confederate officer instruct his men, "Don't show the white men any more quarter than the negroes, because they are no better." After he recognized the futility of continuing to fight, William Bradford fled to the riverbank and held his hands up, "crying at the top of his voice that he surrendered," as bullets flew all around him. Finding no Confederate willing to accept his surrender, he attempted to escape by swimming out into the Mississippi, with "thousands of shots fired at him." Recognizing the futility of swimming under fire in the current, Bradford returned to shore and ran up the bluff, "holding up his hands still crying that he surrendered." Eventually, he found a Confederate soldier willing to accept his surrender. Marched toward Jackson with the other prisoners, Bradford was pulled aside the night after the battle and "taken about 50 yards from the roadside and deliberately shot . . . and his body left unburied upon the ground where he fell."[36]

Wounded earlier in the battle, Forrest did not occupy his usual position at the vanguard but only entered the fort after the massacre was under way. Conflicting accounts suggest that Forrest either encouraged his troops to take no prisoners or actively tried to prevent the slaughter. To a large degree, assessing whether responsibility for the massacre rested with Forrest or his troops creates a false dichotomy. Even if he did not give a specific order instructing his soldiers to ignore offers to surrender, Forrest and his men shared a common animosity toward black and Southern-born Union soldiers. Enraged by their collective failure to take Fort Anderson in Paducah, they were more than ready to carry out Forrest's repeated threat that no quarter would be offered if a demand to surrender were refused. Not unsurprisingly, the precise death toll at Fort Pillow also remains contested. The most thorough scholarly calculations indicate that between 277 and 295 soldiers, nearly half of the Federal garrison, were killed, a rate much higher than that of a typical Civil War battle. The death toll was particularly acute for black soldiers, nearly two-thirds of whom lost their lives.[37]

Forrest denied that a massacre had taken place at Fort Pillow, claiming that "in my operations since the war began I have conducted the war on civilized principles." Isham Harris, the deposed Confederate governor of Tennessee who had attached himself to Forrest, claimed that most of the Union soldiers at Fort Pillow refused to surrender. Although "a few, black and white, threw down their arms and made signs of surrender," their deaths were justified because "in the heat, din, and confusion of a fire of such close quarters there was no chance of discrimination." Jefferson Davis defended Forrest, claiming that "instead of cruelty, General Forrest, it appears, exhibited forbearance and clemency far exceeding the usage of war under like circumstances."[38]

When news of the massacre reached the Northern press, the outcry was swift and furious. The *Chicago Tribune* claimed that "the whole civilized world will be shocked by the great atrocity at Fort Pillow," arguing that such brutality was the natural outgrowth of a slave society. The *State Journal* concurred, claiming that "such are the atrocities which men have been educated by slavery to commit." An initial military investigation conducted in late April found Forrest guilty of "violations of the laws and usages of civilized war and of those obligations of common humanity which even barbarians and heathen tribe, in some sort observe," and a subsequent congressional investigation came to the same conclusion. Their widely disseminated report concluded that Forrest's rebels had committed murder, not war.[39]

Despite the outcry, the Lincoln administration struggled to craft a meaningful response to the massacre. The more radical elements within the Republican Party called for a policy of retaliation and no quarter. Frederick Douglass thought that the massacre would instill in black soldiers "an eagerness for the chance to avenge their slaughtered brethren." A divided cabinet gave Lincoln conflicting advice about how to proceed. Salmon Chase advised Lincoln to follow through on his Order of Retaliation, issued a year earlier, which promised "for every soldier of the United States killed in violation of the laws of war, a rebel soldier shall be executed." Edwin Stanton urged Lincoln to demand that Confederates hand over Forrest for trial, and if they refused, "such measures will be taken by way of retributory justice for the massacre of Fort Pillow, as are justified by the laws of civilized warfare." Gideon Welles and others counseled pursuing a trial for Forrest but were less inclined to retaliate if the Confederates did not surrender Forrest for trial. In the end, Lincoln decided against a retaliatory policy, telling Frederick Douglass that "once begun, I do not know where such a measure would stop."[40]

The most significant political consequence of Fort Pillow was the total cessation of prisoner exchange. Although the regular parole and exchange of prisoners under the Dix-Hill cartel had essentially ended after Vicksburg, Confederate and Union officials continued to parole and exchange prisoners on an ad hoc basis throughout the winter. In addition to the Fort Pillow massacre and other episodes of racial atrocities targeting black soldiers, Union officials concluded that Confederates were not living up to the Dix-Hill cartel, including the illegal return to active duty of the Vicksburg and Port Hudson parolees. On April 17, newly appointed General-in-Chief Ulysses Grant ordered Gen.

Grant, Forrest, and Unconditional Surrender

Ben Butler, who had recently assumed the post of exchange commissioner, to halt all exchanges until the Confederacy changed its policy on black soldiers. Grant foresaw the consequences of ending all prisoner parole and exchange. Union and Confederate prisons would become overcrowded. Scant resources for prisoners would be stretched, especially in Confederate prisons, adding to the misery. On the battlefield, soldiers would be less likely to surrender. They would fight more desperately, fearful of ending up in a prison camp with no prospect of release. Commanders would refuse to surrender, knowing that the consequences for themselves and their men were condemnation to a prison camp with an indeterminate sentence. A hard war would only become harder.[41]

About to embark on the Overland Campaign, Grant knew that these consequences would weigh heavily on both armies but that Confederate armies could ill afford to lose manpower. Without paroles, captured Confederates could never return to the battlefield. Although Grant recognized that calls to resume prisoner exchanges came from a humanitarian impulse, he argued that withholding exchanges at this juncture was the quickest way to bring the war to a close. On August 18, 1864, Grant observed, "It is hard on our men held in Southern prisons not to exchange them, but it is humanity to those left in the ranks to fight our battles. Every man we hold, when released on parole or otherwise, becomes an active soldier against us at once either directly or indirectly. If we commence a system of exchange which liberates all prisoners taken, we will have to fight on until the whole South is exterminated. If we hold those caught they amount to no more than dead men."[42]

Despite the official policy, some Union soldiers thought that Forrest's actions placed him and his men beyond the pale and that they would not accept their surrenders. One white officer commanding a black regiment noted that "the massacre of colored troops at Fort Pillow was well known to us, and had been fully discussed by our men. It was rumored, and thoroughly credited by them, that General Forest [sic] had offered a thousand dollars for the head of any commander of a 'nigger' regiment." An Illinois sergeant claimed that "none of Forrest's command will escape death if captured by our troops, whether an order for retaliation is issued or not." Similarly, an Iowa soldier claimed, "I want no prisoners. . . . I say give rebbels [sic] no quarter, and the feeling is the same throughout the army of the west, we will retaliate."[43]

The consequences of the Union censure of Forrest became apparent two months after Fort Pillow at the Battle of Brice's Crossroads on June 10, 1864. Through judicious and skillful use of the terrain, Forrest managed to defeat a larger Union force, and his aggressive tactics prompted a confused Union retreat. In the midst of the chaos, a brigade of African American soldiers mounted a rearguard action to defend the retreating column. Wearing badges proclaiming, "Remember Fort Pillow," echoing the 1835 massacre at the Alamo, the United States Colored Troops (USCT) soldiers had originally been tasked with defending the wagon train, but as the battle turned into a rout, they found themselves at the forefront of the fight. According to their white officer, they were "entirely cut off" and "surrounded by several hundred" Confederates. They "fought with terrible desperation" and, "having broken up their guns in hand-to-hand conflict, unyielding, died at my feet, without a thing in their hands for defense." Another white officer noted that he "fully expected to be killed if captured" because he commanded black soldiers, and that Forrest's conduct at Fort Pillow "made the Federals afraid to surrender." Some white Union soldiers feared what would happen if they were captured alongside black soldiers. According to one Confederate private, white Union soldiers were "endeavoring to force the negroes away and the negroes [were] equally determined on staying with the Yanks. The Yank afraid to be caught with the negro and the negro afraid to be caught without the Yank." If the black troops fought desperately, so too did the rebels. According to one of Forrest's soldiers, at the sight of black troops, "new life, energy and action coursed through our bodies," resulting in a deadly "maddening rush." Refusing to surrender, black troops preferred to die in battle.[44]

Although Brice's Crossroads proved to be a decisive Confederate victory, black soldiers' refusal to surrender infuriated Forrest. He complained to Union general Cadwallader Washburn that white officers commanding black troops "exhorted their men to remember Fort Pillow, and . . . they expected us to murder them." The battle at Brice's Crossroads "was far more bloody than it would otherwise have been[;] both sides acted as though neither felt safe in surrendering, even when further resistance was useless." He had heard that before the battle black troops had pledged on their knees to "show my troops no quarter." Washburn replied that many black soldiers had taken an oath to fight Forrest relentlessly but thought that "the affair of Fort Pillow fully justi-fied" their behavior. He noted that Forrest "must have learned by this time that the attempt to intimidate the colored troops by indiscriminate slaughter has signally failed, and that instead of a feeling of terror you have aroused a spirit of courage and desperation."

In his correspondence with Washburn, Forrest revealed a paradox at the heart of his thoughts on surrender and black soldiers. Echoing official Confed-erate policy, he claimed that "I regard captured negroes as I do other captured property and not as captured soldiers." Ever the slave trader, Forrest knew the

Grant, Forrest, and Unconditional Surrender

value of slave property and the high prices commanded by healthy adult men. He argued, "It is not the policy nor the interest of the South to destroy the negro—on the contrary, to preserve and protect him—and all who have surrendered to us have received kind and humane treatment." In this final clause, Forrest implied that he would treat black soldiers like "all who have surrendered," except that he had earlier established that he would not.[45]

Forrest's subsequent treatment of black soldiers revealed that Fort Pillow was no aberration. On September 23, Col. Wallace Campbell of the 110th USCT received reports of Confederate attacks all around Athens, Alabama. Five miles north of town, rebel troops besieged a railroad trestle, and after sundown, Confederates occupied the town. From a captured Confederate soldier, Campbell learned that "General Forrest, with his entire force, had invested the place, his force being estimated at from 10,000 to 12,000, with nine pieces of artillery." Outnumbered, Campbell ordered a general retreat to Fort Henderson, burning Federal property in town to prevent it from falling into Forrest's hands. The next morning began with an artillery barrage "from three different sides, casting almost every shell inside the works," while Campbell and his men sheltered in the fort's underground bombproofs. At 8:00 A.M., the firing stopped long enough for a courier to bring a message from Forrest: "I demand an immediate and unconditional surrender of the entire force. . . . I have a sufficient force to storm and take your works, and if I am forced to do so the responsibility of the consequences must rest with you." Forrest ended his demand with the official Confederate policy on Union prisoners: if Campbell surrendered, "all white soldiers shall be treated as prisoners of war and the negroes returned to their masters."

Facing a repeat of Fort Pillow, Campbell rejected Forrest's demands. The messenger tasked with carrying the reply returned with grim news. Forrest "was determined to take the fort, and if he was compelled to storm it no lives would be spared." Awaiting an attack, Campbell received a second courier from Forrest, this time asking if he would be willing to meet outside the fort, as "my only objective is to stop the effusion of blood that must follow the storming of the place." In their brief meeting, Forrest informed Campbell about the size and composition of his force, adding that if Campbell wanted to inspect and verify these numbers, he could do so. Campbell agreed, hoping that such "'dilly-dallying' with General Forrest" would buy him time for reinforcements to arrive. Unfortunately for Campbell, the expected reinforcements never arrived, and his inspection revealed that Forrest had more than 10,000 men. Facing such odds, Campbell concluded that it "would be worse than murder to attempt to hold the fort," as an attack would "result in the massacre of the entire garrison."

Many of the officers under Campbell's command viscerally disagreed with his assessment. After their exchange, they launched a formal complaint "in order that the responsibility of the surrender may rest upon the proper persons." In a letter signed by thirty-two officers, they argued that the fort was adequately built, supplied, and staffed to sustain a ten-day siege and that Campbell had failed to adequately consult with them before surrendering. They concluded that "the surrender was uncalled for by the circumstances, was against our wishes, and ought not to have been made." They hoped that their superior officers would conduct "a thorough and immediate investigation" into Campbell's conduct so that "our names may not be placed in the list of cowards in the general summing up of our nation's history." Their letter attracted the attention of many of the Union Army's senior officers in the region, including William T. Sherman and George H. Thomas, both of whom endorsed further investigation. Gen. John Starkweather, Campbell's immediate superior, concluded that it was "a disgraceful surrender, not only on account of it in itself, but because it infused a spirit of disappointment and demoralization into the balance of his command." Some Union soldiers in Alabama also concluded that Campbell surrendered prematurely. One Michigan soldier whose unit had been sent to reinforce Fort Henderson noted that "our boys would have fought their way through to the fort at Athens but the cowardly cuss that had command of it surrendered the fort." Eager to defend his honor, Campbell asked for a court of inquiry, which was delayed by the peripatetic troop movements in the war's final months. Recognizing that the investigation was unlikely to find in his favor, Campbell quietly resigned in May 1865.[46]

The enlisted men surrendered at Fort Henderson had even greater cause to complain. As at Fort Pillow, Southern Unionists and African Americans made up most of the garrison. In their complaint about Campbell's command, the officers noted that "so far from there being any disposition on the part of the men to surrender or to avoid a fight, it was just the reverse. . . . The soldiers were anxious to try conclusions with General Forrest, believing that in such a work they could not be taken by ten times their number." Familiar with the outcome at Fort Pillow and with Confederate policy on black soldiers, the men inside Fort Henderson recognized the peril in their situation. "When told that the fort had been surrendered, and that they were prisoners, they could scarcely believe themselves, but with tears demanded that the fight should go on, preferring to die in the fort they had made to being transferred to the tender mercies of General Forrest and his men." The black soldiers, most of whom had been slaves in Alabama and Mississippi only a couple of years earlier, had every reason to expect that they would be killed in the aftermath of the surrender. However, the need of the Confederates for manpower apparently outweighed their desire for racial violence. According to Pvt. Joseph Howard of the 110th USCT, the surrendered black troops were sent to Mobile to help construct the city's defenses. En route, "the rebels robbed us of everything we had. . . . They searched our pockets—took our clothing, and even cut the buttons off what little clothing they allowed us." At Mobile, they were "kept at hard labor and inhumanely treated. If we lagged, or faltered, or misunderstood an order, we were whipped and abused—some of our own men being detailed to whip the others."[47]

On the day after taking Fort Henderson, Forrest turned his attention to a fortified railroad trestle a dozen miles north of Athens. Built earlier that year by Union soldiers to secure a vital supply line, the Sulphur Trestle Fort protected a 300-foot-long stretch of railroad that spanned 72 feet above a narrow creek. Occupying higher ground on adjacent hills, Forrest's artillery fired 800 shots into the earthen fort in two hours, and Confederate soldiers occupied a nearby ravine, effectively pinning down the Federal defenders. The Union garrison, more than 1,000 strong at the start of the day, had already lost at least 200 men, including 3 commanding officers, one of whose last words were "Do not surrender the fort." By noon, Forrest concluded that the Union garrison had been sufficiently battered to demand their surrender. The command of the fort had passed to 9th Indiana Cavalry's Maj. Eli Lilly, who would go on to found the pharmaceutical company that bears his name. Conditions within the fort were dire. Out of ammunition, Lilly could see "within the fort, the ground was strewn with dead and wounded." Under a flag of truce, he received Forrest's emissary, who delivered an ultimatum for the immediate and unconditional surrender of the fort, but if "this demand is not instantly complied with, General Forrest can not be held responsible for the conduct of his men." Upon reading Forrest's demands, Lilly retorted that he "would never surrender under a threat; that it was a humiliation his command would not bear and one that should never be asked by a soldier." However, "it was true his forces had suffered heavily" and "they had done their whole duty." He would, therefore, agree to surrender "on honorable terms," but not under the implied threat contained in Forrest's message. Having failed to secure a surrender, Forrest's emissary asked Lilly to negotiate with Forrest directly. There Lilly rebuked Forrest, claiming "that he did not believe that General Forrest could not control his men, and if he did not he would be held responsible." The main question here, as in earlier surrenders, was Forrest's treatment of African American soldiers and Southern Unionists.

As the garrison consisted in roughly equal measures of soldiers from Lilly's 9th Indiana Cavalry, the 3rd Tennessee Cavalry, and the 111th USCT, Lilly could anticipate how the soldiers would react to a surrender. According to Lilly, Forrest promised to treat all Federal soldiers as prisoners of war. After conferring with the other officers in the fort, Lilly agreed to surrender. Forrest burned the fort and the trestle, taking 800 Federal soldiers prisoner. Despite his pledge to the contrary, Forrest immediately segregated the Union prisoners. Replicating the arrangement from Fort Henderson, Forrest sent black soldiers to Mobile to work as manual laborers. White officers, like Lilly, were sent to Enterprise, Mississippi, where they stayed until paroled in December 1864. Enlisted white soldiers were sent to Cahaba Prison. Released in April 1865, many of them perished when the steamboat *Sultana*, overloaded with freed Union prisoners, exploded, killing an estimated 1,800 men.[48]

In the aftermath of the surrenders at Athens and Sulphur Creek, some Union officers in Alabama sought to reassure their commanding officers that they had no intention of surrendering to Forrest. On the evening of September 25, Col. George Jackson of the 9th Indiana wrote, "We have but [a] small force here to hold out against a superior force, but will hold out to the last. Surrender is not in our vocabulary." Other Union officers expressed a more nuanced view of the merits of the two surrenders. Gen. John Starkweather, who had been highly critical of the surrender of Fort Henderson, praised the men who had surrendered at Sulphur Creek, claiming they were "brave men [who] were compelled finally to surrender to a vastly superior force after suffering heavy loss." Forrest himself seemed to agree with the assessment that the garrison at Sulphur Creek had surrendered with honor. He noted in his official report that "the enemy [at Sulphur Creek] suffered severely in this assault," as "almost every house was perforated with shell, and the dead lay thick along the works of the fort."[49]

The surrenders at Athens and Sulphur Creek proved to be the last that Forrest compelled in the Civil War. As a tactical tool, demanding unconditional surrender had proven to be efficient and effective, allowing Forrest to play a larger role in the western theater than the size of his command would indicate. Once asked how to be an effective commander, Forrest quipped, "Get 'em skeered and then keep the skeer on 'em." Forrest's tactical use of unconditional surrender formed a key component of his campaign of terror in 1863 and 1864: his foes were afraid of what would happen were they to surrender and they were afraid of what would happen if they refused. A journalist attached to Grant observed that the Union general had little fear of his Confederate opponents, except Forrest. "If Forrest was in command," he observed, Grant "at once became apprehensive, because the latter was amendable to no known rules of procedure, was a law onto himself for all military acts, and was constantly doing the unexpected at all times and places." Therein rested the fundamental difference in Forrest's and Grant's philosophies of surrender. As a "law onto himself," Forrest saw compelling an enemy to surrender as a manifestation of his dominance. Grant conversely used surrender as a tool to avoid unnecessary bloodshed and a route to reconciliation.[50]

TO THE LAST MAN

Surrender and the Hard War

The year 1864 marked the nadir of surrender's acceptability. With the demise of prisoner exchange, Confederate and Union soldiers alike dreaded indeterminate detention in prisoner of war camps, where the likelihood of survival proved no better than on the battlefield. Surrender proved particularly deadly for black soldiers, guerillas, and Southern Unionists, all of whom risked summary execution upon capture. This widespread aversion to surrender changed the way that the war was fought, from the decisions made by individual soldiers to the choices made by officers all the way up the ranks. To the extent that they had a choice, soldiers increasingly chose death over surrender. Muster reports from 1864 suggest that the ratio of killed to captured soldiers had shifted significantly. In 1862 and 1863, when the Dix-Hill agreement regularly paroled captured soldiers, the soldiers captured in a battle usually outnumbered those killed. After Dix-Hill's demise, these figures came to parity, suggesting that soldiers were less willing to surrender and more willing to fight to the bitter end. While the end of the Dix-Hill cartel was only one factor in the transition to a "hard war" in 1864, the increasing dread with which soldiers held prison made them fight in situations where they would have surrendered a year earlier.

Civil War historians have long recognized that the conflict took a brutal turn in 1864. Advocates of the "hard war" hypothesis have pointed to the destruction of Sherman's March to the Sea and Grant's unrelenting Overland Campaign as indicative of the conflict's increasing ferocity. Historian Mark Grimsley has argued that the transition to hard war began in February 1864 and that it continued until the war's end. Grimsley's chronology roughly coincides with the end of prisoner exchange. However, the reopening of prisoner exchange in early 1865 suggests that hard war did not last until the final

Confederate surrenders. Instead, the Union government made a conscious decision to adopt a more conciliatory stance after Lincoln's reelection; the fall of Savannah, Columbia, and Fort Fisher; and the passage of the Thirteenth Amendment. Once Confederate defeat became inevitable, the Lincoln administration wanted to provide Confederates with whatever incentive it could to entice their surrender.[1] This chapter explores how the culture of surrender underwent a radical transformation between the end of prisoner exchange in April 1864 and its resumption in February 1865.

Even before the Union moratorium on prisoner parole and exchange, many Confederates saw that the tenor of the war had changed. The rate of prisoner exchange slowed to a crawl after the Union victories at Vicksburg and Gettysburg. However, since most officials on both sides believed that the exchange would resume shortly, not until the end of 1863 did the consequences becoming apparent. In November 1863, Braxton Bragg instructed his soldiers prior to the Battle of Missionary Ridge that "the enemy does not intend to carry out in good faith the cartel agreed on between his Government and the Confederate States for the exchange of prisoners of war." Bragg blamed the breakdown of the exchange regime on a strategic decision by the Union to starve the Confederacy by burdening it with hungry prisoners. "Such a cruel proceeding so opposed to the laws of humanity and an enlightened civilization," he argued, "is a virtual acknowledgment by the enemy of his inferiority, and it shows a craft and cunning worthy of the Yankee in imposing upon us the maintenance of thousands of his prisoners, that they may consume the subsistence which should go to the support of our gallant men and their families." Soldiers "should know that if taken prisoners those who survive their cruel treatment will be forced to languish in Northern dungeons until the close of the war, subjected to the taunts and barbarity of a merciless foe." Rather than surrender, Bragg urged his "brave and patriotic Southern soldiers" to choose an "honorable death on the field of battle, nobly fighting for the cause of freedom." Commenting on Bragg's order, the New York Times noted that "he fully intended that the order should have the effect of making his men fight more desperately," but that it likely fell on deaf ears. The newspaper observed that subsequent to the order more than 7,000 Confederates surrendered in battles near Chattanooga, concluding that "the fear of capture will not compel the rebel soldiers to fight to the death; it has just the contrary effect." The Times analysis proved only half right: by the start of 1864, soldiers on both sides dreaded imprisonment but also feared the battlefield. Even veteran soldiers recognized that the nature of combat had changed.[2]

While Bragg ignored the role that the Confederate policy on black soldiers played in the exchange regime's breakdown, his subordinate Gen. Patrick Cleburne drew attention to the war's increasing brutality and how questions of race would shape the Confederate future. On January 2, 1864, Cleburne predicted that "some black catastrophe is not far ahead of us." The war thus far had "spilled much of our best blood," and "our soldiers can see no end to this state of affairs except in our own exhaustion" and were "sinking into a fatal apathy." Cleburne argued that if the Confederacy continued on its current trajectory, surrender and subjugation were the inevitable result. Subjugation to the Union would mean "the loss of all we now hold most sacred—slaves and all other personal property, lands, homesteads, liberty, justice, safety, pride, manhood."[3] Although Cleburne's proposed solution, arming black slaves to fight for the Confederacy, proved unfeasible, unpopular, and probably misguided, his description of surrender's consequences reflected both the war's increased brutality and a growing aversion to a negotiated settlement. Although he fundamentally disagreed with Cleburne's proposal, Jefferson Davis articulated a similar vision of the war's potential outcome. In a speech to the Confederate Congress on May 2, 1864, Davis argued that the Union would continue to attempt to "subjugate or exterminate" Confederate soldiers, who would "prefer any fate to submission to their savage assailants." Davis linked the Confederacy's unrelenting military perseverance to the collapse of the prisoner exchange and attributed the rapidly increasing death rates in prison camps not to their overcrowded conditions, poor sanitation, and inadequate rations but to "the hopelessness of release from confinement." Listening to Davis's speech, Confederate congressmen could only conclude that their president expected the war to escalate into increasing cycles of violence, having given up on foreign alliances or negotiated independence. As "every avenue of negotiation is closed against us," Davis told them, their only option was to "apply every available element of power" in defense of the Confederacy.[4]

Confederates saw other evidence that the Union had abandoned prisoner exchange. In December 1863, Gen. Ethan Allan Hitchcock appointed Gen. Benjamin Butler, probably the most hated man in the South, as commissioner of exchange. Although Butler believed that he could reopen regular prisoner exchanges through diplomacy, his appointment prompted outrage, leading Confederate Secretary of War James Seddon to express "surprise and indignation that the Government of the United States should select for any position of dignity and command a man so notoriously stigmatized by the common sentiment of enlightened nations." Confederate Commissioner Robert Ould refused to work directly with Butler, citing Jefferson Davis's proclamation outlawing Butler for his conduct in New Orleans, and directed his correspondence to Butler's assistant. Ould informed Union officials that exchange negotiations would be nearly impossible so long as someone "so obnoxious as General Butler" held the post of commissioner.[5]

With the exchange cartel's demise, soldiers had to face Hobson's choice of fighting to the death or ending up in a prison with no prospect of release. During the Overland Campaign in May and June 1864, Massachusetts native Darius Starr sometimes contemplated what would happen were he to be taken prisoner. As a sharpshooter, Starr often worked alone, making him particularly vulnerable to capture. "Perfectly still," Starr wrote in his diary on May 9, 1864. "Don't know what it can mean. I'm afraid the army has moved, and I can't tell which way." Rather than finding the silence comforting, he worried that he was stranded and longed to be out of the service: "Wish I was home. I would give a hundred dollars for a discharge. Almost made up my mind to wound myself, & then concluded that I would not." Surrounded and captured two days later by North Carolina cavalry, Starr was "robbed of everything that our guards could find on us, except our clothes." Sent to the recently opened prison at Andersonville, Starr developed chronic diarrhea and complained of painful sores and lice. Although he heard rumors about the possibility of parole, Starr never gave them much credence. "Haven't been at all well for a long time & haven't kept up my diary," he wrote on August 17. "There has been much talk about an exchange but it seems to amount to nothing." Two weeks later he was dead. As one Michigan cavalryman noted in late 1864, "It was no good time to be taken prisoner."[6]

For those who did manage to surrender, life as a prisoner of war had changed dramatically since the collapse of the exchange regime. Prisoner of war camps, which had been nearly empty at the height of the Dix-Hill cartel, quickly became overcrowded. Union prisons, for instance, held only 1,286 prisoners at the start of 1863, at the height of the exchange regime, but a year later in 1864, approximately 35,000 prisoners languished, with little hope of relief.[7] Just as the commencement of the exchange regime resulted in the closing of both Union and Confederate prisons, its demise prompted the creation of new prisons. Union officials opened new prisons at Point Lookout (August 1863), Rock Island (December 1863), and Elmira (July 1864). Confederates followed a similar path, reopening Belle Isle (May 1863) and opening new prisons at Cahaba

(June 1863), Danville (November 1863), Andersonville (February 1864), and Millen (September 1864). Hastily constructed to meet the rapid overcrowding in existing prisons, these later prisons created the stuff of nightmares.

Offering little shelter or sanitation, these newly constructed prisons quickly exceeded capacity. Designed to house no more than 10,000 men, Andersonville, the most notorious of this latter generation of prisons, held 33,000 inmates by August 1864. Entering Andersonville in May 1864, shortly after it opened, Connecticut soldier Robert Kellogg described the desperation soldiers felt passing through the gates: "As we entered the place, a spectacle met our eyes that almost froze our blood with horror, and made our hearts fail within us. Before us were forms that had once been active and erect;—*stalwart men*, now nothing but mere walking skeletons, covered with filth and vermin."[8] When he first entered Andersonville two months later on July 8, 1864, Pennsylvanian Erza Ripple recalled that "the effect was stunning and very disheartening." Captured in a failed assault on James Island in Charleston harbor, Ripple estimated that the prison now held about 25,000 prisoners within its twenty-six-acre enclosure. "What a sinking feeling of the heart there was when we came to realize that this was to be our home—no one knew how long— perhaps until the end of the war, whenever that might be." Although Ripple suffered tremendously during his two months at Andersonville (when he was transferred to new prison in Florence), in a sense he was lucky: of the 41,000 Union soldiers imprisoned in Andersonville between February 1864 and April 1865, only 26,000 lived to recount their experiences.[9]

Union and Confederate officials compounded prisoners' suffering by imposing additional regulations, including limiting the length of letters home, expanding the list of contraband for packages sent by prisoners' families, and prohibiting access to sutlers. In retaliation for reports that Union prisoners were not receiving adequate rations, Federal officials cut those issued to Confederates by a third in April 1864. This new ethos of retaliation came to the forefront during the summer of 1864 during the Union bombardment of Charleston. Starting on June 14, 1864, Confederate officials brought fifty high-ranking Union prisoners from Macon to Charleston to, as the *Mercury* put it, "share in the pleasures of the bombardment . . . in that portion of the city most exposed to the enemy's fire."[10] Union officials quickly cried foul. "I must . . . protest against your action in thus placing defenseless prisoners of war in a position exposed to constant bombardment," wrote Gen. John G. Foster to his Confederate opposite. "It is an indefensible act of cruelty." In retaliation, Foster had requested that "an equal number of rebel officers of equal rank may be sent to me, in order that I may place them under the enemy's fire as long as

Surrender and the Hard War

our officers are exposed in Charleston." By the end of the summer, each army had brought more than 600 prisoners to Charleston. The imprisoned Union soldiers were held inside the city, and Confederate prisoners were near the Union battery on Morris Island. Many of them believed that they had been brought there as part of a reopening of prisoner exchange, only to discover that they were being used as human shields. Captured at Spotsylvania in 1864, Confederate James McMichael rejoiced at the news that he was being sent from Fort Delaware to Charleston, assuming that within days he could return to his home in central Georgia. "This is retaliation in the extreme," McMichael recorded in his diary when he learned the real purpose behind the voyage. Miraculously, prisoner casualties on both sides proved remarkably low during the siege, despite heavy shelling. After six and half weeks, by mutual agreement the original fifty prisoners on each side were exchanged, while the remainder were relocated. Union prisoners went to Columbia and Florence, and Confederate prisoners went to Fort Pulaski, before returning to Fort Delaware. While the use of prisoners of war in Charleston harbor proved exceptional, it revealed how the treatment of prisoners had changed in 1864.[11]

In the largest prisoner exchange during Grant's moratorium, the 100 men liberated at Charleston included some high-ranking prisoners. Among the five Union generals exchanged was Truman Seymour, who had also been part of Robert Anderson's Fort Sumter garrison in 1861. Seymour had surrendered at the Wilderness and would later witness Lee's surrender at Appomattox. Notable Confederates included generals James J. Archer, who surrendered on the morning of July 1 at Gettysburg, and Meriwether Jeff Thompson, who had surrendered when overwhelmed by a Union cavalry raid in Kentucky. Usually segregated from enlisted men into separate camps, officers experienced few of the horrors that plagued the larger camps. Thompson observed that he faced fewer hardships during his year in Union prisons than he would have had in the field and that "as a prisoner I was universally treated with respect." Yet even under comparatively mild conditions, officers emerged from prison transformed. Mary Boykin Chesnut observed that Archer, who had attended college with her husband, was almost unrecognizable after his year in prison. Once known for his "girlish and pretty" visage (college classmates nicknamed him "Sally"), Archer now appeared "grim" with "a hard face, black-beard, sallow, with the saddest black eyes." Chesnut attributed his new appearance, "weary-looking—mind and body," to having been "deadened by long imprisonment."[12]

Many prisoners captured in 1864 wished they had died instead. Union courier John Hadley was taken prisoner while unconscious and wounded at the Wilderness. When he awoke in a Confederate field hospital, Hadley "felt a little more willing to 'give up the ghost' just then than I ever expect to be again." He feared that if he recovered from his injuries, he "would be sent South in the hot season to some prison-pen, to starve or die of epidemic." Foreseeing only more suffering and death, Hadley "had absolutely no hope" and "felt actual regret that the injuring force had not been a little stronger." Hadley so feared what would happen were he sent to a Confederate prison that he attempted to escape from the hospital, despite his injuries.[13]

Without the prospect of exchange, prisoners had greater incentive to escape, and attempts dramatically increased in 1864. In February 1864, more than 100 prisoners escaped from Richmond's Libby Prison, and more than half made it safely to Union lines. Despite its remote location in south-central Georgia, Andersonville saw more than 350 prisoners attempt to escape in 1864, although almost all of these were eventually recaptured. In November 1864, Union prisoners at Salisbury attempted a mass breakout, rushing the prison gates and seizing the guard's weapons, before Confederates regained control, killing approximately 250 prisoners in the process. Historian Lorien Foote has recently calculated that 2,800 soldiers escaped from Confederate prisons in the winter of 1864 and spring of 1865.[14] Confederate prisoners at Johnson's Island tried repeatedly to escape in 1864, venturing out onto the ice during the winter months and constructing makeshift rafts in the summer. More frequent escape attempts prompted enhanced prison discipline, which only made the camps more unbearable. So long as exchange seemed out of reach, inmates experienced escalating cycles of brutality, cruelty, and inhumanity. Prisoners who did escape told harrowing tales of prison life, widely reprinted in newspapers, which only contributed to the dread that soldiers had of prison. In June 1864, *Harper's Weekly* and *Frank Leslie's Illustrated*, the North's most popular illustrated news magazines, published depictions of emaciated men who looked like living corpses that horrified soldiers on the front lines and families on the home front alike. Based on photographs taken of Union prisoners paroled from Belle Isle due to their poor health, the nightmarish images forced soldiers to think twice about surrendering.[15]

The aversion of Union soldiers to surrender only increased toward the end of 1864 when they became more fully aware of conditions in Confederate prison camps. Although newspaper accounts had long detailed the camps' deplorable state, coming face-to-face with prisoners held in such camps made a lasting impression and deepened soldiers' antipathy to raising the white flag. Rice Bull recalled his horror when Sherman's army liberated the Confederate prison at Millen, Georgia. Visiting the prison on December 3, 1864, he noted that the prisoners "had no tents or blankets" and had to dig "holes or caves in the earth" for shelter. Recalling his brief captivity at Chancellorsville, Bull "felt thankful that it was not my fate to be taken to one of these hells." Bull heard many of his fellow soldiers assert upon seeing the conditions at Millen that "they would never be taken prisoner; they would prefer to be shot than put in such a place."[16]

While the situation for captured soldiers deteriorated significantly across the board in 1864, African Americans, Southern Unionists, and guerillas bore the worst of it. While most soldiers faced the horrors of prison upon surrendering, blacks, Unionists, and guerillas confronted a likely death sentence. In the aftermath of the Fort Pillow massacre, such outlawed soldiers concluded that since the black flag had been raised against them, they were under no obligation legally or morally to accept an enemy's surrender. They would fight to the death, knowing that they would receive no quarter.

The new paradigm was apparent in the small North Carolina town of Plymouth only a week after the massacre at Fort Pillow and Grant's moratorium on prisoner exchange. Occupied by Union forces since May 1862, Plymouth hosted a garrison of 3,000 soldiers, including many recently recruited African Americans and Southern Unionists, some of whom had deserted from Confederate service. The garrison's commander, Gen. Henry Wessells, a protégé of Winfield Scott and a veteran of the Mexican War, had spent the past year solidifying Union control of eastern North Carolina and engaging in significant recruiting efforts. Leading a force several times larger, Gen. Robert F. Hoke, nearly thirty years Wessells's junior, quickly surrounded the town on April 17, 1864. Two recently constructed Confederate ironclads, the CSS *Albemarle* and the CSS *Neuse*, sank or drove off the Union gunboats on the Roanoke River. By the morning of April 20, Hoke had captured most of the town and had control of the river. Bottled up in Fort Williams, within firing range of the Confederate ironclads and Hoke's three artillery battalions, Wessells recognized that once the Confederates began their final assault, casualties would likely prove disastrous. Under a flag of truce, Hoke demanded his surrender "in consideration of my untenable position" and "the impossibility of relief." Although he inferred a threat of "indiscriminate slaughter," Wessells declined to surrender, arguing that he could not capitulate "with honor" as he still commanded a "strong garrison without damage" and "had not suffered sufficiently yet." Hoke replied, "I will fill your citadel full of iron; I will compel your surrender, if I have to fight to the last man." Returning to his garrison, Wessells prepared for the worst. In his official report, he noted that once the Confederates began shelling the fort, "this terrible fire had to be endured without reply, as no man could live at the guns. . . . This condition of affairs could not long be endured without a reckless sacrifice of life; no relief could be expected, and in compliance with the earnest desire of every officer I consented to hoist a white flag." Only a few hours after he had met with Hoke, Wessells "had the mortification of surrendering my post to the enemy with all it contained."[17]

Most of Wessells's soldiers expressed stoic resignation at his decision to surrender. Vastly outnumbered and besieged on four sides, one soldier noted, "We could not do much against such odds so we were obligated to surrender." Rather than relief, however, some Union soldiers expressed anger and resentment. Capt. John Donaghy noted that when news of the surrender reached his men, they wanted to destroy their weapons to prevent them from falling into enemy hands. Although he silently shared their antipathy to surrender, he believed that "as the General had surrendered us we had no right to do such a thing." He noted that "the men seemed disappointed when I directed them to lay down their arms unharmed. I had never studied military law in regard to surrendering, but I learned afterwards that I had done right in the matter." Although Donaghy prided himself on acting within the confines of military law, he struggled with his emotional response to surrender. "To have to surrender affected me greatly," he observed; "I felt like crying, but by an effort did not do it." Another officer noted that after the surrender, one soldier had managed to hold on to his weapon and considered killing Hoke, only to be stopped by another soldier who feared what would happen to them if the Confederate general came to harm. The officer concluded that the intervention was "good luck because had a Reb been killed after the surrender, they would have killed us all."

Donaghy knew that they were bound for a Confederate prison camp with little likelihood of parole or exchange. Regular prisoner exchanges had stopped months earlier, and news that Grant had halted all future exchanges had reached Plymouth just before the battle. Many of the soldiers under Wessells's command expressed horror at the surrender because, as one soldier put it, rebel prisons had become "synonymous in the minds of Union soldiers with suffering and death." Some refused to surrender, preferring to die on the battlefield. Lewis Higley of the 85th New York "had often said he would never be taken prisoner." When ordered to stack arms, Higley refused and was "mercilessly shot to death" by a Confederate. Although few Union soldiers shared Higley's resolution, their fear of prison was not misplaced. Most were sent to

Andersonville, where they arrived the day before survivors of the Fort Pillow massacre.[18]

While most Northern-born white soldiers at Plymouth accepted the consequences of surrender, African Americans and Southern Unionists (known locally as Buffaloes) knew that they were unlikely to be afforded prisoner of war protections. Not only was the news of the Fort Pillow massacre on the forefront of their minds, but local Confederate troops had demonstrated that they had little regard for the lives of Buffaloes or black soldiers. A month before the Plymouth surrender, a Confederate soldier boasted about executing a captured black cavalryman, noting that his brigade "never takes any negro prisoners. . . . Officers and men were perfectly enthusiastic in killing the 'd—d rascals.'" Knowing the probable outcomes were he taken captive, Alec Johnson, a black cook with the 85th New York, "refused to surrender, and fell fighting on his own account, pieced with bullets." A pharmacist from New Orleans named Appleton, who had deserted from Confederate conscription to enlist as a hospital steward with the 85th New York, reached a similar conclusion about what would happen were he taken prisoner. "Surrender mean death to him," a fellow soldier noted, "and when our flag went down, he, in his desperation, swallowed a dose of morphine to end his life." The immediate intervention of Union doctors stopped his suicide attempt. Taken prisoner alongside the rest of the garrison, Appleton attempted to disguise his appearance by shading his face with a slouch hat, but he was recognized by a rebel soldier. Separated from the other prisoners, Appleton's fate was unknown, although his comrades surmised that he was killed. One Union officer noted that after the surrender, "the ranks were searched for deserters from the rebel army, a number of whom were detected and taken away. We never knew their fate, but suppose them to have been shot."[19]

Fearing execution, many of the Buffaloes and white USCT officers attempted to blend into other units, hoping to avoid identification. In their efforts to pass for Northern soldiers, Buffaloes assumed the names and identities of men who had fallen earlier in the battle. One Union officer noted that "there were some white natives who had enlisted in our army as North Carolina state volunteers, and they had only too good reason to know that they would receive no mercy from their captors, so they distributed themselves among other organizations." Another noted that "as soon as our flag was hauled down the officers and men of the 2d Loyal North Carolinians—Buffaloes they were called—made a change, the officers doffed their uniforms and donned those of a private, as they did not wish to be recognized by the Rebs." A USCT officer,

Captain Marvin, adopted a similar tactic and donned a private's uniform, as "he did not wish to be known as an officer of colored troops."[20]

The black recruits themselves, however, could not so easily disguise their identities. Many attempted to escape the fort before the surrender, only to be relentlessly pursued by Confederate soldiers. One Union soldier noted that "there were about twenty negro soldiers at Plymouth, who fled to the swamps when the capture of the place became certain; these soldiers were hunted down and killed." Another recalled that throughout the afternoon after the surrender, the captured Union soldiers could "hear the crack of rebel rifles along the swamps, where they were hunting down the colored troops and loyal North Carolinians. I heard a rebel Colonel say, with an oath, that they intended to shoot every Buffalo . . . and negro they found in our uniform." Black recruits who remained in the fort for the surrender fared little better than those who attempted to escape. The 2nd U.S. Colored Cavalry's Samuel Johnson noted that "upon the capture of Plymouth by the rebel forces all the negroes found in blue uniform, or with any outward marks of a Union soldier upon him, was killed." Johnson saw some black soldiers "taken into the woods and hung." Others he saw "stripped of all their clothing" before being shot on the riverbank or "having their brains beaten out by the butt end of the muskets in the hands of the rebels." Johnson himself only escaped execution by donning a "suit of citizen's clothes." Forced to work as a military laborer, he subsequently escaped to Union lines. He was one of the few Union soldiers present to escape death or a lengthy prison term.[21]

Echoing their statements after Fort Pillow, Confederate officials denied that a massacre had taken place at Plymouth. Most Union soldiers and the Northern public, however, concluded that rebels no longer took the sanctity of surrendering soldiers seriously. The *New York Tribune* claimed that the Plymouth massacre "only proves that what was supposed to be an exceptional barbarity at Fort Pillow, has been adopted as the deliberate policy of the rebels." In raising the proverbial black flag, Union soldiers believed, Confederates had signaled their intention to no longer accept the surrender of soldiers on the battlefield. Expecting no quarter, soldiers increasingly fought to the death in situations where only a year or two earlier surrender would be expected. In July 1864, the *Delaware County American* reported the death of George Fetters of the 6th Pennsylvania Cavalry. Surrounded by Confederates, "on his refusing to surrender, he was ruthlessly shot down. He was stripped of everything but his shirt, and left to die." Union soldiers discovered Fetters two days later still alive but severely dehydrated and "sweltering in his [own] blood." African American troops in particular feared the consequences of surrendering.

Horace Porter, Grant's personal secretary, noted that "the black boys . . . all had a notion that their lives would not [be] worth praying for if they fell into the hands of the enemy."[22] This sentiment was reflected and reinforced three months later during the siege of Petersburg, when Confederate soldiers systemically targeted black soldiers.

Eager to end the lengthy siege of Petersburg, Union engineers spent three weeks constructing a 510-foot tunnel underneath Confederate fortifications, filling it with 320 barrels of gunpowder. Detonated at 4:44 A.M. on July 30, 1864, the explosion killed 300 rebel soldiers and created a crevice nearly 200 feet long, 60 feet wide, and 20 feet deep. Initially intended to lead the Union charge until a last minute change, African American troops and their white officers entered the fight with few illusions about how they would be treated. With the memory of Fort Pillow and Plymouth still fresh, Lt. Richard M. Gosney of the 28th USCT observed that the black troops went into battle "not expecting any quarter, nor intending to give any."[23] The regiment's white officers likewise knew that they would not be afforded prisoner of war status if captured; one Confederate noted that they lacked the "insignia of rank," as "they had learned that our men did not readily give quarter to officers of negro regiments and preferred when caught to pass as privates of white regiments."

If USCT soldiers did not expect to receive quarter at the Crater, they did not intend to offer any either. Entering the battle around 8:00 A.M., black soldiers charged into the crowded and chaotic melee, yelling, "Remember Fort Pillow!" and "No Quarter!" As both Confederate and Union soldiers refused to accept the surrender of the other, the battle devolved into a bloodbath. One Confederate soldier recounted that "nothing in war could have exceeded the horrors that followed, no quarter was given and for what seemed a long time fearful butchery was carried on. There was little firing, the men were too crowded but they stabbed with their bayonets and clubbed with their muskets till utterly exhausted. . . . Some of the white men were spared, but very few negroes." In the midst of the battle, a Confederate officer directed his men not to accept Union soldiers' surrender, telling them to "show them no quarter, boys," as "they raised the black flag on us and showed none." The absence of surrender in the midst of combat led to one of the more usual conversations in the conflict. A Confederate officer, "standing in the crater, in the midst of the horrid carnage, . . . said to a Federal colonel who was near him, 'Why in the h—don't you fellows surrender?' . . . The yankee replied quickly, 'Why in the h—don't you let us?'"[24] One Confederate wrote to his wife after the battle that black Union soldiers "threw down the[i]r arms to surrender, but were not allowed to do so." Another noted that USCT soldiers pleaded, "We will surrender.

Where is the rear?" only to be told, "There is no such thing as a rear." A Union soldier overhead a Confederate yelling, "Save the white men but kill the damn niggers." Although Confederate soldiers expressed their intention to refuse any surrender, especially of black soldiers, some USCT soldiers were taken captive. Confederates paraded the 1,500 black and white prisoners taken at the Crater through the streets of Petersburg. Marching four abreast, they were "assailed by a volley of abuse from men, women and children."[25]

The Crater epitomized how the Civil War had devolved into a hard war by August 1864. With the option to surrender effectively off the table, especially for African Americans, combat became increasingly brutal. Increasingly both Union and Confederate soldiers feared capture more than death. During the siege of Atlanta that same month, Sherman's men believed that they would be executed if captured by Confederates. One reported rumors that "rebs killed after the surrender the prisoners they took" and concluded that "we must not be taken prisoners. I confess that I don't expect any mercy if captured." Another said, "I don't want to be captured on this trip, for I expect every man of us the rebels capture will get a 'stout rope and short shift.'"[26]

The massacres at Plymouth and the Crater reflected how racial animosity between USCT and Confederate soldiers transformed the place of surrender on the battlefield. The specter of the black flag loomed menacingly, forcing soldiers to fight with greater desperation. For instance, at the battle of Jerusalem Plank Road in June 1864, Georgia sharpshooter Joseph Edwards found himself "alone, out there in the middle of that opening," separated from the rest of his unit and surrounded by Union soldiers. Only a year or two earlier, such a scenario would have almost inevitably concluded with the isolated soldier throwing his weapon down in surrender, and indeed Edwards noted in his memoirs that "I suppose the Yankees thought I was going to surrender." However, in Edwards's mind, surrender was no longer an option because of the way in which the war had evolved in the past year. "I would have surrendered," Edwards recalled, "but I heard that they had a negro provost guard, and allowed them to take revenge out of their prisoners for our boys killing negro prisoners. I concluded quickly that I had rather be killed there than to fall into those negro[e]s' hands." To that end, Edwards scampered across an open field, in full view of Union troops, and somehow eluded the Union barrage. "There must have been hundreds of shots fired at me," he boasted.[27] Edwards was not alone in fearing what would happen to him under the care of USCT guards. One New Jersey officer noted that "the Rebel prisoners are very fearful of being left to the charge of colored

Surrender and the Hard War

troops as they fear their own acts of inhumanity will be repaid. The Nigs are all anxious to kill but not take prisoners, and their cry is Ft. Pillow." When a Confederate prisoner who had "refused to be marched to the rear by a Nig guard" rebuffed a second order, "the Nig ran him through with a bayonet killing him instantly."[28] Although documented cases of black soldiers abusing or killing Confederate prisoners were relatively rare, they shaped how rebel soldiers fought in 1864, believing that a fate worse than death awaited them at the hands of black men in blue.

The black flag also transformed how Confederate guerillas fought in 1864, transforming an already brutal mode of warfare into barbarity. Although the Union Army had always treated guerillas differently from conventional soldiers, the Lieber Code condemned all guerilla warfare as contrary to the laws of war and removed any possible prisoner of war protections for irregular combatants. This blanket prohibition covered the entire spectrum of paramilitary fighters, including sanctioned ones such as the Partisan Rangers. In 1864, Union generals routinely ordered their subordinates to kill rather than capture Confederate guerillas and to execute those who did surrender. "When any of Mosby's men are caught," Grant instructed Sheridan in August 1864, "hang them without trial."[29] Subject to execution upon capture, Confederate guerillas had little incentive to surrender and increasingly fought to the death. Moreover, prospective Confederate guerillas increasingly gravitated toward more radical forms of irregular warfare, concluding that if the Union did not recognize them as legitimate soldiers under the laws of war, they were not bound by those laws. If they could not surrender, guerillas felt emboldened to torture, arson, and pillage with abandon.

Missouri witnessed some of the worst of this new face of guerilla warfare. While the state had suffered from endemic guerilla warfare for years, many residents claimed that the calibre of violence and degree of brutality escalated in 1864. One noted in August 1864 that the fights between pro-Confederate guerillas and Union soldiers were "rendered horrible by their ferocity. No quarter is being given, no mercy shown." That summer, the epicenter of guerilla violence in Missouri shifted from William Quantrill to his former lieutenant "Bloody" Bill Anderson. Unlike Quantrill, who had a field command derived from the Confederate Partisan Ranger Act, Anderson denied that he answered to any authority other than himself. "I have killed many. I am a guerilla," Anderson boasted. "I have never belonged to the Confederate Army, nor do my men." That summer, Anderson's band brought terror to western Missouri, looting Unionist communities and torturing and killing countless Union soldiers and sympathizers. It was reported that Anderson's men developed a fondness for mutilating their victims, including scalping and cutting off ears and noses. "From this time forward I ask no quarter and give none," Anderson proclaimed. "Every Federal soldier on whom I put my finger shall die like a dog. If I get into your clutches, I expect death. You are all to be killed and sent to hell. That is the way every damned soldier shall be served who falls into my hands."[30]

The murder of twenty-six unarmed Union soldiers in Centralia provided the capstone to Anderson's black flag campaign. On the morning of September 27, 1864, Anderson's band rode into Centralia, robbed a passing stagecoach, and stopped a northbound train by piling wood on the tracks. Some eighty strong (including not-yet-notorious Frank and Jesse James), Anderson's men swarmed onboard, yelling, "Surrender! Surrender!" They frantically searched the passengers, pocketing their spoils and killing those who offered resistance or attempted to conceal valuables, before setting the train on fire. Among the passengers were Union soldiers on furlough from Sherman's army after the siege of Atlanta. "Surrender quietly, and you shall be treated as prisoners of war," one of Anderson's men told the soldiers. "We can only surrender," came the reply, "as we are totally unarmed." Separated from the rest of the passengers, the Union soldiers were ordered to remove their uniforms, "stripped of all save their under-clothing." Only then did Anderson identify himself, asking if the party included an officer. No sooner had Sgt. Thomas Goodman stepped forward than Anderson's men fired their revolvers at the rest of the men in line. The sole survivor, Goodman could hear the guerillas' "demonic yell" over the sounds of gunfire.[31]

Held as a hostage rather than a prisoner of war, Goodman received regular verbal abuse and physical threats from Anderson's men, many of whom expressed surprise that Anderson had let him live. Shortly thereafter, Union cavalry militia tracked down Anderson's band, only to be overwhelmed when the guerillas charged headlong into the dismounted Union line, who found themselves "surrounded before they could have possibly found time to reload their emptied pieces." To Goodman's horror, the Union militia surrendered, "surrendered as we did at Centralia, with assurances of humane treatment." Shutting his eyes to avoid seeing the "carnival of blood," Goodman reopened them after the executions stopped to see that Anderson's guerillas had not only killed the surrendered Union militiamen but had decapitated many of the dead, arranging the heads in a macabre tableau. Some were "stuck upon their carbine points"; others were mounted on "the tops of fence stakes and stumps around the scene." A Union officer who discovered the scene the following day noted, "Most of them were shot through the head, then scalped, bayonets thrust through them, ears and noses cut off, and privates torn off and thrust in the mouths of the dying."[32]

The black flag also shaped the outcome and aftermath of the Battle of Saltville in October 1864, one of the few instances where Confederate guerillas fought black Union soldiers. Launched from Kentucky, the Union cavalry raid into western Virginia targeted a Confederate saltworks guarded by a small Confederate garrison composed mainly of local militia and reserves. Leading a guerilla company, Champ Ferguson came to the garrison's aid. Although he and his men sometimes fought alongside or in conjunction with Confederate regulars, Ferguson, like Bill Anderson, did not have a commission from the Confederate government and believed himself independent of its authority. As soon as the enemy came into sight, the rebel soldiers noticed that the Union raiders included the 5th Colored Cavalry. "The cry was raised that we were fighting negroes," one noted, "the first we ever met." The enraged Confederates focused their hatred and attention on the black soldiers, who responded by charging headlong into the rebel line. Although, as one Union officer noted, "the rebels were firing on them with grape and canister and were mowing them down by the scores," the dismounted black cavalrymen "kept straight on." Another officer observed, "I have seen white troops fight in twenty-seven battles, and I never saw any fight better." Driven by their devotion to the Union cause and their awareness of the Confederate black flag, the 5th Colored Cavalry soldiers fought with both desperation and purpose.

Despite their numerical advantage, Union forces abandoned their attack at sunset when they had exhausted their ammunition, leaving behind hundreds of wounded soldiers. Knowing what would happen to them when Confederates occupied the battlefield, wounded black soldiers tried desperately to follow the retreating Union line. One soldier recalled seeing "one man riding with his arm off, shot through the lungs, and another shot through the hips," all trying urgently to evade capture. By sunrise the next morning, Ferguson's guerillas began patrolling the battlefield and "shooting every wounded negro they could find." Ferguson led the massacre himself, "pointing his revolver down at the prisoners that were laying on the ground." While the death toll at the Saltville massacre remains unclear, the evidence suggests that Ferguson's guerillas killed fifty wounded black soldiers.[33]

Few soldiers articulated the dilemma soldiers faced in 1864 better than John Malachi Bowden, a private in the 2nd Georgia. A veteran of Fredericksburg, Gettysburg, and Spotsylvania Courthouse, Bowden had seen many soldiers taken prisoner and did not wish to add himself to their number. At the Battle of New Market Heights in September 1864, his regiment was ordered to hold Fort Gilmer "at all hazards," an order that ostensibly precluded surrender. With a Union attack imminent, Bowden pledged with a fellow soldier "not to be captured, but to cut our way out or fight to the death." As Bowden recounted in his memoirs, "My purpose was to hold the Fort or die, just as we had been ordered." Even when the fort's fall became inevitable, Bowden maintained that "I had still had no intention to surrender, and began trying to reload my gun. The barrel had become very hot from constant firing, and when the ball was about half way down, it became lodged or jammed, and I was unable to move it. I was standing close to one of the cannons near the entrance to the Fort. My gun was choked, and the enemy was within twenty steps of us. To run, it was too late. To surrender was no part of my programme." Despite his determination not to surrender, when Union soldiers occupied part of the fort and called out, "Fall in here, Johnnie Rebs," Bowden dutifully "fell in among the others."[34]

Although Bowden's memoirs imply that the entire fort fell, in truth only Bowden's segment of the fort became briefly occupied during the battle, and Confederates retained control of Fort Gilmer. Bowden's memoirs also omitted one significant feature of his eventual surrender: he neglected to mention that the Union soldiers whom he feared would "crack his head, or run their bayonets through him" were African American, who after Fort Pillow and the Crater had their own reasons for fearing capture. While some of the assaulting black soldiers managed to infiltrate the fort, most found themselves pinned down in a ditch by rebel troops eager for "a chance to shoot a nigger." Confederates lit exploding artillery shells and rolled them off the fort's parapet into the ditch, killing dozens of USCT soldiers. After a third of the Union force was killed or mortally wounded, the remaining soldiers were, in the words of one officer, "rendered perfectly helpless" and "compelled to surrender."[35]

Soldiers' hostility to surrender spilled over to political rhetoric in the 1864 election. Republicans accused Peace Democrats of shamefully surrendering to Confederate demands. Describing the peace plank in the Democratic platform, the *New York Times* argued that it amounted to a "hopeless and helpless surrender of the Union." Similarly, cartoonist Thomas Nast depicted the consequence of "compromise with the South" as a shameful surrender to Jefferson Davis.

By characterizing any policy outside a full and rigorous prosecution of the war as a shameful surrender, Republican rhetoric reflected Union soldiers' opposition to surrender. As Lincoln noted shortly after his reelection, "No attempt at negotiation with the rebel leader could result in any good." The war would be decided on the battlefield, not at the surrender table.[36]

A similar dynamic played out in the South, where Confederates increasingly equated surrender with ruin and devastation at the hands of rapacious Northerners. Jefferson Davis often reiterated that the only future open to the Confederates came through victory on the battlefield and that he would never surrender or compromise for anything less than independence. While Davis did not face an electoral challenge in 1864, North Carolina governor Zebulon Vance did: newspaper publisher William Woods Holden, who advocated North Carolina negotiating a separate peace. Vance argued that Holden's scheme amounted to a "surrender to the hangman." Long the voice of Southern radicalism, the Charleston Mercury rejected any compromise on the questions of emancipation or Confederate independence. In September 1864, the paper denounced any form of negotiated peace that fell short of maintaining slavery and recognition of Confederate independence. Reunion with the North, the Mercury declared, amounted to the "surrender of your strongholds to your worst enemy—your house to the habitual pilferer—your sword to those who have murdered your children in cold blood—your honor to those who have dishonored your women and stole the tombs of your dead. . . . It is the surrender of your slaves. . . . It is the surrender for a brief respite of quiet." Instead, the newspaper urged its readers to continue "fighting, struggling, dying for the cause of civilization, religion and good morals." The newspaper reiterated this sentiment four months later in February 1865, claiming, "For every proposition to surrender the great ideas on which this war was inaugurated, we encounter a rebuff. Must we then abandon our principles and go down with the double sham of surrender first and defeat afterwards? Forbid it Heaven!"[37]

If 1864 marked the epitome of hard war, 1865 witnessed a shift toward greater magnanimity, at least by the Union. The turning point seems to have coincided with the Hampton Roads Peace Conference. Held on February 3, 1865, aboard the River Queen near Fort Monroe, the conference marked the most direct interaction between the leaders of the Union and Confederate governments during the war. Organized by Francis P. Blair, who hoped to craft a reunification of the Union and the Confederacy through a joint invasion of Mexico, the meeting brought together Confederate vice president Alexander Stephens, Senator Robert Hunter, and Assistant Secretary of State (and former Supreme Court justice) John Campbell with President Lincoln and Secretary of State Seward. After nearly four years of war, all five men had doubts that the conference could bring about a peaceful resolution. Old friends from their time together in Congress twenty years earlier, Lincoln and Stephens greeted each other warmly. By mutual consent they agreed that this would be an informal conference, without an official transcript. Although Lincoln quickly dismissed Blair's fanciful Mexican filibuster, he entertained multiple proposals from the Confederate delegates for a peaceful end to the war. Lincoln laid out three conditions for peace: Confederates must lay down their arms, recognize the authority of the Union ("The restoration of the Union is a sine qua non with me," Lincoln told them), and recognize slavery's end. Lincoln shared with the Confederates a copy of the Thirteenth Amendment, abolishing slavery, which had recently passed Congress, hinting that Confederates could help shape the transition to free labor were the war to end soon. Hunter, the most militant of the three Confederate delegates, took offense at Lincoln's peace terms, saying they amounted to "an unconditional surrender on the part of the Confederate States and her people." Seward rejected Hunter's interpretation of the Union position, claiming that nothing in Lincoln's statement amounted to "unconditional submission to conquerors, or as having anything humiliating about it." On the contrary, Seward claimed that "the Northern people were weary of war" and "desired peace and a restoration of harmony." At an impasse, the conference ended after four hours with nothing approaching a consensus for a political solution. If peace were to come, it would be the product of victory on the battlefield.[38]

Historians have often dismissed the Hampton Roads Peace Conference as inconsequential; Lincoln himself concluded that "the conference ended without result." However, in two contradictory ways, the conference transformed the discourse on surrender and shaped the war's final chapters. First, it contributed to a reopening of prisoner exchange. Just before the conference's conclusion, Stephens broached the subject with Lincoln, asking Lincoln to authorize a special exchange for his nephew, John Stephens, who had been captured at Port Hudson and held for the past twenty months at Johnson's Island. Lincoln assured him that he would and encouraged Stephens to broach the subject of a more general prisoner exchange with Grant before he returned to Richmond.[39]

Although Stephens was unaware of it, Grant had over the previous month taken steps to reopen prisoner exchange. On January 7, 1865, he dismissed Benjamin Butler from his post as exchange commissioner, removing that particular barrier to negotiations with the Confederate commissioner. By late January, Grant had reached an agreement with Confederate officials to resume a general exchange. The week of the Hampton Roads conference, Grant had sent a flurry of letters to Union prison administrators, indicating his intention to parole as many as 3,000 prisoners a week. A quick census of Union prisons indicated that they held more than 66,000 Confederate soldiers. Not wanting to strengthen Lee's army, Grant informed prison officials that they should prioritize injured prisoners and prisoners from Union-occupied territory for exchange. Less than a week after Hampton Roads, the first significant prisoner exchange in more than a year took place at City Point, and exchanges would continue with only occasional interruption until the war's conclusion.[40]

Grant decided to reopen prisoner exchange despite not resolving the issues that led to its demise. Confederates continued to refuse to grant black prisoners equal standing or to account for the numerous irregularities in their application of the Dix-Hill cartel's regulations. Instead, Lincoln and Grant hoped that the reopening of exchange would signal their intention to treat surrendering Confederates magnanimously. It was a message that Lincoln reiterated to Grant, Sherman, and Rear Admiral David Dixon Porter aboard the *River Queen* on March 28, 1865. According to Porter, "Lincoln came down to City Point with the most liberal views toward the rebels. . . . He wanted peace on almost any terms. . . . His heart was tenderness throughout, and, as long as the rebels laid down their arms, he did not care how it was done." Lincoln wanted to avoid unnecessary bloodshed and hoped that Grant and Sherman could compel Lee's and Johnston's armies to surrender. As to the terms of surrender, Lincoln indicated that he would be amendable to almost any conditions that the Confederates required, so long as the generals did not offer any political guarantees. "Let them surrender and go home," Lincoln told them; "they will not take up arms again. Let them all go, officers and all, let them have them have their horses to plow with and, if you like, their guns to shoot crows with. . . . Give them the most liberal and honorable of terms."[41]

While Lincoln adopted a more conciliatory stance after Hampton Roads, Confederates concluded that the conference's failure indicated that the only options available to them were fighting to the bitter end or surrendering unconditionally. At a rally in Richmond held upon the commissioners' return, Jefferson Davis and Virginia governor William "Extra Billy" Smith told the assembled masses that the Confederacy would not accept anything short of full independence and slavery. Virginia, Governor Smith told them, "would sacrifice everything that remained to her, soon than surrender." Following Smith at the podium, Davis said, "We had now learned the terms on which the enemy are willing to accord peace. We are required to make an unconditional surrender." Such a surrender would be disastrous for the white people of the South, as a vindictive North would exact its retribution and Southerners would be forced to take "what a conqueror may choose to give the conquered." Other Confederate leaders tended to follow Davis's lead, even those who had fought with him in the past. "Having made . . . a fair and honest effort to obtain peace by negotiation [at Hampton Roads]," observed North Carolina governor Zebulon Vance, "there is only one thing left for us to do. We must fight, my countrymen, to the last extremity, or submit voluntarily to our own degradation."[42]

Surrender and the Hard War

7

A CONVULSION AT APPOMATTOX

Robert E. Lee, Ulysses S. Grant, and the Uneasy Peace

Historian Bruce Catton titled the 1953 Pulitzer Prize–winning final volume of his Army of the Potomac trilogy *A Stillness at Appomattox*. Catton's choice of title reflected his belief that something singular and sacred transpired in Wilmer McLean's parlor between Union general Ulysses S. Grant and Confederate general Robert E. Lee. Yet despite its prominence in the title, Catton devoted only the book's two final pages to events in Appomattox Courthouse. In Catton's recounting, once flags of truce appeared on April 9, 1865, "no one could doubt that Lee was going to surrender." Both armies fell under the spell of "the enormous silence," a phrase Catton also used as the title of the book's culminating chapter. As a final image, Catton described Grant arriving at the McLean house, asking if Lee had arrived, and ascending the porch steps. Everything afterward—the surrender negotiations themselves, the stacking of arms, and the distribution of paroles—Catton left to the reader's imagination.[1]

Bruce Catton's retelling of Lee's surrender drew upon and reinforced one of the central myths of Appomattox: that it was a unique event, without parallel or precedent during the Civil War or even in American history. Yet Appomattox was the product of four years of conflict in which surrender had often played a prominent role and was the first in series of surrenders that would signify Confederate defeat. Far from an isolated event, Appomattox reflected the experience of earlier surrenders and shaped those that came later. Placing Appomattox within the long history of Civil War surrenders reveals an event more complex and contentious than popular memory suggests. Far from a stillness, Lee's surrender at Appomattox created a tumultuous thunder that reverberated throughout his army and across the Confederacy.

Many of the participants at Appomattox drew on their prior experiences with surrender. Union general Ulysses S. Grant had secured surrenders at Fort Donelson and Vicksburg, victories that had made him famous and had prompted his promotion. While Grant brought his experience accepting Confederate surrenders to Appomattox, many of his officers could sympathize with the surrendering enemy, having themselves been forced to raise the white flag. Indeed, among the highest ranks of Grant's army were veterans of the major Union surrenders, including Fort Sumter (Samuel Wylie Crawford and Truman Seymour), San Augustin Springs (Alfred Gibbs), and Harpers Ferry (Samuel Armstrong). Deeper in the ranks, one could find hundreds of Union soldiers who had surrendered and spent time in Confederate prisons, including many who had only recently returned to arms after the reopening of prisoner exchange. Lee's army drew on a similar wealth of experience. Lee himself had witnessed the aftermath of Twiggs's surrender at San Antonio. More importantly, one of every five soldiers in Lee's army had spent time in a Union prison, and they brought these memories with them to Appomattox. Some former prisoners, captured at the height of the exchange regime in 1862 and early 1863, had experienced only brief confinement. However, many former prisoners in Lee's army had surrendered later in the war, after the exchange regime's collapse, had suffered for months in increasingly overcrowded camps, and had only returned to service in early 1865 with the resumption of regular exchanges. For such men, the trauma of confinement remained fresh, and they were not eager to repeat it. Far from neophytes to surrender, both armies at Appomattox brought a profound understanding and appreciation of how surrender worked and what raising the white flag meant. Their diverse experiences with surrender colored their expectations and interpretations of Appomattox.

Months before Appomattox, a few Confederate officials believed that the best course of action was surrender. Foremost among them was former U.S. vice president and Confederate secretary of war John C. Breckinridge. Convinced by early 1865 that Confederate defeat was inevitable, Breckinridge argued that "the Confederacy should not be captured in fragments," but "we should surrender as a government, and we will thus maintain the dignity of our cause, and secure the respect of our enemies, and the best terms for our soldiers." He recognized that surrender carried some risk, particularly for those who might face prosecution for treason. Nonetheless, Breckinridge maintained that "this has been a magnificent epic, in God's name let it not terminate in a farce." Jefferson Davis, however, steadfastly refused to consider any outcome short of complete Confederate independence. Davis's intransigence grew out of both a stubborn faith in Confederate destiny and his belief that his moral and political obligations to his office precluded surrender when it would result in his country's demise. As Davis told John Campbell, the Confederate "Constitution did not allow him to treat for his own suicide." Reluctant to cross Davis, the Confederate Congress ignored pleas by Breckinridge, Robert M. T. Hunter, and others to seek a political resolution that would stop the bloodshed. The war would continue, Davis believed, until Confederate independence had been achieved.[2]

In an odd confluence of interests, Abraham Lincoln agreed with Jefferson Davis that the Confederacy could not surrender. Maintaining his position on Confederate illegitimacy, Lincoln had refused to engage in direct political negotiations with Richmond throughout the war. Lincoln believed any kind of diplomatic relationship, even for the purpose of accepting Confederate surrender, would amount to formal recognition. With this in mind, Lincoln gave Grant careful instructions only to meet with Lee "for the capitulation of General Lee's army or some minor or purely military matter," and that he was "not to decide, discuss, or confer upon any political question."[3] As a consequence of Lincoln's and Davis's positions, the Confederate government would not and could not surrender; only Confederate armies could. At the start of 1865, Confederates fielded seven major distinct armies or departments, plus dozens of "independent" commands and guerilla bands. Once Davis's government abandoned Richmond and the already tenuous lines of communication broke down completely, each of these remaining armies functioned nearly autonomously. Before the Union government could proclaim victory, it would have to negotiate surrenders with each of these rebel armies.

This confluence of Union and Confederate policy had significant consequences for Lee's surrender at Appomattox and for the surrenders to come after it. Although Lee's Army of Northern Virginia held special symbolic and strategic value, its surrender would only sacrifice a portion of the Confederacy's military resources, leaving the other armies intact. Political policies that limited surrender negotiations to purely military affairs effectively constrained the field of options available to Lee and Grant, simplifying and expediting the surrender process. Armed with Lincoln's instructions at City Point to provide liberal terms, Grant could concede to whatever conditions Lee required, so long as they did not venture into the political sphere. Consequently, negotiations at Appomattox and most other terminal surrender sites tended to be brief and without significant rancor. The significant exception to this, as will be demonstrated in Chapter 8, occurred when generals exceeded their mandates not to incorporate political questions into surrender negotiations.

By February 1865, Robert E. Lee had concluded that his war could not be won on the battlefield. He privately expressed his reservations about prolonging the war unnecessarily, believing that continuing to fight when ultimate defeat loomed only produced unnecessary bloodshed. The siege of Petersburg, now in its ninth month, had weakened and depleted his army. After the Hampton Roads conference, Lee visited Robert M. T. Hunter, one of the Confederate commissioners, to assess Lincoln's disposition. He listened to Hunter's complaints about Davis's intransigence and urged him to seek a political peace if he could "secure better terms than were likely to be given after a surrender at discretion." Lee balked, however, when Hunter suggested that he confront Davis or publicly support a political settlement, arguing that "if he were to recommend peace negotiations publicly it would be almost equivalent to surrender." Although Lee "never said to me he thought the chances [for victory] were over," Hunter believed that "the tone and tenor of his remarks" spoke volumes.[4]

Those who knew Lee best observed a palpable change in his demeanor in February 1865. Summoned to Lee's headquarters at 2:00 in the morning, Gen. John Brown Gordon found him "entirely alone, . . . standing at the fireplace, his arm on the mantel and his head resting on his arm as he gazed into the coal fire burning in the grate." Gordon noted that the burdens of command manifested themselves in Lee's body as he had never seen before. "I had known before I came that our army was in desperate straits," Gordon recalled, "but when I entered that room I realized at once, from the gravity of the commander's bearing, that I was to learn of a situation worse than I had anticipated." Lee had spent the previous hours mulling over "a long table covered with recent reports from every portion of his army" and wanted to know Gordon's assessment. Together, the two men went through the reports for two hours, Lee highlighting the key passages. "The revelation was startling," Gordon noted. "Each report was bad enough, and all the distressing facts combined were sufficient, it seemed to me, to destroy all cohesive power and lead to the inevitable disintegration of any other army that was ever marshalled." Gordon had known that Union forces outnumbered Confederates, but he was "not prepared for the picture presented by these reports of extreme destitution—of the lack of shoes, of hats, of overcoats, and of blankets, as well as of food," leaving many rebel soldiers unable to shoulder a weapon. In Lee's calculations, only 35,000 of 50,000 soldiers in the Army of Northern Virginia were fit for combat, compared with 150,000 well-supplied Union troops in the region. Asked for his assessment, Gordon provided Lee with three options. Gordon recommended that Lee "make terms with the enemy, the best we

Lee, Grant, and the Uneasy Peace

can get." Alternatively, Gordon suggested that Lee "abandon Richmond and Petersburg, unite by rapid marches with General Johnston in North Carolina, and strike Sherman before Grant can join him," or he could attempt to fight his way out of Petersburg. Lee reluctantly admitted that he shared Gordon's assessment. Asked if he had shared his views with either President Davis or the Confederate Congress, Lee demurred, claiming that he "scarcely felt authorized to suggest to the civil authorities the advisability of making terms with the Government of the United States."[5]

Lee's deference to civilian government severely limited his options. Proscribed by both honor and Davis's policy from discussing surrender until compelled to do so, Lee weighed the merits of Gordon's final two options. After a visit to Richmond to meet with Davis, Lee again summoned Gordon to plan their next steps. "Of President Davis," Gordon recalled, Lee "spoke in terms of strong eulogy: of the strength of his convictions, of his devotedness, of his remarkable faith in the possibility of still winning our independence, and of his unconquerable will power." Davis refused to consider peace negotiations, nor would he contemplate abandoning Petersburg, which would necessitate the capital's evacuation, leaving "but one thing that we could do—fight." Lee tasked Gordon with orchestrating a concentrated attack on Union lines. The ensuing Battle of Fort Stedman on March 25 demonstrated the futility of attempting future offensive assaults. Less than a week later, a Union victory at the Battle of Five Forks compromised the Southside Railroad, Petersburg's and Richmond's main supply artery. The following day, on April 2, Lee telegraphed Davis that Petersburg would have to be abandoned and that Richmond should be evacuated as soon as possible.[6]

Lee's departure from Petersburg put the Army of Northern Virginia on the path to surrender. Beaten down after months of siege, Lee's army limped westward in a vain effort to resupply at Danville before reuniting with Joseph Johnston's Army of Tennessee, which was then licking its wounds in Smithfield, North Carolina, after its defeat at Bentonville. Plagued in retreat by Grant's larger, better supplied, and more maneuverable army, the Army of Northern Virginia suffered from a series of disastrous defeats, most significantly at Sailor's Creek on April 6, where Lee lost one-fifth of his remaining army. These defeats on the battlefield were only one factor in the rapid collapse of Lee's army. Between Five Forks and Appomattox, the Army of Northern Virginia shrank by nearly half; only a portion of its losses were the result of combat. Malnourished for months and without rations since they left Petersburg, many rebel soldiers could not maintain the forced marches, fell by the roadside, and were subsequently captured by pursuing Union cavalry. Soldiers who deserted during the Appomattox Campaign cited multiple factors that drove them to abandon their regiments. Hunger and exhaustion played a significant role and helped to blur the lines between soldiers who chose to desert and those who physically could not continue.[7]

In combat, Confederate soldiers demonstrated a renewed willingness to surrender. At Five Forks, Namozine Church, and Sailor's Creek, thousands of Confederate soldiers threw up their hands rather than fight in what many now believed were pointless battles. Union soldiers noted that rebels seemed relieved to have been taken prisoner. Charles Mattocks, a sharpshooter from Maine, noted on April 3, "I should judge from the number of Rebel deserters and voluntary prisoners that the hopes of the Confederacy are about exhausted." Captured at the Wilderness, Mattocks had recently been exchanged after nearly eleven months in Confederate prisons and had returned to his regiment only four days earlier. Shortly before the surrender at Appomattox, Mattocks observed that "the enemy are in full retreat. Many of them are falling into our hands. They are sadly 'demoralized' and many of them will soon find that 'last ditch.'"[8] On April 6, Philip Sheridan informed Grant that his cavalry had "routed them handsomely" at Sailor's Creek, capturing "several thousand prisoners," including eight generals. "If the thing is pressed," Sheridan noted, "I think that Lee will surrender." When his message was forwarded to Lincoln, the president added, "Let the thing be pressed."[9]

While most of Lee's army showed increased willingness to surrender, others deserted, fearing what would happen if and when they surrendered. This fear seemed particularly prevalent in units with many former prisoners of war, especially those only recently exchanged. Nearly half of Richmond's Orange Light Battery had spent some time in a Union prison, including thirty-three soldiers captured at Spotsylvania Courthouse in May 1864 and confined at Fort Delaware. When a handful were exchanged in February 1865, they bore news that seven of their comrades had died in prison and that the remainder continued to languish in confinement. Convinced that a surrender would result in an indefinite prison sentence, many of the soldiers conspired to desert rather than be taken captive. Alexander Kean, a member of the Orange Light Battery, noted that "for many days prior to Lee's surrender there were rumors that there would be a surrender. There was a great unrest among the troops and the whole country was overrun with deserters from our army. Many men in my company deserted, fearing that when the surrender took place—and not one of us doubted it would soon come—they would be imprisoned." By the

Lee, Grant, and the Uneasy Peace

time of Lee's surrender, only twenty-one members of the Orange Light Battery remained to take their paroles.[10]

Like Lee and his army, Jefferson Davis and the rest of the Confederate government sought refuge in the west. After abandoning Richmond on April 2, the mobile rebel cabinet relocated to Danville. There Davis issued a lengthy proclamation, "To the People of the Confederates States," a bold if delusional statement about his vision for the Confederate future. "We have now entered upon a new phase of a struggle," Davis argued,

> the memory of which is to endure for all ages and to shed an increasing luster upon our country. Relieved from the necessity of guarding cities and particular points, important but not vital to our defense, with an army free to move from point to point and strike in detail the detachments and garrisons of the enemy, operating on the interior of our own country, where supplies are more accessible, and where the foe will be far removed from his own base and cut off from all succor in case of reverse, nothing is now needed to render our triumph certain but the exhibition of our own unquenchable resolve. Let us but will it, and we are free.[11]

Historians have hotly debated what Davis meant by a "new phase of a struggle." Some scholars have suggested that Davis intended to transform the war into a guerilla conflict, enabling Confederate resistance to continue long after the fall of Richmond. Others have suggested that Davis simply meant that Lee's army, no longer burdened with the defense of Petersburg and Richmond, could now fight a conventional war in the open. Still others have dismissed Davis's comments altogether as the inconsequential pronouncements of a political leader struggling to maintain power and legitimacy. They note that Davis also promised to defend "every foot" of Confederate territory, a demonstrable absurdity, given events on the ground.[12] If the Confederate war effort did enter a new phase during the first week of April 1865, it concerned the relationship between military leaders and civilian government. Although Davis remained the titular head of the Confederacy until his capture in Irwinville, Georgia, on May 10, his ability to effectively communicate government policy to generals in the field largely evaporated once he fled Richmond. With the exception of Johnston's surrender at Bennett Place, Davis had no direct influence on the location, timing, or terms of Confederate surrenders. His generals would decide the fate of their armies without Davis's input.

Two days after Davis's proclamation that the Confederate war effort would continue indefinitely, Gen. William Pendleton counseled Lee that "the cause had become so hopeless" that he should consider surrendering. Earlier that day Pendleton had met with a cadre of generals, including Gordon, Edward Porter Alexander, and Longstreet, who begrudging agreed that surrender provided the only reasonable option left and appointed Pendleton, Lee's West Point classmate, to present their case to the general. As Alexander described it, "The prospect of being surrendered had suddenly become a topic of general conversation. Indeed no man who looked at our situation on a map, or who understood the geography of the country, could fail to see that Gen. Grant now had us completely in a trap." Pendleton pleaded with Lee to approach Grant for terms to prevent pointless further bloodshed. Seated beneath a large pine tree, Lee listened thoughtfully before rejecting the proposal. "I trust it has not come to that," Lee argued. "We certainly have too many brave men to think of laying down our arms." Moreover, Lee noted, "if I were to intimate to General Grant that I would listen to terms, he would at once regard it as such an evidence of weakness that he would demand unconditional surrender, and sooner than that I am resolved to die. Indeed, we all must determine to die at our posts."[13] Pendleton's recounting of the conversation may not have captured Lee's words verbatim, but it undoubtedly reflected his unwillingness to surrender prematurely.

Later that same evening, Lee received the first of four letters from Grant that would result in his surrender at Appomattox Courthouse. Grant chose his words with great care, intending to project both strength and magnanimity: "The results of the last week must convince you of the hopelessness of further resistance on the part of the Army of Northern Virginia in this struggle. I feel that it is so, and regard it as my duty to shift from myself the responsibility of any further effusion of blood by asking of you the surrender of that portion of the Confederate army known as the Army of Northern Virginia."[14] As historian Elizabeth Varon has observed, Grant's language drew upon not only his own prior experience with surrender but also the long history of surrender in the United States. His usage of the phrase "further effusion of blood" echoed and evoked George Washington's message to Lord Cornwallis at Yorktown in 1781 in which he expressed his "ardent desire to spare the further effusion of blood." Grant himself had used the phrase in his correspondence with General Pendleton prior to Vicksburg's surrender. Indeed, it formed the backbone of surrender discourse throughout the Civil War, appearing as a rhetorical device at the surrenders of Fort Sumter, San Augustin Springs, Fort Pulaski, Fort Jackson, Fort Macon, Port Hudson, Cumberland Gap, and Fort Pillow.[15] Its ubiquity reflected the common understanding that a desire to avoid an imminent massacre formed the foundation of an honorable surrender.

Lee, Grant, and the Uneasy Peace

Grant's brief message also placed the onus on Lee to decide upon the immediate future course of the war. By requesting and not demanding his surrender, Grant allowed Lee some room to negotiate and save face, while simultaneously transferring responsibility for the decimation of Lee's army were the request denied. If Grant expected Lee to accept this initial gambit, he was mistaken. After reading Grant's letter, Lee handed it to Longstreet without comment. Longstreet, who had equivocated over the past couple of days about the merits of surrender, read the note and returned it to Lee, muttering, "Not yet." In his written response to Grant, Lee challenged his assessment about the "hopelessness of further resistance," although he shared "your desire to avoid useless effusion of blood." Before he could submit to Grant's request, Lee would need further details on "the terms you will offer on condition of its [the Army of Northern Virginia's] surrender."[16] Lee's brief message, like Grant's, served several purposes. In neither accepting nor explicitly rejecting Grant's suggestion, Lee communicated a willingness to entertain surrender in the future without compromising his negotiating position. Furthermore, his query about terms might buy his army time to escape, as he hoped Grant would forestall a major engagement with the possibility of surrender still in the air.

The following morning, April 8, Grant penned his response to Lee. "Peace being my great desire," Grant wrote, "there is but one condition I would insist upon, namely, that the men and officers surrendered shall be disqualified for taking up arms against the Government of the United States until properly exchanged." This final point, both Grant and Lee knew, was a fiction designed to appeal to Lee's sense of honor; although the soldiers would be paroled on the battlefield, not unlike at Vicksburg, they would never be exchanged. Beyond this, so long as it did not touch upon political questions, everything was negotiable. "I will meet you," Grant concluded, "at any point agreeable to you, for the purpose of arranging definitely the terms upon which the surrender of the Army of Northern Virginia will be received."[17] In the meantime, Grant ordered his forces to vigorously continue their pursuit of Lee's army. That afternoon a detachment from Sheridan's cavalry led by George Armstrong Custer and Wesley Merritt seized Appomattox Station, the railroad depot southwest of Appomattox Courthouse, capturing artillery and supplies for Lee's army and effectively cutting off his escape to the west.

Although Grant had written his second message at daybreak, Lee did not receive it until sunset. Rejecting his staff officer Charles Venable's suggestion to ignore it, Lee penned a confusing and meandering response that reflected the chaotic disarray of his army. He claimed that his earlier message did not signal his intent to surrender, only to inquire about possible terms. "To be frank," Lee wrote, "I do not think the emergency has arisen to call for the surrender of this army, but as . . . the restoration of peace should be sole object of all," he proposed a meeting the following morning, not "with a view to surrender the Army of North Virginia" but to "tend to the restoration of peace."[18] Lee did not articulate how a "restoration of peace" differed in form or substance from surrender, although he may have envisioned some kind of broader political settlement. If so, Lee would have been exceeding his authority, as Jefferson Davis had made clear his intention to continue the war effort.

That evening, while he awaited Grant's response, Lee held a final meeting with his officers to assess the situation. According to Gordon, "The last sad Confederate council of war . . . met in the woods at his headquarters and by a low-burning bivouac-fire. There was no tent there, no table, no chairs, and no camp-stools. On blankets spread upon the ground or on saddles at the roots of the trees, we sat around the great commander." After the disaster at Sailor's Creek, only Gordon, Pendleton, Longstreet, and Fitzhugh Lee remained of Lee's corps commanders. Hearing cannon fire from Appomattox Station, they knew that Union forces not only were pursuing them but blocked their intended route. The only question remaining was if they could somehow break free of the Union stranglehold. The subdued discussion reflected the resignation that had overcome Lee's army. At daybreak, they would make one final effort to break through the Union cordon to rendezvous with Johnston; if that failed, Lee would meet with Grant to surrender. Few of them, Lee included, expected the plan to succeed. Later that evening, well after midnight, Pendleton visited Lee in his quarters and was surprised to find him "dressed in his neatest style, new uniform, snowy linens." When asked about his apparel, Lee explained stoically that the day would likely end with him "as General Grant's prisoner, and thought I must make my best appearance."[19]

While Lee fretted over the likely outcome of the next morning's attack, Grant pondered what to make of his opponent's last letter. Suffering from a debilitating migraine, he soaked his feet in a tub of hot water and applied mustard plasters to his neck and wrists. Unable to focus his eyes, Grant had an aide read Lee's letter aloud. "Peace," as far as Grant could tell, suggested a political settlement, something that Lincoln had expressly prohibited. "I have no authority to treat on the subject of peace," Grant wrote, but "I am equally anxious for peace with yourself, and the whole North entertains the same feeling." Grant then reiterated his terms for surrender: "The terms upon which peace can be had are well understood. By the South laying their arms they will hasten that most desirable event, save thousands of lives, and hundreds of millions of property

Lee, Grant, and the Uneasy Peace

not yet destroyed." Grant closed his letter noting that he was "seriously hoping that all our difficulties may be settled without the loss of another life."[20]

The following morning proceeded as Lee had anticipated. The daybreak attempt to break the Union cordon failed. Sheridan observed that as soon as "the hopelessness of a further attack" became apparent, "the gray lines instinctively halted." Observing the developing situation from a ridge west of Appomattox Courthouse, Lee rejected a proposal by Edward Porter Alexander to use the remaining artillery ammunition, arguing that the infantry's disorganized state precluded any effective action at this point. "Then, general," Alexander argued, "we have choice of but two courses: to surrender, or to order the army to disperse, and, every man for himself, to take to the woods and make his way either to Johnston's army in Carolina, or to his home, taking his arms, and reporting to the governor of his State." Alexander pressed Lee to take the second option, arguing that "if there is any hope for the Confederacy, it is in delay. But, if this army is surrendered to-day, the Confederacy is gone. The morale of this army has sustained both the people at home and the other armies. Our surrender would demoralize all." On a strategic level, Alexander observed that their surrender would allow Grant to turn his army, "one hundred thousand men, released from duty here, against Johnston, Taylor, and Kirby Smith, they will all go, one after the other, like a row of bricks." Lee listened carefully to Alexander's proposal, but he had already made up his mind about how to proceed. "I appreciate that the surrender of this army is, indeed the end of the Confederacy," he said. "But that result is now inevitable, and must be faced." Ordering the army to disperse and live off the land, Lee argued, would make them "little better than bands of robbers." The ensuing devastation of the South proved too high a price to pay. Lee assured Alexander that Grant would provide generous terms and that he would surrender the army later that day.[21]

By ten o'clock that morning, flags of truce appeared along both Union and Confederate lines, signaling a cease-fire, although Grant and Lee did not meet in the McLean parlor until approximately 1:30 in the afternoon. Early that morning Grant had embarked on a circuitous twenty-two-mile ride to Sheridan's lines and consequently had not received Lee's message until just before noon. "When the offer reached me," Grant noted in his memoirs, "I was still suffering with the sick headache, but the instant I saw the contents of the note I was instantly cured."[22] The five-hour interval between the cease-fire and Lee's departure from the McLean house at the conclusion of the surrender conference allowed soldiers ample time to come to grips with the inevitability of surrender before they learned what terms Lee and Grant had agreed to. While most historians have focused on what transpired in Wilmer McLean's parlor that afternoon, the situation outside may have been more dramatic.

More than a few soldiers expressed surprise and confusion when they learned of the cease-fire. An Alabama surgeon claimed that when news of the cease-fire reached Mahone's division, the soldiers were incredulous, as "they had not thought of surrender." This surprise seems have been more prevalent among Union soldiers, some of whom believed that Lee would never surrender. When he heard from a Confederate messenger under a flag of truce that Lee intended to surrender, Maine's Joshua Chamberlain felt blindsided. "Surrender? We had no rumor of this," he recalled. The revelation prompted "a tumult of heart and brain" as Chamberlain sought to master his emotions. By contrast, most Confederates soldiers had anticipated surrender, resigned themselves to its inevitability, and prepared for its eventuality. One Richmond artillerist noted in his diary on April 8 that "the question of our surrender is now one of time only."[23]

For Confederates, the cease-fire brought to a halt the almost incessant marching that had commenced with the abandonment of Petersburg. More than a few men had not slept or eaten in days. They were physically and mentally exhausted, and the pause brought forth a panoply of emotions. Pvt. John Wilson Warr of the Palmetto Sharpshooters noted that when "the news reached us 10 1//2 o'clock all fighting ceased and grate [sic] confusion took place among our men. Some were wishing they had never been borned[,] some were crying[,] cursing[,] some praying." One North Carolinian recalled a similar scene; hearing news of the cease-fire, "some broke into tears, some threw down their guns, others broke them against trees." For many Confederates, this initial anger tempered to anxiety, depression, and resentment. One Georgia soldier who witnessed Lee riding to the McLean house noted that "doubt, sadness, [and] gloom, settled upon our hearts" as they awaited his return.[24]

The lengthy cease-fire engendered palpable apprehension among both Union and Confederate soldiers. A New Jersey soldier recalled that "the hours dragged slowly along; anxiety was intense. Every man knew that the truce indicated a continuance of negotiations for surrender and that the end could not be long delayed." Although most expected the negotiations to culminate in Lee's surrender, the terms remained uncertain, especially to the enlisted men and officers who had not been privy to the contents of Lee and Grant's correspondence. If the negotiations failed, hostilities could immediately resume. Only returned to duty a month earlier, "after a long absence as a prisoner," rebel captain John C. Gorman noted that "eager hopes hung on

Lee, Grant, and the Uneasy Peace

the interview between the opposing great commanders of the two armies. Peace might follow this interview. It might end in resumption of hostilities, in fiercest battle, in terrible carnage. The two armies were plainly visible to one another."[25]

Some soldiers took the lengthy cease-fire as an opportunity to converse with the enemy, most often by yelling across the expanse that separated them but occasionally by venturing into the no-man's-land between the pickets. The most significant of these gatherings took place in the village, not far from the courthouse and the McLean residence, where Confederate and Union generals, most of them prewar army acquaintances, awkwardly passed the time. "For the first time in four years prominent officers on both sides, who had not met, except in battle, during that time, mingled together," recalled Union general John Gibbon. Although someone thoughtfully passed around a whiskey flask, "no one felt like talking much." The small circle included Confederates James Longstreet, Henry Heth, John Gordon, and Cadmus Wilcox and Union officers Philip Sheridan, Wesley Merritt, and Edward Ord, some of the highest-ranking and best-informed individuals in either army. Privy to much of the correspondence between Lee and Grant, these men had a much greater sense of the negotiating landscape than almost anyone at Appomattox. Nonetheless, "all wore an air of anxiety," Gibbon recalled, "though all seemed hopeful that there would be no further need of bloodshed." Although Lee's conference with Grant lasted less than two hours, "to those of us, who were waiting outside," Gibbon noted, "the time dragged slowly along."[26]

Not all Confederates waited patiently to hear the results of Lee's conference with Grant. Fearing that Grant would exact harsh terms, including lengthy prison terms, some Southerners used the cease-fire to escape Appomattox.[27] This fear was particularly pronounced among soldiers who had only recently been exchanged and had experienced the nadir of prison life. South Carolinian Berry Benson told his brigade commander that "I had been in prison once, and I was not going to again." With his officer's tacit approval, he escaped through the lines to Johnston's army in North Carolina, arriving just prior to Johnston's surrender. Chaplain John Paris observed that the appearance of flags of truce prompted intense "excitement among the officers and men. . . . Many propose to fight out to the bitter end rather than Surrender. Others are determined to take to the bushes and thus take care of themselves." Fearing indefinite detention, Paris "made my arrangements to take to the woods, reach my family if possible," only to be dissuaded by an officer who appealed to his sense of duty.

While Paris felt obliged to remain, others believed that their duty to their country and cause required them to continue the struggle elsewhere. "My first and only duty was to my country," wrote South Carolinian David Gregg McIntosh, "as long as I could be of service to her I should avoid surrender." McIntosh led like-minded rebels, who tore off their military insignias, through the woods, evading Union patrols. Upon hearing of Lee and Grant's conference, Gen. Martin Gary defiantly proclaimed that "South Carolinians did not surrender." With a small escort, Gary escaped through the lines on horseback, intending to rendezvous with Jefferson Davis. Similarly, Ham Chamberlayne, a Virginia artillery officer, could not stomach the spectacle, noting that many soldiers "refuse to attend the funeral at Appomattox C.H. & as soon as the surrender was certain we cut or crept our way out. . . . I am going to Johns[t]on's Army & and if they can do nothing here, I am off for Raymond & thence to Texas. . . . I am not conquered by any means & shall not be while alive."[28]

By April 19, Chamberlayne, Gary, and McIntosh had all traveled as far as Charlotte, where Jefferson Davis had established a temporary headquarters. There McIntosh, weighing his options, wrote to Jefferson Davis for guidance. He explained that he "made my escape . . . believing a Surrender of that army to be imminent, and not wishing to be included in the Surrender." McIntosh wanted Davis's "opinion as to how my Status as an officer" had been affected. When Davis failed to respond, McIntosh reluctantly returned home.[29] Chamberlayne rode on, venturing into Mississippi, before he concluded that continued resistance was futile. Gary continued on with Jefferson Davis as an escort until the party reached his mother's home of Cokesbury, South Carolina, where he decided to remain.

How many Confederates joined McIntosh, Gary, and Chamberlayne in escaping during the cease-fire remains unclear, although the evidence suggests that they numbered in the hundreds. The departure of so many "diehard" Confederates (to use historian Jason Phillips's term) further fragmented Lee's already decimated army. Those that remained, only 10,000 men by Lee's estimation, represented an intriguing remnant of the Army of Northern Virginia. Maintaining profound faith in Lee's leadership and willing to abide by whatever settlement Lee could negotiate, these remaining Confederate soldiers found solace in the fact that if Lee could marshal the courage to surrender, they could as well. Those who saw Lee before the surrender conference, astride Traveller and garbed in an immaculate uniform, took comfort in his patrician bearing. "We are all satisfied with Uncle Robert," one Virginian noted. "He always did right."[30]

Lee, Grant, and the Uneasy Peace

Tasked with finding a suitable location for surrender negotiations, Lee's aide Charles Marshall selected Wilmer McLean's house, the grandest residence in the hamlet of Appomattox Courthouse. Fronted by a wide staircase that opened onto a white-columned porch, the three-story brick Greek Revival house stood not far from the courthouse, just off the stage road connecting Richmond and Lynchburg that ran through town. Marshall discovered, to his amusement, that the home's owner had "lived on the battle-field of Bull Run, but had remove to Appomattox Courthouse to get out of the way of the war."[31] Having selected a site, Marshall retrieved Lee and Col. Orville Babcock, his equivalent on Grant's staff. The three men waited in the parlor for about half an hour before Grant's arrival, Babcock nervously checking the window every few minutes.

Every description of the surrender conference noted the physical difference between Lee and Grant. By the time that Grant wrote his memoirs in 1885, their study in contrast had become such a clichéd element in the surrender narrative that he too included it. Grant noted that "as I had not expected so soon the result that was then taking place, and consequentially was in rough garb. I was without a sword, as I usually was when on horseback on the field, and wore a soldier's blouse for a coat, with the shoulder straps of my rank to indicate to the army who I was." By contrast, "General Lee was dressed in a full uniform which was entirely new, and was wearing a sword of considerable value. . . . In my rough travelling suit, the uniform of a private with the straps of a lieutenant-general, I must have contrasted very strangely with a man so handsomely dressed, six feet high and of faultless form." Although many commentators have sought to divine some insight into Lee's and Grant's characters and mentality based on their appearance at Appomattox, the most straightforward analysis suggests that Lee had little faith in that morning's offensive and believed surrender inevitable, while Grant did not expect Confederates to capitulate so soon. As Grant noted in his memoirs, Lee wore "an entirely different sword from the one that would ordinarily be worn in the field." Grant had dressed for battle; Lee, for a funeral.[32]

A more meaningful and purposeful distinction between the two commanders also became evident upon Grant's arrival. Whereas Lee had only Charles Marshall accompany him to the convention, Grant brought most of his senior officers and aides. A dozen men escorted Grant into the McLean parlor, including Robert Todd Lincoln, the president's son, and Ely Parker, a Seneca Indian on Grant's staff who would draft the final copy of the surrender agreement. As historian Elizabeth Varon has pointed out, Lee may have been attempting to shield his generals from the humiliation they might have experienced in attending the surrender conference, while Grant sought to share the honor as broadly as possible. Moreover, Grant may have sought to ensure that the surrender negotiations had sufficient witnesses to corroborate his version of events. Many of the participants recorded an account of the surrender negotiations in the McLean parlor. Unfortunately, Lee himself did not, but his aide Charles Marshall did, nearly thirty years after the fact. Of the Union accounts, Grant provided the fullest description in his memoirs, which, like Marshall's version, dates from a couple of decades removed. Although the various accounts generally agree on the sequence of events and the contents of the negotiations, they subtly differ in their interpretations, reflecting both the perspectives of the individual authors and the interval that separated the event from its documentation.[33]

Most accounts mention, often in passing, that Grant commenced the surrender conference with an informal conversation about their common experience in Mexico. Marshall recounted that "General Grant greeted General Lee very civilly, and they engaged for a short time in conversation about their former acquaintance during the Mexican war. Some other Federal officers took part in the conversation, which was terminated by General Lee saying to General Grant that he had come to discuss the terms of the surrender of his army." Historians have often dismissed this conversation as Grant's awkward and failed attempt to put Lee at ease. Yet Grant may have been not only trying to allude to their previous acquaintance but also signaling to Lee a prior common experience with surrender. Horace Porter's account adds a small but potentially significant detail to the conversation: Grant mentioned that their prior meeting had occurred "while we were serving in Mexico, when you came over from General Scott's headquarters to visit Garland's brigade, to which I then belonged." Although specifically dating this meeting requires some speculation, this prior encounter most likely took place just prior to the battle of Chapultepec, as the members of Winfield Scott's and Zachary Taylor's armies coordinated the assault on the Mexican fortress. The subsequent Mexican surrender paved the way for the American occupation of Mexico City and victory in the overall conflict. If Grant intended any particular subtext about the disposition of the Appomattox surrender, it appears to have been lost on Lee.[34]

At Lee's urging, Grant sat down at a small oval table to put his proposed terms to paper. Handed a pencil and a manifold order book by Ely Parker, Grant wrote out in simple, plain language his proposed settlement that reflected his prior correspondence with Lee and Lincoln's admonition to

Lee, Grant, and the Uneasy Peace

provide liberal terms. In form, what Grant produced resembled a letter more than a formal legal document; indeed, its appearance and opening sentence suggest that it is merely another entry in an ongoing correspondence:

Appomattox Court House, Va.

Apl. 9th 1865

Gen. R.E. Lee

Comdg. C.S.A.

Gen. In accordance with the substance of my letter to you of the 8th inst., I propose to receive the surrender of the Army of Northern Virginia on the following terms, to wit: Rolls of all the officers and men to be made in duplicate, one copy to be given to an officer to be designated by me, the other to be retained by such officer or officers as you may designate. The officers to give their individual paroles not to take up arms against the Government of the United States; and each company officer sign a like parole for the men of their commands. The arms, artillery, and public property to be parked and stacked, and turned over to the officers appointed by me to receive them. This will not embrace the side-arms of the officers, nor their private horses. This done, each officer and man will be allowed to return to his home, not to be disturbed by U.S. authority so long as they observe their paroles and the laws in force where they may reside.

Very Respectfully,

U.S. Grant, Lt. Gen.

In his memoirs, Grant claimed, "When I put my pen to the paper I did not know the first word that I should make use of in writing the terms. I only knew what was in my mind, and I wished to express it clearly, so that there could be no mistaking it." Although Grant claimed to have composed the terms on the spot, the similarity between the original draft and Grant's earlier correspondence with Lee suggests that considerable premeditation factored into his prose. Moreover, as historian Joan Waugh has pointed out, Grant drew heavily on his experiences accepting the surrenders of Fort Donelson and Vicksburg. Looking over the original draft with Ely Parker, Grant made a few minor corrections before handing it over to Lee for his inspection.[35]

Pulling out his steel-rimmed spectacles, Lee read over the draft silently and made one slight modification to the text. At the top of the second page,

Lee added "until properly exchanged" to Grant's original. Historians have often described this addition as a mere correction, with Lee inserting words that Grant had mistakenly omitted. Indeed, Horace Porter's account suggests this interpretation.[36] However, an alternative reading of these three added words reveals a more meaningful change in the agreement's meaning and military consequences. In Grant's original draft, Lee's soldiers would be paroled after pledging never to "take up arms against the Government of the United States." It made Appomattox distinct from earlier surrenders—sending Confederates home unmolested "so long as they observe their paroles." Lee's modification, however, opened up the possibility that these parolees might be subsequently exchanged to resume Confederate service. If Grant intended to signal that Appomattox delineated a transition to peace (at least for the Army of Northern Virginia), Lee's changes brought the language of the agreement into line with earlier surrenders. Knowing that Lee's troops would never be exchanged, Grant permitted Lee's modification to stand.

Reading over Grant's terms, Lee must have been relieved that they contained none of the elements that diehards within his army feared. Nothing in the tone or substance of the agreement sought to humiliate Confederates or compel their submission to an unconditional surrender. Soldiers and officers (including Lee himself) would not spend any time in a Union prison but would be immediately paroled and allowed to return home. The soldiers' private property would be respected. Finally, the agreement's final sentence implied that soldiers would receive some immunity from prosecution for their participation in the Confederacy. Lee readily admitted to Grant that the terms would "have a happy effect on the army."

Although he generally approved of the terms, Lee pointed out that "their army was organized a little differently from the army of the United States": whereas Union cavalry and artillery used government-owned horses, Confederates owned their horses. Lee asked if enlisted men could retain their horses. Grant initially refused, citing that the surrender terms only mentioned officers, but almost immediately reconsidered and told Lee that he would instruct his officers to allow paroled Confederates to retain their horses, reasoning that they would help them "put in a crop to carry themselves and their families through the next winter." Furthermore, Grant reasoned, most Confederate horses, beaten down from excessive use and poor forage, had negligible military value and would prove more of a burden than an asset to his army. While Grant and Lee agreed on this point, neither believed it necessary to modify the surrender agreement to reflect the disposition of Confederate horses. Lee trusted that Grant would stand by his word.

Lee, Grant, and the Uneasy Peace

Satisfied, Lee instructed Charles Marshall to craft his acceptance, while Ely Parker, "whose handwriting presented a better appearance than that of anyone on the staff," made ink copies of the agreed terms. Lee's acceptance, like Grant's terms, took the form of a letter:

Headquarters Army of Northern Virginia

April 9, 1865

General:—I received your letter of this date containing the terms of the surrender of the Army of Northern Virginia as proposed by you. As they are substantially the same as those expressed in your letter of the 8th inst., they are accepted. I will proceed to designate the proper officers to carry the stipulations into effect.

R.E. Lee, General.[37]

According to Horace Porter, Lee edited Marshall's original draft, removing extraneous formalities and thereby producing an acceptance that mirrored Grant's concise and direct prose. While official copies were made, Lee had one final request: "His army was in a very bad condition for want of food . . . [and] his men had been living for some days on parched corn exclusively." Could Grant spare rations for his famished army? Lee admitted that he did not know how many of soldiers remained. "I have not seen any returns for several days," Lee told Grant, "so that I have no means of ascertaining our present strength," although he knew his army had shrunk significantly since Petersburg due to "many stragglers and some deserters." Conferring with Sheridan, Grant asked if 25,000 rations would suffice, and Lee said he thought that "ample . . . and it will be a great relief, I assure you."[38]

Having secured generous terms for his army, Marshall recalled, "at last General Lee took leave of General Grant." The two men "mounted our horses, which the orderly was holding in the yard, and rode away, a number of Federal officers, standing on the porch in front of the house, looking at us." Union artist Alfred Waud's illustration of Lee's departure captures the scene: The Confederate general is astride Traveller, his eyes forward and posture erect. Marshall trails a respectful distance behind. Union soldiers look on reverentially, one of them doffing his slouch hat to Lee. On the porch of the McLean house, Union officers watch Lee ride away; one of them (presumably intended to be Grant) is a few steps below the others. Grant later recalled that Lee's "whole bearing was that of a patriotic and gallant soldier, concerned alone for the welfare of his army."[39]

FIGURE 2. Alfred Waud, "Robert E. Lee leaving the McLean House following his surrender to Ulysses S. Grant" (Library of Congress, Prints & Photographs Division, LC-DIG-ppmsca-21320)

News of Lee's surrender spread rapidly through both armies. Although they had anticipated the outcome, Confederate soldiers could not help but be overwhelmed by its emotional impact. William Abernathy of the 17th Mississippi recalled that "no man can describe what followed. Some sat at the roots of trees and cried as if their hearts would break. Some grasped the rifle that they had carried for years and smashed them. Some cursed bitters, some prayed." When the initial shock had dissipated, their anger and heartbreak morphed into profound sadness. At twilight, the soldiers from his regiment "gathered around the old flag and each of us took off a piece, and when the dawn of another morning came, there was no part of the old flag left." As they divided the fragments of their regimental flag, "we gave way to womanish tears as we did so, and shall I say it, cried bitterly." One Confederate noted simply that it was *"the saddest day of my life."*[40]

For many Confederates, Lee's surrender posed something of an existential crisis. Over the past four years, Lee had become the embodiment of all their hopes and dreams. Many Confederate soldiers invested Lee with almost mystical qualities, a military sage who would lead them to victory. With his surrender, they struggled to make sense of what their sacrifices meant. "To think we have been toiling, suffering, bleeding for our country and for the freedom to govern our states as we wish and then to be forced to surrender," noted one Confederate in his diary on the afternoon of the surrender. "I have feeling we are not being true or loyal to our countless comrades who gave up their lives during this four years."[41] That same afternoon, Rev. William Wiatt, a Virginia chaplain, articulated his own doubts in his diary: *"Has God forsaken us? Is our Confederacy ruined?"* Unable to hold back his tears, Wiatt hoped that Lee's surrender amounted to a divine test of their humility and that God would in "time grant unto us deliverance & prosperity & honor." Most Confederates, however, could not muster Wiatt's faith that Lee's surrender prefaced a Confederate resurgence. When news of Lee's surrender reached one South Carolina regiment, some of whom had enlisted prior to Fort Sumter, "we looked in each other's faces, where blank and fathomless despair was written, nor said one word—our hearts were too full for language. We vainly strove to comprehend the reality of our situation but our intellects were stunned by the heaviness of the blow and we could only murmur stupidly and meaninglessly the word 'surrendered!' It sounded like a knell of damnation."[42]

Lee's conduct at Appomattox helped surrendered Confederates temper their despair. The number of soldiers who noted seeing Lee at Appomattox suggests that the general made a conscious choice to be observed that afternoon, recognizing that his standing would encourage a peaceful transition to civilian life. Charles Marshall noted that "when General Lee returned to his lines, a large number of men gathered around him." After Lee described the terms of surrender, "great emotion was manifested by officers and men, but love and sympathy for their command mastered every other feeling." One of the officers greeting Lee upon his return recalled that "the troops crowded around him, eagerly desiring to shake his hand. . . . Sympathy, boundless admiration and love for him filled their hearts. They pressed up to him, anxious to touch his person or even his horse, and copious tears washing from strong men's cheeks the stains of powder." Yet even Lee, known for his stoicism, could not contain his emotions. One soldier noted that Lee "looked so careworn and aged. The boys broke out in their usual cheer of welcome, but his only response was shading his face with his hat, and bowing his head almost to the mane of his familiar old gray horse, Traveller, and I could see the tears trickle down his face."[43]

News of Lee's surrender also brought a cathartic release among Union troops. A New Jersey soldier recalled that "instantly the wildest excitement prevailed. The feelings that had been so long suppressed burst forth in the wildest cheers. Guns were fired and caps darkened the air."[44] Relieved that he would not have to face battle again, William H. Smith addressed a letter home to Michigan from "the Glorious Field where Genrl Bob Lee Surrendered." A veteran of Bull Run, Antietam, Gettysburg, and the Wilderness, Smith had seen more than his fair share of combat, but nothing had prepared him for the closure and overwhelming release that Confederate surrender engendered. "I am so 'happy' I don't know what to say. . . . Well at last we have realy broken the 'Back Bone' of the Rebelion." For Smith, Union victory helped to create meaning of the sacrifices he and other soldiers had made over the past four years and in particular in the march from Petersburg. "We have had a hard time of it I assure you," Smith wrote, "but I feel well repaid. Many are barefoot as the country is rough and stony. The soles of my boots are worn off and for the past two days I have marched with my feet wound in pieces of cotton tenting. My feet are quite sore, but I was bound to see the 'last ditch,' and I believe we have found it. For I now consider the Rebellion virtually over." Pleased when he learned the terms, Smith thought that it "should be the policy of all in authority to conciliate as far as possible without sacrificing our own honor." The raucous celebrations prompted a Pennsylvania sergeant to note, "I never seen a crazier set of fellows anywhere."[45]

Although officers attempted to keep soldiers within their lines, some Union and Confederate soldiers did fraternize that afternoon. One Pennsylvania cavalryman noted in his diary that no sooner had news of Lee's surrender spread than "we were soon all mixed up, shaking hands, giving the Johnnies grub & coffee and getting tobacco." He found the experience surreal, noting that "it seemed more like meeting of dear old friends after long absence than of men ready to kill or be killed a few hours previously." Another Union soldier recalled that they "shared their provender with their fallen foeman until every haversack was empty. The sweet aroma of real coffee staggered the Confederates, condensed milk and sugar appalled them, and they stood aghast at just a little butter which one soldier, more provident than his fellows, happened to have preserved."[46] Hardly widespread, these episodes appear far more frequently in Union than Confederate sources, suggesting that Union soldiers felt more inclined to record their magnanimity than rebels were to note Union charity.

Grant quickly put a damper on Union celebrations. In his memoirs, Grant claimed that "when news of the surrender first reached our lines our men commenced firing a salute of a hundred guns in honor of the victory. I at once sent word, however, to have it stopped. The Confederates were now our prisoners, and we did not want to exult over their downfall." Intriguingly, as Caroline Janney has recently observed, no contemporary source made note of this order, suggesting that if Grant tried to restrict celebrations, few soldiers paid attention. Although he only hints at it in his memoirs, Grant may have had more pragmatic reasons for restraint beyond a concern for surrendered Confederates' emotional well-being. Some Union officers worried that embittered rebels might reject Lee's surrender and riot, a reaction that Union celebrations might provoke. Over the next several days, as Lee's army received their paroles, fraternization between Union and Confederate soldiers often contained an undercurrent of rage, one that could surface if a Confederate felt provoked.[47]

Grant's efforts not to shame Confederates mirrored his conduct at Fort Donelson and Vicksburg. Eschewing formalities, he neither required nor desired an elaborate ceremony to mark the surrender. By the time that Confederate troops came to stack arms, both he and Lee had left Appomattox. By curtailing Union celebrations and liberally sharing rations after his meeting with Lee on April 9, Grant helped to pave the way for sectional reconciliation. Although historians have sometimes overemphasized Appomattox as a site of national healing, many Confederates did express genuine appreciation for Union generosity. One Confederate noted with approval that Federals showed "no evidence of a disposition to crow over us . . . indulging in no boast, no firing of guns, no cheers that we heard. Never in all [of] history was a captured army treated with such respect." He also appreciated their behavior during the surrender ceremony when Confederates stacked arms, noting that "General Grant and his men treated us nobly, more nobly than was ever a conquered army treated before or since. The conduct of the Federals on this occasion was soothing and comforting beyond anything that words can express."[48]

Before he departed for Washington on the morning of April 10, Grant decided to have one final meeting with Lee. Conversing on horseback between the lines, Grant asked for Lee's help in preventing future bloodshed. Since no "man in the Confederacy whose influence with the soldiery and the whole people" exceeded Lee, Grant argued, peace would be hastened "if he would now advise the surrender of all the armies." Lee refused, arguing that he could not recommend such a course of action without first consulting Jefferson Davis.[49] Although he could not bring himself to counsel surrender then, this conversation may have influenced Lee's decision on April 20 to advise Jefferson Davis that he should direct the remaining Confederate commands to stand down. Nearly two weeks after his surrender, Lee concluded that further resistance would damage the South irreparably. "From what I have seen and learned," Lee wrote, "I believe an army cannot be organized or supported in Virginia, and as far as I know the condition of affairs, the country east of the Mississippi is morally and physically unable to maintain the contest unaided with any hope of ultimate success." Lee also counseled against a guerilla war, arguing that it would be both ineffective and counterproductive: "A partisan war may be continued, and hostilities protracted, causing individual suffering and the devastation of the country, but I see no prospect by that means of achieving a separate independence." Lee closed his letter by evoking the now-familiar formulation: "To save useless effusion of blood, I would recommend measures be taken for suspension of hostilities and the restoration of peace."[50] On the run, the Confederate president may not have received Lee's letter. If he did, Davis did nothing to act on it.

Grant paid one final visit to the McLean house to meet with his generals before his departure for Washington. Lee and Grant had each designated three commissioners to orchestrate the mechanics of surrender. As he had at Vicksburg, Grant trusted that his subordinates would dutifully exercise their charge. His three designates, John Gibbon, Wesley Merritt, and Charles Griffin, had only a skeletal framework upon which to organize the surrender, as Lee and Grant's agreement offered few specifics. The three Union commissioners met with their Confederate partners (Longstreet, Gordon, and Pendleton) that afternoon. The six men first met in the Clover Hill Tavern but, finding it a "bare and cheerless place," retired to the McLean parlor. Although not mythologized like Grant and Lee's meeting, this conference had significant consequences for the shape and disposition of Confederate surrender. If Lee and Grant decided on April 9 that the Army of Northern Virginia would surrender, the six commissioners decided on April 10 what that surrender would look like.

Only one of the six commissioners described the proceedings in any detail. According to John Gibbon, the commissioners quickly agreed to a number of important provisions: soldiers would "stack their arms, deposit their flags, sabres, pistols, etc., and from thence march to the homes," and they would be allowed to keep private property, including horses. The only contentious point in their meeting concerned who ought to be included in Lee's surrender. All present knew that a substantial portion of the Army of Northern Virginia had fallen behind during Lee's march from Petersburg to Appomattox, including those who deserted and those physically unable to continue. Moreover, Gibbon noted that "a part of the cavalry had made its escape toward Lynchburg just about the time the surrender took place," and Confederate officers probably suspected that some rebel soldiers had absconded since the initial cease-fire the previous day. Did Lee's surrender encompass those soldiers as well as those still in Appomattox Courthouse? Rising to his feet, John Gordon argued that "as they had been treated to so much liberality, . . . he considered his personal honor required him to give the most liberal interpretation to every question that came up for discussion." Presumably, Gordon meant that he hoped that surrender would encompass the entirety of the Army of Northern Virginia. Longstreet, who during Gordon's histrionics had "sat still and said nothing," made a more practical suggestion: "the surrender should include all troops belonging to the army except such cavalry as actually made its escape" and any artillery more than twenty miles from Appomattox Courthouse. The other commissioners quickly assented to Longstreet's proposal, and all six men signed the accord. With this "final agreement," Gibbon noted, "it only remained to carry out its provisions."[51]

While his commissioners worked out the mechanics of surrender, Lee contemplated how to explain the surrender to his army. As with much of Lee's official correspondence, Charles Marshall crafted the first draft of Lee's farewell address. Assigned the task on the evening of April 9, Marshall found it unusually thorny: how to explain concisely and sympathetically the surrender and thank the troops for their commitment and sacrifice. When, by 10:00 A.M. the following morning, Marshall had not yet completed the address, Lee sequestered him in his personal ambulance until he had finished, posting an orderly outside so that he would not be disturbed. After his meeting that morning with Grant, Lee examined Marshall's draft, cut "an entire paragraph," and made "one or two verbal changes" before sending it off to be copied. Manuscript copies, transcribed by Confederate clerks and signed by Lee, were distributed to corps commanders.[52]

Historians commenting on Lee's farewell address have emphasized Lee's clarity and brevity in explaining Confederate defeat. Lee attributed Union victory to superior numbers, not to any deficit in Confederate efforts or dedication. Drawing on tropes of Southern manhood and honor, Lee maintained that Confederates had fought with "unsurpassed courage and fortitude." Some have seen in Lee's words the foundational text of the Lost Cause, an explanation of Confederate defeat that emphasized rebel bravery against overwhelming Federal manpower and resources.[53] Yet one significant element of Lee's address has thus far eluded historians. Lee states that that soldiers could return home "until exchanged," suggesting that he did not necessarily see the Appomattox surrender as terminal. The reference in his farewell address to exchange suggests that Lee's insistence on the addition of the phrase "until properly exchanged" to the April 9 surrender agreement did not amount to a mere formality, but that he held out some faint hope that his soldiers could be returned to service. However, if any rebel soldiers saw hope for a resurrected Army of Northern Virginia in Lee's message, they did not comment on it.

Most Confederate soldiers first heard the words of Lee's address when their commanding officers read them aloud on the evening of April 10. Many soldiers wanted copies of Lee's address as a memento of Appomattox. Although mass-produced copies soon appeared (and would remain a feature of Lost Cause commemoration), impatient soldiers frantically produced hand-written transcriptions. Georgian Herman Perry "sat down and copied it on a piece of Confederate paper, using a bass-drum head for a desk." Perry asked Lee to autograph his copy, which he kept as a treasured token. He recalled that Lee had "tears in his eyes when he signed it for me, and when I turned to walk away there were tears in my own eyes too." Lee's conduct at Appomattox made him "the greatest man that ever lives, and as a humble soldier of the South, I thank Heaven that I had the honor of following him."[54]

Most of the Union army had left Appomattox on April 11, leaving a portion of the 5th Corps to accept the surrender of Confederate arms the next morning. Joshua Lawrence Chamberlain, tasked with overseeing the ceremonial stacking of arms, stood at the forefront of the Union line. The column of Union soldiers stretched along the Richmond-Lynchburg Stage Road, past the courthouse, with its terminus near the McLean house. Over the next six hours, surrendered Confederates marched four abreast past the Union soldiers, stacking their weapons and draping their regimental flags upon them. The parade stopped periodically for Union wagons to remove the discarded piles.[55]

Historians have traditionally relied heavily on Chamberlain's account of the surrender ceremony. He saw the surrender as a moment of reconciliation, a rite of passage that transformed honorable opponents into reunited citizens. He lavished praise on defeated Confederates, describing them as "the embodiment of manhood: men who neither toils and sufferings, nor the fact of death, nor disaster, nor hopelessness could bend from their resolve; standing before us now, thin, worn, and famished, but erect, and with eyes looking level into ours, waking memories that bound us together as no other bond;—was not such manhood to be welcomed back into a Union so tested and assured?" In Chamberlain's account, the critical moment came when his men saluted the surrendering Confederates, who returned the gesture, "honor answering honor." Once the guns were stacked and the battle flags surrendered, Confederates could resume their duties as American citizens. "Now that is my flag (pointing to the flag of the Union)," one Confederate general told Chamberlain, "and I will prove myself as worthy as any of you."

Chamberlain's propensity for self-promotion and exaggeration may have distorted his vision of the surrender proceedings, underestimating the level of anger and resentment among Confederate soldiers. Chamberlain provides only one voice of dissent, when a disgruntled Confederate officer (whom some scholars identify as former Virginia governor Henry Wise) vocally rejected reconciliation, claiming that "there is a rancor in our hearts which you little dream of. We hate you, sir." Chamberlain presents this outburst as anomalous, the product of someone "so disturbed in mind" as to be dismissed.[56] Yet a few Confederate accounts suggest that the ceremony did little to foster sectional reconciliation. Virginian J. E. Whitehorne wrote in his diary that he "saw lots of fine looking Northern officers. Had to march between two columns of the enemy, one on each side. They did not look at us, did not look defiant, did not make disrespectful remarks. Our men marched up boldly and stacked arms and did not seem to mind any more than if they had been going on dress parade." While Chamberlain interpreted Union soldiers' demeanor as a sign of respect, Whitehorne concluded that "the Yanks are afraid of us now. . . . If we meet one in the road he will always get out of our way. They . . . look like they are afraid we will jump on them."[57]

Most Confederate soldiers, however, found neither reconciliation nor resentment when stacking arms. They described the ceremony only in passing in their diaries and correspondence, suggesting that they attributed little meaning to the event. "Soon after sunrise," Kena King Chapman wrote in his diary, he "marched over to Appomattox C.H. and stacked arms in front of a corps of the enemy. Were then marched back to camp." Thomas Devereux's diary expressed a similar nonchalance: "Next day we stacked arms and the Army of Northern Virginia was a thing of the past." For both Chapman and Devereux, their minds were focused less on the symbolic importance of stacking arms as they were on their imminent journey home. One Confederate noted, "I do not know what we are going to do. We have no money, no niggers, and we have no credit. What we are to do, God only knows."[58]

News of Lee's surrender spread rapidly across the North. Secretary of War Edwin Stanton received word from Grant no later than 9:00 P.M. that evening and sent the Union general a congratulatory telegram at 9:30. To mark the occasion, Stanton ordered a 200-gun salute fired "at the headquarters of every army department, and at every post and arsenal in the United States . . . on the day of the receipt of this order." By the next morning, newspapers across the North proclaimed Lee's surrender. The headlines in the *New York Times* proclaimed, "Thanks to God, the Giver of Victory. Honors to Gen. Grant and His Gallant Army," while those in the *Boston Herald* proclaimed that the "Surrender of. Gen. Lee" amounted to "The Death Blow of the Rebellion!"[59] Writing in his diary on April 10, New Yorker George Templeton Strong recalled that "a series of vehement pulls at the front door bell roused me to consciousness" late the previous evening. Although he tried to go back to sleep, news of Lee's surrender kept Strong awake most of the night. Reading the newspaper accounts the next morning, he praised Grant's magnanimity, believing his policies would expedite eventual Confederate defeat. "Every officer and every private who goes home on parole," Strong argued, spreads the news that "surrender was unavoidable; that the Confederacy was overmatched; that fighting was a useless waste of life; that the rebel cause was hopeless. Each will be a fountain of cold water on whatever pugnacity and chivalry may yet survive in his own home and vicinage." Lee's army, Strong concluded, "can bother and perplex none but historians henceforth forever."[60]

Among the most complex reactions in the North to the news of Lee's surrender were those from Confederate prisoners. Although the resumption of regular prisoner exchanges earlier in the year had thinned their ranks, tens of thousands of captured Confederates remained in Union prisoner of war camps, with no clear timetable for their release. Among them was Mississippi captain Gart Johnson, who by the time of Lee's surrender had spent five months at Johnson's Island. When he enlisted in 1861, Johnson recalled, "I never gave much thought to being captured." However, when he found himself "cut off and surrounded" in a minor skirmish in September 1864, "the alternative was surrender or die. I chose the former, and threw my sword as far as I could send it." Like his fellow prisoners, Johnson longed to return either to his regiment

Lee, Grant, and the Uneasy Peace

or home. "When the news came of Lee's surrender," Johnson recalled, "we were sad and glad at the same time: sad to know that it had to be, and glad to know that we would soon see our own loved ones at home." For Johnson, the hope that Lee's surrender might expedite his release proved unreliable, as he remained in prison until mid-June.[61] Other prisoners responded to news of Lee's surrender with despair and renewed commitment to the Confederate cause. On the evening of April 9, James McMichael, a prisoner at Fort Delaware, learned what had happened earlier that day. In his diary he wrote, "*Bad news.* Gen. Lee has been forced to surrender his army to Gen. Grant. Woe be to the Confederacy! Now for the first time I consider our cause hopeless." Although some of his fellow prisoners promptly took the oath of allegiance to secure their freedom, McMichael steadfastly refused. Only in early May, after subsequent Confederate surrenders, did he reconsider his position. "It appears from what we hear that our government has ceased to exist," he noted. "Our armies have all been forced to surrender and disband. Most all the prisoners are taking the oath and being released. I am at a loss to know what to do." He only became convinced of complete Confederate defeat in mid-June and took the oath. "Of course," he recorded in his diary, "I am delighted at the idea of getting out of prison."[62]

While the news spread rapidly across the North, large portions of the collapsing Confederacy did not learn of Lee's surrender for some time. The decimation of Southern communications networks, including telegraphs, railroads, and the Confederate postal service, created pockets where news about the war's progress arrived sporadically. In many of these isolated communities, news of Lee's surrender came from paroled Confederate soldiers traveling home. David Dodge, a North Carolina teenager, lived in one such community. By the spring of 1865, he observed that "the trains on the railroad near us stopped running, the bridges were burnt, and the telegraph wire was cut" and consequently "the outside world could not have been more non-existent to shipwrecked mariners on the loneliest island in untraveled seas." Although rumors about the machinations of Lee's and Johnston's armies abounded, Dodge held little stock in their veracity. On the evening of April 15, six days after Lee's surrender and three days after arms were stacked, Dodge observed six men dressed in Confederate gray. He initially mistook them for deserters, a common phenomenon in the North Carolina piedmont, but Dodge found their lack of weapons perplexing, as deserters usually retained their guns. To a man, they bore the signs of a long travail. "One was barefooted, another hatless, while the garb of all was in a sad plight," Dodge recalled. "Mud covered them from head to heel, and they had evidently been on a long tramp." When they told Dodge's mother that they belonged to Lee's army, she initially rebuked them, saying, "In days like these Lee's men ought be with Lee's army." With a doleful face, one of veterans told her, "He hasn't any army, madam. . . . *Lee has surrendered.*" Dodge's family greeted the news with disbelief ("General Lee would never surrender!") and accused the men of being deserters, as "you ask us to believe the impossible." Ruefully, the men produced their paroles, documents that "prove us to be no deserters, but true Southern soldiers, who followed Lee to the last."

Over the next few days, several other bands of Appomattox parolees passed Dodge's family farm. While they pitied the surrendered soldiers, feeding them from the meager reserves of their cupboard, they rejoiced at "the last sight of armed Confederates, for a spirited little band of horsemen drew up at the gate." Refusing to accept the surrender, these diehards sought to make "their way to Johnston" or "cross the Mississippi and join Kirby Smith." Looking back on the encounter years later, Dodge recalled the contradictory emotions these committed Confederates engendered. "Their buoyancy and hopefulness gave us strength," Dodge noted, as they rode "bravely forward on their hopeless mission." Drawing hope from hopelessness reflected the paradox embedded in Confederate defeat. For young men like Dodge, not quite old enough to serve in the Confederate military himself, the sight of such stalwart nationalism in the face of collapse helped to cultivate a lifelong commitment to the Lost Cause.[63]

Of the Civil War's terminal surrenders, Lee's capitulation to Grant at Appomattox Courthouse overshadows all those that came after it in popular understandings of the conflict's conclusion. Not only was Appomattox first, but it featured the war's two most prominent military leaders. Retold countless times, the story of Appomattox remains deeply familiar. More so than other Civil War surrenders, Appomattox developed a robust mythology, a panoply of anecdotes that helped to embellish and create meaning in an otherwise straightforward episode. Some of these are rooted in reality: for instance, the disparity between Lee's immaculate uniform and Grant's disheveled one. Other parts of the Appomattox lore, including Lee offering Grant his sword and Grant refusing, and the surrender negotiations taking place under an apple tree, are complete fabrications, persistent myths that get retold despite repeated debunkings. The most powerful and persistent Appomattox myth, as historian Greg Downs has recently observed, is that Lee's surrender brought the war to a close, a distortion that colors our view of subsequent surrenders

Lee, Grant, and the Uneasy Peace

and persistent hostility by white Southerners against Federal authority during Reconstruction.[64]

Appomattox set the stage for the Confederate surrenders that followed. Lee's surrender gave other Confederate generals tacit permission to follow suit. Many of the subsequent surrenders used the Appomattox terms as a template for their own negotiations. Yet, in significant ways, the circumstances at Appomattox differed from those of later Confederate surrenders. Only at Appomattox was the surrender immediately preceded by significant military action and in which the surrendering army had no route of escape. Only at Appomattox did the two contending armies camp in such close proximity. Only at Appomattox did Confederates ceremonially stack their arms. These attributes distinguished Appomattox as a unique site of surrender, albeit one that allowed the participants to craft their own interpretations of its meaning.

In a 1906 magazine article, Grant's former aide Horace Porter articulated what for many has become the dominant cultural memory of Lee's surrender:

> The scene at Appomattox was characteristically American, and the manner in which it was conducted reflected lasting credit upon both the illustrious soldiers who directed. There was nothing theatrical, no indulgence in mock heroics, no posing for effect, no offering or demanding of swords, and no stilted speeches. The conference was less like a formal procedure of surrender and more like a business meeting between two practical Americans charged with the settlement of affairs involving great responsibilities. Grant's magnanimity, his prompt proffer of generous terms to spare Lee the necessity of suing for them, the delicate courtesy with which he endeavored to avoid wounding the feelings of a conquered antagonist, commanded the admiration of friend and foe alike.[65]

For Porter, Lee and Grant's pragmatism made Appomattox "characteristically American," stripped of the pretense and formality that he associated with European excess. More importantly, Porter saw Appomattox as a site of reconciliation and healing, creating the framework for American prosperity in the decades to follow.

For all the power of Porter's interpretation, not all who participated in the surrender shared his vision of its significance. Many Confederate soldiers distinguished between the military surrender and their commitment to Confederate values. Alabaman Cullen Battle noted that Appomattox was "not the surrender of principles, involving a weight of turpitude that no honorable man could bear; but a surrender in which honor was earned and the moral grandeur of the South rose to heights unknown before."[66] For Battle, who would return home to found the Knights of the White Carnation, a white supremacist terrorist organization that predated the formation of the Ku Klux Klan, surrender changed little. Although Appomattox marked the beginning of the end for the Confederate nation, many paroled soldiers left with their commitment to Confederate values of white supremacy and Southern distinctiveness intact and reinforced.

DYING IN THE
LAST DITCH

Joseph Johnston, Richard Taylor, Nathan Bedford
Forrest, and the Fall of the Cis-Mississippi Confederacy

Historians have often treated Appomattox as the de facto conclusion to the war, with subsequent events acting as an extended denouement or coda, implying that once Lee surrendered, the other Confederate officers would follow suit in time. Indeed, "Appomattox" is often used a shorthand for the end of the Confederate national experiment. More recently, some historians have downplayed the end of the Civil War as a significant turning point, arguing that the end of formal hostilities only shifted violence into new forms and venues, including paramilitary organizations like the Ku Klux Klan. Both of these tropes trivialize the series of Confederate surrenders that took place after Appomattox. Examining post-Appomattox surrenders reveals greater complexity and contingency in Confederate defeat than historians have often supposed. The war ended not with a bang or whimper but with a succession of negotiated settlements, each dependent on particular local circumstances and the idiosyncratic desires and objectives of Confederate and Union officers. Even after Appomattox, Confederate officers continued to worry about surrendering dishonorably. Furthermore, Confederate officers did not make the decision to surrender independently but were often driven by the actions of their soldiers, who had their own ideas about how their war should end. Just as Lee's surrender at Appomattox had been shaped by the rampant desertions from his army in the flight from Petersburg, subsequent surrenders demonstrated how the choices of individual soldiers could prompt surrender and influence its terms. In negotiating these surrenders, Federals and Confederates drew upon four years of experience with surrender: many of the soldiers who stacked arms had surrendered before, and officers came to the surrender table as veterans, not neophytes. However, all recognized that the surrenders that brought an end to the war had a different character. Rather than surrendering to fight another day, raising the white flag in 1865 meant going home and abandoning hope for an independent Confederacy.

Even after Lee's surrender, Confederate stalwarts maintained that their remaining armies could secure their independence. In North Carolina, Joseph Johnston commanded more than 30,000 men. Reorganized and consolidated at Smithfield, North Carolina, the Army of Tennessee had suffered significant setbacks at Averasboro and Bentonville at the hands of William Tecumseh Sherman's army, but it remained (at least compared with the Army of Northern Virginia) well fed and supplied. To Johnston's south, two Confederate departments had thus far managed to retain some pockets of resistance to Union occupation. Headquartered at Tallahassee, Sam Jones's Department of Florida and South Georgia had more than 8,000 men under arms. In north Georgia, William Wofford commanded approximately half that number. Although neither Jones nor Wofford could reasonably expect to prevail in open battle, their diffuse commands extended over hundreds of miles. To Johnston's west, several more substantial Confederate forces remained in the field. Commander of the Department of Alabama, Mississippi, and East Louisiana, Gen. Richard Taylor retained more than 12,000 soldiers. Son of Mexican War hero and president Zachary Taylor and brother-in-law of Confederate president Davis, Taylor could call upon two adjacent commands. Headquartered in Mobile, Dabney Maury's Department of the Gulf included approximately 4,000 men, and M. Jeff Thompson's Northern Sub-District of Arkansas had more than 7,000 soldiers. Interspersed among these larger departments, districts, and armies were more than a dozen smaller "independent" commands, including William Holland Thomas's Legion of Cherokee in the mountains of western North Carolina; Thomas Munford's Maryland cavalry brigade, which had split off from Lee prior to Appomattox; John S. Mosby's Partisan Rangers in Virginia's Shenandoah Valley; and Nathan Bedford Forrest's Cavalry Corps, which by April 1865 had found a home in Taylor's Department of Alabama, Mississippi, and East Louisiana.[1] Finally, all the remaining Confederate armies, Johnston's included, paled in comparison with Kirby Smith's force in the Trans-Mississippi Department. Effectively cut off after the surrender of Vicksburg in July 1863, the Trans-Mississippi Confederacy served as the great hope for committed Confederate nationalists and diehard rebels after

Richmond's fall and Lee's surrender. The Confederacy could be reborn, they believed, from the bastion of Texas, and the territory that had temporarily fallen to the Union could be reclaimed. Although the size of the Confederate forces in the Trans-Mississippi remained unclear—Kirby Smith claimed anywhere from 20,000 to 50,000, depending on his audience—the idea that the remaining rebel armies could be united to continue the struggle proved an irresistible lure.

Jefferson Davis stood at the fore among those who believed that the setback of Lee's surrender could be overcome. In his memoirs, Davis noted that although "I was fully sensible of the gravity of our position, seriously affected as it was by the evacuation of the capital, the surrender of the Army of Northern Virginia, and the consequent discouragement which these events would produce, I did not think we should despair. We still had effective armies in the field, and a vast extent of rich and productive territory." If only rebel armies could be concentrated, Davis believed, they could rally and use the extensive domain still under Confederate control to prolong the conflict and hopefully secure their independence. "In two or three weeks," Davis told them, the Confederacy could muster "a large army in the field" by concentrating smaller commands and "bringing back into the ranks those who had abandoned them." Although he had contentious relationships with both Joseph Johnston and Edmund Kirby Smith, Davis saw them as key components in the Confederate future.[2]

Davis shared his vision with his cabinet and assembled generals (including Johnston and Beauregard) at a meeting in Greensboro, North Carolina, nearly a week after Lee's surrender at Appomattox. Recent setbacks, Davis told them, had definitely hurt, but "I do not think we should regard them as fatal. . . . I think we can whip the enemy yet if our people will turn out." If Davis expected rousing support for renewing the war effort, the response he received must have been disappointing. Asked for his views, Johnston tried to temper Davis's enthusiasm. "Our people are tired of the war, feel themselves whipped, & will not fight," Johnston claimed. "Our country is overrun, its military resources greatly diminished, while the enemy's military power & resources were never greater." His own army, Johnston argued, could not withstand another major engagement. Not only did Sherman's army possess greater numbers, but Johnston's men had been deserting in droves. "Since Lee's defeat," Johnston told Davis, "they regard the war as at an end." If he attempted to rendezvous with Kirby Smith, Johnston argued, his entire army would desert before he arrived in Texas: "I shall expect to retain no man beyond the bye road or cow path that leads to his home. My small force is melting away like snow before the sun." Eager to find an ally, Davis asked Beauregard for his assessment, only to find that he too found the situation hopeless. When Johnston suggested that he contact Sherman, "proposing an interview to arrange terms of surrender & peace," Davis was dismissive, claiming that "I am not sanguine to the ultimate results."[3]

Had Jefferson Davis been more perceptive of his surroundings, he would have found confirmation of Johnston's assessment of the situation. Ever since rumors of Lee's surrender had reached Greensboro, Confederate soldiers concluded that their war had ended. Gen. Alfred Iverson, demoted to garrison duty in Greensboro after his disastrous performance at Gettysburg, reported on April 14 "the desertion of numbers of the troops. . . . The disposition of the command is not good, there being much demoralization." Iverson noted that almost all of the Virginians had left and that those soldiers who remained could not be counted on. Another Confederate general stationed in Greensboro reported on the same day "a material alteration in the morale of the troops" since news of Lee's surrender. "Desertions are becoming very numerous. About 200 men of one battalion abandoned their post last night, and the remaining force state openly their intention to return to their homes." Desertions had become so frequent that he could no longer assess how many men he had under his command.[4]

Jefferson Davis's refusal to contemplate surrender even after Appomattox made him only the most prominent of an entire class of Confederates who maintained their conviction in rebel invincibility and eventual victory. As historian Jason Phillips has observed, their self-deception grew out of a fanatical devotion that allowed them to ignore or dismiss the ample evidence around them that the Confederacy's days were numbered. For the most part, these men were not delusional—they recognized that Lee's surrender was a tremendous blow to Confederate morale and military capacity—but held out hope that eventual victory would be theirs. Upon hearing of Lee's surrender, one diehard in Johnston's army reaffirmed his belief "that we will whip this fight yet." Determined to never surrender, diehards saw every setback as an opportunity to reaffirm their commitment to the Confederate cause. Even after all the Confederate forces east of the Mississippi had laid down their arms, one soldier in Kirby Smith's Texas declared, "We are NOT whiped [sic], we CAN and we MUST fight; subjugation never." Although diehards never amounted to more than a fragment of the Confederate army, by April 1865 they had gravitated toward other rebels who shared their devotion, forming pockets of profound resilience in an army that most considered broken beyond repair. These committed

Fall of the Cis-Mississippi Confederacy

enclaves would have an outsized impact on the shape of Confederate surrender in April and May 1865.[5]

Despite Davis's misgivings, Joseph Johnston went ahead and invited Sherman to confer on the terms of his surrender. Leaving the conference with Davis's cabinet in Greensboro, Johnston rejoined his army on the evening of April 13, his journey back delayed by "one of the accidents now then inevitable on the North Carolina railroad." During his absence, the Army of Tennessee, under the temporary command of William J. Hardee, had marched through Raleigh and west through Chapel Hill en route for Greensboro. Ever since he had taken command of the Army of Tennessee in February 1865, Johnston had concluded that Confederate defeat was inevitable and that his primary duty therefore was "to obtain fair terms of peace." After he received news of Lee's surrender on April 11, Johnston intensified his focus on an honorable surrender. Although he initially attempted to hide news of Appomattox from his soldiers, rumors of Lee's surrender had arrived in camp before official confirmation. One officer knew that the rumors were true when Johnston commuted the sentence of a deserter who was to be executed. "Then I knew, was positively certain, that the war was over," the officer recalled. "I knew that General Johnston, on one hand, would not relent so long as there was a necessity of preserving discipline, and that, on the other hand, he would not sacrifice a life unnecessarily." Sparing the deserter's life meant "that there would be no prolongation of the struggle."[6]

Civilians who watched Johnston's army march through Raleigh and Chapel Hill expressed dismay at their beleaguered condition and worn countenance. Viewed as a safe location within the Confederate interior, the North Carolina piedmont had attracted thousands of refugees from across the South, some of whom had not seen assembled rebel soldiers since they sent them off in the summer of 1861. Most found the sight deeply disturbing, as the soldiers before them bore only passing resemblance to the vigorous young men who had rallied to the Confederate cause four years earlier. In Chapel Hill, one resident described the "straggling bodies of Confederate soldiers" as mere "fragments of the once powerful army of Tennessee." The soldiers were threadbare and exhausted, one young woman observed, and hard marching had left them "so worn out they fall down on the sidewalks and sleep." One Raleigh woman described the tramping soldiers as "the funeral procession of the Southern Confederacy!" Yet despite the haggard appearance of these soldiers, some onlookers managed to find hope that they could still rally. A young woman at St. Mary's

School in Raleigh recorded in her scrapbook that "the confederate soldiers came marching in each one with a blooming sprig of lilac tucked in his hat, like plumes, though almost barefoot, wearing ragged and worn uniforms. Unshaved and gaunt they were but unconquered still." In both Raleigh and Chapel Hill, the community came out to witness the spectacle. "The whole population of our town poured out to see these war-worn men; to cheer them; to feed and shelter them," wrote Chapel Hill resident Cornelia Phillips Spencer. "They were our soldiers—our own brave boys. The cause was desperate, we knew—the war was nearly over—our delusions were at an end; but while we had it, our last loaf to our soldiers—a cheer, and a blessing, with dim eyes, as they rode away."[7]

Sherman learned of Lee's surrender before sunrise on April 12, one day after Johnston did. "I hardly know how to express my feelings, but you can imagine them," he wrote to Grant upon hearing the news. Praising Grant's terms as "magnanimous and liberal," Sherman hoped that Johnston would follow "Lee's example." His army, Sherman reported, rapidly pursued Johnston's and he hoped that the news of Lee's surrender might encourage his men to pick up the pace.[8] Later that day, Sherman received an unexpected communication from North Carolina governor Zebulon Vance, delivered by two former governors, William Graham and David Swain. With Sherman's army approaching Raleigh, Vance hoped to avoid the destruction visited upon Columbia and asked for safe passage to discuss "the suspension of hostilities" and "the final termination of the existing War." Sherman greeted the commissioners warmly, invited them to dine with him, and expressed a desire to bring the war to a swift conclusion on terms that would not dishonor Confederates. When Graham and Swain did not return to Raleigh promptly, Vance interpreted their absence as evidence that the mission had failed, and fearing being taken prisoner, he rode out of the city at midnight bound for Greensboro. Sherman entered the North Carolina capital the next day, accepting the keys to the statehouse from Swain and Graham.[9]

In his memoirs, Sherman recalled his state of mind on April 12 and 13. After hearing of Lee's surrender, "we all regarded the war as over, for I knew well that General Johnston had no army with which to oppose mine. So that the only questions that remained were, would he surrender at Raleigh? or would he allow his army to disperse into guerilla bands, to 'die in the last ditch,' and entail on his country an indefinite and prolonged military occupation?" Sherman recalled Lincoln's admonition at City Point to provide generous terms to Confederates and allow them to return home unhindered. Committed to bringing the war to a swift conclusion, Sherman received only sporadic reports of Confederate resistance, mostly rearguard actions designed to slow his pursuit. He suspected that, if pressed, Johnston would surrender.[10]

On the morning of April 14, Sherman received confirmation that Johnston had no intention of continuing the struggle unnecessarily. In a letter written the previous evening, Johnston admitted to Sherman that "the results of the recent campaign in Virginia have changed the relative military condition of the belligerents." In order "to stop the further effusion of blood and devastation of property," Johnston asked for a cease-fire "to permit the civil authorities to enter into the needful arrangements to terminate the existing war." Although Sherman welcomed the overture, he recognized that what Johnston proposed did not exactly amount to a surrender but was a cease-fire to enable civilian peace negotiations. Since his directions from Lincoln precluded such forays into the political sphere, Sherman chose to ignore this part of Johnston's letter. In his response, Sherman agreed to halt his army and to meet with Johnston under the "same terms and conditions as were made by Generals Grant and Lee at Appomattox Court-House." Sherman closed with a pledge that could be read as either an olive branch or a threat: "I really desire to save the people of North Carolina the damage they would sustain by the march of this army through the central or western parts of the State."[11]

On April 16, Sherman received Johnston's reply agreeing to meet with him the following day at a point midway between their armies. Just before he departed the next morning, Sherman received a telegram informing him of Lincoln's assassination. "Dreading the effect of such a message at that critical instant of time," Sherman ordered the telegraph operator to secrecy, hoping that news of the assassination would not complicate the surrender negotiations. Escorted by a small cavalry squadron, Sherman encountered Johnston and his aides along Hillsborough Road, not far from Durham Station, a small railroad depot between Hillsborough and Raleigh.[12] The two generals retired to a nearby farmhouse owned by James Bennitt, a yeoman farmer who had lost a son and a son-in-law during the war. (Although the owner of the house spelled his name Bennitt, the meeting site has traditionally been referred to as Bennett Place.)[13]

During the four-hour interval between hearing of Lincoln's death and entering the Bennett farmstead, Sherman struggled to make sense of the assassination's implications for his negotiations with Johnston. Although he thought it unlikely that Lee or Johnston had been directly involved, he did not discount the idea that someone in the Confederate government, including Jefferson Davis, had orchestrated the events in Ford's Theater and the simultaneous attack on Secretary of State William Seward. If so, did the assassination mean that the Confederates intended to continue the war by other means? What worried him most was how the soldiers would respond when they heard the news.

He could not predict how Confederate soldiers would react, but he knew that his own soldiers venerated Lincoln, and he "feared that some foolish woman or man in Raleigh might say something or do something that would madden our men, and that a fate worse than that of Columbia would befall the place." Sherman had creeping doubts that the assassination had thrown the prospects for a peaceful surrender into jeopardy.

Leaving their aides outside, Sherman and Johnston sat at the only table in the Bennett parlor. "As soon as we were alone together," Sherman recalled, "I showed him the dispatch announcing Lincoln's assassination, and watched him closely. The perspiration came out in large drops on his forehead, and he did not attempt to conceal his distress." Johnston denied any involvement in the assassination, describing the murder as "a disgrace to the age." Sherman told Johnston that he must know that further military resistance would prove catastrophic and that "since Lee had surrendered, he could do the same with honor and propriety." Johnston agreed that "any further fighting would be 'murder'" rather than war, but to Sherman's surprise he did not immediately offer to surrender his army. In his memoirs, Johnston recalls telling Sherman that he could not surrender his army under the Appomattox terms, as "our relative positions were too different from those of the armies in Virginia to justify me in such a capitulation." Unlike Lee's army, which faced an imminent attack and had no immediate route of escape, the bulk of Johnston's army camped more than twenty miles from the vanguard of Sherman's army and had several possible avenues to retreat. Instead, Johnston proposed that "we might arrange terms that would embrace *all* the Confederate armies . . . embracing [my] own army, that of Dick Taylor in Louisiana and Texas, and of Maury, Forrest, and others, in Alabama and Georgia." When pressed, Johnston admitted that he did not have authority to surrender all Confederate armies but assured Sherman that he could quickly obtain it. Eager to return to their headquarters before news of Lincoln's assassination became widespread, Sherman and Johnston adjourned their meeting, pledging to return to the Bennett farm the following day to continue negotiations.[14]

When Sherman returned to Raleigh that evening, he found rumors of Lincoln's assassination rife among the ranks and instructed his officers to suppress any retaliation that soldiers might unleash on Raleigh's civilian population. Hoping to dispel any errant rumors, Sherman issued Special Field Order 56, informing his men of President Lincoln's assassination and the attack on Secretary Seward. Although some threatened "to exterminate the South race" in vengeance, Union soldiers demonstrated remarkable restraint. Despite angry words uttered that night, both Union and Confederate sources indicate that

Fall of the Cis-Mississippi Confederacy

Sherman's men chose not to channel their rage against Raleigh's civilians. Nonetheless, Sherman noted that "I saw and felt that one single word by me would have laid the city in ashes, and turned its whole population houseless upon the country, if not worse." Raleigh residents felt the same tension; one noted that "hundreds of people sat up during the entire night, expecting every moment mob violence."[15]

If Sherman faced challenges controlling his army that evening, they paled in comparison with Johnston's when he returned to Hillsborough. News of his meeting with Sherman had spread rapidly, prompting many of his soldiers to contemplate whether they wanted to linger until they had been surrendered. Just as Lee's army witnessed an exodus of diehards bent on continuing the struggle, the Army of Tennessee saw soldiers desert in droves, hoping to serve as escorts to Jefferson Davis in Charlotte or rendezvous with Kirby Smith in Texas. One Confederate noted in his diary that no sooner had rumors of a surrender begun to spread than "disorganization was complete. Horses and mules were everywhere taken without the least regards to ownership. . . . The flags of the brigade were burned by the men in the certainty of surrender. . . . With that day the army perished—a mob remained." A cadre of junior officers urged Johnston to surrender soon because "they could not control their men [much] longer." One colonel wrote that "various rumors have just come into camp regarding the surrender of this army, which has already induced some men to leave, and it is probable that others will do so in the course of the night." Desertion was highest among the North Carolina regiments, as soldiers departed for home by moonlight, often taking army horses and mules with them.[16]

At twilight, Johnston wired Secretary of War John Breckinridge, requesting that he join him in Hillsborough to confer before the following day's meeting with Sherman. Breckinridge arrived well after midnight, accompanied by Governor Zebulon Vance and Postmaster General John Reagan. If Johnston expected a collegial and productive meeting, that notion was quickly dispelled. Gen. Wade Hampton, Johnston's cavalry commander, rebuked Vance for his foray into negotiations with Sherman, stopping just short of calling Vance a traitor and a coward. Only hours earlier, Hampton had nearly gotten into a fight with Union cavalry general Judson Kilpatrick as they waited outside the Bennett House, and his temper had not cooled. When no one came to his defense, Vance welcomed Johnston's invitation to leave the room, spending the cold evening trying to sleep on the lawn outside, bitter and frustrated that he had not been allowed to defend his conduct or participate in ensuing negotiations. Once Vance had left the room, Johnston shared the news of Lincoln's assassination. Most agreed that the president's murder only provided more incentive to surrender, as the protections offered by parole inoculated the soldiers, if not the politicians, from prosecution for complicity. Working through the night, Johnston discussed with Breckinridge, Reagan, Hampton, and his other generals what terms he should ask for the following day, with Reagan dutifully taking notes of their suggestions.[17]

The following morning, Johnston and Breckinridge rode to meet Sherman at the Bennett farmhouse, leaving Reagan in Hillsborough to finish his memorandum. Sherman initially objected to Breckenridge's inclusion, as he was empowered to negotiate with military, not political, leaders, but demurred when Johnston pointed out that in addition to his role as Confederate secretary of war, Breckenridge also held a commission as a major general and was, for the purposes of this meeting, serving in that capacity. Eager to conclude negotiations, Sherman shared a bottle of whiskey with the Confederates, a move intended to put them at ease. As soon as he finished his dram, however, Breckinridge began to lecture Sherman on the "law of war, laws governing rebellion and laws of nation." Outnumbered in the room, Sherman found Breckinridge's grandstanding almost amusing, telling them, "See here, Gentlemen, who is doing this surrendering, anyway? If this thing goes on, you'll have me sending an apology to Jeff Davis."

Johnston insisted that he had authority to surrender all Confederate armies, not only his own, but that he would require some concession on Sherman's part. Johnston argued that the major roadblocks to peace were concerns about "their political rights after surrender." Sherman replied that his understanding of Lincoln's amnesty policy and Grant's terms at Appomattox secured political rights to Confederate soldiers and officers, although he was unwilling to address the legal disposition of rebel political leaders. Midway through their discussions, a courier arrived delivering Reagan's memorandum, which Johnston handed to Sherman for inspection. Frustrated by their slow progress, Sherman dismissed Reagan's lengthy and verbose treatise and wrote his own terms, which he believed conformed to Lincoln's instructions at City Point. Passing the written terms to Johnston for inspection, Sherman said that both armies should remain in their current positions until the terms could be approved by President Andrew Johnson.[18]

Reading over the proposed terms, Johnston and Breckinridge must have been amazed at Sherman's generosity. Vilified across the Confederacy as a barbarian for his conduct in Georgia and South Carolina, Sherman now offered more than either Confederate anticipated. The document that Sherman and Johnston signed at Bennett Place on April 18, 1865, has often been mistakenly characterized as a surrender agreement, a sequel to Grant and Lee's agreement at Appomattox Courthouse. Yet it was both more and less than that. In his "Basis of Agreement," Sherman articulated not so much terms for Confederate surrender, but a framework to bring the war to a speedy conclusion. It provided for the disbandment of Confederate armies, the recognition of Southern state governments, the reestablishment of Federal courts in the South, and a pledge for "the people and inhabitants of all the States to be guaranteed, so far as the Executive can, their political rights and franchises, as well as their rights of person and property . . . so long as they live in peace and quiet, abstain from acts of armed hostility, and obey the laws in existence at the place of their residence." Sherman recognized that neither he nor Johnston had the authority to bring about a general peace and amnesty; the document concludes with the supposition that its terms required the approval of their "respective principals." In this respect, the Bennett Place agreement had a fundamentally different character than that negotiated at Appomattox Courthouse. Whereas the latter took effect immediately, the former required political approval.

Historians have often concluded that Sherman overstepped his authority in offering such generous terms, especially when it ventured into political questions of amnesty and property and voting rights. Instead, they argue that Sherman should have offered Johnston the same terms that Lee accepted at Appomattox Courthouse.[19] Yet these criticisms may underestimate the complexity of Sherman's situation, which in many ways proved more precarious than that which Grant faced less than two weeks earlier. Lincoln's assassination and the elevation of Andrew Johnson to the presidency had changed the political landscape in complex ways, many of which Sherman could only dimly perceive from his vantage point in North Carolina. Sherman had no way of knowing if the new administration would continue Lincoln's amnesty policies or how political tides had shifted in Washington. Sherman's pressing concern at Bennett Place was not to allow Johnston to leave without some kind of agreement. Sherman knew that if Johnston's army broke apart into guerilla bands, the war would continue for months, if not years. As Sherman's subordinate Gen. John Schofield observed, "It must be remembered that Johnston's army was not surrounded, and its surrender could not have been compelled. Unless the terms of capitulation could be made such as the troops themselves would be willing to accept, they would, it was apprehended, break up into guerilla bands of greater or less strength and carry on the war in that way indefinitely."[20]

Moreover, the "Basis of Agreement" did not commit the Union government to any particular course of action; if its terms were rejected by either side, hostilities could resume.

When Sherman returned to Raleigh that evening, he forwarded the terms of the agreement to Washington. In the accompanying letter, Sherman highlighted that it amounted to "an absolute submission of the enemy . . . in such a manner as to prevent their breaking up into guerilla bands." Moreover, he hoped that bringing a swift end to the Confederacy would expedite the demobilization of his own army, allowing his men to return to civilian life. Indeed, Sherman estimated that, if the agreement were approved, he would like to begin the march north on May 1, with his troops mustering out shortly thereafter. Not trusting so significant a communication to the telegraph, Sherman tasked Maj. Henry Hitchcock with delivering the message in person, a round-trip that would take at least five days. In the meantime, Sherman and his army would wait to see if President Johnson would approve his terms.

Just before sunrise on April 19, General Johnston arrived at his headquarters in Greensboro to find his army dispirited and in disarray. His meetings with Sherman, Johnston observed in his memoirs, "produced great uneasiness in the army. It was very commonly believed among the soldiers that there was to be a surrender, by which they would be prisoners of war, to which they were very averse." Most of his soldiers had already resigned themselves to surrender's inevitability. "For the last four days we have been expecting Genl. Johnston to surrender the army," one soldier wrote his sister on April 20. "There is no other hope for it but to surrender eventually. I am firmly convinced of this fact." Unlike Lee's troops, Johnston's men were in a military limbo because they would have to wait to see if the Bennett Place terms had been approved by the Union and Confederate governments. This stagnation and uncertainty bred resentment, frustration, and anger. "Demoralization," one Confederate wrote in his diary, "is utter and complete; there is no spark of fight left in the troops." Order within the ranks evaporated, as soldiers refused to perform guard duty and officers felt powerless to discipline them. According to Johnston's estimate, nearly 8,000 men deserted between April 19 and 24. While most of these soldiers simply went home, unwilling to wait for formal recognition and a parole, a significant minority sought to rendezvous with western Confederate armies to continue the struggle.[21]

Wade Hampton, Johnston's cavalry commander, stood foremost among those who repudiated the Bennett Place agreement. When Johnston returned to Hillsborough after his second meeting with Sherman, Hampton told him not to include him in any surrender agreement. In a letter to Jefferson Davis the following day, April 19, Hampton argued that Johnston fundamentally misunderstood the military situation. His men, Hampton informed Davis, "are not subdued, nor do they despair." Hampton was persuaded that he could rally Confederate forces east of the Mississippi, regroup in Texas, and "show that we are not conquered." Hampton offered to assist in Davis's flight west: "If you desire to go in that direction it will give me great pleasure to escort you." The plan's impracticality and improbability of success, which required riding more than 800 miles through Union-occupied territory, outweighed in Hampton's mind the evil that would befall them were they to accept surrender. "No suffering which can be inflicted by the passage over our country of the Yankee armies can equal what would fall on us if we return to the Union," Hampton wrote. "We shall live under a base and vulgar tyranny. No sacrifice would be too great to escape this train of horrors." Hampton concluded his letter to Davis with the assertion, "My own mind is made up as to my course. I shall fight as long as my Government remains in existence; when that ceases to live I shall seek some other country, for I shall never take the 'oath of allegiance.'" If he could find no refuge in Texas, then Hampton would exile himself to Mexico. A few days later, Hampton wrote Davis a second letter reiterating his offer to escort him to Texas, but Davis did not respond to either message.[22]

Davis's failure to respond to Hampton's offer reflected the critical dysfunction at the top of the Confederate command. Davis and the remaining part of his cabinet limped along the railroad line from Greensboro to Charlotte, arriving in the latter city on April 19. The glacial pace of their retreat not only revealed the crumbling communications and transportation infrastructure but also reflected Davis's paralysis in the face of defeat. Shortly after his arrival in Charlotte, Davis learned of Lincoln's assassination and, on April 22, with the arrival of Breckinridge and Reagan, of the Bennett Place terms. In a cabinet meeting that evening, Davis solicited their reactions. To a man, they advised Davis to accept the terms and more broadly that the war was over. Secretary of State Judah P. Benjamin told him, "The Confederacy, is, in a word, unable to continue the war by armies in the field, and the struggle can no longer be maintained in any other manner than by a guerrilla or partisan warfare," a route that Benjamin saw as worse than defeat. "We have been vanquished in the war," he concluded and should accept Sherman's generous terms. Breckinridge endorsed Benjamin's condemnation of guerilla warfare, claiming that "ineffective hostilities may be prosecuted, while the war, wherever waged, will probably degenerate into that irregular and secondary stage, out of which greater evils will flow to the South than to the enemy." With deep reluctance, Davis telegraphed Johnston on April 24, tersely informing him, "Your action is approved."[23]

If Joseph Johnston experienced any relief from Davis's telegram, it proved ephemeral. Only an hour later, Johnston received two messages from Sherman. As Johnston noted in his memoir, "In one of them he informed me that the Government of the United States rejected the terms of peace agreed upon by us; and in the other he gave notice of the termination of the armistice in forty-eight hours." Earlier that morning, Major Hitchcock had returned from his mission to Washington, unexpectedly accompanied by Grant, who informed Sherman that Johnson and his cabinet had rejected the terms. Grant instructed Sherman that he was authorized to offer Confederates the Appomattox terms, but if Johnston did not accept them, Sherman was to resume the offensive.[24]

Johnston recognized immediately that if the cease-fire expired, his army was in no position to meet Sherman's on the battlefield, as desertions over the past week had crippled his capacity to wage war. He wired Breckinridge in Charlotte for counsel, adding that "we had better disband this small force to prevent devastation to the country." Breckinridge quickly replied, although the words sound more like Davis's or Hampton's, who had just arrived in Charlotte to offer his services. "Can you not bring off the cavalry and all the men you can mount from transportation and other animals, with some light field pieces?" the reply asked. "Such a force could march away from Sherman and be strong enough to encounter anything between us and the Southwest." Recognizing that such a course of action would necessitate a rigorous pursuit by Federal cavalry and the decimation of the countryside, Johnston demonstrated unusual independence in rejecting the guidance from Charlotte. On the morning of April 25, Johnston replied, "We have to save the people, spare the blood of the army, and save the high civil functionaries. Your plan, I think, can only do the last. . . . Commanders believe the troops will not fight again. We think your plan impracticable." Unwilling to allow the cease-fire to expire, Johnston wrote to Sherman, asking to meet to negotiate terms of surrender. Sherman agreed and scheduled a meeting for the following day (April 26), again at the Bennett farmstead.[25]

When they met for the third time in the Bennett parlor, Sherman and Johnston both recognized their limited negotiation options. Sherman had already been discredited in the Northern media for his initial terms and had been given explicit instructions to use the Appomattox Courthouse terms as a template. Johnston also felt under substantial pressure to come to some agreement, recognizing that his army was on the verge of disintegration. Yet despite these pressures, Johnston had difficulty agreeing to surrender under the same terms that Lee had accepted. The major hang-up in negotiations appears to have been

Johnston's concern that his soldiers would be paroled without adequate rations or transportation. "The disbanding of General's Lee's army," Johnston noted, "has afflicted this country with numerous bands having no means of subsistence but robbery." Fearing that the dissolution of his army would create anarchy and chaos, Johnston lobbied Sherman for some provision to guarantee that his soldiers could return home without the need to pillage. Sherman replied that he was only authorized to offer the Appomattox terms and that alternatives would likely be rejected. Sherman's subordinate, Gen. John Schofield, provided a solution to this dilemma: Johnston would sign two agreements, the first with Sherman surrendering his army and the second a few days later with Schofield (who would succeed Sherman in local command once Sherman departed for Washington) to provide transportation and rations to paroled Confederates. Eager to have the terms approved, Sherman immediately took the surrender agreement to Grant in Raleigh for his imprimatur, and Grant added his signature to the document.[26]

Orchestrated by General Schofield, the North Carolina surrender took on a cant slightly different from what transpired in Virginia a few weeks earlier. As at Appomattox Courthouse, surrendered Confederates received Federal rations. Sherman authorized the distribution of a quarter-million rations, more than enough to sustain Johnston's army during the parole process and the journey home, a generosity Johnston considered an "enlightened and humane policy" that would ease the transition to peacetime. Schofield, Sherman, and Johnston wanted to ensure that Confederate soldiers' return home progressed in a more orderly fashion than had happened after Appomattox. Unlike Lee's army, much of which came from eastern states, Johnston's force drew predominantly from western states and faced a much longer journey home. To facilitate transportation, Confederate horses would be "loaned to the troops for their march to homes, and for subsequent use in their industrial pursuits." Confederate soldiers from Arkansas and Texas would be provided water transportation home. Moreover, Confederate units were encouraged to make the journey home intact, preserving the discipline that all but disappeared from Lee's army after their parole. To this end, Confederates were permitted to keep one-seventh of their weapons in order "preserve order and protect citizens en route," pledging to turn over these weapons to Federal authorities once they returned home.[27]

Unlike at Appomattox Courthouse, there would be no formal surrender ceremony or parade in North Carolina. Instead, on May 1 the Federal authorities opened a parole office in Greensboro where surrendered soldiers could apply for and receive their paroles. The first Confederates in line to receive their paroles were Rear Admiral Raphael Semmes, formerly captain of the CSS *Alabama*, and his "Naval Brigade," sailors who had less than a month earlier attached themselves to Johnston's army. Semmes enthusiastically sought his parole because his conduct in the Confederate navy had been branded by some in the North as piracy, and he thought that the parole document's pledge "not to be disturbed by the United States authorities" might provide some degree of amnesty from prosecution. Over the next two days and taking their turns by unit, 36,971 Confederates received paroles in Greensboro.[28]

Despite Schofield's concerted efforts, the process of paroling Johnston's troops proved, in his words, "embarrassed by utter confusion and anarchy." Many of Confederates refused to turn over their weapons, preferring to bury or destroy them rather than deposit them in Federal hands. Henderson Dean, a soldier in the 66th North Carolina, had often expressed his aversion to surrender, noting that "I hade sworn that the Yankees should not never take me prison[er] that I would die first." When it came time to stack his Springfield rifle, he recalled all the miles and battles they had shared. Rather than allow it to fall into Union hands, Dean buried his rifle under a fence rail, hoping that its burial site would remain undisturbed. Others simply abandoned their arms along the roadside. Schofield complained to Sherman that "General Johnston found it impossible to deliver all the arms and other public property at Greensborough, and we were compelled to receive them wherever the troops chose to throw them down." One Confederate involved in the parole process noted that only 8,000 rifles were surrendered, less than a third of the number expected.[29]

Before they took their paroles, Confederate soldiers had ample time to consider their options. They had been in camp nearly two weeks with little to do except discuss whether to accept the terms of surrender, receive their paroles, and return home, or to continue fighting. Texan Samuel T. Foster waited impatiently to see the terms of surrender. Foster had enlisted in the fall of 1861 and had been taken prisoner in January 1863 after the surrender of Fort Hindman. After brief stints in Camp Chase and Fort Delaware, Foster benefited from one of last significant exchanges under the Dix-Hill cartel in May 1863. Wounded at Missionary Ridge, Foster remained with the Army of Tennessee throughout the Atlanta and Carolinas campaigns. On April 16, the day before Johnston and Sherman's initial meeting, Foster noted in his diary, "Every one suppose[s] this army is to be surrendered shortly and of course there is great excitement about it. The whole army (or at least as far as I know) are badly demoralized." The following day, he added, "No one knows what Genls Johns[t]on and Sherman have done, yet all suppose it is a surrender. Everything very quiet. All hands talking about how they will go to Texas." Foster knew about the terms that Lee's army had received at Appomattox Courthouse and expected they would receive the same. "None calculate to go to prison," he wrote. "All expect to be paroled, and go home as soon as the surrender is made." Although his own imprisonment had been brief and mild, Foster knew that prison conditions had deteriorated since and had no desire to spend even a day in captivity. As an officer, Foster attempted to keep his men in line, only to discover that "discipline is very loose. Everyone doing pretty much as he pleases." In part to dispel the boredom of camp, Foster attempted to drill his company, "just to see if the men would drill." Most of the time, Foster and his men sat "in camp passing rumors from one Brigade to another all day—Some say that the thing is settled and some say that the difficulty has hardly begin yet—so it goes." The scuttlebutt fell into predictable patterns: that they had been surrendered and would go home on parole; that fighting would resume shortly; that the United States had gone to war with Mexico or France, and that a joint Union-Confederate army was in the works (sometimes with Robert E. Lee commanding); that slavery had been abolished in the Confederacy; that reunion had been established while preserving slavery. In the end, Foster believed little of it, noting that there were "no rumors from any source that can be relied upon."

Not until the night of April 27 did Foster hear any news worthy of serious thought, when General Johnston announced the results of his military convention with Sherman. By Foster's estimation, no one slept that evening: "a dreadful night, all hands up and talking over the situation. They go over and over the war again, count up the killed and wounded, then the results obtained—It is too bad! If crying would have done any good, we would have cried all night." Over the next several days, Foster filled his diary with memories of the last four years: battles he had fought in, marches he had suffered through, and friends he had lost. "And what does it amount to? Has there been anything gained by this sacrifice?" he asked himself. Only on May 3 did his mood shift from despair to relief. "After turning in our guns, and getting our parol[e]s, we fell relieved," Foster noted. "No more picket duty, no more guard duty, no more fighting, no more war. It is all over, and we are going home. HOME after an absence of four years from our families and friends."

Despite his misgivings, Samuel Foster welcomed surrender, as it brought a close to a grueling war. Most of his fellow Confederates shared this sentiment, eager to end that chapter of their lives and begin the next one. Foster recognized, however, that diehard components in Johnston's army rejected any surrender as dishonorable. These men, Foster noted, saw themselves as "still not whip[p]ed and evince a determination to fight it out some way, or leave the country, rather than go back into the Union." The exodus had begun even before the final terms had been announced. "Before the Expiration of the Armistice," one Confederate noted, "our men 'began to leave—without leave'—and desert in squads." Some feared that surrender would mean imprisonment and concluded that it would be "far better to die—fighting—in hot blood—than endure the horrors—of "scant food'—'death line'—'freezing to death'—as thousands of our men—had so suffered and—died." South Carolina artilleryman Charles Hutson remembered that many men chose "to make our way home and thence to Texas, without being hampered by the Paroles." Although only a fraction of Johnston's army, those who chose to depart without a parole in their pockets often did so accompanied by other men from their regiment, suggesting a high degree of social pressure to either accept or reject surrender.[30]

A disproportionate number of Confederates rejecting surrender in North Carolina came from the Trans-Mississippi, including a handful of Texans who had volunteered prior to Twiggs's surrender in 1861. More than half of the 8th Texas Calvary, popularly known at Terry's Rangers, elected to join Taylor's or Kirby Smith's armies. James Blackburn, who had fought with the Rangers since the beginning, recalled that his company held a conference and "decided unanimously to go to Dick Taylor and to start at once." They dispersed into smaller bands to elude notice by Union forces, and Blackburn believed that "most of them made their escape and were never paroled at all, but are still to say, soldiers of the Confederate government." Blackburn's band made it to Tennessee, where they learned that "General Taylor had surrendered his army." They held another "council of war" and elected to push westward and "offer our services to General Kirby Smith." Splintering into squads of three or four men to cross the Mississippi, Blackburn and the other Rangers arrived too late to aid Kirby Smith. Without an army to fight for, Blackburn went home.[31]

Reflecting the pattern established at Appomattox Courthouse, some of those who refused to accept surrender became the first to embrace postwar paramilitary terrorism. On April 26, Munson Buford, a South Carolina cavalryman, decided to join Gen. Wade Hampton's quest to "join Gen. Kirby Smith's army beyond the Mississippi, the last remnant of the Confederate armies that had not surrendered," rather than submit to the terms of surrender agreed to that morning. Before Hampton, Buford, and other South Carolinians could reach the Trans-Mississippi, however, "everything had gone to pieces, Kirby

Fall of the Cis-Mississippi Confederacy

Smith's army included." Nonetheless, Buford took great pride in the fact that "General Hampton had not surrendered, and neither had I." Upon his return home, Buford helped to establish the Ku Klux Klan in Newberry County, a site of intense racial violence during Reconstruction. Wade Hampton himself openly supported the Klan in South Carolina and used paramilitary violence to terrorize political opponents in his 1876 gubernatorial campaign.[32]

Part of the confusion that emerged during Johnston's surrender concerned which Confederate soldiers fell under its aegis. Johnston commanded not only the Army of Tennessee but also the Confederate Department of South Carolina, Georgia, and Florida and the Department of North Carolina and Southern Virginia. Unlike the Appomattox Courthouse settlement, which established a twenty-mile cordon, Johnston's surrender could be read to include not only the army he commanded directly but all remaining Confederate forces east of the Chattahoochee River. Not unsurprisingly, Union officials embraced this broader interpretation, while Confederates not directly attached to Johnston's command argued for a more limited interpretation. For these Confederates scattered across the Southeast, Union officers had to negotiate separate surrender agreements. In the largest of these, Samuel Jones surrendered 8,000 soldiers in Florida to Edward M. McCook on May 10. Two days later at Kingston, Georgia, William Wofford surrendered 6,000 soldiers to Henry Judah. For both Jones and Wofford, the size of their forces on paper vastly exceeded what they could actually muster, as most of their soldiers had gone home or broken into partisan bands functioning outside Confederate control. Both men welcomed the opportunity to relieve themselves of commands in a war they thought lost.[33]

Some of the remaining Confederate forces in the East did not learn of Johnston's surrender until much later. In western North Carolina, what one soldier referred to as "the most inaccessible part of the Confederacy," William Holland Thomas's Legion of Indians and Highlanders (officially the North Carolina 69th) continued to fight, apparently unaware of Johnston's surrender. They engaged in a skirmish with Union troops near White Sulphur Springs (modern Waynesville) on May 6. In his initial parley with Lt. Col. W. C. Bartlett, Thomas initially refused to surrender, attempting to intimidate the Federal officers with twenty Cherokee bodyguards who were "stripped to the waist and feathered off in fine style." Indeed, Thomas began their negotiations by demanding Bartlett's surrender, claiming that if "he did not immediately surrender and make haste to get away from Waynesville, he would turn his Indians upon the Yankee regiment and have them all scalped." After two lengthy days of negotiations, Thomas concluded that his cause had lost, agreeing to surrender on May 9, exactly a month after Lee's surrender at Appomattox Courthouse. Some of the smaller Confederate commands in the Southeast had to seek out Union forces to accept their surrender. Not receiving confirmation of Johnston's surrender until the first week of May, Gen. B. J. Hill had to approach the nearest Federal outpost in Dalton, Georgia, about surrendering his two undersized regiments of new recruits from north Georgia and Alabama. "I am an old soldier, and have been fighting in this revolution for four years, and have always considered myself as a gentleman and soldier, and I wish to do nothing but what is strictly honorable," Hill wrote, eager to reach a settlement that would not bring shame to him or his men. "I have no wagons, nor ambulances, and my command are rather poorly armed," he admitted. On May 16, Hill marched into Chattanooga with the small remnant of his brigade, surrendering them under the same terms that Lee had received at Appomattox Courthouse and Johnston had received at Bennett Place. Throughout the month of May, Confederate soldiers arrived at Federal outposts in dribs and drabs to surrender and receive their paroles.[34]

Johnston's surrender left three major Confederate commands still in the field: Richard Taylor's Department of Alabama, Mississippi, and East Louisiana; M. Jeff Thompson's Northern Sub-District of Arkansas; and Edmund Kirby Smith's Trans-Mississippi Department. Union invasions had effectively segregated these commands from each other and from the Confederacy's political leadership, transforming them into semiautonomous potentates. In this balkanized Confederacy, news traveled slowly, distorted and mangled by fractured lines of communication and transportation. From his headquarters in Meridian, Richard Taylor had little direct contact with other Confederate commands, except Kirby Smith, whom he loathed, once calling him "stupid, pig-headed and obstinate." Taylor had a reputation for level-headed but bold action, a reputation he earned during the Red River campaign in the spring of 1864, the last decisive Confederate victory of the war.

Taylor had two able and trusted lieutenants in his department. He entrusted the defense of Mobile to Gen. Dabney Maury. A West Point graduate and Mexican War veteran, Maury had demonstrated his competence and bravery at Pea Ridge and Corinth. Maury and Taylor had been close friends prior to the war, and the diminutive Virginian had his superior's full support and trust. Taylor also leaned heavily on Nathan Bedford Forrest, who had found a home for his cavalry corps in Taylor's department. In the year since Fort Pillow, Forrest's reputation had only grown. Northerners continued to vilify him as a butcher and barbarian, while Confederates rallied behind a figure they saw as the embodiment of the cavalier ideal. Like Maury, Forrest had an excellent relationship with Taylor, whom he once praised as "the biggest man in the lot. If we'd had more like him, we would have licked the Yankees long ago."[35]

Of these three, Union officials seemed most concerned about Forrest, who many believed would never surrender. Not only had Forrest demonstrated a visceral aversion to surrender, but calls to prosecute him for the Fort Pillow massacre might push him into waging a guerilla war long after other Confederates had raised the white flag. During the surrender negotiations at Bennett Place, Sherman wrote to Grant that Confederates accused of war crimes should be held accountable and that he would "use my influence that rebels shall suffer all the personal punishment prescribed by law." Facing prosecution and possible execution, such men would never surrender and would form "bands of desperadoes" led by "such men as . . . Forrest . . . who know not and care not for danger and its consequences." Sherman echoed this sentiment in a letter home, noting that for men like Forrest, "nothing is left for them but death or highway robbery." Gen. George Thomas shared Sherman's belief that Forrest would never surrender. After hearing rumors that Forrest intended to continue fighting in Texas, Thomas ordered a subordinate to "inform" Forrest that "if he attempts such a reckless and bloodthirsty adventure he will be treated thereafter as an outlaw, and the States of Mississippi and Alabama will be so destroyed that they will not recover for fifty years."[36]

When news of Johnston's surrender reached him, Taylor had suffered two major setbacks in the past month. Gen. James H. Wilson's cavalry had swept into central Alabama, repeatedly overwhelming and outmaneuvering Forrest's threadbare command. On April 2, 1865, at the Battle of Selma, both Forrest and Taylor barely managed to escape before Union forces captured the city. According to Taylor, "Forrest fought as if the world depended on his arm." The shame of recent defeats had only enraged Forrest, who repeatedly plunged himself into the fray, suffering a sabre wound before concluding that Selma could not be defended. "Forrest appeared, horse and man covered with blood," Taylor recalled, "and announced the enemy at his heels, and that I must move at once to escape capture." Taylor fled on the last train out of Selma; before slipping into the darkness, Forrest and his men set fire to 25,000 bales of cotton stockpiled in the city to prevent them from falling into Union hands. Taking control of the city, Wilson systematically destroyed what had been one of the Confederacy's main manufacturing sites.[37]

In Selma's aftermath, Forrest again demonstrated an aversion to the commonly accepted paradigms of surrender. According to Federal reports, during their retreat, Forrest and his personal escort found a detachment of Union soldiers "asleep in a neighboring field. . . . He charged them in their sleep, and refusing to listen to their cries of surrender, killed or wounded the entire party, numbering twenty-five men." One of the wounded survivors claimed that this massacre amounted to "a repetition of Fort Pillow." Forrest's partisans disputed this characterization, claiming that Federal soldiers fired first and that "not a single man was killed after he surrendered."[38] As at Fort Pillow, the absence of a significant number of unwounded prisoners suggests that the Federal version of events would have been the more likely scenario. Either way, Forrest continued to draw Northern ire for his apparent barbarism and bloodlust, reinforcing his notoriety established at Fort Pillow although tarnishing his reputation for invincibility.

Taylor's command suffered its second disaster only a week after the fall of Selma, when Union forces occupied Mobile, one of the Confederacy's best-fortified cities. Mobile's defenses included a ring of forts along the bay that needed to be taken before the city itself could be assaulted. In August 1864, Admiral David Farragut's victory at the Battle of Mobile Bay laid the groundwork for the siege and surrenders of Fort Gaines, Fort Powell, and Fort Morgan. But Mobile's most formidable sentinels stood unmolested until the end of March 1865, when Gen. Edward Canby assembled 45,000 men in a carefully planned attack on the city's remaining fortifications. Investing both Spanish Fort and Fort Blakely simultaneously on April 1, Union forces vastly outnumbered their combined garrison of 6,500 men. Despite these imbalances, rebel soldiers demonstrated remarkable resilience to the Union sieges. Slowly encroaching on Spanish Fort, Canby ordered a bombardment and assault on April 8, with Union soldiers breaking through the first line of rebel breastworks at 5:00 P.M. One Iowan recalled that "we here witnessed the spectacle of dying in the last ditch, as quite a number of the rebels refused to surrender and were shot in their ditches, and on the other hand quite a number of them who were taken prisoners ought, in justice to our men, to have been killed, as they would first fire at our men after being ordered to surrender, then throw up both hands and surrender." Recognizing that he could no longer defend the site, Gen. Randall Gibson spiked his guns and evacuated his remaining soldiers under the cover of nightfall. The following morning, the combined Union forces prepared to assault Fort Blakely.[39]

Overshadowed by events at Appomattox Courthouse earlier that afternoon, the attack on and surrender of Fort Blakely on April 9 demonstrated how the tension between race and surrender continued to shape combat a year after Fort Pillow. Led by three brigades of USCT soldiers, the Federal assault on Fort Blakely managed to overwhelm Confederate defenders in less than an hour. As soon as the first black soldiers emerged from their siege trenches, signaling the start of the assault, a Confederate officer ordered his men to "lay low and mow the ground—the damned niggers are coming." Crossing the open field that separated Union trenches from the first line of Confederate fortifications, black soldiers came under heavy fire. "Greater gallantry," one Union general noted, "could hardly be desired" as the USCT soldiers, "burning with an impulse to do honor to their race, . . . rushed forward with intense enthusiasm, in [the] face of a terrible fire."[40]

Once inside the first line of fortifications, USCT soldiers raised the now-familiar battle cry of "Remember Fort Pillow!" Most of the undersized garrison fled, hoping either to escape the fort or to surrender to white Union soldiers, from whom they expected better treatment. "The colored troops [were] so worked up by the time they got in the fort that their officers couldn't control them," one white Illinois soldier noted, and they were "determined to do as the rebels had done with the colored troops at Fort Pillow. Kill them, surrender or no surrender! They had to bring up a division of white troops to stop them." When white Union soldiers followed the USCT into the fort, desperate Confederates sought them out as sanctuary from unrestrained violence at the hands of the USCT. One Union soldier noted that "many of the enemy garrisoning these works threw down their arms and ran toward their right to the white troops to avoid capture by the colored soldiers fearing violence after surrender."[41]

After the battle, some Confederates claimed that USCT soldiers had engaged in a retaliatory massacre at Fort Blakely, indiscriminately killing rebel prisoners. Little evidence supports this claim: unlike at Fort Pillow, the number of captured soldiers vastly exceeded the number killed. However, Confederate soldiers did believe that USCT soldiers would execute them if they were captured and took extraordinary steps to avoid surrendering to black soldiers. Moreover, the zeal with which black soldiers attacked amazed and alarmed white Union soldiers, who believed they needed to restrain the USCT to prevent a massacre. When Confederates tried to escape by fleeing into Mobile Bay, USCT soldiers relentlessly pursued them. "Lots of them ran into the bay and were drowned or shot by the colored troops," noted an Iowan sharpshooter. "We tried to stop the killing of the rebels, but had to stand back, for the colored troops had blood in their eyes and meant to have revenge for the murder of their comrades at Fort Pillow." Conversely, USCT soldiers accused surrendering Confederates of not abiding by the conventional laws of surrender. When one Alabama regiment found itself overwhelmed by Minnesotans, there was "nothing left for us except to run up a white flag." As soon as the rebels dropped their weapons, however, "the negro troops rushed over our works, brandishing their guns in great rage, accusing us of having fired upon them after we surrendered." After USCT soldiers shot one Mississippi officer, "it looked as though we were to be butchered in cold blood," and Confederates contemplated reclaiming their rifles to "die fighting to the last."[42]

Although Confederate casualty figures for Fort Blakely are imprecise, the vast majority of the rebel garrison chose to surrender rather than attempt to escape or sacrifice their lives to a lost cause. Of the nearly 4,000 Confederates defending Fort Blakely, only 250 were killed, with an equal number estimated to have escaped from the massive fort into the adjacent swamps or waterways. For many of the 3,400 Confederates who surrendered, the fall of Fort Blakely evoked memories of Vicksburg. Indeed, nearly all of the Confederate regiments and many of the Union regiments who fought at Fort Blakely had participated in the surrender at Vicksburg nearly two years earlier. When an Ohio officer demanded the surrender of Confederates in one corner of the fort, a Missouri soldier asked, "To whom do we surrender?" When the reply came that the officer commanded the 83rd Ohio, the Confederate wryly quipped that "I believe we did that once before." Indeed, for some soldiers in the 4th Mississippi, this was their third experience surrendering, having laid down arms at Fort Donelson and Vicksburg. Although veteran prisoners, surrendered rebel soldiers bristled at having African American soldiers guard them. Confederate prisoners, one Union officer noted, demonstrated "an unreasonable dread of the colored soldiers; huddling together in heaps, and acting as if their captors were wild beasts." Escorted to Ship Island prison by USCT detachments, many Confederates believed that their captors would execute them. "The rebels were very indignant at being subjected to such a disgrace as they considered it and they seemed to be terable afraid of the darkeys," one Union soldier noted. "I supposed they knew that the darkeys didn't owe them much sympathy."[43]

Richard Taylor knew that the loss of Selma and Mobile meant that Confederate defeat, at least in his department, proved inevitable. He could no longer supply what remained of his army, and his sphere of influence extended to only a handful of counties along the Mississippi-Alabama border. Between them, Forrest and Maury commanded only 8,000 men, far fewer than necessary to mount a meaningful defense against the encroaching Union armies. Shortly after his flight from Selma to Meridian, Taylor heard of both Lee's surrender and Lincoln's assassination. He decided not to hide this information from his soldiers, most of whom had heard rumors already. Although resigned to eventual defeat, Taylor did not believe that Lee's capitulation and his own recent defeats necessitated his own surrender. "The surrender of Lee left us little hope of success," Taylor noted in his memoir, "but while Johnston remained in arms we must be prepared to fight our way to him. Again, the President and civil authorities of our Government were on their way to the south, and might need our protection. Granting the cause for which we had fought to be lost, we owed it to our own manhood, to the memory of the dead, and to the honor of our arms, to remain steadfast to the last."[44]

Although Taylor believed that he could not surrender, he saw few practical options before them. He could not march his army west to rendezvous with Kirby Smith, "with the Mississippi impassible for troops." Dabney Maury, reorganizing what remained of his force from Mobile into three brigades in preparation, recommended that they "march eastward and join Johnston" in his campaign against Sherman. But Forrest refused to leave Mississippi, and with Canby's army and Wilson's cavalry between them and Johnston, such a reunion also seemed doomed to failure. On April 14, Taylor wired Jefferson Davis asking how he should progress: "Decision should be had at once as to which of the courses to adopt. Ignorant of the policy of the Government, I cannot decide." When he received no response, he resent the message on April 20, to the same effect. Unable to move from his enclave in Meridian, Taylor took what steps he could to hold his army together.[45]

On April 22, Taylor received word of Johnston's first convention with Sherman at Bennett Place. Since that convention called for all Confederate forces to lay down their arms, Taylor immediately wrote to his Union counterpart Edward Canby to secure his inclusion in the pact. A week later, on April 29, Canby and Taylor meet at the Magee farm, ten miles north of Mobile. Reflecting the relative strengths of their commands, Canby arrived "escorted by a brigade with a military band, and accompanied by many officers in 'full fig,'" while Taylor arrived with one aide clad in "rusty suits of Confederate gray," traveling via railroad handcar, "the motive power of which was two negroes." The two generals quickly agreed to a forty-eight-hour truce, ostensibly to await confirmation that the Union and Confederate governments had approved of the Bennett Place convention. That done, Taylor recalled, "we then joined the throng of officers, and although every one present felt a deep conviction that the last hour of the sad struggle approached, no allusion was made to it." Canby offered his guest "a bountiful luncheon," complete with the "joyous poppings of champagne corks." The military band began to play "Hail, Columbia," until Canby intervened, requesting "Dixie" in its stead. Taylor insisted that the band resume its initial tune in "hope that Columbia would be again a happy land, a sentiment honored by many libations." Canby and Taylor departed believing that their chapter in the war had ended.[46]

Unfortunately for Canby and Taylor, their celebrations proved premature. Shortly after his return to Meridian, Taylor received word from Canby that his government had rejected the peace settlement and that he would therefore be required to resume hostilities within forty-eight hours. Canby suggested, however, that they could avoid "any further effusion of blood" if Taylor would be willing to surrender under the Appomattox terms. Recognizing that he had no other option, Taylor agreed to Canby's terms. In his memoirs, Taylor characterized his role in the surrender as an executor fulfilling the terms of a will: "The military and civil authorities of the Confederacy had fallen, and I was called to administer on the ruins as residuary legatee. It seemed absurd for the few there present to continue the struggle against a million of men. We could only secure honorable interment for the remains of our cause." As one Texas senator passing through Taylor's department observed, by the time of the surrender, Taylor's "army was reduced to a mere skeleton by desertion." On May 4, 1865, the same day that President Lincoln was laid to rest in Springfield, Illinois, Taylor met with Canby in Citronelle, Alabama, to surrender what remained of his department. Local lore recalls that their final meeting took place under a large white oak, although contemporary sources situate their conference at a nearby doctor's house. Negotiations took the entire afternoon, as Taylor lobbied for better terms, only to acquiesce to Grant's Appomattox terms. Taylor and Canby agreed to hold the formal surrender and parole on May 8 at Meridian.[47]

As had been the case in earlier Confederate surrenders, many of Taylor's officers and men rejected the idea of surrender, lobbying their commander to keep fighting or deciding to break out on their own. One officer, a veteran of the recent disaster in Mobile, recalled that "at Meridian several hundred officers of all grades and whose commands were greatly diminished . . . were willing and anxious to fight to the last in any manner they could." John Bell Hood, himself en route to Kirby Smith's Texas, urged Taylor to join him and bring whatever portion of his command he could muster west across the Mississippi. Taylor believed that such efforts were undoubtedly doomed to failure. Moreover, he worried that if his army disintegrated before a formal surrender and without the protections provided by parole, "they will be hunted down like beats of prey, their families will be persecuted, and ruin thus entailed not only upon the soldiers themselves, but also upon thousands of defenseless Southern women and children." On May 2, prior to his second meeting with Canby, Taylor wrote to his officers, urging them to remain vigilant. He pledged to "make every effort to secure an honorable and speedy cessation of hostilities." They had an obligation to promote the surrender as the only honorable course of action available. "You will explain to your troops," Taylor told them, "that a surrender ... will not be the consequence of any defeat ... but is simply, so far as we are concerned, yielding upon the best terms and with a preservation of our military honor to the logic of events."[48]

Of his officers, Taylor suspected that Nathan Bedford Forrest would prove the least amenable to surrender. In the weeks since his defeat at Selma, Forrest had been behaving oddly, demonstrating little of his usual vigor. Encamped at Gainesville, Forrest hoped to reorganize his remaining troops, get fresh mounts and supplies, and plot his next moves. There his soldiers heard details of Lee's surrender at Appomattox and that Johnston was negotiating his surrender to Sherman in North Carolina. This news was mixed with other rumors: that Jefferson Davis sought to continue the fight in Texas, that Abraham Lincoln had been assassinated, and that General Taylor intended to surrender. In response, Forrest issued a curious announcement to his soldiers on April 25. Decrying a "morbid appetite for news and sensation[al] rumors," Forrest dismissed claims that Lee had surrendered or that Taylor intended to meet with Canby to surrender, telling his men that "no credence should be given to such reports." Conversely, he informed them that "southern sources" indicated that "General Lee has not surrendered" and that "Grant has lost in battle and by desertion 100,000 men." Confirming Lincoln's assassination, Forrest characterized the military convention between Sherman and Johnston not as a surrender but as a peace treaty "for the purpose of adjusting the difficulties and differences now existing between the Confederate and United States of America." Forrest pledged that his men would never "ground your arms except with honor." He closed his proclamation by urging his men to demonstrate patience and fidelity, as "a few days more will determine the truth or falsity of all the reports now in circulation"[49]

Many of Forrest's men feared that they would be prosecuted for their conduct at Fort Pillow if they surrendered to Federal authorities. They proposed fleeing to Texas, where Kirby Smith's army remained in the field, or seeking asylum in Mexico. One of Forrest's soldiers noted, "When the determination of the commander [Taylor to surrender] was made known to the men, they were bowed down with unutterable grief. . . . They gathered in groups under the forest-trees at Gainesville, and in low tones told of their despair. Many wept like children. Then came reaction; a sudden fever seemed to seize the men. There were their arms and horses. They would go to the Trans-Mississippi Department and continue the struggle for Southern independence." Another claimed that "many of General Forrest's men begged him to lead them to Mexico. With tears and entreaties they crowded around him and told him they could not brook the thought of surrender and would follow him anywhere, even to the end of the earth." If these diehards expected Forrest to lead them in their western adventure, they were sorely disappointed. "What could not be accomplished here could never be done in the thinly settled West," Forrest told them. His refusal helped to discourage rampant desertion among his men; if Forrest could accept surrender, so could they. His decision prompted them to realize "the hopelessness of their cause; and, with grim determination which had carried them so gloriously through the war, they decided to go home and to face the consequences, whatever they might be." Forrest similarly dismissed political leaders who encouraged him to continue fighting. On May 3, Forrest met with Mississippi governor Charles Clark and former Tennessee gover- nor Isham Harris, who urged him to take his soldiers west to Texas. Forrest dismissed the idea, saying, "Men, you may all do as you damn well please, but I'm a-going home." Continuing to fight against such overwhelming odds, Forrest understood, would prove disastrous. "To make men fight under such circumstances," he told them, "would be nothing but murder." When the two governors lobbied Forrest to reject the surrender agreement, he offered one final rebuke: "Any man who is in favor of a further prosecution of this war is a fit subject for a lunatic asylum."[50]

On May 9, Union general E. S. Dennis arrived at Forrest's headquarters in Gainesville to oversee the paroling of his cavalry. That morning, Forrest rode with his aide Maj. Charles Anderson, expressing "his bitter distaste for surrender" and that "the idea of going to Mexico was alluring to him." Major Anderson rebuked his superior, saying that if Forrest did go to Mexico, "his men would have to suffer the humiliation of surrender." Moreover, they would suffer "added humiliation to be compelled to bear the bitterness of surrender without your example and inspiration." Anderson's words evidently touched a nerve, as Forrest decided to reject the Mexican adventure, saying "I will share the fate of my men."[51] Although probably apocryphal, this story reflected something

Fall of the Cis-Mississippi Confederacy

of the conflict that Forrest felt about surrender. He had since his escape from Fort Donelson steadfastly refused to surrender, viewing any capitulation as dishonorable and unmanly. Now, however, he could see no alternative, short of abandoning his men. Faced with these options, Forrest reluctantly embraced surrender as the lesser of two evils.

That afternoon, while they awaited their paroles, Forrest's men received hastily printed copies of his farewell address. Printed on flimsy paper "of all colors and qualities," his words were probably composed by Anderson, who often served as Forrest's amanuensis. They reflected an unusual generosity and compassion, traits that Forrest had pointedly eschewed in his own surrender negotiations. "The armies of Generals Lee and Johnston having surrendered," they read, "you are the last of all the troops of the Confederate States army, east of the Mississippi River, to lay down your arms." Forrest argued that they should embrace the surrender as a sign that the Federal government did not intend to punish Confederates, noting, "The terms upon which you were surrendered are favorable, and should be satisfactory and acceptable to all. They manifest a spirit of magnanimity and liberality on the part of the Federal authorities, which should be met, on our part, by a faithful compliance with all the stipulations and conditions therein expressed. . . . Obey the laws, preserve your honor, and the government to which you have surrendered can afford to be, and will be magnanimous."

Knowing that many of his soldiers still harbored fantasies about joining Kirby Smith in Texas, Forrest counseled against such recklessness. "That we are beaten is a self-evident fact," he told them, and "any further resistance on our part would be justly regarded as the very height of folly and rashness." Those who refused paroles or violated their terms, he warned, would probably be arrested and imprisoned. Given Forrest's at-times brutal and unforgiving conduct throughout the war, his farewell address embraced uncharacteristically generous sentiments. "Civil war, such as we have just passed through, naturally engenders feelings of animosity, hatred and revenge," Forrest told them. "It is our duty to divest ourselves of all such feelings, and so far as in our power to do so cultivate friendly feelings towards those with whom we have so long contented. . . . Whatever your responsibilities may be to government, to society, or to individuals, meet them like men." In his closing, Forrest counseled them to "obey the laws, preserve your honor, and the government to which you have surrendered can afford to be, and will be magnanimous."[52]

Nathan Bedford Forrest embraced surrender as a route to peace in May 1865 after more than three years of openly disdaining surrender and threatening to raise the black flag to compel terrified Union garrisons into capitulation. If he reflected on this change of heart, Forrest did not comment on it publicly. His soldiers, however, saw his acceptance of the terms of surrender and parole as an indication that defeat did not mean dishonor and that they could resume their civilian lives without shame. When one of Forrest's soldiers received his parole the following day, he noted that he left military life "if not with victory, at least and above all, with honor."[53]

9

WITHOUT A
GOVERNMENT

Jeff Thompson, Edmund Kirby Smith, and the
Slow Death of the Trans-Mississippi Confederacy

True to his word, Jefferson Davis never surrendered. When he found himself surrounded by Union cavalry on the morning of May 10 near Irwinville, Georgia, Davis had spent the past two weeks in a sluggish trek south from Charlotte, North Carolina, in a vain effort to reach the Trans-Mississippi Confederacy. In Davis's version of events, recorded in his memoirs, "a trooper galloped up and ordered me to halt and surrender, to which I gave a defiant answer," prompting the Union cavalryman to aim his carbine at the fugitive Confederate president. In what would have been a suicidal move, Davis contemplated charging the mounted soldier, dislodging him from the saddle, and escaping astride his horse. Before Davis could enact his rash scheme, Varina Davis intervened, throwing her arms around him, thus preventing the Union soldier from firing but also foiling her husband's plan to escape. Although Union and Confederate accounts offer conflicting versions of events that morning (particularly with regard to whether Jefferson Davis had donned his wife's shawl in an effort to conceal himself), all descriptions referred to their culmination as Davis's capture, never his surrender. Although Civil War soldiers often used the words "captured" and "surrendered" as synonyms, both Davis's and his Union captors' universal preference for the former language over the latter suggests that his imprisonment was not the product of a voluntary surrender but the involuntary detention of a fugitive. This rhetoric served the purposes of both captor and captive. With a $10,000 bounty on his head, Davis had been labeled a criminal fugitive by the Federal government, which suspected that he had some role in Lincoln's assassination. Unlike soldiers, he would not be eligible for parole and allowed to return home. His involuntary capture would also signal the absolute collapse of the Confederate government. Jefferson Davis also had good reason to prefer the language of capture over surrender. Not only did it permit him to uphold his pledge never to surrender, but it also allowed him to claim that he was being held against his will during the two years he spent in prison. Although the idea would have horrified Davis, his capture in the Georgia woods demonstrated a kind of ironic justice. As historian Yael Sternhell has pointed out, Davis's capture, pursued by men on horseback, mirrored the plight of runaways hunted by slave patrols.[1]

Davis's capture did not bring an end to the Confederacy. Although its eastern armies had laid down arms and its president was held prisoner, west of the Mississippi, Confederate forces did not immediately fold but persisted for weeks before surrendering. Compared to that of their eastern brethren, the surrender of the Confederacy's western armies proved much more chaotic and explosive. Although their terms of surrender built on the model established by Grant and Lee, the routes taken to arrive at these settlements demonstrated little of the decorum or civility that characterized the surrenders at Appomattox Courthouse, Bennett Place, or Citronelle. Long after the Army of Northern Virginia raised the white flag, some Trans-Mississippi generals steadfastly refused to abandon their quest for Confederate independence, even if their new republic only included Texas and parts of Louisiana and Arkansas. Others knew that Confederate defeat was inevitable but did not believe that they could honorably surrender until compelled to on the battlefield. Even more so that in the East, the decisions of rebel soldiers, both individually and in aggregate, shaped the timeline and contours of Confederate surrender. By deserting their posts, refusing to stack arms, and fleeing to Mexico, they, as much as their commanders, determined how and when western armies surrendered.

In February 1865, Edmund Kirby Smith appointed Meriwether Jeff Thompson to command the Northern Sub-District of Arkansas. Although theoretically the district was within Kirby Smith's Trans-Mississippi Department, Union occupation of central Arkansas meant that Thompson's jurisdiction extended only to a small corner of the state, cut off from Kirby Smith's army in Texas and surrounded on all sides. Thompson's highest priority upon assuming his post, however, was not facing these external threats but establishing law and order in northeast Arkansas. Although guerilla warfare had been endemic in Arkansas throughout the conflict, its intensity and brutality had only escalated in 1864 and 1865. Rampant desertion crippled regular Confederate units in the region, and chronic food shortages threatened the civilian population with famine.[2] With a skeletal staff of ten men, Thompson sought to rid his district of guerillas; attending to the Federals would take second priority. "I determined to exterminate or drive out of the Sub District all Guerrilla Bands, and independent companies," Thompson wrote, "for they were not only irritating the whole people by their acts, but were demoralizing all good soldiers by their freedom from restraint and discipline." By his own estimation, Thompson only had "a few hundred true men, and more than ten thousand demoralized men" in his department.[3]

Thompson's military career frequently intersected with critical junctures in the development of surrender. In 1861, Thompson accepted a brigadier general's commission in the Missouri State Guard, a pro-Confederate creation of secessionist governor Claiborne Jackson, and took an active role in some of the earliest prisoner exchange agreements with John C. Frémont and Henry Halleck. When Frémont declared martial law in August 1861, Thompson responded with his own proclamation, promising to "hang, draw, and quarter a minion of Abraham Lincoln" for every Confederate sympathizer executed under Frémont's order. In 1862 and 1863, Thompson led repeated raids into Missouri from northwest Arkansas, taking hundreds of prisoners and earning him the nickname of "Swamp Fox of the Confederacy." In a retaliatory Union raid, Thompson surrendered near Pocahontas, Arkansas, on August 1863. Taken during the nadir of prisoner exchange, Thompson spent a year in Federal prisons, including Johnson's Island and Fort Delaware. He devoted his time in prison to writing poetry and dismissed the harshness of captivity, noting that he did not "suffer as much as I have when in the field with my command." Sent to Charleston as part of the prisoner-hostage crisis there in July 1864, Thompson was one of only fifty Confederates exchanged. He returned in time to participate in Sterling Price's unsuccessful Missouri raid in September and October 1864, where he fought under Jo Shelby.[4]

News of Lee's surrender took more than a week to reach Thompson. "The terrible news from the East has been received," Thompson wrote to Kirby Smith on April 18, "and the loss of the grand Old Dominion, with the noble Lee, and the remnant of the heroic Army of Northern Virginia, is a most disheartening misfortune." As a "true Southron," Thompson pledged to vigorously continue the struggle but worried that his subordinate officers had become demoralized. He expected that desertions would only increase as news from the East spread, and "if the 'worse comes to worst,' I will collect all true men around me and we will make our way to your headquarters."[5] Thompson had little faith in the loyalty and commitment of Confederate soldiers in Arkansas, and his efforts over the past few months to rein in paramilitary violence proved largely unsuccessful.

Two weeks later, on April 30, Thompson received a demand to surrender from Gen. J. J. Reynolds. Reynolds had penned his demand on the same day that Thompson had written to Kirby Smith, but Thompson's peripatetic headquarters made it difficult for the Union couriers to locate him. In a defiant and contemptuous tone, Thompson asserted that he must "most positively decline," arguing that despite Lee's surrender, he continued to believe "firmly in the justness of our cause and our ability to succeed in the course." He would be willing to sacrifice as many men as needed on the altar of Southern independence and would fight until victory had been secured or "until my Government or superior officers bid me stop." To this end, he would "meet the shock and bear the brunt as our forefathers did in '76," regardless of the consequences.[6]

Not long after he refused Reynolds's demand to surrender, Thompson received a second, more harshly worded ultimatum from Gen. Grenville Dodge that clearly articulated the choices Thompson faced. Enclosing reports from recent Union victories and Confederate surrenders, Dodge offered Thompson the same terms that Lee had accepted at Appomattox. Accepting them, Dodge promised, would bring "an end to the further destruction of life and property in North Arkansas." However, "should you not accept these terms," Dodge warned, Thompson's soldiers would "immediately be declared outlaws, and no terms thereafter granted to them."[7] As with the earlier demand to surrender, this message took more than a week to reach Thompson. This time, however, he proved more amendable to negotiating. Thompson's change of heart seems to have been brought about by his failure to rally Confederate support in Arkansas. He recognized that were Union forces to engage him, "it would have been perfectly impossible" to mount a defense, "for I could not have concentrated five hundred men, from the ten thousand subject to orders." Between May 7 and May 11, Thompson bombarded Dodge's representative, Lt. Col. Charles W. Davis, with a series of letters, inquiring about the precise terms of surrender and parole Lee had received, how surrender would affect soldiers' families, and how and when civil authority would resume. Most pressing, however, was whether his men could pass into Confederate lines after the surrender. In his letter to Davis, Thompson argued that "many of those I am called on to surrender will prefer to go to Texas or Louisiana to remaining in neighborhoods where private animosities will keep the community in a tumult after the military authorities are withdrawn." Although Thompson framed this request with an eye to preventing postwar community violence and protecting soldiers' families, he undoubtedly also had in mind that many

Slow Death of the Trans-Mississippi Confederacy

of his soldiers had declared that they would never live in the United States and were determined to emigrate to Texas or Mexico.

Thompson eventually accepted the proffered terms but insisted that the Confederacy would in time prevail. Ignorant of Jefferson Davis's capture the previous day, Thompson wrote to Dodge on May 11 that "though dark clouds now obscure our prospects, yet I have every faith in our ultimate success, am only induced to surrender now to spare the people of this already desolated country the horrors of an invasion." Although Union officials thought it an unnecessary complication, Thompson insisted on mustering his diffuse command at two locations where he could personally supervise their surrender and parole, ordering soldiers in the eastern half of his district to assemble at Wittsburg on May 25 and those in the west to rendezvous at Jacksonport on June 5. He insisted on this prolonged schedule, claiming that it would take weeks for the news to spread throughout his command. Thompson closed with a curious coda: while a "strict compliance . . . will be expected that those who desire to accept these terms . . . those who do not so desire will be gone out of the sub-district before these times." Unlike Lee, Johnston, or Taylor, each of whom sought to keep their commands together during their surrenders, Thompson actively encouraged diehards to leave Arkansas prior to their surrender. Indeed, no sooner had he agreed to surrender than he sent dispatches to "warn all parties who did not desire to surrender to immediately leave the district."[8]

On the morning of May 25, a small delegation of Union officers arrived at Wittsburg on the USS Arkansas to accept Thompson's surrender. En route, they wondered how many soldiers Thompson had in his command and, of those, how many would show up to receive their paroles. Estimates ranged from fewer than 400 men to an entire division. A cabin boy noted that "nobody knew just how many men he had in his command. The way his soldiers fought, you'd think they were a whole division. That was one of the reasons that I was glad I was going to be on hand at his surrender, so I could learn firsthand how many men there really were in his army." When they arrived, he saw Thompson on the bank, "astride a white horse, straight as a ramrod." Approximately 2,000 men lingered around Thompson, which the cabin boy described as "a sorry-looking lot . . . ragged and thin, and their faces pinched from hunger." While Union officials expressed disappointment that so few Confederates came to Wittsburg to receive their paroles, Jeff Thompson wished that he had arrived at the surrender site alone. He had attempted to persuade those accompanying him not to surrender but to make their way to Texas. "I would be proud," Thompson told them, "if I was the only man there to surrender on the 25th for I had positively promised none but myself." News of Taylor's surrender and Davis's capture, however, had just reached them, persuading many of Thompson's men to accept the paroles and return home.[9]

When the steamship's gangplank lowered, Colonel Davis and the other Union officers stood at attention on the main deck. Thompson promptly called his men to attention, eliciting a radical transformation in their disposition. "The ragged soldiers were a different body of men," one Union observer noticed. "They leaped into line, shoulders straight, heads held high, and in their eyes, deep-set in their sunken faces, flashed the undying spirit and pride in the Confederacy." The sight alarmed some of those onboard the *Alabama*. One "began to wonder what would happen if the warriors of the Swamp Fox should suddenly decide that they weren't quite ready to surrender, if they should resolve to bag a few more Yankees before laying down their guns." With his men at attention, Thompson dramatically bounded up the gangplank on his horse, dismounted, and strode to the table to sign his parole. Thompson's nearly 200 officers followed on foot and diligently had their paroles recorded. Unlike at Appomattox, Union and Confederate officers showed no interest in fraternization, reflecting "a sullen undercurrent" onboard.

The tension only increased when the first enlisted man marched onboard to receive his parole and surrender his weapon. Walking slowly to the table, the rebel soldier "looked Colonel Davis straight in the eye, and then strode swiftly to the rail and tossed his gun into the river." At the act of defiance, one Union officer began to draw his sword, but Davis attempted to dissipate the situation, promising food and transportation home to Thompson's famished and footsore soldiers. "The hold of his steamboat is filled with supplies," he told them. "Each of you may take away as much as you can carry." Davis's gesture immediately changed the disposition of the surrendering rebels, although many of them continued to prefer a watery burial for their weapons rather than surrender them to the Union, as the "sound of guns striking the water" punctuated the afternoon. After signing their paroles, they stuffed their pockets and hats with food. Even Thompson found humor in the sight of men with "one pocket... filled with salt, another with coffee, another with sugar, the hat with hard bread, drink the vinegar, put the bar of soap under one arm, the bacon under the other, the candles and rice and dried apples, etc. as best they could in their hands." Over the course of the day, more Confederates arrived on the shore, and by sundown, more than 2,000 rebels had received their paroles.[10]

The drama of Thompson's Wittsburg surrender reappeared in a slightly different mode at his second surrender at Jacksonport on June 5. More than twice as many soldiers encamped themselves on the town's waterfront to receive their paroles. Among the Union officers on board the *Arkansas* to supervise the paroles was Gen. Alexander Shaler, who had run the Johnson's Island prison during Thompson's detention there and, after his capture at the Wilderness, had been exchanged for Thompson in August 1864. Also present was Hans Mattson, a veteran of the Union surrender at Murfreesboro and the Confederate surrender at Vicksburg. Mattson noted in his journal that while the assembled rebel soldiers looked desperate and threadbare, Thompson arrived "dressed in a suit of snowy white, from the plume in his hat to the heel of his boot, and with a white sword-belt and white gloves." At as Wittsburg, very few of the surrendering Confederates stacked their arms, preferring to leave them at home.[11]

That evening, Thompson assembled his paroled soldiers to address them one final time. Unlike most Confederate generals, who offered their farewell remarks in writing as Lee had done at Appomattox, Thompson addressed them in person. Standing on top of a barrel to be seen and heard over the crowd, Thompson delivered an address that differed not only in its mode but in its message. While most Confederate officers followed Lee's template in praising their men for their sacrifice, Thompson took the opportunity to blame his soldiers for their shortcomings and cowardice. Rather than fight bravely and uphold their obligations to the cause, they had abandoned their posts as deserters. "Many of the 8,000 men I now see around me," Thompson said, "have been skulking for the last three years in the swamps" rather than fighting. Placing the blame for Confederate defeat at their feet, Thompson proclaimed that "I now come to surrender you and hope you will make better citizens than you have soldiers." When a soldier pleaded for Thompson to "Talk to us like gentlemen, Sir!" Thompson doubled down, threating to "take the top of his head off, if he interrupted me." Knowing that at least some of the soldiers present had fought bravely, Thompson sought not to paint with too broad a brush. "I know there are some gentlemen here," he said, "and I know there are some damned, sneaky cowardly dogs." He instructed those men who had left their guns at home to immediately surrender them to the nearest Federal outpost and told them that they deserved whatever punishment they received. Not unsurprising, Thompson's soldiers left the surrender ceremony embittered and angry that their commander had challenged their honor at their moment of defeat.[12]

Jeff Thompson's surrenders at Wittsburg and Jacksonport demonstrate that not all Confederate surrenders at the end of the war followed the same script. Unlike Lee, Johnston, or Taylor, Thompson actively encouraged his soldiers not to participate in the surrender but to flee west to join Kirby Smith. With this in mind, he consciously delayed the issuance of paroles to give diehards time to leave his department. Also in a departure from earlier surrenders, Thompson condemned rather than praised his men, telling them that they should be ashamed of their conduct. He attributed their surrender to a fatal deficiency in Confederate nationalism rather than the necessity of succumbing to overwhelming Union power, as Lee, Johnston, and Taylor had done. Although Thompson's surrenders marked a departure from Confederate surrenders in April and May, they foreshadowed some of the chaos, miscommunication, and profound bitterness that would characterize the surrenders to come.

In the second week of May 1865, Union colonel John T. Sprague waited impatiently in Shreveport for Edmund Kirby Smith to return. The trip from St. Louis to the Confederate Trans-Mississippi capital had taken two weeks, far longer and more complicated than anticipated, and he was eager to report to Gen. John Pope about his mission to compel a Confederate surrender west of the Mississippi. As soon as he learned of Lee's surrender at Appomattox Courthouse, Pope had wired Grant to congratulate him and ask if he recommended using the Appomattox terms as a model to demand Kirby Smith's surrender. Grant approved Pope's suggestion, deferred to his judgment about the specifics, and added that "by judicious management" Kirby Smith "might be induced to give up the contest" and "might want to get out of the country himself."[13] As soon as he received Grant's approval, Pope assigned Sprague, his chief of staff, to deliver the demand for surrender. Now that Lee had surrendered, Pope expected that other Confederate armies would quickly follow suit and that Sprague would promptly return with Kirby Smith's capitulation. This assumption proved disastrously in error.

An Old Army veteran, Sprague understood surrender. Stationed in Texas in 1861, Sprague had been taken prisoner in Twiggs's capitulation. Upon his parole, Sprague delivered an address titled "The Treachery in Texas" to the New-York Historical Society. He told them in June 1861 that the experience had left him with "a degree of embarrassment almost unsurmountable." Although he spent most of the conflict away from the front lines, serving as New York's adjutant general, Sprague never forgot the lingering shame. Insisting on delivering Pope's message in person, Sprague was repeatedly delayed before he received Confederate approval to travel up the Red River to Shreveport. Crossing into Confederate territory on May 8, Sprague traveled upriver via steamboat, sharing the vessel with Simon B. Buckner, who had surrendered Fort Donelson in 1862 and now served as Kirby Smith's chief of staff. Also on board were "several exchanged or paroled soldiers" from Lee's army who were headed home, their war over. Sprague hoped that Pope's letter and developments over the past month would make Kirby Smith's path forward clear: Lee had surrendered at Appomattox (April 9); Johnston had surrendered to Sherman at Bennett Place, North Carolina (April 26); and Gen. Edward Canby had accepted the surrenders of generals Thomas Howell Cobb (April 20) and Richard Taylor (May 4). Sprague had known both Kirby Smith and Buckner from the Old Army and expected them to bend to the logic of events.[14]

Kirby Smith read Pope's message closely. Although he had anticipated its contents, he refused to respond immediately, explaining that he was scheduled to meet with western Confederate governors in Marshall, Texas, twenty miles west of Shreveport. Kirby Smith asked Sprague to wait in Shreveport for him to consult with civil authorities. Before he left, Kirby Smith "admitted the force of recent events," and Sprague indicated "a warm and benevolent desire to avoid the further effusion of blood and the infliction of needless suffering."[15] Yet when he returned a week later, Kirby Smith told Sprague that he could not surrender. In a lengthy "Memorandum for Col. Sprague," Kirby Smith articulated his reasoning. He argued that "my army was menaced only from a distance, that it is large and well-supplied, and in an extensive country full of resources." Unlike Lee's worn and exhausted army, surrounded at Appomattox, his force faced no immediate military threat and had ample food and resources. Considering the differing circumstances of the two armies, the Appomattox terms, Kirby Smith argued, "were not such as a soldier could honorably accept." Reiterating the now-familiar definition, Kirby Smith explained that "an officer can honorably surrender his command when he has resisted to the utmost of his power, and no hopes rest upon his further efforts." Given the condition of his army, he reasoned that "it cannot be said that the duty imposed upon me [not to surrender unnecessarily] has been fulfilled to the extent required by the laws of honorable warfare."

Unlike some of his subordinates, who harbored fantasies about the Trans-Mississippi Confederacy continuing to fight indefinitely, Kirby Smith did not hold unrealistic expectations about the military prospects before him. Barring foreign intervention, a highly unlikely proposition at this point, he did not expect to obtain Confederate political independence. However, since he was in a stronger military position than Lee, Kirby Smith believed that he deserved better terms. Furthermore, he interpreted the Federal government's insistence on the Appomattox terms as an indication that it intended to "humiliate a people who have contended gallantly." Kirby Smith proposed alternative terms, including immunity from prosecution, a full restoration of political rights, and the freedom to leave the country unhindered. Any less liberal terms,

Kirby Smith argued, would be contrary to "the laws which custom has made binding amongst nations and military men" and would engender continued resistance and rebellion.[16]

Although Kirby Smith would never admit it to Sprague, recent months had decimated his army. Unpaid for over a year, most of the men had become deeply disillusioned. Listless and disaffected, many had begun plundering the local populace. On April 8, Gen. John Bankhead Magruder wrote to Kirby Smith from Houston that "great outrages are being perpetrated on citizens" by soldiers in central Texas. Since most soldiers in the Trans-Mississippi came from Texas regiments, many found the lure of returning home irresistible, deserting rather than enduring the monotony of camp life. This dissatisfaction only intensified on April 20 when news of Lee's surrender reached Texas. "Lee's surrender burst like a thunderbolt upon the Trans-Mississippi Department," recalled one Missouri cavalryman, as a flurry of emotions and stages of grief consumed them: "A great horror came first, then unbelief, then fleeting resolutions of hate and defiance, then a great reaction, followed by timidity and despair." Confederate officers attempted to rally their men, pledging to continue the struggle. Kirby Smith, Magruder, and Texas governor Pendleton Murrah each issued proclamations urging fidelity to the Confederate cause, claiming that Johnston's army and Jefferson Davis would soon arrive, and they could reconstitute the Confederacy in the West. Except on the most diehard of rebel soldiers, these efforts appeared to have had little effect, as desertion rates only increased. When news of Johnston's and Taylor's surrenders arrived in early May, the scant discipline that remained entirely vanished. In Galveston, approximately 400 soldiers plotted munity. Rumors spread that Shreveport would be set aflame and looted. Although all could see the writing on the wall, little consensus developed about how to approach the imminent demise of the last vestige of the Confederacy. By the time Kirby Smith returned from his conference with Confederate governors, only the most diehard rebels remained at their posts, and many of them had no interest in surrender. "The men were gathered in groups everywhere," one Louisiana soldier noted, "discussing the approaching surrender. Curses deep and bitter fell from lips not accustomed to such language, while numbers, both officers and men, swore fearful oaths never to surrender." Even if victory proved out of reach, they could not stomach the unbearable humiliation of surrender.[17]

While Kirby Smith understood that his army continued to collapse with each passing day, he had only a faint awareness that many of his senior officers had been plotting against him. Shortly after Kirby Smith agreed to meet with Sprague, Gen. Sterling Price conferred with his subordinates about the possibility of arresting Kirby Smith, fearing that the meeting would culminate in surrender. A few days later, while Kirby Smith sought council from rebel governors in Marshall, a cabal of officers, including generals Thomas James Churchill, Alexander Hawthorn, and Jo Shelby, met nearby to plot how to overthrow Kirby Smith if he chose to surrender. The ringleader of the planned coup, Jo Shelby argued that the army "no longer has any confidence in General Smith." They should depose Kirby Smith and rally what men remained, along with "fugitives from Lee and Johnston" to create one vast Confederate army, which he estimated would number 100,000 soldiers. They would await President Davis's arrival, as "he alone has the right to treat of surrender." If that failed, Shelby argued, they should march into Mexico and intervene in the ongoing Mexican civil war to either "reinstate Juarez or espouse the cause of Maximilian. It makes no difference which." Whatever happened, Shelby adamantly refused to consider negotiations that culminated in their surrender. "Surrender is a word," he concluded, "which neither my division nor myself understand." To replace Kirby Smith, Shelby proposed Simon Buckner, who had the "rank, reputation, [and] the confidence of the army." Through loyal aides, Kirby Smith caught wind of most of these Byzantine machinations. To temper his critics, Kirby Smith told anyone who would listen that he had no intention of surrendering.[18]

John Sprague was probably only dimly aware of the rapid dissolution of Kirby Smith's army and his officers' plots against him. He did see, however, that the alternative terms that Kirby Smith proposed fell far outside those he was empowered to accept. His mandate, he told Kirby Smith, only included the power to negotiate for a military surrender consistent with the Appomattox terms, not to reach a political settlement. At an impasse, Sprague concluded that further negotiations would prove fruitless and decided to depart for Union lines. As their boat left Shreveport, an aide who had accompanied Sprague noticed that the tenor of rebel soldiers along the levee had changed since their arrival. They had become a "murderous gang . . . hurrahing, yelling, firing off their revolvers" to signal their hostility to the Union envoy. He felt grateful that Kirby Smith had sent a company of Missouri sharpshooters to escort them. That morning, Kirby Smith also left Shreveport, bound for Houston, where he intended to prepare the Trans-Mississippi Department for an imminent Union invasion. While in transit, Kirby Smith left Buckner in temporary command while he relocated his headquarters.

Sprague began his return journey to St. Louis, believing his mission to be a failure. Crossing into Union lines, Sprague received two unexpected revelations. First, a telegram from Pope ordered him to abandon his mission "unless you have made, or are actually in process of making, arrangements with General E. Kirby Smith for the surrender of his forces." The political and military situation had evolved quickly since Sprague's departure, Pope indicated, and "it is not now of consequence whether General Kirby Smith surrenders or not." Jefferson Davis had been captured, and Canby had accepted Taylor's surrender.[19]

Second, Sprague heard that Simon Buckner was traveling to Baton Rouge to surrender the Trans-Mississippi Department. The decision to surrender was not prompted by a reconsideration about the merits of capitulation so much as it was a response to the rapid disintegration of Kirby Smith's army. Fifty thousand strong at the time of Sprague's meeting with Kirby Smith, rebel soldiers had heard rumors of an impending surrender and interpreted Kirby Smith's departure as a signal that the war had ended. Although a few maintained that they would continue the war in Texas or Mexico, most simply walked away, ignoring their pleading officers and commandeering whatever military supplies they believed they were owed. No sooner had Kirby Smith left for Houston than riots broke out in Shreveport and Mansfield. On May 17, Gen. James Slaughter wrote from Brownsville that "great dissatisfaction exists among the troops on this frontier, at least one half [of whom] have already or will desert their colors. They say 'We are whipped.' . . . War meetings have been held, speeches made, but all without the desired effect." Assessing the state of the Trans-Mississippi Department on May 19, one of Buckner's subordinates observed that "the major portion of the command [have] deserted camp and gone to their homes," taking with them "all the government animals and most of the wagons," thereby "completely paralyzing the present military organization." Within a week, the actions of soldiers in west Louisiana and Texas had overturned Kirby Smith's refusal to surrender on terms he believed dishonorable and pushed Buckner to capitulate while he still had an army to surrender.[20]

Accompanied by generals Sterling Price and Joseph Brent, Buckner hastily traveled down the Red River from Shreveport to Baton Rouge and from there to New Orleans under Union escort. Canby arrived the same day from Mobile. Meeting at the St. Charles Hotel, the generals were joined by many junior officers and onlookers, hoping to witness the final significant Confederate surrender. Among those present was Richard Taylor, who, two weeks after his own capitulation, wanted to provide Buckner with support and counsel. Canby offered the Appomattox terms, which Buckner accepted, signing the final agreement on May 26.[21]

The irony that it fell to Simon Buckner to offer the final significant Confederate surrender of the war was not lost on contemporaries. His conduct at Fort Donelson in 1862, surrendering the fort to Ulysses S. Grant after Floyd and Pillow abandoned it, had earned Buckner both the distinction of presiding over the first major Confederate surrender and a reputation for bravery and honor. One Missouri cavalryman, critical of Buckner, observed that "he had the mournful satisfaction of surrendering the first and the last army of the subjugated and destroyed South." As at Fort Donelson, the burden of surrender only fell to Buckner by default when his superior officers either abdicated their posts or were unable to act. In a letter to his wife, Buckner reflected on the relationship between his surrenders at Fort Donelson and Baton Rouge. "My action at Fort Donelson was but an illustration of what I did here," he wrote. His surrender of the Trans-Mississippi army, he argued, reflected the same principles that drove him to surrender three years earlier: the desire to maintain order and to prevent needless bloodshed. Although the Trans-Mississippi did not face the same immediate threat that the garrison at Fort Donelson did, Buckner argued that its absolute collapse necessitated his action. "Before you can judge the propriety of my surrender," Buckner wrote, one must understand how little of his army remained: "The troops were deserting by divisions, and were plundering the people as well as the government property." He could not consult with Kirby Smith, then en route to Houston, and had to act. "Having once taken the position to surrender," he wrote, "I think it more becoming to my character to act with proper dignity." Although he could have fled Texas for Mexico, Buckner argued that honor dictated that he remain.[22]

Meanwhile, Kirby Smith's trip from Shreveport to Houston had taken far longer than anticipated. He did not arrive at the site of his proposed new headquarters until May 27, one day after Buckner surrendered the entire department. Enraged but impotent, Kirby Smith issued a convoluted farewell address on May 30. "The day after I refused the demand of the federal government to surrender this department," he explained to his scattered soldiers, he left Shreveport for Houston with the intention of concentrating his forces. From such a position of strength, Kirby Smith argued, he could have continued to fight or if necessary surrender under terms "alike honorable to soldier and citizen." Using language that expressed a similar sentiment in milder tones than Jeff Thompson's rant in Jacksonport, Kirby Smith blamed them for the disgraceful surrender. "Soldiers! I am left a commander without an army—a general without troops. You have made your choice.—It was unwise and unpatriotic, but it is final." He urged them to return to their homes and families, to obey the law, and to rebuild their lives. Having dismissed his soldiers, Kirby Smith traveled from Houston to Galveston, where he added his signature to Simon Buckner's on the surrender agreement.[23]

On May 17, a week after Jefferson Davis's capture, Grant provided Phil Sheridan with new orders: head west and "force the surrender of the Confederates under Kirby Smith." Although Grant provided Sheridan with wide latitude about how he approached Kirby Smith, he did instruct him that if Kirby Smith did not immediately surrender, "he and his men were not entitled to the considerations due to an acknowledged belligerent." Grant claimed that Davis's capture and the collapse of the Confederate government had changed the nature of the conflict: without a government, even one never recognized as legitimate, Kirby Smith's men were no longer soldiers but "outlaws." They would have one final chance to accept surrender under the same terms that Lee and Johnston had accepted, after which the option to surrender would be closed. By the time that he arrived in New Orleans, Sheridan received word from Canby that Kirby Smith's army had surrendered. He quickly came to the conclusion, however, that "the surrender was not carried out in good faith, particularly by the Texas troops," since many of them "had marched off to the interior of the State in several organized bodies, carrying with them their camp equipage, arms, ammunition, and even some artillery, with the ultimate purpose of going to Mexico."[24]

While surrenders east of the Mississippi had witnessed a trickle of soldiers dissent, fleeing before receiving their paroles to continue fighting, only in the Trans-Mississippi did a large organized body of soldiers systematically refuse to surrender. The process had started in Thompson's Northern Sub-District of Arkansas, when hundreds left for Texas prior to the surrenders at Wittsburg and Jacksonport. It reached its culmination in Texas after Buckner surrendered Kirby Smith's army, when a rebel regiment elected to march into Mexico rather than stack arms. Sources vary widely on the number of men who joined the Mexican Expedition, ranging from 150 to more than 1,000, with the lower figure probably more reliable. Most came from Missouri, although their ranks included scattered diehards from across the Confederacy. While in absolute terms, this amounted to only a sliver of Kirby Smith's army, the degree of organization in this remnant was unprecedented. Led by Jo Shelby, members of the Mexican Expedition saw themselves as the rightful heirs of the Confederacy, men who had refused to surrender their weapons, their flag, or their cause. As Shelby told them just after news of the Shreveport surrender, "You have been betrayed! The generals whom you trusted have refused to lead you. . . . We are the Army and the Cause. To talk of surrender is to be a traitor."[25]

Viewing themselves as protectors of order and civil society in the chaotic landscape of post-surrender Texas, Shelby's regiment marched across the state to San Antonio before beginning their final march to the Rio Grande border. At the Menger Hotel, adjacent to the Alamo, Shelby met with former Confederate leaders, many of whom had already surrendered, including generals Sterling Price, Thomas Hindman, and John Bankhead Magruder; Missouri governor Thomas Reynolds; Louisiana governor Henry Watkins Allen; and Texas governor Pendleton Murrah. Also staying at the hotel was Edmund Kirby Smith, who had registered under a pseudonym and had barricaded himself in his room. Hoping to lure Kirby Smith from his refuge, Shelby summoned his regimental band to the street below Kirby Smith's window and had them play "Hail to the Chief" and "Dixie." When music failed to elicit a response from the drawn curtains, Shelby told the assembled crowd to "shout for him until you are hoarse." Eventually Kirby Smith emerged on the balcony, bewildered and frightened by the fracas outside. Shelby greeted him as the "ranking officer of the Trans-Mississippi Department," claiming that the men below "are your soldiers, and we are here to report to you. Command and we will obey." They were all that remained of his army, "that little band which knows neither dishonor nor surrender." Although Kirby Smith declined command of the expedition, he did elect to join the exodus to Mexico.[26]

Now swelled by the addition of other former soldiers, political exiles, and refugee families—all those who "could not brook the idea of surrendering"— Shelby's column departed San Antonio on June 25. Their route to the Rio Grande meandered through arid wasteland, "made dreary by mesquite and chaparral" and populated largely by rattlesnakes and bandits. A pursuing Federal cavalry brigade, part of Sheridan's force sent to secure the border, came within five miles of them but inexplicably did not engage. On July 4, 1865, in the border town of Eagle Pass, Shelby's men raised their flag one final time before burying it with a plume from Shelby's hat in the "depths of the Rio Grande," weighing it down with stones. Crossing into Mexico, they unsuccessfully offered their services to the French-backed Emperor Maximilian, claiming that they preferred "exile to surrender."[27]

The Mexican Expedition marked the culmination and apotheosis of a particular thread of surrender thought among diehard rebels. They had no illusions that by refusing to surrender they could advance the Confederate political cause. They did believe, however, that life after surrender within the United States would prove inhospitable and intolerable. This sentiment held particular weight for the political leaders who attached themselves to the expedition, who feared prosecution for their wartime actions. A dearth of sources makes assessing why individual soldiers joined Shelby's march difficult, although one soldier's memoirs offer insight into his motivations. Enlisting in 1861 at the age of nineteen, Thomas Westlake fought primarily in Sterling Price's cavalry. He reluctantly surrendered in late 1864, during the nadir of prisoner exchange, only offering himself up when "the bullets were whizzing so close to me I saw that if I did not Surrender I would be killed." Westlake found his prison experience dehumanizing and disheartening. "There has been a great deal said about the Brutal treatment of federal prisoners in Southern prisons," he recalled, but "it could not have been any worse [than] that the Southern Prisoners Received at the hands of the Thieves, murder[er]s, and cowards in charge of Northern prisons." Exchanged in Virginia in March 1865, he traversed the Confederacy to return to his regiment, now in Texas, a trip that included a clandestine crossing of the Union-controlled Mississippi. When Shelby asked for volunteers to go to Mexico rather than surrender, Westlake was the only soldier from his regiment to step forward. While the others accepted surrender as an inevitability, Westlake proclaimed that "I finally determined never to surrender to the Federals again if I could do otherwise."[28] While scant records make generalizing from his experience difficult, Westlake, like many Confederate soldiers, drew upon four years of intimate familiarity with surrender in deciding how his war would end.

In the decades after the war, many a former Confederate vied to call himself the last rebel to surrender. Edmund Kirby Smith, Richard Taylor, and William Holland Thomas, among others, all claimed or were granted that mantle.[29] Being "last" mattered because it implied a deeper commitment to the Confederate cause; even when everyone else had given up, the sole survivor had continued the struggle. The value former Confederates attached to the last surrender helps to explain the periodic appearance in Southern newspapers of stories describing Confederate soldiers who had gone into hiding before Appomattox and only emerged months, if not years, later, unaware that the war had ended. These fanciful accounts, unsupported by any collaborating evidence, appealed to defeated Confederates' romantic inclinations. The most widely reprinted of these anecdotes concerns four rebel soldiers who emerged from Virginia's Dismal Swamp on August 1866 and "did not know the war was over." Southern newspapers labeled their commander, Col. Tewksbury, as "the last man to surrender of all the Confederate forces," although some incredulous editors added their suspicions that the story was mostly likely fabricated.[30]

Fictions aside, two late Confederate surrenders do have legitimate claims to be the last to raise the white flag. On June 23, 1865, two months after Appomattox, Stand Watie rode to the outskirts of Doaksville, Indian Territory (modern Oklahoma), to surrender to two junior Federal officers. Watie had two sources of authority. Born in Georgia in 1806, he had grown up among the slave-holding Cherokee elite, who remained politically powerful even after Indian removal. From an early age, he had been an active player in contentious tribal politics, adding his signature to the Treaty of New Echota in 1835 and culminating in his selection as principal chief of the Cherokee Nation (South) in 1863. He also held a general's commission from the Confederacy. An 1861 treaty between the Confederacy and the western Cherokee created an unusual place for Native Americans within the Confederate military. Although pledged to mutual defense, Native soldiers would not be required to fight outside Indian Territory. Consequently, Stand Watie's Civil War consisted primarily of battles with Unionist natives, including other Cherokees, punctuated by raids into Kansas. Although Watie was theoretically subordinate to Kirby Smith, his status as the leader of a dependent nation meant that his men did not necessarily fall under the protections offered by the Trans-Mississippi Department's surrender.[31]

The document that Stand Watie signed with Lt. Col. Asa C. Matthews on June 23, 1865, was both a surrender agreement and a peace treaty. While Watie pledged that his men would return home and cease hostilities, the document created significant obligations for the Federal government. In exchange for laying down arms, Waite's men would "be protected by the United States authorities in their person and property not only from encroachments on the part of white, but also from the Indians who have been engaged in the service of the United States." Watie's insistence on this protection reflected his fear that the end of the Civil War would only exacerbate conflict between and within Native nations.[32] Although normalized relations in Indian Country would take another year to come to fruition, Watie's treaty marked the final Civil War surrender within the United States.

The final Confederate surrender took place more than four months later and 4,000 miles away in Liverpool, England, when Confederate commander James Iredell Waddell surrendered CSS *Shenandoah* to British navy captain James Paynter on November 5, 1865. Built in 1863 for the East Indian tea trade, the clipper ship was purchased by Confederates in October 1864 and began its short career as a commerce trader, traveling around the Cape of Good Hope into the Indian Ocean and ultimately to the North Pacific whaling grounds. In the Arctic waters off the Aleutian Islands, CSS *Shenandoah* preyed on American whaling vessels, taking nearly two dozen prizes in June 1865. After taking a New Bedford whaler on June 22, Waddell first heard of Lee's surrender, although he and most of the crew did not take the report seriously. One of the ship's officers dismissed the report, arguing that while Lee may have sacrificed a portion of his command, "as to his surrender of whole army and his treating with General Grant for peace, I do not believe one single word." Convinced that the Confederacy remained alive and well, the *Shenandoah* continued to raid whalers in the Bering Sea, taking more than a dozen prizes over the next few days. Not until August 2, when they took the whaler *Barracouta*, did Waddell admit that the Confederacy had been defeated. An officer described it as the "darkest day of my life. . . . Our dear country has been overrun, our President captured, our armies & navies surrendered, our people Subjugated!"[33]

Now convinced that the Confederacy had fallen months before, Waddell immediately determined that they must surrender. He ordered the crew to lower its rebel flag, store the cannons below deck, and refit the ship to look like a merchant vessel. Rather than sail his ship into San Francisco, only a few days' voyage away, Waddell thought that they would receive better treatment in a non-American port. Although international law permitted commerce raiding during wartime, Waddell worried that his actions after the fall of the Confederacy could be interpreted as piracy, a crime punishable by hanging. His crew agreed, writing a petition to their captain that "we can not reasonably expect any good treatment if we fall in the hands of the U.S. government," urging him to surrender the ship anywhere else. After considering Cape Town, Waddell settled on Liverpool, a destination that would take them 9,000 miles and three months to reach.

When the *Shenandoah* arrived at the mouth of the River Mersey on November 6, a harbor pilot refused to steer the ship into Liverpool docks without its flag flying, prompting Waddell to order its Confederate colors raised one final time. Eager to surrender his ship to British authorities, Waddell demanded that the pilot enter the port at low tide, resulting in a temporary grounding on a sandbar. Once freed at high tide, Waddell anchored his ship adjacent to the HMS *Donegal*, to whom he surrendered. In a letter to the British foreign secretary, Waddell pleaded for mercy, arguing that his situation was unprecedented and that he and his men should not be judged too harshly. As "I am without a government," Waddell felt obliged "to surrender the ship . . . to her Majesty's Government for such disposition as in its wisdom should be deemed proper." Despite protests from the United States, a British government inquiry concluded that the vessel had not violated any laws of war and paroled its crew.[34]

The surrenders of the Stand Watie's Cherokee and the CSS *Shenandoah* in Liverpool are unique not only because of their chronological place at the end of a long series of Confederate surrenders, but also because they situated surrender in an international context that implied greater formal recognition of the Confederacy than ever before. The Union administration's longtime fear that accepting Confederate surrender might imply some degree of recognition of the Confederacy's legitimacy seems to have vanished after Jefferson Davis's capture. Watie's treaty with the United States recognized him as both the leader of a dependent Indian nation and a Confederate officer and created a framework of reciprocal obligations, characteristic of international diplomacy more than a military surrender. Similarly, the British government, which had never formally recognized the Confederacy during the war itself, provided some modicum of recognition when it accepted CSS *Shenandoah*'s surrender in Liverpool. In these final notes of the Confederate funeral dirge, the formality of surrender eased the transition to peace.

10

NEVER SURRENDER

Remembering (and Forgetting) Civil War Surrenders

Over the past two decades, historians have deepened our understanding of how Americans have remembered and commemorated the Civil War. Path-breaking works by David Blight, Fitz Brundage, Karen Cox, Caroline Janney, and others have demonstrated deep disjunctures in how Americans, Northern-ers and Southerners, black and white, have chosen to remember the conflict. If the war ended in 1865, fights over what the war meant and how it should be in-scribed on the landscape have raged ever since. Current debates over the place of the Confederate flag and the propriety of buildings named after and statues of Confederate generals reflect long traditions of using Civil War symbols as signifiers in modern culture wars.

Within this context, surrender sites present something of an anomaly. Unlike battlefields, where a common language of commemoration developed by the end of the nineteenth century, surrender sites remained curiously un-memorialized. Indeed, many significant surrender sites have been thoroughly neglected in the commemorative landscape. Against a widespread paucity of surrender monuments and commemoration, a few sites stand out as places where Americans attempted to make sense of surrender. At Fort Sumter, Vicksburg, Appomattox Courthouse, and Bennett Place, idiosyncratic and often controversial monuments reflected both local and national debates about the meaning of surrender and of the Civil War more broadly. Surrender sites have remained contentious locations because unlike battlefields, whose monuments and commemorations have tended to highlight the bravery of both Union and Confederate soldiers, surrender sites exposed the surren-dering party to dishonor and humiliation. While those men who fought in the Civil War accepted that one could honorably surrender, subsequent gen-erations grew increasingly uncomfortable with surrender, repudiating it as un-American and weak.

This aversion to commemorating surrender first manifested itself in a celebration marking the fourth anniversary of the fall of Fort Sumter. On the morning of Friday, April 14, 1865, more than 5,000 people assembled on Charleston's docks awaiting ferries to take them to Fort Sumter. Two months earlier, Confederate flags had flown proudly over the city. Sherman's approach had prompted P. G. T. Beauregard, who had presided over Sumter's bombardment and had accepted Anderson's surrender, to evacuate the city on February 15, 1865. Three days after Beauregard's departure, Charleston's mayor surrendered the city unceremoniously to one of Sherman's subordinates. Ever since, Union flags had flown over the city, much of which lay in ruins, as the prolonged shelling from Union gunboats since August 1863 had reduced the city to a shell of its former grandeur, leaving more than one visitor to compare it to the recently excavated ruins of Pompeii. The crowds on the docks had come to celebrate the fourth anniversary of the fort's surrender and the raising of one final Union flag over the city. Robert Anderson, now promoted to general for his heroism during Sumter's shelling, had returned to hoist the flag he had lowered during the fort's surrender.

General Anderson had arrived in Charleston only a couple of days earlier, traveling aboard the *Arago*, a chartered steamship from New York with other dignitaries handpicked by Lincoln to participate in the ceremony. Their number included Rev. Henry Ward Beecher, who would give the keynote address; *Liberator* editor William Lloyd Garrison; and British abolitionist George Thompson, who shared a stateroom with Garrison during the voyage. Each of their lives, a *New York Times* reporter wryly noted, would not have been worth "the price of the rope which would have served to hang him, if he had simply 'put in an appearance'" in Charleston a few months earlier. Joining them on board were approximately sixty others, including politicians, judges, military officials (including several of the soldiers who had surrendered with Anderson at Sumter), and reporters from the major New York and Chicago newspapers. While some of the others on board saw the planned ceremony as a symbolic end to the war—the eventual defeat of the Confederacy a fait accompli—for Beecher, Garrison, and Thompson, the return of the Union flag to Fort Sumter was the final nail in slavery's coffin.

Few of the men aboard the *Arago* were as overjoyed to make the journey to Charleston as William Lloyd Garrison. A pariah for most of his thirty years of public life for his radical opposition to slavery and demands for immediate emancipation, Garrison must have felt vindicated to be selected to participate in such a symbolically important ceremony. Nearly sixty years old, Garrison had become a venerated figure, a far departure from the young man who in 1835 had been dragged through the streets of Boston by a mob enraged by his fiery rhetoric. In a letter to his wife written during the second day of their voyage, Garrison remarked, "All on board have been very courteous and attentive to [fellow radical abolitionist] George Thompson and myself, and are manifestly pleased that we are on board." He also noted that they had been blessed with "a fair wind, a bright sky, and a slight undulation of the waves," culminating in "a splendid sunset" and "a night so brilliant and entrancing that I did not turn into my berth until a late hour." Furthermore, he had thus far avoided any signs of the seasickness that usually afflicted him. Considering all aspects of the voyage, Garrison concluded that "there was nothing to be desired in the matter of favorable omens."

Garrison took great pleasure at conversing with the *Arago*'s other passengers. "There is no stiffness of manners," he wrote. "Everyone is ready for conversational interchange." An anomaly on a ship packed with politicians and military men, Garrison believed that they shared a common aversion to slavery, noting that "though we are heterogeneous in the professions and pursuits of life, yet there is entire harmony on the slavery question." He was particularly impressed with Robert Anderson, with whom he had several conversations. Garrison found him to be "a very amiable and modest man . . . quite religious in his spirit." Indeed, in a comparison that probably would have shocked Anderson, a Kentucky native, career soldier, and former slave owner, Garrison claimed that he "reminds me more of John Brown than any one."

En route to Charleston, the *Arago* stopped briefly at Fort Monroe, located at the southern tip of the Virginia peninsula, where the waters of the James River join the Chesapeake Bay before flowing into the Atlantic. Held by the Union throughout, Fort Monroe had been where in the early months of the war fugitive slaves had pushed Benjamin Butler to formulate his contraband policy, a doctrine that paved the way for thousands of runaway slaves to lay a claim to freedom. There the distinguished passengers met briefly with Secretary Stanton before traveling on to Port Royal, south of Charleston, where they witnessed the fruition of Butler's contraband policy, meeting with former slaves. For abolitionists aboard, the sight brought tears to their eyes. Beecher's assistant noted the significance of a "company of world-famed abolitionists, speaking for the first time in their lives on the soil of Calhoun, to an audience of tearful, prayerful, thankful, emancipated slaves."

Cruising into Charleston harbor, the *Arago* passed Fort Sumter, which one passenger noted resembled a "Coliseum of ruins." After four years of war, the island fort had become "battered, shapeless, overthrown . . . [a] monument to the broken rebellion." After arriving in Charleston, the dignitaries were escorted to their hotel by a large contingent of newly freed African Americans, creating a procession a mile long. After four years of war, the Charleston Hotel on Meeting Street had lost some of its antebellum charm (one member of the party noted that cannonballs had created "eighteen new windows"), but some hasty repairs and patriotic bunting had made it into a suitable headquarters for the upcoming celebration.

Touring Charleston the next day, the *Arago*'s passengers witnessed a city transformed. Not only were its buildings in ruins and were weeds poking up through the cracked pavement, but the tenor of the city, once the birthplace of the Confederacy, had changed. The city swarmed with black and white Union soldiers enjoying a respite from four years of fighting, Northern merchants eager to reestablish trade networks severed by the war, newly freed blacks testing the limits of their freedom, and white Southern civilians, mostly women, who ventured out of their homes only when necessary, horrified at much of what they saw outside their doors. Some of the men who had left the city when Beauregard evacuated had recently returned, and some of these had taken the oath of allegiance, pledging their loyalty to the United States.

Over the next two days, other steamships brought visitors eager to observe the return of the Union flag to Fort Sumter. Among the last to arrive was the *Oceanus*, which like the *Arago* had voyaged from New York. Many of its 200 passengers were congregants at Henry Ward Beecher's Brooklyn church, having spent $150 for the privilege of hearing him preside over the flag raising. Entering the harbor, the *Oceanus* passed Fort Wagner, where nearly two year earlier the soldiers of the 54th Massachusetts Volunteer Infantry, one of the first black regiments in the Union Army, bravely assaulted the entrenched Confederate position, losing nearly half of the regiment, including its white commander, Robert Gould Shaw. In deference to the sacrifices of the 54th Massachusetts, the passengers on the *Oceanus* stood in silence aboard the upper deck, doffing their hats in salute. When they saw Fort Sumter, their reverential silence was transformed into song, as the passengers began to sing the doxology in celebration. Sailors on gunboats nearby heard their chorus and joined in, taking "up the strain and manning the yards pour[ed] forth a thundering cheer."

The *Oceanus* bore more than Beecher's excited parishioners; it also carried news that transformed the meaning of the next day's flag-raising ceremony. Calling to the nearby sailors, the passengers on board yelled, "General Lee has surrendered!" The news of Lee's surrender spread quickly throughout Charleston. The *New York Times* reported, "The reception of the news of LEE's surrender . . . occasioned the liveliest demonstration. At the theatre, where the glorious victory was announced, the audience was wild with enthusiasm.

Dense crowds filled the spacious parlors of the Charleston Hotel and gave vent to the widest latitude of jubilancy over the great event." Politicians who had come to Charleston aboard the *Arago* gave speeches honoring "General Grant, the old flag and President Lincoln," which were "cheered lustily."

After the previous night's celebrations, many of those attending the flag-raising ceremony at Fort Sumter awoke bleary-eyed and fatigued. The *New York Times* noted that the "revelry and congratulations were kept up until a late hour, the joy extending into many households which had received information of the glorious news." Starting an hour before sunrise, naval vessels "dressed in a profusion of bunting" ferried participants from the city's docks to Fort Sumter, with the last trip bearing Anderson, Beecher, and Garrison arriving just after noon. Although the exterior of the fort had survived, its interior had become "a mass of debris composed of concrete, brick and sand in which was imbedded tons of iron missels [sic]." An elevated speaker's podium had been erected in the center of the parade ground, festooned with myrtle and streamers. Soldiers composed the majority of those in attendance, including black soldiers from the 54th Massachusetts, some of whom had fought at Fort Wagner. Also in attendance were the son of Denmark Vesey, executed in 1822 for organizing a slave revolt, and Robert Smalls, a former slave who stole a Confederate warship, the CSS *Planter*, in 1862, and would later represent South Carolina in Congress.

When it came time for Anderson to raise the flag, the usually taciturn military officer shed a few tears, as did many in the audience. At the sight of the torn and battered flag, "the amphitheater saluted it with five thousand voices, and the battlements replied with two hundred guns." One observer claimed that "it was the most exciting moment of my life when that flag went up." A *New York Times* correspondent noted that four years earlier, "our national ensign, floating in its pride and power over the battlements of Fort Sumter, was assailed and trailed in surrender." Today "the identical flag that was lowered in humiliation, was raised with appropriate ceremonies." When the cheering subsided, Anderson found his voice enough to say that he "was here to fulfill the cherished wish of my heart through four long, long years of bloody war, to restore to its proper place this dear flag."

The task of finding meaning in the flag's return fell to Henry Ward Beecher in what would be the afternoon's longest oration. Speaking for more than two hours, Beecher needed to stop midway, telling the band to play a song to allow those "to get up that are sitting down, and you to sit down that have been standing; and I will sit down too, and rest a moment." Beecher's speech bore the marks of weeks of preparation, and some revision since his arrival in Charleston, referring to the "desolation . . . in yonder sad city." Over the course of the afternoon, Beecher touched on many topics, including the righteousness of the Union cause, the role of God in the abolition of slavery, the legacy of the American Revolution, the future of Southern manufacturing, the origins of the Civil War, and the importance of the Constitution. Nowhere in his speech, however, did Beecher mention surrender, either Robert Anderson's four years to the day earlier or Robert E. Lee's, which many in the audience had spent the previous night celebrating. Beecher briefly alluded at the beginning of his speech to the bravery of Robert Anderson "and a small heroic band" who "did gallant and just battle for the honor and defense of the nation's banner." That the battle ended in Anderson surrendering Fort Sumter went unsaid.

The absence of even one mention of the word "surrender" in the many thousands of words that Beecher uttered that afternoon, at an event commemorating a surrender, suggests that he felt there was something unmanly or un-American about surrender. He was not alone. None of the other speakers at the flag-raising ceremony uttered the word "surrender." Nor did Judge Advocate General Joseph Holt in a dinner address that evening, a speech that rivaled Beecher's for its scope, if not quite its length.[1] The difficulty that Beecher and others had in coming to terms with the idea of surrender is surprising, given how ubiquitous surrenders were during the conflict. Despite the ubiquity of surrender during the Civil War, during in the 150 years since its conclusion, generations of Americans have struggled, like Beecher, to articulate what those surrenders meant.

If events at Fort Sumter in 1865 demonstrated the difficulties that Unionists had in discussing surrender, Confederates had an even harder time that spring and summer in coming to terms with surrender and defeat. Many Confederate civilians recoiled in horror at the news of Lee's and subsequent surrenders. When the news reached her in Louisiana, Sarah Wadley noted in her diary that it made her "depressed almost to despair." Other Confederate women responded to the news with defiance. Sarah Morgan recorded in her diary that while others cried when they learned of Appomattox, she "would not, satisfied that God will still save us, even though all should apparently be lost."[2]

No sooner had Lee surrendered to Grant than white Southerners began to develop a rationale that squared these terminal surrenders with Southern ideas of honor, a rationale that came to be known as the Lost Cause. A robust interpretation of Confederate defeat that shaped Southern (and indeed national) discourse about the Civil War for decades to come, the Lost Cause dictated that the Confederacy fought for states' rights, not for the preservation of slavery; that emancipation destroyed a civilized society in which contented slaves loyally served their owners; and that the military defeat of the Confederacy was the consequence of overwhelming Union numerical superiority. Indeed, a central tenet of the Lost Cause was that Union military superiority made Confederate defeat inevitable. Therefore, the argument went, if the Confederacy could not have won, then it did not really lose. Instead, Confederate soldiers should be praised for their bravery in the face of certain defeat. For postwar white Southerners, the Lost Cause became a kind of civil religion, with Robert E. Lee and Stonewall Jackson its reigning deities.[3]

Lost Cause advocates struggled to find a way to wrestle Confederate surrenders into their narrative. Lee's farewell address became something of a foundational text, a concise explanation of how they could reconcile honor and surrender. In one of the earliest manifestations of the Lost Cause, in 1866 journalist Edward Pollard reprinted (in a volume appropriately titled *The Lost Cause*) the entirety of Lee's address, in which Lee praised his men for "four years of arduous service, marked by unsurpassed courage and fortitude." They had been compelled to surrender, not for lack of "valor or devotion," but because of the Union Army's "overwhelming numbers and resources." Even in surrender, Lee is the hero of Pollard's narrative, possessing a "Roman manhood" after his final meeting with Grant. Remarkably, Pollard was also generous to Grant in his account of surrender. Having damned Grant as an alcoholic and a butcher for the majority of his text, Pollard praised him for behaving "with a magnanimity and decorum that must ever be remembered to his credit even by those who disputed his reputation in other respects." In defeat, Pollard's Lee emerges victorious. Even though the Confederacy was defeated, the honor of its men and their cause was not. "The Confederates have gone out of this war," Pollard observed, "with the proud, secret, deathless, dangerous consciousness that they are the Better Men."[4]

While the Lost Cause gave white Southerners a way to minimize any dishonor attached to surrender, white Northerners too tended to downplay its significance. Recognizing that surrenders, especially those at the end of the conflict, posed acute problems for white Southerners, white Northerners interested in the politics of reconciliation tempered their discussions and commemorations of surrender events. Even in an era when waving the "bloody shirt" functioned as a hallmark of Republican electoral politics, many of those same Republicans opted to remain silent on the topic of surrender.

Few Northerners were as instrumental in the crafting a Northern interpretation of surrender as Ulysses S. Grant. Having accepted the Confederate surrenders at Fort Donelson, Vicksburg, and Appomattox, Grant occupied a unique position to articulate how surrenders contributed to Union victory. However, when given the opportunity, Grant minimized their importance. Nowhere was this more evident than in the *Personal Memoirs of U. S. Grant*, published in December 1885, five months after Grant's death from throat cancer. Issued in two volumes, the 1,231-page text became an immediate literary sensation, praised for its compelling, clear, and direct prose. The text focuses primary on Grant's military career during the Mexican War and Civil War, providing relatively little coverage of his childhood, Reconstruction, or his two terms in the White House. Throughout the two volumes, Grant unflinchingly champions the superiority of the Union cause, the merits of free labor, and the immorality of slavery. Given Grant's prominent role in so many Civil War surrenders, he devotes relatively little space in the memoirs to reflecting on their meaning. Instead, he uses surrenders as vehicles to articulate the reconciliation of the North and the South.[5]

The first volume of his memoirs ends with the Confederate surrender at Vicksburg. Describing the surrender negotiations at Vicksburg, Grant quotes a letter he wrote to Confederate general Pemberton noting that "men who have shown so much endurance and courage as those now in Vicksburg, will always challenge the respect of an adversary, and I can assure you will be treated with all the respect due to prisoners of war." When it came time for the Confederate garrison to lay down arms, Grant was careful to note that "our whole army present witnessed this scene without cheering." In victory, Grant portrayed his army as magnanimous and generous: "Our soldiers were no sooner inside the lines than the two armies began to fraternize. Our men had had full rations from the time the siege commenced, to the close. The enemy had been suffering, particularly towards the last. I myself saw our men taking bread from their haversacks and giving it to the enemy they had so recently been engaged in starving out. It was accepted with avidity and with thanks." While Grant noted the importance of the Confederate surrender at Vicksburg, along with the victory at Gettysburg, in rallying Northern sentiment for continuing the war effort, he was careful not to shame either the Confederate command or soldiers in the process.

Grant demonstrated a similarly light hand in describing Lee's surrender at Appomattox. Offering a minimalist account of the surrender negotiations, Grant only occasionally commented on the broader meaning and significance of the events. He noted when romantic accounts of his meeting with Lee, then in wide circulation, were in error. He observed, for instance, that "the much talked of surrendering of Lee's sword and my handing it back, this and much more that has been said about it is the purest romance." Grant conspicuously avoided attributing too much meaning to anything that transpired during surrender negotiations. Their meeting ended without drama: "Lee and I then separated as cordially as we had met, he returning to his own lines, and all went into bivouac for the night at Appomattox." In a similar vein, Grant ordered his troops not to celebrate the surrender, as it would shame Confederate soldiers—an order that would foreshadow decades in which white Northerners and white Southerners alike found reasons to not remember or observe Civil War surrenders.

Conversely, some African Americans saw the anniversary of Lee's surrender at Appomattox as an event worthy of commemoration. As early as 1866, "Surrender Day" became one of several competing holidays celebrated by African Americans to signify their transition from slavery to freedom. By 1890, the holiday had become an established part of the African American calendar, at least in central Virginia. When questioned about its meaning, one Mecklenburg County man said, "We do it because we held that our real deliverance was accomplished by the 'surrender.' If Lee had never been beaten and the confederacy never crushed, the [emancipation] proclamation would have been no avail." Not unsurprisingly, former Confederates bristled at Surrender Day celebrations, viewing them as an effort by African Americans to shame former rebels. When black residents of Hampton, Virginia, many of whom were Union veterans, marched on April 9, 1866, a white mob assaulted the procession.[6]

The desire by both white Northerners and white Southerners to forget or ignore surrenders most tangibly manifested itself in how these sites were memorialized. Most Civil War monuments date to the decades prior to the war's semicentennial. Starting as soon as the war was over and reaching its apex starting in the 1880s, white Americans, both North and South, erected monuments on battlefields and town squares to recognize the soldiers' sacrifice. Veterans groups such as the Grand Army of the Republic and the United Confederate Veterans played prominent roles in building monuments to their fallen comrades. Women's groups also contributed significantly to monumentalizing the Civil War landscape, particularly in the South, where organizations such as the Ladies' Memorial Association and the United Daughters of the Confederacy (UDC) erected thousands of monuments. State and local governments joined in this flurry of Civil War commemoration. As early as 1863, states such as Vermont passed measures to authorize towns to build monuments to the local dead, offering state funds to help in construction.[7]

Nowhere was this flurry to commemorate the recent conflict more evident than on its battlefields. By 1888, the twenty-fifth anniversary of the battle, the fields at Gettysburg were littered with more than 300 monuments. Two years later, Congress passed legislation authorizing the formation of National Military Parks. By 1900, five Civil War sites had received this designation: Chickamauga and Chattanooga, Shiloh, Gettysburg, Vicksburg, and Antietam. Operated by the War Department, the National Military Parks were intended not only to preserve historic locations, now increasingly adorned by monuments, but also to serve as sites where military officers could be instructed, drawing upon the lessons of the Civil War.[8]

The monuments erected on these sites reflected a common visual vocabulary, shared by both the North and the South, about the proper way to commemorate martial valor. The most common monuments depicted the common soldier, usually standing at parade rest, his hands resting on the barrel of his rifle. By 1890, more than 200 such monuments had been erected across the country, not only on battlefields, but also in town squares and cemeteries. Sometimes the statues were mass produced, and the differences between Union and Confederate soldiers were recognizable only by minor alterations in uniforms and the inscriptions on their belt buckles. The sentinel soldier monuments were joined on the commemorative landscape by thousands of obelisks, columns, and plaques.[9]

In this flurry of Civil War commemoration, sites of surrender were largely ignored. Fort Sumter remained in active use as a military fortification. During the 1870s, much of the rubble in the fort was cleared away and portions of the wall were rebuilt to support a new range of cannons. Not long after the renovation of the fort, however, the site fell into disrepair due to neglect. During the 1890s, the fort was home to one ordnance officer and one lighthouse keeper, who lived in the fort with their families. Between 1899 and 1901 a large concrete structure, known as Battery Huger, was constructed in the middle of the fort to anchor two long-range rifled cannons, an edifice that effectively subsumed the surrender site. While tourists occasionally visited the site, it was not until 1926 that regular ferry service to the island began, and no monuments were erected until 1928.[10]

Both the McLean house, the site in Appomattox where Lee surrendered to Grant, and Bennett Place, in the North Carolina piedmont where Johnston surrendered to Sherman, remained in private hands and in significant disrepair since the surrenders of April 1865. Union officers ransacked Wilmer McLean's house after Lee's surrender, paying McLean for some souvenirs while simply absconding with others. When the McLean family went into debt a few years later, the house was auctioned and was occupied by several different families over the next two decades. In 1891, the house was purchased by Myron E. Dunlap, who bought it with the intention of moving it to Chicago to be exhibited at the World's Columbian Exposition. He carefully dismantled the house, crafting detailed blueprints along the way. When the plan to relocate the house to Chicago fell through, Dunlap hatched a scheme to move it to Washington, D.C. That plan also failed to come to fruition, leaving the McLean house a pile of bricks and rotting wooden siding. Vandals and souvenir hunters ransacked the ruins over the next several decades as the structure became overwhelmed in weeds and brush.

Although veterans' groups from both the North and the South made periodic efforts to preserve the location, little official action was taken in the fifty years after the event to commemorate or maintain the site of Lee's surrender. In 1893, after the dismantling of the McLean house, the War Department erected a series of iron plaques to mark the location of important events associated with the surrender. The only large monument on the site was a granite plaque erected in 1905 by North Carolina Confederate veterans, with the support of the state's legislature. Notably, the monument did not commemorate the surrender, a word that does not appear on the plaque, but North Carolinians' role in firing "the last volley" of the Civil War. In 1926, the Appomattox Chapter of the UDC erected a smaller plaque not far from the site of the courthouse; the inscription read,

HERE ON SUNDAY APRIL 9, 1865
AFTER FOUR YEARS OF HEROIC STRUGGLE
IN DEFENSE OF PRINCIPLES BELIEVED FUNDAMENTAL
TO THE EXISTENCE OF OUR GOVERNMENT
LEE SURRENDERED 9000 MEN THE REMNANT
OF AN ARMY STILL UNCONQUERED IN SPIRIT
TO 118000 MEN UNDER GRANT.

The plaque embodied many of the major tropes of the Lost Cause's version of Appomattox. It praised Lee's soldiers and the cause they fought for, although naming that cause only obliquely while dramatically inflating the size of Grant's army and undercounting the number of soldiers under Lee's command. Lost Cause histories of the war often exaggerated the disparities between Union and Confederate forces and thereby justified rebel defeat, but rarely so boldly. While a few Lost Cause organizations dotted the landscape at Appomattox with the occasional monument, Union organizations and the Federal government saw less value in the site. In 1926, a congressionally appointed battlefield preservation committee concluded that although Appomattox Courthouse had sentimental appeal, unlike battlefields, it had no potential for tactical instruction and advocated that preservation funds be allocated elsewhere.[11]

Bennett Place shared a fate similar to that of Appomattox. The small farmhouse remained in the Bennitt family until 1890, when it was sold to Brodie Duke, the oldest son of tobacco magnate Washington Duke. The black sheep of the family with a penchant for risky speculation and a proclivity for scandal, Brodie Duke purchased the site as an investment and built a protective wooden shell over the tiny structure. Sometime after 1908, Brodie Duke sold the property to Samuel Morgan, a Durham fertilizer dealer, who also hoped to turn the property into a historic tourist attraction. Morgan, like Duke, failed in his efforts, and the building fell into significant disrepair. A year after Morgan's death in 1920, Bennett Place burned to the ground in a fire rumored to have been started either by migrant workers squatting on the site, not far from the railroad tracks, or from sparks from a passing train. Only the stone chimney remained standing.[12]

During the golden age of Civil War commemoration, Vicksburg presented something of an exception to the general neglect of surrender sites. Although Vicksburg was one of the sites chosen by Congress for preservation as a National Military Park in 1899, the legislation makes it clear that the intention was to preserve the site because of the siege and defense of the city, not the surrender. Like other battlefields, Vicksburg became littered with hundreds of monuments, representing both the Union and Confederate soldiers who fought there. Among the largest was the Illinois State Memorial. Dedicated in 1906, the memorial was modeled on the Roman Pantheon. Set on top of a hill, the structure had forty-seven steps, one for each day of the siege. Bronze plaques lining its interior named the 36,000 soldiers from Illinois who participated in the Vicksburg campaign. More typical of the monuments erected at Vicksburg was a marble statue dedicated in April 1893. Paid for in large measure by white women from Vicksburg, the statue was carved in Italy but bore many of the hallmarks of typical Civil War statuary: a Confederate soldier, rifle in hand, at relaxed attention. Its dedicatory plaque noted that it had been placed "in memory of the men from all the States of the South who fell in defense of Vicksburg . . . a defense unsurpassed in the annals of war for heroism, endurance of hardships and patriotic devotion." At the dedication ceremony, former Confederate general Stephen D. Lee made it clear that the monument was intended to commemorate the heroic defense of Vicksburg. The Confederate soldiers' bravery, he told the crowd, which included veterans who had participated in the defense, was only "vanquished by starvation and overwhelming odds." Repeating the Lost Cause mantra that the Confederacy had been defeated only because of the Union's vast numerical superiority, Lee said that Vicksburg represented a "fiery furnace" from which its soldiers emerged with their "honor untarnished."[13]

Despite the proliferation of Union and Confederate monuments at Vicksburg, one site became dememorialized: the site of Pemberton's surrender to Grant. On July 4, 1864, the one-year anniversary of the surrender, Union soldiers stationed in Vicksburg erected a marble obelisk to commemorate the surrender, one of the earliest Civil War battlefield monuments. They had salvaged the obelisk from a local tombstone maker who had intended it to grace the tomb of a Mexican War veteran. In 1867, after vandals had substantially defaced it, the monument was moved to the Federal cemetery. It was replaced by an unusual monument, an upturned 42-pounder cannon approximately ten feet in height. The inscription on the replacement monument described the site as the "site of the interview" between Grant and Pemberton, omitting that the interview resulted in Pemberton's surrender.[14]

Surrender sites were conspicuously absent during the semicentennial celebrations that occurred between 1911 and 1915. No events were held at Fort Sumter in 1911, although there was a minor debate about the location of the flag that Major Anderson had lowered in 1861 and raised in 1865. The War Department claimed to have the original flag housed in the dark corner of a private office, inaccessible to the general public, while a family in Lowell, Massachusetts, also claimed to have it. Shortly before the anniversary of the firing on and surrender of Fort Sumter, the *Richmond Times-Dispatch* noted, "The long-reunited nation will not celebrate this anniversary. Few men who heard the thunder of that battle are still among us." Similarly, no official celebrations seem to have been held at Bennett Place, Appomattox, or Vicksburg. The absence of any official ceremony at Vicksburg in 1913 was particularly striking, considering the enormous celebration held a day earlier at Gettysburg, where more than 50,000 elderly veterans from both armies had converged for a reunion. Joining them were an equally large number of observers and well-wishers, including President Woodrow Wilson.[15]

By the time of the U.S. entry into World War I, the golden age of Civil War commemoration had come to a close. With every passing year, the ranks of Civil War veterans thinned. Yet it was during the 1920s that the long neglect of surrender sites began to be rectified. Driven in part by the boom in tourism created by the automobile, surrender sites became viable destinations. Nowhere was this more true than in Charleston, which started in the 1920s to advertise itself as "America's Most Historic City." Protecting its antebellum dwellings of

Remembering Civil War Surrenders

the planter class as "sacred relics" while moving to demolish black Charleston in the historic district, boosters hoped to attract tourists by selling them a romanticized version of the Southern past. New luxury hotels, such as the Francis Marion, were constructed to accommodate tourists.[16]

The development of Fort Sumter as a tourist site grew out of this broader effort to construct Historic Charleston. Regular ferry service began in 1926, and within a year, several competing companies vied for the tourist trade. On the island, tours were led by "Colonel" William Robert Greer, who advertised himself as the last living Confederate soldier to have served at the fort. It was during this period that the first monuments were added to the site. In 1928, the Flagpole Monument was added, dedicated in "honor of Major Robert Anderson and the 128 men of his command." Erected at the bequest of Anderson's daughter and with congressional approval, the monument unobtrusively began the process of returning the site to its Civil War condition. It also began a rapid monumentalization of the site. Unlike battlefields, where ample real estate rewarded monuments built on an epic scale, the limited space available on Sumter necessitated smaller commemorations. A year after the addition of the Flagpole Monument, the Charleston Chapter of the UDC added a plaque to commemorate the Confederate soldiers who defended the fort after Anderson's surrender. In contrast to the Flagpole Monument, which did not mention surrender, the plaque honored "the Confederate garrison of Fort Sumter who during 4 years of continuous siege and constant assaults from April 1861 to February 1865, defended this harbor without knowing defeat or sustaining surrender," sending the implicit message that the Confederate garrison was braver than the Federal garrison they replaced. Three years later, in 1932, a small garrison monument was also added, dedicated to the "memory of the garrison defending Fort Sumter," listing the roster of the Federal soldiers. In 1943, the two rifled guns installed after the Spanish-American War were removed, long since obsolete, and in 1948, the site became a national monument. Its initial management plan called for the removal of all of the modifications made to the site since 1865, with the exception of Battery Huger and the recently erected monuments.[17]

Driven by similar motives to attract tourists, the Durham Chamber of Commerce pushed for a monument at Bennett Place. Although the 1921 fire had leveled the homestead, save for its chimney, they believed that it had the potential to attract tourists. In 1923, the North Carolina state legislature, at the urging of the Durham chamber, created the Bennett Place Memorial Commission, tasked with building a monument to national unity on the site. Tapped to head the commission was local tobacco magnate Julian Shakespeare Carr.

Carr had served in the 3rd North Carolina Calvary and had surrendered with Lee at Appomattox. Afterward he became a partner in one of the state's largest tobacco manufacturing firms and established himself as one of the richest and most influential men in the state. As commander-in-chief of North Carolina's United Confederate Veterans, "General Carr" had presided over the dedication of many Civil War monuments, including the Silent Sam monument at the entrance to the campus of the University of North Carolina in Chapel Hill. A committed white supremacist, Carr once boasted that "less than 90 days perhaps after my return from Appomattox, I horse-whipped a negro wench, until her skirts hung in shreds, because . . . she had publicly insulted and maligned a Southern lady." The Memorial Commission eventually settled on an unusual design to commemorate the surrender; it consisted of two Corinthian columns, representing the Union and the Confederacy, topped by a lintel engraved with the word "UNITY" in large letters.

While Carr and other leading businessmen backed the design, the local chapter of the UDC (ironically the Julian Carr Chapter) objected. Members argued that the monument and the ceremony dedicating it would dishonor their ancestors and that an unostentatious plaque, installed without fanfare, would be more appropriate. Carr replied that he thought the monument celebrated both Northern and Southern values and would serve as a beacon of Durham's development since the surrender. Unpersuaded, the UDC, as well as many Confederate veterans, chose not to participate in the dedication ceremony.[18]

Presiding over the dedication of the Unity Monument in November 1923, Julian Carr told the assembled crowd that the new monument symbolized the "sincerity of the South's purpose to keep her pledge of devotion to the Union." In response to the criticism that the monument had received from the UDC, Carr wanted to assure them that surrender did not dishonor the South. "Speaking as a Confederate soldier who followed Lee to Appomattox," Carr told them, "no Confederate soldier has ever been asked to sacrifice the principles for which he fought. The basis of our surrender was, lay down our arms, as General Lee told us in his Farewell at Appomattox; to go home and make good citizens in peace as we had made brave soldiers in war. No Confederate soldier has ever surrendered nor has ever been asked to surrender the principles for which he fought." For Carr, like other Lost Cause spokesmen, those principles were not the defense of slavery, but states' rights. "Over-whelmed in numbers, he lay down his arms and sheathed his sword, but he has never run away from, nor repudiated the principles for which he stood and for which he fought four long years of bloody war, and these principles today rule the world and they are the foundations on which all civilized governments have their being—self-determination." His evocation of "self-determination" linked the Lost Cause mantra of states' rights to President Woodrow Wilson's Fourteen Points, thereby associating the Confederate cause with the American national cause. The underlying message of Carr's speech was that there was nothing dishonorable about Johnston's surrender at Bennett Place or any Confederate surrender, because at a deeper level, Confederates never surrendered their principles and those principles continued to live on. Indeed, for Carr and for many others assembled at the dedication, the ideology behind the Confederacy had not surrendered; it was victorious. Defeat, he argued, had brought only honor to the Confederacy. "We lost," he told them, "but we won."[19]

The tensions that manifested themselves over the Bennett Place Unity Monument resurfaced a decade later when boosters and politicians from Appomattox planned to erect a monument at the McLean house. In March 1930, Congressman Henry St. George Tucker and Senator Claude A. Swanson, both Virginians, introduced bills to erect a peace monument on the surrender site. Passed several months later, the legislation authorizing the monument allocated $100,000 for its construction, placing the final decision over its design in the hands of the Commission of Fine Arts, the body with oversight of monuments in Washington, D.C. When members of the commission joined local politicians on a tour of the site in September 1931, they found very little evidence of the community that had existed in 1865. In their initial report, issued shortly thereafter, the commission suggested rebuilding the McLean house as the centerpiece of any monument at Appomattox. Ignoring this suggestion, the War Department called for American architects "of standing and reputation" to submit designs for a monument to "an undivided Nation and a lasting peace." The winning design, of 186 submitted, was essentially a more elaborate version of the Bennett Place Unity Monument. As at Bennett Place, the design received robust criticism from members of the UDC, one of whom wrote to the War Department that she was horrified that the site where "Constitutional government and Lee were crucified in 1865" would receive any monument at all. If Appomattox needed a monument, she argued, it should show how the Union had unjustly terrorized white Southerners, including images of "Beast Butler and his Negro Troops" and the burning of Columbia. Another UDC member concurred, saying that "the very name of Appomattox must forever bring a stab of pain to the heart of a Southerner." The commander-in-chief of the United Confederate Veterans joined in the criticism, saying, "Who can view this monument without opening afresh the memory of the circumstances which gave rise to its erection, the hot, burning antagonisms, the fierce desire to kill, the death of fathers, husbands, brothers, the privations, the sufferings, the oppressions of those times, the memory of which the 70 years have done so much to obliterate." In a letter published in the *Richmond Times-Dispatch*, a University of Virginia professor asked "why any State should welcome the erection of a monument on her soil to memorialize her own defeat and subjugation." The Confederate Southern Memorial Association issued a statement condemning the proposed monument as "an insult to General Lee and to every Southern soldier who fought and died for the Confederate cause." In response to the overwhelming Southern white criticism of the proposed monument, the Commission of Fine Arts rejected the proposed design and reiterated its recommendation that a reconstructed McLean house would serve as a proper monument for the site. Lacking consensus, the site of Lee's surrender would remain largely unmemorialized for another two decades.[20]

The years leading up to the Civil War's centennial were marked by increasing foreignness and hostility toward the idea surrender. During World War II, President Franklin D. Roosevelt evoked Grant's demands of "unconditional surrender" when demanding the same of Germany and Japan. At a press conference following the Casablanca conference with Winston Churchill, Roosevelt told reporters, "We had a general called U.S. Grant. His name was Ulysses Simpson Grant but in my, and the Prime Minister's early days, he was called 'Unconditional Surrender Grant.' The elimination of German, Japanese and Italian war power means the unconditional surrender of Germany, Italy and Japan." Roosevelt's interpretation of Civil War surrenders, particularly at Appomattox, differed significantly from those offered either by Edward Pollard or by Grant in his memoirs. In Roosevelt's version, Grant exercised absolute control of the surrender, dictating to Lee what he would and would not accept and requiring Lee's absolute submission. In evoking Grant, Roosevelt created a doctrine of "unconditional surrender" far harsher and more inflexible than anything Grant considered.[21]

While demanding harsher forms of surrender from its enemies, the United States became increasingly intolerant of surrender by its own soldiers. The American aversion to surrender reached its clearest distillation in the Code of the United States Fighting Force, the military's official code of conduct. Drafted in 1955 after the Korean War, the code prohibited American soldiers from surrendering, requiring them to affirm that "I will never surrender of my own free will. If in command, I will never surrender the members of my command while they still have the means to resist." It dictated that even when "isolated, cut off or surrounded, a unit must continue to fight," even when vastly outnumbered. The code only countenanced surrender when "certain death [was] the only alternative."[22] The code signified that surrender, in any form, was un-American and shameful. Indeed, at the height of the Cold War, the prospect of nuclear holocaust appeared preferable to surrendering to Communist domination. During the Cuban Missile Crisis in October 1962, President John F. Kennedy addressed the nation on live television and declared, "The cost of freedom is always high, but Americans have always paid it. And one path we shall never choose, and that is the path of surrender, or submission."[23]

It was against this Cold War background that the United States celebrated the Civil War's centennial. In 1957, Congress authorized the creation of a Civil War Centennial Commission to coordinate with state commissions and the federal government (especially the Park Service) for what was expected to be a major celebration of national strength and reconciliation in the face of the Communist threat. Karl Betts, the Civil War Centennial Commission's executive director, said in April 1960 that national unity would be the central theme of the upcoming commemoration. "There was glory and honor for all who fought in the war," he observed; "they were all good Americans." In valorizing both Union and Confederate soldiers equally, Betts and Ulysses S. Grant III, the general's grandson and Centennial Commission chairman, hoped to avoid introducing into the commemoration any divisive issues, especially the emerging civil rights movement, which had recently reawakened sectional tensions in the aftermath of the *Brown v. Board of Education* decision; the Montgomery bus boycotts; and the sit-in movements.[24]

Despite Betts's and Grant's intentions to the contrary, the civil rights movement shaped and informed the Civil War's centennial from the very beginning. The commission had invited state commission members to a planning conference, held in conjunction with the anniversary of Fort Sumter, at Charleston's Francis Marion Hotel. Prior to the conference, Betts received a letter from the New Jersey state commission that "one of our members, Mrs. [Madaline] Williams, is a Negro. She has expressed concern over her reception by hotel people in South Carolina. Naturally we do not want to be separated from one of our members. Please advise me what we can expect." Betts argued that the commission had no power to compel the hotel to accept African American guests—a position that Grant later supported—and that the commission had no responsibility for the equal treatment of black delegates. In response, New Jersey threatened to boycott the event, a boycott that other Northern states quickly endorsed. Roy Wilkins, executive secretary of the National Association for the Advancement of Colored People, criticized Betts for the commission's "abysmal mishandling of this affair." Recently inaugurated president John F.

Kennedy, who hoped to avoid either endorsing segregation or publicly embracing integration, wrote a critical letter to Grant, saying that as a government agency, "the Commission has the responsibility to see that all of its members and guests are treated on a basis of equality." Kennedy's letter prompted robust condemnation in the Southern press and by politicians such as Strom Thurmond, who said that the president had no authority to "bring about integration in Charleston." The purpose of the committee, Thurmond argued, was to "commemorate the observance of the War Between the States. It is not for the purpose of starting another war." The centennial was prevented from being derailed before it began when, at the suggestion of commission member and historian Bell Wiley, the conference was moved from the segregated Francis Marion Hotel to an integrated Federal navy facility located just outside the city. Despite the new location, racial tensions continued to frame the opening of the Civil War centennial, as black delegates worried about their safety and Southern speakers at the conference used the event to defend the region's racial policies. Indeed, with news of Yuri Gagarin's space flight dominating newspaper headlines and racial tension dividing the commission, the particulars of 1861 were largely forgotten in their commemoration in 1961.[25]

Although some of the early centennial events, especially battle reenactments such as Bull Run, were well attended, after 1961, most Americans had lost interest in the anniversary of the Civil War. By the time of the Appomattox commemoration in April 1965, the entire enterprise had largely been forgotten. In the years since the effort to erect a peace monument in 1931 failed, the site at Appomattox had been transformed, in part to prepare for the centennial. In 1940, the site became a national historic monument. In April 1950, Robert E. Lee IV and U.S. Grant III met in front of a crowd of 10,000 to dedicate a reconstructed McLean house. Historian Douglas Southall Freeman, famous for his laudatory biography of General Lee, gave the keynote address at the dedication, arguing that the house stood as a "shrine to peace."[26] By 1965, however, the Virginia Centennial Commission demonstrated little interest in commemorating Appomattox, because after the rush of public enthusiasm in 1961 had abated, centennial events had been poorly attended. One member of the Virginia commission suggested that instead of celebration, he "would rather see the place draped in crepe." Local organizers in Appomattox County, however, eager to attract tourist dollars, pushed on with plans for an ambitious commemoration. In the years leading up to the anniversary, they entertained proposals for a "mammoth historical spectacle" replete with fireworks, a more subdued theatrical production, and a massive parade of flags, emphasizing "peace and unity."

Remembering Civil War Surrenders

After much debate, local and state officials finalized a program in mid-March 1965, only a few weeks before the event. It was a decidedly low-key affair, and only a few thousand people turned up, far fewer than event organizers had hoped. White Virginians comprised the vast majority of those in attendance. Welcoming the crowd, Virginia's segregationist governor Albertis S. Harrison connected the surrender at Appomattox to the contemporary fight over integration. "The beliefs and principles for which the Confederate forces fought are still with us," he argued. "They were not surrendered at Appomattox. They have not been surrendered since." Here Harrison drew the same distinction that Julian Carr made decades earlier: Confederate surrender meant laying down arms, but not principles, which lived on unconquered in the hearts of every true white Southerner.

Historian Bruce Catton delivered that afternoon's keynote address. The author of *A Stillness at Appomattox*, Catton was a compromise selection, as event organizers originally wanted either President Lyndon B. Johnson or former president Dwight D. Eisenhower to deliver the keynote address, but both declined the invitation. Catton told a crowd before a reconstructed McLean house that the surrender was "the final act in an unforgettable story" that heralded a new age of reconciliation. "We have one country now," Catton argued, "brought at a terrible price, cemented everlastingly together because at the end of our most terrible war the men who had fought so hard decided they had had enough of hatred." Media coverage characterized the ceremony as uninspired; the *Washington Post* noted that the two biggest cheers were for the introduction of Robert E. Lee's great-grandson and when the band played "Dixie." In a slightly more charitable note, *Time* noted that while few people attended, events at Appomattox Courthouse lacked the crass commercialization evident earlier in the centennial.[27]

A similar narrative unfolded at Bennett Place a couple of weeks later. In the thirty years since Julian Carr had dedicated the Unity Monument at Bennett Place, the Durham boosters' hopes that it would attract tourists had largely gone unfulfilled. The property was rarely visited by tourists and largely ignored by locals. Despite these shortcomings, a committed contingent of Durham boosters hoped that the site would attract visitors during the Civil War centennial. Starting in 1958, they raised money to reconstruct the Bennitt farmhouse. Reusing timbers from a condemned building of a similar vintage, they rebuilt the farmhouse upon the original foundation, as well as a detached kitchen and smokehouse. Completed in 1962, the reconstructed site became a North Carolina State Historic Site.[28]

A month before the Bennett Place centennial, President Lyndon Johnson urged Americans to attend the celebration, saying that the site symbolized the "spirit of national unity." Johnson signed off on a congressional joint resolution that praised the "negotiations between General William T. Sherman and General Joseph E. Johnston when those opposing commanders in their search for peace met at the Bennett House." Nowhere in either the lengthy joint resolution or President Johnson's statements when signing it did the word "surrender" appear. Instead, the site and the celebration were dedicated, like the 1923 monument, to "national unity."[29] At the ceremony itself, Vice President Hubert Humphrey repeated the central theme of the final year of the centennial, national unity, managing to speak for nearly an hour without mentioning the word "surrender." Sherman and Johnston met at Bennett Place, Humphrey argued, in search of "peace with honor," a phrase that would take on additional meaning within the context of the Vietnam War. They had "the courage and the vision to place their trust in the strength of an ideal—that ideal was unity." Humphrey devoted the majority of his speech to addressing the lessons that could be learned from Bennett Place and its aftermath. He focused particularly on how Reconstruction revealed the dangers of "radicalism." Evoking a Lost Cause interpretation, Humphrey told a mostly white local audience that radicalism during Reconstruction was not unlike the "senseless, revengeful extremism that even today, if left unchecked, could bring our great democracy to its knees." During Reconstruction, Humphrey argued, Americans learned "the bitter lesson that the spirit of regional vindictiveness and political opportunism contribute nothing to the general welfare of the country." Only a month after the "Bloody Sunday" beatings of civil rights marchers on the Edmund Pettus Bridge, Humphrey hoped that the lesson of Bennett Place would be that the "senseless struggle of . . . race against race will be ended." Only "an undivided America" could, he argued, carry "the burden of freedom" to the world. Few members of the audience were likely persuaded by Humphrey's remarks. With them, the Civil War centennial ended its lengthy death rattle.[30]

In the fifty years since the Civil War centennial, very little has changed to transform how the surrender sites have been commemorated. In 1970, a small visitors' center was added at the Bennett Place site, although the location remains rarely visited except by local schoolchildren and the most dedicated Civil War buffs. In recent years, state budget cuts have threatened to close the monument, although thus far it has managed to remain open, albeit with reduced hours and staffing. During the 1990s, the National Park Service began a process of reinterpreting how slavery contributed to the origins of the Civil War. Long criticized by historians for neglecting to incorporate slavery into its Civil War sites, the National Park Service introduced its new interpretive schema at the Fort Sumter Visitors Center in 1995. This change was not without controversy, as the Park Service was flooded with letters from the Sons of Confederate Veterans and other groups decrying the change as "demonizing and slandering" the South.[31]

If the sesquicentennial (2011–15) provided an opportunity to reinterpret the Civil War for the general public, surrender sites received little of the attention lavished on battlefields. In contrast to the centennial, sesquicentennial events emphasized the role of slavery as the cause of the war and the role of African Americans in its progress and outcome. Greater attention was also paid to the role of women, guerillas, and Southern Unionists, groups that were largely ignored during the centennial. Unlike the centennial, no national body coordinated events, and the degree of state-level commitment to celebrating the anniversary varied tremendously. Although the sectional bitterness that arose during the centennial did not reappear fifty years later, much of the enthusiasm was also missing. On April 14, 2011, the National Park Service and the Fort Sumter–Fort Moultrie Historical Trust staged reenactments of Anderson's surrender at Fort Sumter throughout the day, although crowds rarely numbered more than 300 visitors, who participated with "measured enthusiasm" and "applauded politely." The anniversary of the surrender at Vicksburg went largely unnoticed. Although the National Park Service held events, they were sparsely attended, and the local population ignored them almost entirely. With the Lost Cause still alive and well in Vicksburg—Old Courthouse Museum downtown still refers to the conflict as the "War Between the States" and describes the Emancipation Proclamation as "wartime propaganda"—there was little interest in commemorating the town's darkest hour. Far more people attended the local blues concert or Independence Day fireworks.[32]

Both Bennett Place and Appomattox attempted to capitalize on the sesquicentennial. In Durham, Bennett Place Historic Site renovated its small museum for the anniversary. Funded largely by private donations, the new exhibits updated the site's interpretation, emphasizing the role of slavery in the Civil War and placing the April 1865 events into a broader context. An even bolder effort to capitalize on the sesquicentennial took place in Appomattox. In 2012, the Museum of the Confederacy opened a branch in Appomattox adjacent to the National Historic Site. The new museum drew on the Richmond-based Museum of the Confederacy's ample collections related to the surrender, including Robert E. Lee's sword, jacket, gauntlets, and pen. As with earlier efforts to commemorate the site, the opening ceremonies were marred by controversy and protests. Groups including the Sons of Confederate Veterans and the Virginia Flaggers (a group dedicated to the public display of the Confederate flag) protested the absence of the Confederate battle flag on the site. They noted that the "reunification promenade" in front of the museum included fourteen state flags but did not include a Confederate battle flag. Their protest included a small plane that circled over the new museum, trailing an enormous Confederate flag behind it. In response, the museum's executive director said that he had no plans to add a Confederate flag to the site. "Appomattox is a metaphor for the reunification of the country," he said. "To put the Confederate flag into that display would be a historical untruth."[33] While some protesters objected to the absence of a Confederate flag outside the museum, others objected to how the flag was displayed within the museum. Some visitors who attended a pre–grand opening tour of the museum were offended by a cardboard cutout of drag queen RuPaul wearing a sequined dress patterned after the Confederate battle flag. The accompanying display described the myriad cultural uses to which the Confederate flag had been put over the past 150 years, including a "Dukes of Hazzard" serving tray. Although the display was promptly taken down after only six hours on display, some neo-Confederate visitors felt that its inclusion had compromised the site forever.[34]

For their 2015 events, both Appomattox Courthouse and Bennett Place hosted surrender reenactments, in stark contrast to the centennial, when organizers bristled at the idea of publicly performing a manifestation of Confederate defeat. More than 6,000 people descended on Appomattox Courthouse to witness the reenactment. Many of the reenactors had participated in dozens of events during the sesquicentennial, and for most of them, this marked their final time donning a uniform during the anniversary.[35] Coupled with the reenactments were a series of speeches by Virginia politicians and historians. Senator Tim Kaine claimed that Appomattox should be remembered for Grant's magnanimity, for the destruction of slavery, and for the national unity it created, while Governor Terry McAuliffe used the event to urge citizens to vote.[36]

While most of the speakers repeated familiar platitudes about how the site should be remembered, historian and University of Richmond president Edward Ayers used the occasion to challenge the myth of Appomattox. The problem with the dominant narrative, Ayers argued, was that "it allowed everyone to be a hero." The willingness of Grant, both at Appomattox and in his memoirs, to extend a generous hand to Lee and his army, while decrying the cause for which they fought, helped in the "severing of the cause and of the fight that established the bargain that the white North and the white South would hold to for the next 150 years." Ayers concluded his address by urging the audience to recognize Appomattox as both an ending and a beginning. Although it marked the symbolic end to the Civil War, it was also the beginning of a long process of Reconstruction and the continued struggle for racial justice. "People see in the events at Appomattox what they want to see: testimony to American's shared greatness or testimony to promises unfulfilled," Ayers observed. "Both those things are real."[37]

Events on April 9, 2015, culminated with a nationwide event dubbed "Bells across America." At 3:15 that afternoon, the National Park Service urged schools, churches, temples, public buildings, and historic sites across the country to ring bells for four minutes, one for each year of the war. National Park Service officials recognized that this symbolic end to the sesquicentennial allowed for a multitude of interpretations, an ambiguity they embraced. "The end of the Civil War has different meanings for different people. Each organization may customize this idea to its own situation," a Park Service press release noted. "Some communities may ring their bells in celebration of freedom or a restored Union, others as an expression of mourning and a moment of silence for the fallen. Sites may ring bells to mark the beginning of reconciliation and reconstruction or as the next step in the continuing struggle for civil rights."[38]

The events at Appomattox Courthouse were not without their critics. Writing in *Slate*, cultural critic Jamelle Bouie decried the absence of black voices in the commemoration, claiming that "the real Appomattox wasn't just about reunion; it was about emancipation as well." In the *New Republic*, journalist Brian Beutler argued that Americans have lost sight of the real cost of Appomattox, claiming that "the generous terms of Robert E. Lee's surrender to Ulysses S. Grant at Appomattox Court House foreshadowed a multitude of real and symbolic compromises that the winners of the war would make with secessionists, slavery supporters, and each other to piece the country back together." To properly remember Appomattox, Beutler argued, the federal government should make April 9 a national holiday, as a celebration of emancipation and the surrender not only of Confederate armies but of Confederate values as well. Beutler proposed calling this holiday "New Birth of Freedom Day," presumably unaware that black Virginians had already dubbed it "Surrender Day" 149 years earlier.[39]

In Durham, organizers planned ten days of events called "The Dawn of Peace" to celebrate Sherman and Johnston's three meetings at Bennett Place. They hoped that a robust series of programs would help to bring Bennett Place out of the shadow created by Appomattox. John Guss, Bennett Place Historic Site's manager, who also filled the role of General Sherman during the reenactment, argued that the site was the "Rodney Dangerfield of Civil War history," getting no respect from either historians or the general public. Reenactor Craig Boswell, who portrayed Joseph Johnston, expressed a similar sentiment: "I just want people to know the war did not end in Appomattox." Event organizers hoped that 8,000 people would visit, but heavy rains and thundershowers soaked the reenactors and tamped down attendance.[40]

The surrender reenactments at Appomattox Courthouse and Bennett Place during the sesquicentennial brought these sites more in line with other Civil War locales. Yet they also amounted to an interpretive abnegation. At both sites, the surrender negotiations themselves remained invisible, as onlookers witnessed Grant, Lee, Sherman, and Johnston disappear into the surrender sites, only to emerge hours later, leaving the critical moments unseen. The sesquicentennial occurred against a background of American culture that found itself increasingly hostile to and alienated from the idea of surrender. Donald Trump's inane criticism of John McCain, challenging his status as a war hero because he was captured, and the widespread condemnation of Bowe Bergdahl, the U.S. Army sergeant captured in Afghanistan in 2009, both drew upon a common sentiment that surrender was unpatriotic, a trope frequently invoked in American politics and popular culture. The phenomenally low rates of capture in recent American wars in Iraq and Afghanistan reflected not only the brutality and lethality of modern counterinsurgency but also a popular and military culture that views surrender as fundamentally illegitimate. Against this broader aversion to surrender, Americans found it difficult to make sense of the choices and values that drove so many Americans to surrender during the Civil War.

CONCLUSION

In 2011, demographic historian David Hacker concluded that the oft-cited figure of Civil War fatalities of 620,000 dramatically undercounted the number of men who died in the conflict. Using complex statistical analysis of census figures, Hacker claimed that the real death toll for the war probably exceeded 750,000. Civil War historians quickly adopted this revised figure, not only because of the quality of Hacker's scholarship, but because a higher butcher's bill fit into broader interpretive debates about the nature of combat during the Civil War, debates that began long before Hacker announced his revised numbers. During the late twentieth century, Civil War historians argued whether the Civil War was a total or a modern war. At the heart of this debate was a question of categorization: did the Civil War more closely resemble the limited wars of the eighteenth century or the more devastating conflicts of the twentieth century? More recently, Civil War historians have asked how our view of the Civil War changes if we incorporate the brutality of guerilla warfare, the horrific conditions in refugee camps and prisons, and the butchery of Fort Pillow and the Crater. Does our understanding of Civil War soldiers change when we consider the lifelong suffering from physical and psychological wounds? Dubbed by some as the Civil War's "dark turn," this historiographic development has garnered both praise for its originality and scorn for its apparent presentism. Undergirding both the total war hypothesis and the "dark turn" are questions about civilized and savage warfare.[1]

This study of surrender suggests that the Civil War was both more civilized and more savage than we thought. The ubiquity of surrender throughout the conflict indicates that most Civil War soldiers and officers believed they were fighting in a civilized war, one in which soldiers had the right to surrender and the expectation of humane treatment as prisoners. Take, for example, the case of Thomas Benton Alexander, a Tennessee farmer who surrendered three times over the course of the war. In October 1861, at age twenty-two, Alexander mustered into the Maury Artillery. Sent to reinforce Fort Donelson in February 1862, Alexander surrendered under Simon Buckner shortly thereafter and was imprisoned at Camp Douglas in Chicago until September 1862. Exchanged under the Dix-Hill cartel, Alexander's regiment received an assignment to garrison Port Hudson, north of Baton Rouge. Like Vicksburg, Port Hudson fell under Union siege and surrendered on July 9, 1863, its garrison immediately paroled. Declared exchanged by Confederate officials, Alexander received a posting to Fort Morgan, guarding the entrance to Mobile Bay. There, Alexander surrendered a third time when Fort Morgan fell to Admiral David Farragut in August 1864. Imprisoned at Governor's Island and then Elmira, Alexander was paroled in early March 1865, when prisoner exchange resumed. On furlough until his exchange (which never came), Alexander suggested in his diary that he had no desire to return to the Confederate ranks. After a brief stay at Chimborazo Hospital, Alexander took a train to Charlotte, a journey that should have taken a day but, due to the condition of Confederate railroads, took three. From Charlotte, Alexander meandered more than 600 miles, mostly on foot, across the Carolinas, Georgia, and Alabama before he ended up in Barnesville, Georgia. Unclear about what he should do next, Alexander hired himself to a local farmer as a plowhand. Having largely left the war behind him, Alexander was working in the fields when he first heard rumors of Lee's surrender. On April 24, 1865, more than two weeks after Appomattox, Alexander wrote in his pocket diary, "commenced plowing again[.] was Rumered to Day that they was trying to make peace." Dismissing the rumors as unreliable, Alexander devoted his attention to more pressing matters. He started for home on May 10 and arrived in Nashville a week later. Taking the oath of allegiance, Alexander ended his diary with "18th we marched on towards our home Distance of 20 miles we got home in the Evening at 3.o'ck P.M. our sold[i]er over." He died at the age of ninety, not far from where he was born.

Surrender shaped the entirety of Alexander's war experience. Although some may view his plight as cursed, having been assigned to three doomed Confederate posts, in many ways he was lucky. Even though he spent more than a year in Union prison camps and suffered from several bouts of illness during his imprisonment, Alexander felt that his captors "treated us very well under the circumstances." Since he was not an African American, a Southern Unionist, or a guerilla, Alexander knew that we would receive the full protections afforded to prisoners of war. He benefited from a robust military culture that embraced the fair treatment of prisoners as a hallmark of civilized warfare.

Had he been fighting in a different kind of war, or had he been categorized by the enemy as an illegitimate soldier, Thomas Benton Alexander may not have survived to surrender three times.[2]

As a counterfactual, consider what the Civil War would have looked like if the option to surrender had been taken off the table and men like Thomas Benton Alexander had been compelled to fight rather than being allowed to surrender. Undoubtedly, the death toll would have been much higher, probably exceeding a million. Without the option to surrender, soldiers' experiences in combat would have taken on a more desperate cast and the brutality that characterized combat during the nadir of prisoner exchange in 1864 would have been the baseline. Indeed, removing surrender as an option may have made the experience of the average white soldier more comparable to that of an African American or a guerilla, both of whom were routinely denied the right to surrender. How long would soldiers be willing to fight and democratic institutions to back the war effort if every battle resembled Fort Pillow or the Crater?

If the experience of soldiers like Thomas Benton Alexander demonstrates how the civilizing power of surrender limited fatalities during the Civil War, the specter of barbarism often lurked nearby. Soldiers, civilians, and politicians knew that the Civil War could devolve into a barbaric conflict in which no quarter was given. They could look at the guerilla warfare raging in Kansas, Missouri, and Arkansas and understood that it would not take much for the black flag to replace the white flag. For African American soldiers, the black flag flew over every battle. Denied the protections afforded to legitimate combatants, black Union soldiers went into combat knowing that they could not surrender without risking execution, torture, or enslavement. Many USCT soldiers concluded that since they had been effectively outlawed by the Confederacy, they had no obligation to accept rebel surrenders. Indeed, the absence of surrender defines much of this "dark" war, linking the experiences of USCT soldiers, Southern Unionists, and guerillas.

Recognizing the central role of surrender in the Civil War requires some reconsideration of what being American means. If Americans define themselves as a people who never give up, never compromise, and never surrender, what does it mean that during one of the defining events in the nation's history, Americans surrendered in droves? For many modern Americans, "take no prisoners" and "never surrender" function as mantras, signifying their ideological purity and relentless work ethic. Yet if we are to learn anything from the Civil War generation, we might come to see surrender not as a sign of weakness but as a hallmark of humanity.

Acknowledgments

The idea for this book came to me in a dream. I'm not entirely sure why my unconscious mind thought that researching surrender during the Civil War would prove to be a fruitful topic, but I am very grateful, as writing this book has been both an enjoyable and an educational experience.

Grants from British Academy/Leverhulme Trust, the Carnegie Trust, and the Virginia Historical Society allowed me to do the archival work that underpins this book. I am also grateful to the School of History, Classics, and Archaeology at the University of Edinburgh, which has always been supportive of my research and given me the resources necessary to bring this project to completion.

Although I alone am responsible for any errors in fact or interpretation, I attribute many of this volume's strengths to conversations with friends and colleagues who have generously shared their expertise and insights. A radically incomplete list of those who have helped me along the way includes Bruce Baker, Catherine Bateson, Steve Berry, Fitz Brundage, Pete Carmichael, Catherine Clinton, Frank Cogliano, Adam Domby, Greg Downs, Carole Emberton, Lorien Foote, Sarah Gardner, Judy Giesberg, Lesley Gordon, Susan-Mary Grant, Hilary Green, Fabian Hilfrich, Carrie Janney, Kevin Levin, Robert Mason, Barton Myers, Megan Kate Nelson, Scott Nelson, Angela Riotto, Anne Rubin, Brooks Simpson, Manisha Sinha, Susannah Ural, Elizabeth Varon, Tim Williams, and Cathy Wright. I was also fortunate to present some of my early findings at the Edinburgh American History Workshop and at the annual meetings of the British American Nineteenth Century Historians (BrANCH), the Scottish Association for the Study of America (SASA), and the Society for Civil War Historians.

My family supported me throughout the research and writing process, including trips to surrender sites and museums that masqueraded as family vacations. I dedicate this book to my father, who supported me when I made unconventional choices and taught me never to give up.

Notes

ABBREVIATIONS

B&L   *Battles and Leaders of the Civil War.* 4 vols.
New York: Century, 1887–88.

CWAL   Lincoln, Abraham. *Collected Works of Abraham
Lincoln.* Edited by Roy P. Basler. 9 vols. New
Brunswick, N.J.: Rutgers University Press, 1953.

LOC   Library of Congress, Washington, D.C.

NYHS   New-York Historical Society, New York, N.Y.

OR   *The War of the Rebellion: A Compilation of the Official Records
of the Union and Confederate Armies.* 70 vols. Washington,
D.C.: Government Printing Office, 1880–1901.

ORN   *Official Records of the Union and Confederate Navies
in the War of the Rebellion.* 30 vols. Washington,
D.C.: Government Printing Office, 1894–1922.

PUSG   Grant, Ulysses S. *Papers of Ulysses S. Grant.* 31 vols.
Carbondale: Southern Illinois University Press, 1967–2012.

SHC   Southern Historical Collection, Wilson Library,
University of North Carolina, Chapel Hill

VHS   Virginia Historical Society, Richmond

INTRODUCTION

1. Neely, Holzer, and Boritt, *Confederate Image*, 69, 71; LeBeau, *Currier & Ives*, 82.

2. Wagner-Pacifici, *Art of Surrender*.

3. Sanders, *While in the Hands of the Enemy*, 1; Neal, "Surrendered," 1–2; Rhodes, *History of the United States*, 5:507–8. As recent scholarship on the number of soldiers killed indicates, casualty figures for the American Civil War can be unreliable. See Hacker, "Census-Based Count of the Civil War Dead."

4. "Remarks by the President at the United States Naval Academy Commencement"; Allen, *Until the Last Man Comes Home*, 300; *Public Papers of the Presidents of the United States: Richard Nixon*, 553.

CHAPTER 1

1. Scott, *Memoirs*, 182.

2. Ramsay, *Life of George Washington*, 118; Weems, *History of the Life and Death*, 114. On surrender during the Revolutionary War, see Gruber, "Yorktown"; Krebs, "Ritual Performance"; and Lee, *Barbarians and Brothers*, 169–241.

3. Ahrens, "Nineteenth Century Painting and the United States Capitol."

4. Scott, *Memoirs*, 60; Eustace, *War of 1812*, 61–74.

5. Mansfield, *Life of General Winfield Scott*, 11.

6. Scott, *Memoirs*, 62–63; Peskin, *Winfield Scott*, 24.

7. Scott, *Memoirs*, 65–66, 71–72; Peskin, *Winfield Scott*, 27–28.

8. Elliott, "Some Unpublished Letters of a Roving Soldier-Diplomat"; Peskin, *Winfield Scott*, 63–64.

9. Broers, "'Civilized, Rational Behaviour'?"

10. Marszalek, "Where Did Winfield Scott Find His Anaconda?," 79.

11. *General Regulations for the Army*, 118, 139; Peskin, *Winfield Scott*, 67.

12. Hattaway and Jones, *How the North Won*, 11–12; Reardon, *With a Sword in One Hand*, 6–9; Waugh, *Class of 1846*, 63–64; Hsieh, *West Pointers and the Civil War*, 2–94; Phipps, "Mahan at West Point, 'Gallic Bias,' and the 'Old Army,'" 2–10.

13. Witt, *Lincoln's Code*, 32.

14. *Addresses and Messages of the Presidents*, 2:746

15. Drake, *Biography and History of the Indians of North America*, 161.

16. Jung, *Black Hawk War of 1832*, 180–98; Trask, *Black Hawk*, 295–302; Campbell, "Surrender in the Northeastern Borderlands of Native America," 125–26.

17. Missall and Missall, *Seminole Wars*, 129–30, 134–38; Mahon, *History of the Second Seminole War*, 214–17.

18. Connelly, "Did David Crockett Surrender at the Alamo?"; Hardin, *Texian Iliad*, 127–49; Donovan, *Blood of Heroes*, 207–97; Brands, *Lone Star Nation*, 362–78; Davis, *Three Roads to the Alamo*, 532–63.

19. Brands, *Lone Star Nation*, 398–407, 443–55; De Bruhl, *Sword of San Jacinto*, 210.

20. Greenberg, *Wicked War*, 132.

21. Crist, *Papers of Jefferson Davis*, 3:24.

22. Fry, *Life of Gen. Zachary Taylor*, 299–316; French, *Two Wars*, 77; Hale, "Man without a Country," 674; Eisenhower, *So Far from God*, 185–91; Bauer, *Zachary Taylor*, 199–206.

23. Peskin, *Winfield Scott*, 155.

24. Scott, *Memoirs*, 428–29; Greenberg, *Wicked War*, 169–71.

25. Finney, *Memoirs*, 189, 310.

26. Wineapple, *Ecstatic Nation*, 9–10; Paulus, "America's Long Eulogy for Compromise"; Tetlock, Armor, and Peterson, "Slavery Debate in Antebellum America"; Seager, "Henry Clay and the Politics of Compromise and Non-Compromise"; Bowman, *At the Precipice*, 268–71; Varon, *Disunion!*, 188, 319.

27. *Liberator*, December 14, 1833.

28. Garrison, *No Compromise on Slavery*, 14, 21.

29. Emerson, "American Civilization."

30. Calhoun, "Speech on Slavery," U.S. Senate, *Congressional Globe*, 24th Cong., 2nd sess. (February 6, 1837), 157–59.

31. "How Can the Union Be Preserved?," *DeBow's Review* 21 (1856): 247

32. *State of North Carolina v. Mann*, 13 N.C. 263 (N.C. 1830).

33. Wyatt-Brown, *Southern Honor*; Wyatt-Brown, *Yankee Saints and Southern Sinners*, 183–213; Greenberg, *Honor and Slavery*; Rable, *Damn Yankees!*, 118.

34. Isenberg, *Sex and Citizenship in Antebellum America*, 107; McCurry, *Masters of Small Worlds*, 86; Bardaglio, *Reconstructing the Household*, 27; Jabour, *Scarlett's Sisters*, 136; Berry, *All That Makes a Man*, 38.

35. McGlone, "Forgotten Surrender"; Horwitz, *Midnight Rising*, 176–80; *Life, Trial, and Execution of Captain John Brown*, 49, 72, 80; Mason, *Report of the Select Committee*, 41–44; Redpath, *Public Life of Capt. John Brown*, 203.

36. The scholarship on the secession crisis is extensive. I have relied on Cooper, *We Have the War upon Us*; Potter, *Lincoln and His Party in the Secession Crisis*; Holzer, *Lincoln, President-Elect*; McClintock, *Lincoln and the Decision for War*; Goodheart, *1861*; and Klein, *Days of Defiance*.

37. Potter, *Lincoln and His Party in the Secession Crisis*, 58–60; Freehling and Simpson, *Secession Debated*, 32–50.

38. Wyatt-Brown, *Shaping of Southern Culture*, 182; Wilson, "Crittenden Compromise"; Oakes, *Scorpion Sting*, 46; Duberman, *Charles Francis Adams*, 224; Foner, *Free Soil, Free Labor, Free Men*, 219; *New York Tribune*, December 31, 1860; Cooper, *We Have the War upon Us*, 57, 61.

39. *CWAL* 4:172, 259; Holzer, *Lincoln, President-Elect*; McClintock, *Lincoln and the Decision for War*.

40. Anderson, "Soldiers' Retreat."

41. Anderson, *Artillery Officer in the Mexican War*, 91–96, 179.

42. Hunt, "Narrative and Letter of William Henry Trescot," 532–33.

43. Moore, *Rebellion Record*, 3:266–67; Keyes, *Fifty Years' Observations*, 317; Johnson, *Winfield Scott*, 222.

44. *B&L* 1:40–42.

45. Diary, December 29, 1860, Crawford Papers, LOC; Hunt, "Narrative and Letter of William Henry Trescot," 544; *OR*, ser. 1, 1:3.

46. Crawford, *History of the Fall*, 193–94; Diary, January 11, 1861, Crawford Papers, LOC; Anderson to Pickens, January 11, 1861, Anderson Papers, LOC.

47. Jefferson Davis to Francis Pickens, January 13, 1861, in Rowland, *Jefferson Davis*, 5:36–37; Pickens to Davis, January 23, 1861, Goodyear Collection, Yale University, New Haven, Conn.

48. Doubleday, *Reminiscences*, 116.

49. Williams, *P. G. T. Beauregard*, 2–12, 45–61.

50. *OR*, ser. 1, 1:191, 247, 282–83; Memoirs, Chisolm Papers, NYHS.

51. Doubleday, *Reminiscences*, 112; *B&L* 1:65.

52. McClintock, *Lincoln and the Decision for War*, 200–215; Goodheart, *1861*, 151–56; *CWAL* 4:284–85, 288–90.

53. Farber, *Lincoln's Constitution*, 79–81.

54. Goodheart, *1861*, 152–53; McClintock, *Lincoln and the Decision for War*, 229–31; Keyes, *Fifty Years' Observations*, 378.

55. McClintock, *Lincoln and the Decision for War*, 232–49; Goodheart, *1861*, 161; Symonds, *Lincoln and His Admirals*, 3–36; Thompson and Wainwright, *Confidential Correspondence*, 1:32.

56. *B&L* 1:51.

57. *OR*, ser. 1, 1:241, 245.

58. Klein, *Days of Defiance*, 396–397; *CWAL* 4:324; *OR*, ser. 1, 1:289–91.

59. *OR*, ser. 1, 1:13.

60. *OR*, ser. 1, 1:89–90, 103.

61. *B&L* 1:75, 82; Crawford, *Genesis*, 423–26.

62. Doubleday, *Reminiscences*, 151.

63. Doubleday, *Reminiscences*, 158.

64. *B&L* 1:78; Diary, April 13, 1861, Crawford Papers, LOC.

65. Ringold, "William Gourdin Young and the Wigfall Mission," 31.

66. Crawford, *Genesis*, 439–41.

67. *B&L* 1:78–79; Crawford, *Genesis*, 441–43.

68. Crawford, *Genesis*, 446–48; Doubleday, *Reminiscences*, 171–74.

69. McPherson, *Tried by War*, 22; Donald, *Lincoln*, 292–94; McClintock, *Lincoln and the Decision for War*, 247–49; Carwardine, *Lincoln*, 157–64; Marvel, *Mr. Lincoln Goes to War*, 364.

70. *B&L* 1:81.

71. Bacon, *Letters of a Family during the War for the Union*, 67.

CHAPTER 2

1. Doubleday, *Reminiscences*, 173–74; Crawford, *History of the Fall*, 449.

2. *New York Herald*, April 19, 1861; Doubleday, *Reminiscences*, 173–74; Crawford, *History of the Fall*, 449.

3. Doubleday, *Reminiscences*, 174–76.

4. *New York Herald*, April 15, 1861; McPherson, *Battle Cry of Freedom*, 274; Strong, *Diary*, 185.

5. *New York Herald*, April 16, 1861; Holzer, *Lincoln and the Power of the Press*, 303.

6. Shapiro, "Becoming Union Square," 68–86; *New York Times*, April 20, 1861.

7. *New York Times*, April 21, 1861; *New York Herald*, April 25, 1861.

8. *New York Herald*, April 19, 1861.

9. *CWAL* 4:350, 359; Simon Cameron to Anderson, April 22, 1861; Sitchfield to Anderson, April 22, 1861; Rhinaldo Waters to Anderson, April 23, 1861; Lincoln to Anderson, May 1, 7, 1861, Anderson Papers, LOC.

10. *Charleston Courier*, April 16, 1861; *Richmond Daily Examiner*, April 17, 1861.

11. Heidler, "'Embarrassing Situation,'" 157–72; Brown, "Old Woman with a Broomstick"; Freeman, *R. E. Lee*, 1:414–30; *OR*, ser. 1, 1:579–90, 53:618–28; *Tri-Weekly Alamo Express*, February 13, 1861.

12. Cutrer, *Ben McCulloch and the Frontier Military Tradition*, 5–6, 16, 176.

13. *B&L* 1:34–35; Blackburn, "Reminiscences of the Terry Rangers," 39.

14. *OR*, ser. 2, 1:1–6; *B&L* 1:35.

15. *Philadelphia Inquirer*, March 2, 1861.

16. *B&L* 1:36.

17. Anderson, *Texas, before and on the Eve of the Rebellion*, 31–32; Johnson, *Soldier's Reminiscences*, 132–33; Freeman, *R. E. Lee*, 1:425–30; Rister, *Robert E. Lee in Texas*, 158–61. Anderson shipped Lee's possessions to Virginia, but they were seized en route.

18. Johnson, *Soldier's Reminiscences*, 134; Charles Anderson to Robert Anderson, March 20, 1861, Anderson Papers, LOC.

19. *Independent*, March 14, 1861; *Philadelphia Inquirer*, February 26, March 1, 1861; *Freedom's Champion*, March 2, 1861.

20. *OR*, ser. 1, 1:610, ser. 4, 1:135.

21. *OR*, ser. 2, 1:9–10.

22. *New York Times*, May 13, August 6, 1861.

23. *New York Times*, March 6, 7, 1861.

24. *OR*, ser. 1, 4:37, 45, 51; Armstrong, "Case of Major Isaac Lynde," 2–5.

25. *OR*, ser. 1, 4:5; Wilson, *When the Texans Came*, 43.

26. *OR*, ser. 1, 4:5–6; Wilson, *When the Texans Came*, 43; Nelson, "'Difficulties and Seductions of the Desert.'"

27. *OR*, ser. 1, 4:6, 17–20.

28. *OR*, ser. 1, 4:8–11; Frazier, *Blood and Treasure*, 60.

29. Nelson, "'Difficulties and Seductions of the Desert.'"

30. McKee, *Narrative of the Surrender*, 10, 29, 33; Wilson, *When the Texans Came*, 46, 130.

31. *OR*, ser. 1, 4:19; Josephy, *Civil War in the American West*, 48.

32. *OR*, ser. 1, 4:2, 8–10.

33. *New York Times*, August 29, November 9, 1861; *Ohio State Journal*, reprinted in *Baltimore Daily Exchange*, September 6, 1861.

34. *Journal of the House of Representatives of the United States*, December 4, 1861, 35.

35. Wadsworth, *Incident at San Augustine Springs*, 362; Wilson, *When the Texans Came*, 51.

36. Gould, *History of the First—Tenth—Twenty-Ninth Maine Regiment*, 105; Hawthorne, "Chiefly about War Matters," 53.

37. Hartwig, *To Antietam Creek*, 209.

38. Lowry, *Curmudgeons, Drunkards, and Outright Fools*, 52–54; Hearn, *Six Years of Hell*, 109–12; Teetor, *Matter of Hours*, 13–39.

39. *OR*, ser. 1, 19(1):523, 525; Hartwig, *To Antietam Creek*, 210; Teetor, *Matter of Hours*, 52–57.

40. Hartwig, *To Antietam Creek*, 213; Hearn, *Six Years of Hell*, 132.

41. Willson, *Disaster, Struggle, Triumph*, 45; *OR*, ser. 1, 19(1):720.

42. Sears, *Landscape Turned Red*, 123, 144; Hartwig, *To Antietam Creek*, 236–44, 553; *Boston Evening Transcript*, September 19, 1862; *OR*, ser. 1, 19(1):743; Hull Diary, September 14, 1862, Ohio Historical Society, Columbus.

43. *OR*, ser. 1, 19(1):744; Teetor, *Matter of Hours*, 189–94.

44. *OR*, ser. 1, 19(1):539–40; *B&L* 2:610. Years later, a rumor circulated that Miles was shot by one of his own men in retaliation for the surrender. See Hearn, *Six Years of Hell*, 187, and Teetor, *Matter of Hours*, 203–5.

45. Douglas, *I Rode with Stonewall*, 162; *OR*, ser. 1, 19(1):955. The exact number of Union soldiers surrendered at Harpers Ferry varies between 11,000 and 12,500.

46. Teetor, *Matter of Hours*, 200–201; Simons, *Regimental History*, 36.

47. Robertson, *Stonewall Jackson*, 606; *New York Herald*, September 23, 1862.

48. *OR*, ser. 1, 19(1):799–800.

49. Clark, *Iron Hearted Regiment*, 38–41; *OR*, ser. 2, 4:644–45; Willson, *Disaster, Struggle, Triumph*, 116; Murray, *Redemption of the "Harper's Ferry Cowards*," 43–46; Eisenschiml, *Vermont General*, 44–60; Sanders, *While in the Hands of the Enemy*, 142–44.

50. *Charleston Mercury*, May 1, 1862. On Confederate nationalism, see Quigley, *Shifting Grounds*; Escott, *After Secession*; Faust, *Creation of Confederate Nationalism*; Rable, *Confederate Republic*; and Rubin, *Shattered Nation*.

51. *PUSG* 4:157; *OR*, ser. 1, 7:122–52; Woodworth, *Nothing but Victory*, 77; Grant, *Personal Memoirs*, 1:284–94; *B&L* 1:358–72.

52. Woodworth, *Nothing but Victory*, 115.

53. Vesey, "Why Fort Donelson Was Surrendered"; Hamilton, *Battle of Fort Donelson*, 289–340.

54. Hughes, *I'll Sting If I Can*, 24–25.

55. Broers, "'Civilized, Rational Behaviour'?"; Childs, "Surrender and the Laws of War."

56. Hughes, *I'll Sting If I Can*, 24; Richardson, *Personal History*, 226; Brinton, *Personal Memoirs*, 129; *PUSG* 4:218.

57. Wallace, "Capture of Fort Donelson," 1:428; Grant, *Personal Memoirs*, 1:310–15; *PUSG* 4:290.

58. Brinton, *Personal Memoirs*, 133–34.

59. Richardson, *Personal History*, 233–34.

60. Cooling, *Fort Donelson's Legacy*, 1; Woodworth, *Nothing but Victory*, 118; Crummer, *With Grant*, 43.

61. Tucker, *Unconditional Surrender*, 112–13.

62. Pierson, *Mutiny at Fort Jackson*, 7, 18–22, 26, 32.

63. *Proceedings of the Court of Inquiry, Relative to the Fall of New Orleans*, 198.

64. *Richmond Daily Examiner*, February 21, 1862; McArthur and Burton, *"Gentleman and an Officer,"* 159–65.

65. *New York Times*, March 2, 1862; *Christian Recorder*, March 8, 1862; *Frank Leslie's Illustrated Weekly*, March 22, 1862; *Weekly Vincennes Western Sun*, March 15, 1862; *Burlington Weekly Hawk-Eye*, March 15, 1862; *Congressional Globe* (1862), 1161; Wakelyn, *Southern Unionist Pamphlets*, 100.

66. *Richmond Dispatch*, May 30, 1862.

67. *Richmond Enquirer*, November 13, 1863; Minton, "Defining Confederate Respectability"; Tunnell, "'Patriotic Press.'"

CHAPTER 3

1. Grigsby, *Smoked Yank*, 51.

2. *Hardee's Rifle and Light Infantry Tactics*, 19.

3. The concept of agency has been a powerful if controversial tool for historians trying to understand the experience of disadvantaged peoples, including slaves, women, and the working class. For a critique of agency, see Johnson, "On Agency."

4. Glatthaar, *General Lee's Army*, 327; Sheehan-Dean, *Why Confederates Fought*, 126.

5. Blackburn, "Reminiscences of the Terry Rangers."

6. Blackburn, "Reminiscences of the Terry Rangers," 62.

7. While his identity is a mystery, the German American soldier probably fought in the 32nd Indiana Regiment, often known as the 1st German Regiment, many of whose members were recent immigrants with only limited proficiency in English. See Reinhart, *August Willich's Gallant Dutchmen*, 71–89.

8. Blackburn, "Reminiscences of the Terry Rangers," 62.

9. Wyatt-Brown, *Southern Honor*, 350–61; Wiley, *Life of Johnny Reb*, 308; McPherson, *For Cause and Comrades*, 36–42.

10. Wiley, *Life of Johnny Reb*, 308.

11. Holmes, *Firing Line*, 323–24, 381–90; Ferguson, *Pity of War*, 367–94.

12. McPherson, *For Cause and Comrades*, 77–80; Johnson, "Prison Life at Harpers' Ferry and on Johnson's Island," 242.

13. Hess, *Union Soldier in Battle*, 47.

14. Glatthaar, *General Lee's Army*, 323; Boggs, *Eighteen Months a Prisoner*, 6.

15. Hess, *Rifle Musket in Civil War Combat*, 73, 89, 97, 103–8; Day, *Fifteen Months in Dixie*, 5; Geer, *Beyond the Lines*, 28.

16. Hess, *Civil War Infantry Tactics*, 95–101; *OR*, ser. 1, 19(2):148–52; *California Farmer and Journal of Useful Sciences*, June 6, 1862.

17. Bull, *Soldiering*, 134, 158; Minnich, "Famous Rifles"; Leon, *Diary of a Tar Heel Confederate Soldier*, 60.

18. Eby, *Observations of an Illinois Boy*, 120–24.

19. Hadley, *Seven Months a Prisoner*, 9–18.

20. Sabre, *Nineteen Months a Prisoner*, 10–11.

21. Hess, *Union Soldier in Battle*, 9–15. On the sensory experience of Civil War battles, see Smith, *Smell of Battle*.

22. Byers, *What I Saw in Dixie*, 4.

23. Keiley, *In Vinculis*, 24.

24. Putnam, *Prisoner of War in Virginia*, 9–10; Northrop, *Chronicles from the Diary of a War Prisoner*, 29; Darby, *Incidents and Adventures in Rebeldom*, 101; McElroy, *Andersonville*, 59–60.

25. Gallagher, "Through Battle, Prison, and Disease," 33–34; Putnam, *Prisoner of War in Virginia*, 10.

26. Glatthaar, *General Lee's Army*, 178; United States Sanitary Commission, *Narratives of Privations and Sufferings*, 30; Sabre, *Nineteen Months a Prisoner*, 11.

27. Hunter, *Johnny Reb and Billy Yank*, 301.

28. Eby, *Observations of an Illinois Boy*, 126; Geer, *Beyond the Lines*, 27–28; Bates, *Stars and Stripes in Rebeldom*, 77.

29. Diary, April 13, 1865, Gore Papers, NYHS; Nisbet, *Four Years on the Firing Line*, 312; Mitchell, *Civil War Soldiers*, 25–27, 37–41; Noe, *Reluctant Rebels*, 91–92.

30. Johnston, *Four Months in Libby*, 35; United States Sanitary Commission, *Narratives of Privations and Sufferings*, 155.

31. David Henkel to his brother, November 7, 1863, Henkel Family Papers, VMI Archives, Lexington, Va.; Faust, *This Republic of Suffering*, 102–16; Glatthaar, *General Lee's Army*, 301.

32. United States Sanitary Commission, *Narrative of Privations and Sufferings*, 19–20.

33. Crossley, *Extracts from My Diary*, 11–12.

34. Morey, "Prison Life," 330.

35. *Charleston Mercury*, June 7, 1861.

36. *OR*, ser. 2, 3:8–9.

37. Sears, *Civil War Papers of George B. McClellan*, 53.

38. Mitchell, *Civil War Soldiers*, 37.

39. Corcoran, *Captivity of General Corcoran*, 22–23.

40. Ely, *Journal of Alfred Ely*, 14–16, 25; Corcoran, *Captivity of General Corcoran*, 40.

41. Donald, *Lincoln*, 302.

42. *OR*, ser. 2, 3:131–32; Speer, *War of Vengeance*, 27–28; Carnahan, *Act of Justice*, 67.

43. Bates, *Stars and Stripes in Rebeldom*, 15–16.

44. *OR*, ser. 2, 3:50.

45. *OR*, ser. 2, 1:511, 523, 541.

46. Pickenpaugh, *Captives in Gray*, 45.

47. William A. Coleman to J. C. Coleman, April 20, 1862, and A. G. Hammack to his brother, April 21, 1862, Chase Papers, VHS.

48. Hesseltine, *Civil War Prisons*, 9.

49. *Harper's Weekly*, November 30, 1861.

50. *OR*, ser. 2, 3:150–51, 157, 199; Chase, *Inside Lincoln's Cabinet*, 49.

51. *OR*, ser. 2, 4:266–68.

52. Berlin, Fields, Miller, Reidy, and Rowland, *Slaves No More*, 3–41; Oakes, *Freedom National*, 95–108, 153–66, 179–86, 318–24, 377–80.

53. Barrett, *Civil War in North Carolina*, 90–91; Springer and Robins, *Transforming Civil War Prisons*, 10–11.

54. Sanders, *While in the Hands of the Enemy*, 120.

55. Prokopowicz, "Word of Honor," 35–37; Hesseltine, *Civil War Prisons*, 75–78; Springer and Robins, *Transforming Civil War Prisons*, 11; Sanders, *While in the Hands of the Enemy*, 112–15; Carnahan, *Act of Justice*, 30–32, 61–70.

56. Anders, "Blackwater Incident," 419, 423–26; *OR*, ser. 2, 1:292–374; Kelsey, *Deeds of Daring*, 188–200; Neely, *Fate of Liberty*, 162–75

57. *OR*, ser. 2, 4:556–58.

58. Cline Diary, Notre Dame University, Notre Dame, Ind.

59. Hunter, *Johnny Reb and Billy Yank*, 191, 198, 200, 218–21, 226–27, 306–7, 313.

60. Sheehan-Dean, *Why Confederates Fought*, 126.

61. McElroy, *Andersonville*, 98; *OR*, ser. 2, 4:499, 576.

62. Eisenschiml, *Vermont General*, 50.

63. *New York Times*, August 19, 1861.

64. Witt, *Lincoln's Code*; Dilbeck, "'Genesis of This Little Tablet with My Name.'"

65. Sutherland, *Savage Conflict*, 23–24, 33, 63–66; Witt, *Lincoln's Code*, 191; Mackey, *Uncivil War*, 6–11.

66. Witt, *Lincoln's Code*, 192–93.

67. Sutherland, *Savage Conflict*, 64, 81, 200.

68. *OR*, ser. 2, 4:945–46.

69. *OR*, ser. 2, 5:940–41.

70. *OR*, ser. 2, 6:21–22.

71. Lowe, "Battle on the Levee," 125; Bergeron, "Battle of Olustee," 144; Gautier, *Harder Than Death*, 10–11; Cornish, *Sable Arm*, 158–59; Smith, "Let Us All Be Grateful," 44–46.

72. Wilson, *Black Phalanx*, 315; Smith, "Let Us All Be Grateful," 47; *Charleston Courier*, July 17, 1863.

73. Duncan, *Blue-Eyed Child*, 343; Burkhardt, *Confederate Rage, Yankee Wrath*, 55.

74. Foner, *Fiery Trial*, 254–55.

75. Bates, *Texas Cavalry Officer's Civil War*, 270.

76. Hunter, *Johnny Reb and Billy Yank*, 443, 449–56.

CHAPTER 4

1. Statistics for battlefield casualties are inherently suspect, and one can find many conflicting sets of numbers for Gettysburg. See Busey and Martin, *Regimental Strengths and Losses at Gettysburg*, 125, 260, and Glatthaar, *General Lee's Army*, 283.

2. Hartwig, "Unwilling Witness to the Rage of Gettysburg," 40.

3. Murray, *Redemption of the "Harper's Ferry Cowards,"* 42–74.

4. Memoirs, Blacknall Papers, North Carolina Department of Archives and History, Raleigh; "Twenty-Third Regiment," in Clark, *Histories of the Several Regiments,* 2:231–32, 254–56; *North Carolina Troops,* 7:143.

5. Harris, "Gen. Jas. J. Archer"; Guelzo, *Gettysburg,* 133–34.

6. Doubleday, *Chancellorsville and Gettysburg,* 132.

7. Ernsberger, *Also for the Glory Muster,* 39; Pfanz, *Gettysburg: The First Day,* 99.

8. Sears, *Gettysburg,* 172; Guelzo, *Gettysburg,* 149–50; Hartwig, "I Have Never Seen the Like Before," 168–69; Beecham, *Gettysburg,* 66–68; Harries, "Iron Brigade in the First Day's Battle at Gettysburg," 340–41; Harries, "Sword of General James J. Archer"; *OR,* ser. 1, 27(1):274.

9. Ernsberger, *Also for the Glory Muster,* 40; Hardman, "As a Union Prisoner Saw the Battle of Gettysburg," 39–40; Hawkins, "Sergeant-Major Blanchard at Gettysburg," 214; Pfanz, *Gettysburg: The First Day,* 100.

10. James Coey, "Cutler's Brigade," *National Tribune,* July 15, 1915; Snyder, *Oswego County in the Civil War,* 63; Pfanz, *Gettysburg: The First Day,* 85–87.

11. Dawes, *Service with the Sixth,* 169; Sears, *Gettysburg,* 178; Guelzo, *Gettysburg,* 153; New York Monuments Commission, *Final Report,* 3:1005–6; Hartwig, "Guts and Good Leadership"; Pfanz, *Gettysburg: The First Day,* 104.

12. Vautier, *History of the 88th Pennsylvania Volunteers,* 107; Wynstra, *Rashness of That Hour,* 240; Guelzo, *Gettysburg,* 172; Pfanz, *Gettysburg: The First Day,* 172–75; Blacknall Papers, North Carolina Department of Archives and History, Raleigh; *OR,* ser. 1, 27(1):289, 310, (2):342.

13. Guelzo, *Gettysburg,* 188–92.

14. Wainwright, *Diary of Battle,* 236–37.

15. Hardman, "As a Union Prisoner Saw the Battle of Gettysburg," 36–40.

16. *Maine at Gettysburg,* 43–44; Pfanz, *Gettysburg: The First Day,* 192; Guelzo, *Gettysburg,* 192.

17. Guelzo, *Gettysburg,* 190; Pfanz, *Gettysburg: The First Day,* 267; Dunkelman, *Brothers One and All,* 132–33.

18. Dawes, *Service with the Sixth,* 178.

19. Boone Memoirs, 88th Pennsylvania file, Gettysburg National Military Park, Gettysburg, Pa. A slightly different version appears in Vautier, *History of the 88th Pennsylvania Volunteers,* 219–21.

20. Reed, "Gettysburg Campaign," 188; Dawes, *Service with the Sixth,* 178; *OR,* ser. 1, 27(1):183, 730.

21. New York Monuments Commission, *Final Report,* 1:380.

22. Meredith, "First Day at Gettysburg," 185; Guelzo, *Gettysburg,* 214.

23. Glatthaar, *General Lee's Army,* 274–75; McLaws, "Gettysburg," 68; Pfanz, *Gettysburg: The First Day,* 350–51.

24. Domschcke, *Twenty Months in Captivity,* 28.

25. Fishel, *Secret War for the Union,* 526–28; Sears, *Gettysburg,* 342.

26. Sears, *Gettysburg,* 276; Guelzo, *Gettysburg,* 263–67.

27. Sears, *Gettysburg,* 295–96; Guelzo, *Gettysburg,* 270–72.

28. Styple, *With a Flash of His Sword,* 301.

29. Desjardin, *Stand Firm Ye Boys of Maine,* 112.

30. Stevens, *Reminiscences of the Civil War*, 114–15.

31. Barziza, *Adventures of a Prisoner of War*, 44–45.

32. Sears, *Gettysburg*, 296; Oates, *War between the Union and the Confederacy*, 215–17, 222.

33. Oeffinger, *Soldier's General*, 196; Nelson, *Battles of Chancellorsville and Gettysburg*, 150–51; Martin, *History of the Fifty-Seventh Regiment*, 89.

34. Campbell, "Key to the Entire Situation," 181.

35. Mulholland, *Story of the 116th Regiment*, 409.

36. Hartwig, "Unwilling Witness to the Rage of Gettysburg," 67.

37. Murray, *Redemption of the "Harper's Ferry Cowards,"* 48–49.

38. Willson, *Disaster, Struggle, Triumph*, 169–70; Murray, *Redemption of the "Harper's Ferry Cowards,"* 93–102; Guelzo, *Gettysburg*, 324.

39. Sutton, *Civil War Stories*, 43.

40. Carter, *Four Brothers in Blue*, 313; Guelzo, *Gettysburg*, 303.

41. Coco, *From Ball's Bluff*, 201–5.

42. Cockrell and Ballard, *Mississippi Rebel in the Army of Northern Virginia*, 198.

43. Reardon, "Pickett's Charge," 57; Guelzo, *Gettysburg*, 441–42; Hess, *Pickett's Charge*, 333.

44. *OR*, ser. 1, 27(1):454; Simons, *Regimental History*, 144; Guelzo, *Gettysburg*, 425.

45. McFarland, "Eleventh Mississippi Regiment at Gettysburg," 564; Hess, *Pickett's Charge*, 207.

46. Taylor, *Cry Is War, War, War*, 147; Smith [Brown] to parents, July 4, 1863, Brown Papers, Hamilton College, Clinton, N.Y.; *OR*, ser. 1, 27(1):454.

47. Rice, "Repelling Lee's Last Blow at Gettysburg," 3:389; Hall, "From the Official Report of Norman J. Hall," 3:391.

48. *New York Times*, July 6, 1863.

49. Hess, *Pickett's Charge*, 205, 229; Hartwig, "It Struck Horror to Us All."

50. Hess, *Pickett's Charge*, 270; Simons, *Regimental History*, 138; *OR*, ser. 1, 27(1):462; Page, *History of the Fourteenth*, 156.

51. Reardon, *Pickett's Charge*, 84–107.

52. Coddington, *Gettysburg Campaign*, vii.

53. *CWAL* 6:324.

54. Chamberlain, *Something of the Pettijohn (Pettyjohn) Family*, 16; Gantt, *Gettysburg Prisoners*; Coco, *From Ball's Bluff*, 207; Domschcke, *Twenty Months in Captivity*, 135; Snyder, *Oswego County in the Civil War*, 64; *OR*, 1, 27(3):518; Brown, *Retreat from Gettysburg*, 65–66.

55. Coco, *From Ball's Bluff*, 207; *OR*, ser. 1, 27(2):299.

56. *OR*, ser. 1, 27(3):514.

57. Brown, *Retreat from Gettysburg*, 98–99.

58. Coddington, *Gettysburg Campaign*, 543.

59. Collins, "Prisoner's March from Gettysburg to Staunton."

60. Heaton, "War Experiences of Samuel Wheeler," 58–59.

61. Brown, *Retreat from Gettysburg*, 262; Wallber, "From Gettysburg to Libby Prison," 196; Gantt, *Gettysburg Prisoners*.

62. Coco, *From Ball's Bluff*, 209; Domschcke, *Twenty Months in Captivity*, 31–32.

63. Ransom, *Andersonville Diary*, 13.

64. Domschcke, *Twenty Months in Captivity*, 137; Cavada, *Libby Life*, 49–50; Burch Diary, Wisconsin Historical Society, Madison.

65. Bird, *Stories of the Civil War*, 20, 28–29.

66. Barrett, *Yankee Rebel*, 128, 177, 181.

67. Curran, *John Dooley's Civil War*, 239, 244; Barrett, *Yankee Rebel*, 151; Barziza, *Adventures of a Prisoner of War*, 99–100; Memoirs, 257, Thompson Papers, SHC.

CHAPTER 5

1. Pollard, *Lee and His Lieutenants*, 760.

2. *Harper's Weekly*, March 1, 1862; *PUSG* 4:229; Woodworth, *Nothing but Victory*, 119.

3. *OR*, ser. 1, 16(1):794–96; Trenerry, "Lester's Surrender at Murfreesboro."

4. *OR*, ser. 1, 16(1):805.

5. Wyeth, *Life of Forrest*, 35–36.

6. *State of North Carolina v. Mann*, 13 N.C. 263 (N.C. 1830).

7. Hurst, *Forrest*, 33–67; Wyatt-Brown, *Southern Honor*; Greenberg, *Honor and Slavery*.

8. *OR*, ser. 1, 16(1):809.

9. Hurst, *Forrest*, 108–10; Jordan and Pryor, *Campaigns of Lieut.-Gen. Forrest*, 201; *OR*, ser. 1, 17(1):567–68, 594, 598.

10. Wyeth, *Life of Forrest*, 170; Wills, *River Was Dyed with Blood*, 31; *OR*, ser. 1, 23(1):188–90.

11. *OR*, ser. 1, 17(1):567.

12. *Louisiana Democrat*, July 25, 1866; *OR*, ser. 1, 23(1):291–92; Wills, *River Was Dyed with Blood*, 32; Hurst, *Forrest*, 124.

13. Greenberg, *Honor and Slavery*, 135–45; Wyatt-Brown, *Southern Honor*, 339–51; Hurst, *Forrest*, 17, 64; *Louisiana Democrat*, July 25, 1866.

14. Maynard, "Vicksburg Diary," 47.

15. Maynard, "Vicksburg Diary," 48–51

16. Ballard, *Vicksburg*, 381–82; *ORN*, ser. 1, 25:118.

17. Ballard, *Vicksburg*, 397; *OR*, ser. 1, 24(1):59.

18. *OR*, ser. 1, 24(1):60.

19. *OR*, ser. 1, 24(1):284; Pemberton, "Terms of Surrender at Vicksburg"; Strong, "Campaign against Vicksburg"; Grant, *Personal Memoirs*, 1:554–70; Simpson, *Grant*, 213.

20. Gaskell, "Surrendered at Vicksburg."

21. Richardson, *Personal History*, 333–34; Dana, *Recollections*, 99; Hogane, "Reminiscences of the Siege of Vicksburg," 487–88; Ballard, *Vicksburg*, 403; Simpson, *Grant*, 214.

22. *OR*, ser. 1, 24(1):285; Grant, *Personal Memoirs*, 1:565.

23. Ballard, *Vicksburg*, 398; Waugh, "'I Only Knew,'" 313.

24. Grant, *Personal Memoirs*, 1:571–72.

25. *PUSG* 9:41.

26. Whittington, "In the Shadow of Defeat"; Prokopowicz, "Word of Honor," 50–51; Hesseltine, *Civil War Prisons*, 96–108.

27. *OR*, ser. 1, 32(3):117–19, 145–46.

28. Moore, *Rebellion Record*, 8:41–44; *OR*, ser. 1, 32(1):542–46; Wyeth, *Life of Forrest*, 327–28; Maness, "Ruse That Worked"; Wills, *River Was Dyed with Blood*, 75–77; Ward, *River Run Red*, 111–14; Holley, "Seventh Tennessee Volunteer Cavalry."

29. Craig, *Kentucky Confederates*, 235–36; *OR*, ser. 1, 32(1):547–48.

30. Witt, *Lincoln's Code*, 389.

31. *OR*, ser. 1, 32(1):547–48, 607; Huch, "Fort Pillow Massacre"; Ward, *River Run Red*, 120–24.

32. Moore, *Rebellion Record*, 8:55–56; Dinkins, *Personal Recollections and Experiences in the Confederate Army*, 150–51.

33. *OR*, ser. 1, 32(1):596.

34. *Reports of the Joint Committee on the Conduct of the War*, 120; *OR*, ser. 1, 32(1):614.

35. Wills, *River Was Dyed with Blood*, 109; *Reports of the Joint Committee on the Conduct of the War*, 4; Carroll, *Autobiography and Reminiscences*, 28–29; Cimprich, *Fort Pillow*, 78–79.

36. Wills, *River Was Dyed with Blood*, 110; Cimprich and Mainfort, "Fort Pillow Revisited," 299; *Reports of the Joint Committee on the Conduct of the War*, 4, 21, 43, 46; Cimprich and Mainfort, "Dr. Fitch's Report on the Fort Pillow Massacre"; *OR*, ser. 1, 32(1):589.

37. Cimprich and Mainfort, "Fort Pillow Massacre: A Statistical Note"; Cimprich, *Fort Pillow*, 85, 129.

38. *OR*, ser. 1, 32(1):586, 617; *Richmond Dispatch*, May 20, 1864; Cimprich, *Fort Pillow*, 103.

39. Ward, *River Run Red*, 306–8; *OR*, ser. 1, 32(1):518; Cimprich, *Fort Pillow*, 90, 96–100; Tap, "'These Devils Are Not Fit to Live on God's Earth,'" 116–25.

40. Ward, *River Run Red*, 306–8, 322–23; Cimprich, *Fort Pillow*, 90.

41. Springer and Robins, *Transforming Civil War Prisons*, 15–22.

42. *OR*, ser. 2, 7:607.

43. Morgan, "Reminiscences of Service with Colored Troops in the Army of the Cumberland," 31; Wills, *River Was Dyed with Blood*, 165–66.

44. Moore, "Fort Pillow, Forrest, and the United States Colored Troops in 1864"; Wilson, *Black Phalanx*, 348–49.

45. *OR*, ser. 1, 32(1):586–93.

46. *OR*, ser. 1, 39(1):520–26, 534; S. R. Norton to Hattie Norton, September 27, 1864, Norton Letters, University of Alabama, Tuscaloosa.

47. *OR*, ser. 1, 39(1):524; Berlin et al., *Freedom*, ser. 2, 591–92.

48. Comstock, *Ninth Cavalry*, 7–8; *OR*, ser. 1, 39(1):534.

49. *OR*, ser. 1, 39(1):533, 539, 545.

50. Wills, *River Was Dyed with Blood*, 19; Cadwallader, *Three Years with Grant*, 39.

CHAPTER 6

1. Grimsley, *Hard Hand of War*; Neely, *Civil War and the Limits of Destruction*; Royster, *Destructive War*; Burkhardt, *Confederate Rage, Yankee Wrath*; Mountcastle, *Punitive War*. The idea of "hard war" should be distinguished from the related but distinct notion of "total war." See Hsieh, "Total War and the American Civil War Reconsidered."

2. *OR*, ser. 1, 31(3):701; *New York Times*, December 4, 1863; Sanders, *While in the Hands of the Enemy*, 196.

3. *OR*, ser. 1, 52(2):586–87; Levine, *Confederate Emancipation*, 27–28, 85–87.

4. Crist, *Papers of Jefferson Davis*, 10:378–87.

5. *OR*, ser. 4, 3:335; *OR*, ser. 2, 6:752, 754, 768–69; Trefousse, *Ben Butler*, 140–43; Sanders, *While in the Hands of the Enemy*, 213.

6. Coulter, "From Spotsylvania Courthouse to Andersonville"; Wallace, *Few Memories of a Long Life*, 33.

7. Sanders, *While in the Hands of the Enemy*, 164.

8. Kellogg, *Life and Death in Rebel Prisons*, 56.

9. Ripple, *Dancing along the Deadline*, 18; Marvel, *Andersonville*, 1.

10. *OR*, ser. 2, 7:73, 150–51, 183–84; *Charleston Mercury*, June 14, 1864.

11. *OR*, ser. 1, 35(2):135, 141–48, 174–75, 198; McMichael Diary, September 7, 1864, Emory University, Emory, Ga.; Speer, *War of Vengeance*, 97–112; Duke, *Reminiscences*, 374–79.

12. Memoirs, 248, 275, Thompson Papers, SHC; Woodward, *Mary Chesnut's Civil War*, 632.

13. Hadley, *Seven Months a Prisoner*, 19–32.

14. Sanders, *While in the Hands of the Enemy*, 191; Foote, *Yankee Plague*, 1.

15. *Harper's Weekly*, June 18, 1864; *Frank Leslie's Illustrated Weekly*, June 18, 1864.

16. Bull, *Soldiering*, 193.

17. Jordan and Thomas, "Massacre at Plymouth," 131–45; *OR*, ser. 1, 33:299; Blakeslee, *History of the Sixteenth Connecticut Volunteers*, 57; Gordon, *Broken Regiment*, 137.

18. Smith, "Siege and Capture of Plymouth"; Gordon, "'Surely They Remember Me,'" 341; Donaghy, *Army Experience*, 154; Gordon, *Broken Regiment*, 137.

19. *Charlotte Daily Bulletin*, March 18, 1864; Smith, "Siege and Capture of Plymouth," 343; Donaghy, *Army Experience*, 161–62; Kellogg, *Life and Death in Rebel Prisons*, 40.

20. Donaghy, *Army Experience*, 155; Mahood, *Charlie Mosher's Civil War*, 205; Reed, *History of the 101st Regiment*, 135.

21. Goss, *Soldier's Story*, 61; *OR*, ser. 2, 7:459–60; Jordan and Thomas, "Massacre at Plymouth," 166; Gordon, *Broken Regiment*, 138–44.

22. *New York Tribune*, April 26, 1864; *Delaware County American*, July 13, 1864; Porter, *Campaigning with Grant*, 126.

23. Hess, *Into the Crater*, 128.

24. John Cheves Haskell, "Reminiscences of the Confederate War," 102–3, Haskell Papers, SHC; Hess, *Into the Crater*, 147; Clark, "Alabamians in the Crater Battle," 69.

25. Hess, *Into the Crater*, 164–65; Levin, *Remembering the Battle of the Crater*, 7, 28.

26. Hitchcock, *Marching with Sherman*, 87; Connolly, *Three Years with the Army of the Cumberland*, 298.

27. Reminiscences, Edwards Papers, Duke University, Durham, N.C.

28. Poriss and Poriss, *While My Country Is in Danger*, 109.

29. Sutherland, *American Civil War Guerrillas*, 50–54; *OR*, ser. 1, 43(1):811.

30. Sutherland, *American Civil War Guerrillas*, 73; Fellman, *Inside War*, 184–92; *OR*, ser. 1, 41(2):75; Castel and Goodrich, *Bloody Bill Anderson*, 42–54; Barber and Howe, *Loyal West*, 621.

31. Goodman, *Thrilling Record*, 21–25.

32. Goodman, *Thrilling Record*, 34–35; *OR*, ser. 1, 41(3):488.

33. Mays, "Battle of Saltville"; Mays, *Cumberland Blood*, 113–21; McKnight, *Confederate Outlaw*, 146–47.

34. John Malachi Bowden, "Some of My Experiences as a Confederate Soldier," Bowden Papers, Atlanta History Center, Atlanta, Ga.

35. Alexander, *Fighting for the Confederacy*, 478; Sherman, "Negro as Soldier."

36. *New York Times*, August 31, 1864; "Compromise with the South," *Harper's Weekly*, September 3, 1864; *CWAL* 8:151.

37. Mobley, "Zebulon B. Vance," 440; *Charleston Mercury*, September 30, 1864, and February 9, 1865.

38. Stephens, *Constitutional View of the Late War*, 2:616–18; Harris, "Hampton Roads Peace Conference"; Conroy, *Our One Common Country*; Striner, "Lincoln and the Hampton Roads Conference."

39. *CWAL* 8:285; Stephens, *Constitutional View of the Late War*, 2:618; Avary, "Lincoln Souvenir in the South."

40. *OR*, ser. 2, 8:63, 74, 170; *PUSG* 13:266, 370; Simpson, "Facilitating Defeat," 88–89.

41. Sherman, *Memoirs*, 2:329; Porter, *Naval History*, 794–95; Simpson, *Let Us Have Peace*, 78; Waugh, "'I Only Knew,'" 321–22.

42. Crist, *Papers of Jefferson Davis*, 11:382–89; *OR*, ser. 1, 47(2):1190.

CHAPTER 7

1. Catton, *Stillness at Appomattox*, 379–80.

2. *B&L* 6:494; Davis, *Honorable Defeat*, 46.

3. *OR*, ser. 1, 46(2):802.

4. Hunter, "Peace Commission," 308–9; Grimsley, "Learning to Say 'Enough,'" 48–50; Nolan, "Price of Honor."

5. Gordon, *Reminiscences*, 385–90.

6. Gordon, *Reminiscences*, 393–94.

7. Marvel, *Lee's Last Retreat*, 46–47.

8. Racine, *Unspoiled Heart*, 265, 268.

9. *OR*, ser. 1, 46(3):610; Varon, *Appomattox*, 16.

10. Kean, "In a Uniform of Grey," VHS.

11. *OR*, ser. 1, 46(3):1382–83.

12. Feis, "Jefferson Davis and the 'Guerrilla Option,'" 104–28; Thomas, *Confederate Nation*, 51; Ballard, *Long Shadow*, 56–57.

13. Lee, *Memoirs of William Nelson Pendleton*, 402; Alexander, *Fighting for the Confederacy*, 527; Longstreet, *From Manassas to Appomattox*, 618; Gordon, *Reminiscences*, 433; Marvel, *Lee's Last Retreat*, 133, 144; Varon, *Appomattox*, 24–25.

14. *OR*, ser. 1, 34(1):54.

15. Varon, *Appomattox*, 21; *OR*, ser. 1, 1:2, 14, 30, 60, 113, 129, 137, 149, 301, 640, 642, 4:13, 583, 6:543, 9:277, 24(1):59–60, 26(1):15, 620, 30(2):614, 617, 619, 621, 709, 32(1):547, 596, 600, 621.

16. *OR*, ser. 1, 34(1):54–55.

17. *OR*, ser. 1, 34(1):55; Varon, *Appomattox*, 30–31; Waugh, "'I Only Knew,'" 323.

18. *OR*, ser. 1, 34(1):55.

19. Gordon, *Reminiscences*, 434–35; Lee, *Memoirs of William Nelson Pendleton*, 404.

20. *OR*, ser. 1, 34(1):55; Grant, *Personal Memoirs*, 2:483–84; Varon, *Appomattox*, 38.

21. Alexander, "Lee at Appomattox," 926–27.

22. Grant, *Personal Memoirs*, 2:485.

23. Minor, "Surrender of Mahone's Division," 312; Chamberlain, *Passing of the Armies*, 240; White, "Stray Leaves from a Soldier's Journal," 558.

24. Warr Diary, April 9, 1865, Appomattox Courthouse, Va.; "From Petersburg to Appomattox," 12, Devereux Papers, SHC; Peacock, "Surrender at Appomattox Courthouse," 269.

25. Marbaker, *History of the Eleventh New Jersey Volunteers*, 295; Gorman, *Lee's Last Campaign*, 5, 55.

26. Gibbon, *Personal Recollections*, 318; Sheridan, *Personal Memoirs*, 2:196–201; Varon, *Appomattox*, 46–47.

27. "From Petersburg to Appomattox," 12–13, Devereux Papers, SHC.

28. Dunkerly, *Confederate Surrender at Greensboro*, 110–11; Diary, April 9, 1865, Paris Papers, SHC; McIntosh Diary, April 9, 1865, VHS; Boykin, *Falling Flag*, 62; Chamberlayne, *Ham Chamberlayne—Virginian*, 322; Phillips, *Diehard Rebels*, 169–70.

29. D. G. McIntosh to Jefferson Davis, April 19, 1865, Pegram-Johnson-McIntosh Papers, VHS.

30. Lee to Davis, April 20, 1865, in Dowdey, *Wartime Papers of R. E. Lee*, 938–39; "An Unpublished Piece of History," French Papers, Library of Virginia, Richmond.

31. Marshall, "Appomattox Courthouse," 357.

32. Grant, *Personal Memoirs*, 2:489–90.

33. Varon, *Appomattox*, 55, 58, 267; Cauble, *Surrender Proceedings*, 45–61.

34. Marshall, "Appomattox Courthouse," 358; Porter, *Campaigning with Grant*, 475; Dugard, *Training Ground*, 335–69. Other significant figures from Civil War surrenders who fought at Chapultepec include David Twiggs, Gideon Pillow, Stonewall Jackson, and Joseph Johnston.

35. Grant, *Personal Memoirs*, 2:492; Waugh, "'I Only Knew.'"

36. Porter, *Campaigning with Grant*, 477–78.

37. Grant, *Personal Memoirs*, 2:494; Porter, *Campaigning with Grant*, 480.

38. Grant, *Personal Memoirs*, 2:494–95; Porter, *Campaigning with Grant*, 482–83; Marshall, "Appomattox Courthouse," 359–60.

39. "Robert E. Lee Leaving the McLean House after His Surrender to Ulysses S. Grant," Waud Papers, LOC; Young, *Around the World with General Grant*, 381.

40. Hoopes, "Confederate Memoir of William M. Abernathy," 3:17; Chapman Diary, April 9, 1865, SHC; Fields Diary, April 9, 1865, VHS.

41. Whitehorne Diary, April 9, 1865, SHC.

42. Wiatt, *Confederate Chaplain*, 237–38; Hagood, "Memoirs of the First South Carolina Regiment," 215, University of South Carolina, Columbia.

43. Marshall, "Appomattox Courthouse," 360; Cooke, *Just before and after Lee Surrendered to Grant*, 6; "Recollections of the War," Bahnson Papers, SHC.

44. Marbaker, *History of the Eleventh New Jersey Volunteers*, 296.

45. William H. Smith letter to his friends, April 9, 1865, Smith Papers, University of Washington, Seattle; Wert, *Sword of Lincoln*, 409.

46. Diary of a Union Soldier of the 3rd Pennsylvania Cavalry, April 9, 1865, New York Public Library, New York, N.Y.; Smith, *Antietam to Appomattox*, 593.

47. Grant, *Personal Memoirs*, 2:496; Janney, *Remembering the Civil War*, 42–43; Marvel, *Lee's Last Retreat*, 185.

48. Minor, "Surrender of Mahone's Division."

49. Grant, *Personal Memoirs*, 2:496–97.

50. Lee to Davis, April 20, 1865, in Dowdey, *Wartime Papers of R. E. Lee*, 938–39; Rafuse, *Robert E. Lee and the Fall of the Confederacy*, 248.

51. Gibbon, *Personal Recollections*, 329–31.

52. *B&L* 4:747; *OR*, ser. 1, 46(1):1267.

53. Varon, *Appomattox*, 68–70; Janney, *Remembering the Civil War*, 43–44; Blight, *Race and Reunion*, 37–38.

54. Perry, "Appomattox Courthouse," 61.

55. Varon, *Appomattox*, 77–78; Calkins, *Final Bivouac*, 30–35.

56. Chamberlain, *Passing of the Armies*, 260–66.

57. Whitehorne Diary, April 12, 1865, SHC.

58. Chapman Diary, April 12, 1865, SHC; Calkins, *Final Bivouac*, 36.

59. *New York Times*, April 10, 1865; *Boston Herald*, April 10, 1865.

60. Strong, *Diary*, 290–91; Silber, *Romance of Reunion*, 15–16.

61. Johnson, "Prison Life at Harpers' Ferry and on Johnson's Island."

62. McMichael Diary, April 9, May 2, 7, June 16, 1865, Emory University, Emory, Ga.

63. Dodge, "Home Scenes at the Fall of the Confederacy," 662–64.

64. Downs, *After Appomattox*.

65. Porter, "Lee's Surrender at Appomattox," 976.

66. Battle, *Third Alabama Regiment*, 134, VHS; Storey, *Loyalty and Loss*, 218.

CHAPTER 8

1. Existing records make it difficult to state with any precision the size of Confederate forces in April 1865. The numbers provided here are estimates derived from a number of sources, including Livermore, *Numbers and Losses*, 7; Grimsley, "Learning to Say 'Enough,'" 69; and Dunkerly, *To the Bitter End*, 147.

2. Davis, *Rise and Fall*, 2:679; Johnston, *Narrative*, 397.

3. Mallory Diary and Reminiscences, 70, SHC. Also see Johnston, *Narrative*, 397–98; Reagan, *Memoirs*, 199–200; and Memoirs, Chisolm Papers, NYHS.

4. *OR*, ser. 1, 47(3):799–800

5. Phillips, *Diehard Rebels*, 147–48, 172, 175.

6. Bradley, *This Astounding Close*, 90, 141; Johnston, *Narrative*, 400–401; Cumming, "How I Knew That the War Was Over."

7. Clarke, *Live Your Own Life*, 207; undated scrapbook, St. Mary's School, Raleigh, N.C.; Spencer, *Last Ninety Days*, 52; Silkenat, *Driven from Home*, 178–79; Bradley, *This Astounding Close*, 92.

8. *OR*, ser. 1, 47(3):140, 177.

9. *OR*, ser. 1, 47(3):178; Zebulon B. Vance, "Last Days of the War," in Dowd, *Life of Vance*, 484–85; Bradley, *This Astounding Close*, 114–27.

10. Sherman, *Memoirs*, 2:344.

11. *OR*, ser. 1, 47(3):207–8.

12. Sherman, *Memoirs*, 2:347–49.

13. Menius, "James Bennitt."

14. Sherman, *Memoirs*, 2:349–50; Johnston, *Narrative*, 402–3.

15. Bradley, *This Astounding Close*, 163; Barrett, *Civil War in North Carolina*, 382–83; *OR*, ser. 1, 47(3):238–39; Sherman, *Memoirs*, 2:350–51; Birdsall Diary, April 24, 1865, SHC; Amis, *City of Raleigh*, 63.

16. Hagood, *Memoirs of the War of Secession*, 369; Mullen, "Last Days of Johnston's Army," 108; Bradley, *This Astounding Close*, 168–69; Dunkerly, *Confederate Surrender at Greensboro*, 60.

17. Bradley, *This Astounding Close*, 166–67; Reagan, *Memoirs*, 201–2; Johnston, *Narrative*, 404; Zebulon B. Vance, "Last Days of the War," in Dowd, *Life of Vance*, 487.

18. Sherman, *Memoirs*, 2:352–53; Johnston, *Narrative*, 404–405; Barrett, *Civil War in North Carolina*, 384–85.

19. Bradley, *This Astounding Close*, 173–76.

20. Schofield, *Forty-Six Years in the Army*, 350.

21. Johnston, *Narrative*, 408–10; Hagood, *Memoirs of the War of Secession*, 369; Bradley, *This Astounding Close*, 182–83, 200–202; Dunkerly, *Confederate Surrender at Greensboro*, 85–88.

22. Andrew, *Wade Hampton*, 296–98; Bradley, *This Astounding Close*, 203; *OR*, ser. 1, 47 (3):813–14, 829–30.

23. Davis, *Honorable Defeat*, 171–88; Johnson, *Pursuit*, 133–41.

24. Johnston, *Narrative*, 410–11; Sherman, *Memoirs*, 2:357–59; Grant, *Personal Memoirs*, 2:516–17.

25. *OR*, ser. 1, 47(3):303–4, 835–36; Johnston, *Narrative*, 412.

26. Johnston, *Narrative*, 412–14; Sherman, *Memoirs*, 2:362–63; *OR*, ser. 1, 47(3):304; Schofield, *Forty-Six Years in the Army*, 351–53.

27. *OR*, ser. 1, 47(3):482; Schofield, *Forty-Six Years in the Army*, 352–53; Sherman, *Memoirs*, 2:370–71; Bradley, *This Astounding Close*, 226.

28. "An Incident at the Surrender of General Joseph E. Johnston," Chisolm Papers, NYHS; Semmes, *Memoirs*, 823–31; Diary, May 1, 1865, Semmes Papers, Duke University, Durham, N.C.; Bradley, *This Astounding Close*, 234. Sources vary concerning the number of soldiers paroled at Greensboro. See Sherman, *Memoirs*, 2:370, and *OR*, ser. 1, 37(1):1066, 37(3):482.

29. Dean Reminiscences, 10–11, SHC; *OR*, ser. 1, 47(3):482; Dunkerly, *Confederate Surrender at Greensboro*, 113–14; "An Incident at the Surrender of General Joseph E. Johnston," Chisolm Papers, NYHS.

30. Brown, *One of Cleburne's Command*, 164–74; Schenck Diary, 41, University of North Carolina, Wilmington; Dunkerly, *Confederate Surrender at Greensboro*, 89.

31. Blackburn, "Reminiscences of the Terry Rangers," 172–77.

32. Buford, "Surrender of Johnston's Army"; Diary, April 26, 1865, Buford Papers, SHC; "Capt. M. M. Buford."

33. *OR*, ser. 1, 49(1):369, 49(2):804, 932.

34. Hauptman, *Between Two Fires*, 118–20; *OR*, ser. 1, 49(2):709–10, 754–55, 821–22; W. W. Stringfield, "Sixty-Ninth Regiment," in Clark, *Histories of the Several Regiments*, 3:757–61.

35. Maury, *Recollections of a Virginian*, 224–25; Parrish, *Richard Taylor*, 405.

36. *OR*, ser. 1, 47(3):303, 49(2):569; *Home Letters of General Sherman*, 346.

37. Taylor, *Destruction and Reconstruction*, 219; *OR*, ser. 1, 49(1):360–62; Jones, *Yankee Blitzkrieg*; Wyeth, *Life of Forrest*, 603–6; Wills, "Confederate Sun Sets on Selma."

38. *OR*, ser. 1, 49(1):406; Wills, "Confederate Sun Sets on Selma," 81–82; Wyeth, *Life of Forrest*, 608–9.

39. *OR*, ser. 1, 49(1):278. Fort Blakely is sometimes spelled "Blakeley."

40. Andrews, *History of the Campaign of Mobile*, 200–201; Noles, "Confederate Twilight"; Hearn, *Mobile Bay and the Mobile Campaign*, 182–99.

41. Wiley, *Civil War Diary of a Common Soldier*, 150–51; *OR*, ser. 1, 49(1):289–90; Andrews, *History of the Campaign of Mobile*, 200.

42. *National Tribune*, December 15, 1887; Tarrant, "Siege and Capture of Fort Blakely," 457.

43. Andrews, *History of the Campaign of Mobile*, 201, 209; Wiley, *Civil War Diary of a Common Soldier*, 150–51.

44. Taylor, *Destruction and Reconstruction*, 222.

45. "Terms of Capitulation"; Maury, *Recollections of a Virginian*, 225; *OR*, ser. 1, 49(2):455, 1255.

46. *OR*, ser. 1, 49(2):440, 448; Taylor, "Last Confederate Surrender," 156–57; Taylor, *Destruction and Reconstruction*, 224–25; Parrish, *Richard Taylor*, 439; Heyman, *Prudent Soldier*, 232–34.

47. *OR*, ser. 1, 49(2):531–32, 559; Taylor, *Destruction and Reconstruction*, 226; Jewett, *Rise and Fall*, 55; *New York Times*, May 16, 1865; *New York Herald*, May 14, 1865; *New Orleans Times*, May 7, 1865.

48. Todhunter, "Colonel Todhunter's Account of the Closing Events"; Jewett, *Rise and Fall*, 84; Miller, *John Bell Hood*, 171–72; Taylor, *Destruction and Reconstruction*, 226; *OR*, ser. 1, 49 (2):1275–79; Parrish, *Richard Taylor*, 440–41.

49. Hurst, *Forrest*, 254–55; *OR*, ser. 1, 49(2):1263–64; Morton, *Artillery of Nathan Bedford Forrest's Cavalry*, 312.

50. Young, *Seventh Tennessee Cavalry*, 136–37; Morton, *Artillery of Nathan Bedford Forrest's Cavalry*, 319; Ward, *River Run Red*, 358–60; Carter, *When the War Was Over*, 9.

51. Morton, *Artillery of Nathan Bedford Forrest's Cavalry*, 316–19.

52. Morton, *Artillery of Nathan Bedford Forrest's Cavalry*, 317–19; Hancock, *Hancock's Diary*, 562–65; Diary, May 9–11, Simpson Papers, SHC; Hurst, *Forrest*, 257–58.

53. Hancock, *Hancock's Diary*, 565.

CHAPTER 9

1. Davis, *Rise and Fall*, 2:702; Davis, *Honorable Defeat*, 303–4; Johnson, *Pursuit*, 180–83; Sternhell, *Routes of War*, 192.

2. Sutherland, "Guerrillas"; Moneyhon, "1865"; Mackey, *Uncivil War*, 66–71.

3. Mueller, *M. Jeff Thompson*, 89; Memoirs, 341, 349, Thompson Papers, SHC.

4. Mueller, *M. Jeff Thompson*, 1–88; Memoirs, Thompson Papers, SHC; M. Jeff Thompson to Mrs. Ingraham, March 15, 1864, Thompson Correspondence, NYHS.

5. Thompson to Col. Lurner, April 18, 1865, Thompson Papers, SHC.

6. *OR*, ser. 1, 48(2):249.

7. *OR*, ser. 1, 48(1):229.

8. *OR*, ser. 1, 48(1):232–37; Memoirs, 350–51, Thompson Papers, SHC.

9. Hereford, *Old Man River*, 86–88; *OR*, ser. 1, 48(2):210; Memoirs, 354, Thompson Papers, SHC.

10. Hereford, *Old Man River*, 88–91; Memoirs, 356–57, Thompson Papers, SHC; *OR*, ser. 1, 48(1):237, 48(2):722.

11. Mattson, *Reminiscences*, 87–88.

12. *New York Times*, June 20, 1865; *Harper's Weekly*, July 15, 1865; Memoirs, 360–61, Thompson Papers, SHC.

13. *PUSG* 14:394.

14. Sprague, *Treachery in Texas*; Bundy, "Last Chapter in the History of the War," 113–19.

15. Kirby Smith to Sprague, May 15, 1865, Smith Papers, SHC.

16. "Memorandum for Col. Sprague," Smith Papers, SHC; *OR*, ser. 1, 48(1):186–94.

17. *OR*, ser. 1, 48(2):1271; Edwards, *Shelby and His Men*, 516; Clampitt, "Breakup," 501–34; Tunnard, *Southern Record*, 335–36; Settles, *John Bankhead Magruder*, 279–80; Castel, *General Sterling Price and the Civil War in the West*, 268–70; Jewett, *Rise and Fall*, 201.

18. Edwards, *Shelby and His Men*, 522–25; Edwards, *Expedition to Mexico*, 235–36; O'Flaherty, *General Jo Shelby*, 229–30; Arthur, *General Jo Shelby's March*, 57.

19. Bundy, "Last Chapter in the History of the War," 120–21; *OR*, ser. 1, 48(2):507.

20. James Slaughter to Kirby Smith, May 17, 1865, Smith Papers, SHC; *OR*, ser. 1, 48(2):747; Kerby, *Kirby Smith's Confederacy*, 416–18; Prushankin, *Crisis in Confederate Command*, 212–14; Castel, *General Sterling Price and the Civil War in the West*, 268–71; Jewett, *Rise and Fall*, 215.

21. *New York Times*, June 4, 1865; *OR*, ser. 1, 48(2):581, 591, 600–606.

22. Edwards, *Shelby and His Men*, 451; Stickles, *Simon Bolivar Buckner*, 273.

23. Farewell address, Smith Papers, SHC; *New York Times*, June 22, 1865; Kerby, *Kirby Smith's Confederacy*, 425–26; Ramsdell, *Reconstruction in Texas*, 36–37.

24. Sheridan, *Personal Memoirs*, 208–11; Wahlstrom, *Southern Exodus to Mexico*, 2–3.

25. Edwards, *Expedition to Mexico*, 238–39; Westlake memoirs, 2:131, Watson-Westlake Papers, State Historical Society of Missouri; O'Flaherty, *General Jo Shelby*, 234; Arthur, *General Jo Shelby's March*, 66.

26. Edwards, *Expedition to Mexico*, 252–54; O'Flaherty, *General Jo Shelby*, 242–44; Magruder, "Our Mexican Problem"; Allen, *Recollections*, 325–27.

27. Westlake memoirs, 2:136, Watson-Westlake Papers, State Historical Society of Missouri; Arthur, *General Jo Shelby's March*, 82–83; Davis, *Fallen Guidon*, 63–66; O'Flaherty, *General Jo Shelby*, 245, 266; Jewett, *Rise and Fall*, 214.

28. Westlake memoirs, 1:67, 79, 2:130–31, Watson-Westlake Papers, State Historical Society of Missouri.

29. Taylor, "Last Confederate Surrender"; W. W. Stringfield, "The Last Battle and the Last Surrender," in Clark, *Histories of the Several Regiments*, 5:653–56; *New York Times*, March 29, 1893.

30. The newspaper accounts vary slightly in the timing and number of soldiers involved in this supposed event. See Lawson, *War Anecdotes and Incidents of Army Life*, 1–2; *Chicago Tribune*, August 20, 1866; *Spirit of Jefferson*, September 4, 1866; and *Fayetteville Observer* (Tenn.), September 13, 1866.

31. Hauptman, *Between Two Fires*, 41–61; Franks, *Stand Watie and the Agony of the Cherokee Nation*, 180–82; Knight, *Red Fox*, 269–74; Perdue, "Stand Watie's War."

32. *OR*, ser. 1, 48(2):1100–1101.

33. Baldwin and Powers, *Last Flag Down*, 206–76; McKay, *Sea King*, 1–9, 167–200; Chaffin, *Sea of Gray*, 226–304.

34. Baldwin and Powers, *Last Flag Down*, 276–328; McKay, *Sea King*, 200–28; Chaffin, *Sea of Gray*, 305–60.

CHAPTER 10

1. *New York Times*, April 10, 18, 20, 1865; Moore, Willis, and Cornell, *Fort Sumter Memorial*, 35–45; William Lloyd Garrison to Helen Garrison, April 9, 1865, Anti-Slavery Collection, Boston Public Library, Boston, Mass.; *The Independent*, April 27, 1865; *New York Evangelist*, April 27, 1865; *Philadelphia Inquirer*, April 8, 18, 1865; Holt, *Remarks of Hon. J. Holt at a Dinner in Charleston*; Edwin Stanton to Robert Anderson, March 28, 1865, and W. L. Garrison to Edwin Studwell, April 13, 1866, Goodyear Collection, Yale University, New Haven, Conn.; Janney, *Remembering the Civil War*, 55–56. On the ruins of Charleston, see Nelson, *Ruin Nation*, 1–2.

2. Diary, April 20, 1865, Wadley Papers, SHC; Gardner, *Blood and Irony*, 39; East, *Sarah Morgan*, 606; Rubin, *Shattered Nation*, 123.

3. Nolan, "Anatomy of the Myth"; Foster, *Ghosts of the Confederacy*; Wilson, *Baptized in Blood*; Janney, *Remembering the Civil War*, 43.

4. Pollard, *Lost Cause*, 711–12, 729. On Pollard's treatment of Grant, see Simpson, "Continuous Hammering and Mere Attrition," 148–50; Waugh, "Ulysses S. Grant, Historian," 17–19; Blight, *Race and Reunion*, 214–15; and Schivelbusch, *Culture of Defeat*, 4–6, 10–62.

5. Waugh, "Ulysses S. Grant, Historian," 5–38.

6. Varon, *Appomattox*, 173; Kachun, *Festivals of Freedom*, 118; Brundage, *Southern Past*, 80–81; Blair, *Cities of the Dead*, 23–24; Janney, *Remembering the Civil War*, 90, 120.

7. Janney, *Burying the Dead but Not the Past*; Cox, *Dixie's Daughters*; Gannon, *Won Cause*; *Acts and Resolves Passed by the General Assembly of the State of Vermont*, 6.

8. Brown, *Public Art*, 17–18; O'Connell, "Public Commemoration of the Civil War and Monuments to Memory," 79; Smith, *Golden Age of Battlefield Preservation*.

9. Brown, *Public Art*, 23–35; Savage, *Standing Soldiers, Kneeling Slaves*, 162–80.

10. Ferguson, *Overview of the Events at Fort Sumter*, 42–50; Comstock, *Short History*, 8–9.

11. Marvel, *Lee's Last Retreat*, 81; Marvel, *Place Called Appomattox*, 311–12; Janney, "War over a Shrine of Peace," 93–97; Appomattox Court House National Historical Park, National Register of Historic Places Registration Form (1989); Loewen, *Lies across America*, 317–20. The UDC plaque was moved prior to the centennial from its original location to a spot near the Confederate cemetery in Appomattox Courthouse. At some point (no one is sure when), the last line describing the number of soldiers under Grant was chiseled from the plaque, although the outline of the letters remains visible.

12. Jim Wise, "Events Mark Bennett Place's Role in Ending the Civil War," *News & Observer*, April 25, 2012; Anderson, *Durham County*, 106; McCullough, *North Carolina's State Historic Sites*, 40. On Brodie Duke, see Silkenat, *Moments of Despair*, 130–32.

13. *Appeal-Advance*, April 27, 1893.

14. Smith, *Golden Age of Battlefield Preservation*, 14–16.

15. *New York Times*, April 9, 13, 1911; *Richmond Times-Dispatch*, April 9, 1911; Blight, *Race and Reunion*, 383–87.

16. Brundage, *Southern Past*, 183–226; Yuhl, *Golden Haze of Memory*; Brown, *Civil War Canon*, 170–74.

17. Comstock, *Short History*, 9–13; Ferguson, *Overview of Events at Fort Sumter*, 51–52.

18. Anderson, *Durham County*, 276–77; "Unveiling of Confederate Monument at University," Carr Papers, SHC.

19. Carr, *Peace with Honor*.

20. Janney, "War over a Shrine of Peace."

21. Strozier, "Tragedy of Unconditional Surrender"; *Public Papers of the Presidents of the United States: F. D. Roosevelt*, 12:39.

22. "The U.S. Fighting Man's Code," Library of Congress, http://www.loc.gov/rr/frd/Military_Law/pdf/US-fighting-code-1955.pdf.

23. "U.S. Imposes Arms Blockade on Cuba on Finding Offensive Missile Sites; Kennedy Ready for Soviet Showdown," *New York Times*, October 23, 1962.

24. Cook, *Troubled Commemoration*, 1–89.

25. Cook, *Troubled Commemoration*, 89–121.

26. Marvel, *Place Called Appomattox*, 317–19.

27. Harrison Speech, April 9, 1865, and Catton Speech, April 9, 1965, Records of the Virginia Civil War Commission, Library of Virginia, Richmond; Shackel, *Memory in Black and White*, 48; Kammen, *Mystic Chords of Memory*, 603; Cook, *Troubled Commemoration*, 206–7, 224; "This Hallowed Ground."

28. Anderson, *Durham County*, 277; Vatavuk, *Dawn of Peace*.

29. *Times-Union* (Henderson, N.C.), March 31, 1965; Public Law 89-7, March 29, 1965, *United States Statutes at Large* 79 (1965): 24–25.

30. Speech, Bennett Place, April 25, 1965, Humphrey Papers, Minnesota Historical Society; Bodnar, *Remaking America*, 223–24; Shackel, *Memory in Black and White*, 48.

31. "N.C. Budget Crunch Affecting State Historic Sites," March 13, 2002, wral.com; "Panel Suggests Cutbacks at N.C. Cultural Sites to Save $2M," *News & Observer*, February 15, 2012; Pitcaithley, "Public Education and the National Park Service."

32. Cook, Noe, Shoaf, Weber, and Sutherland, "Historians' Forum"; Kytle, "Fort Sumter Sesquicentennial"; Campbell Robertson, "With Civil War's Rancor Faded, Reasons to Celebrate," *New York Times*, July 3, 2013.

33. "Museum of the Confederacy Opens in Appomattox," *Richmond Times-Dispatch*, April 1, 2012.

34. Martha M. Boltz, "The Civil War: Controversy Swirls around the Museum's Confederate Flag," *Washington Times*, March 29, 2012.

35. "Re-enactors Leave 2015 Behind, Charge into Past at Appomattox Court House," *News & Advance* (Lynchburg), April 10, 2015; "More Than 1,000 Attend End of Civil War Commemoration at Appomattox," *Richmond Times-Dispatch*, April 9, 2015; "More Than 6,000 Turn Out for Appomattox Sesquicentennial Observance," *Roanoke Times*, April 9, 2015.

36. "On 150th Anniversary of the End of the Civil War."

37. Ayers, "Not Forgotten."

38. National Park Service press release, February 2, 2015, https://www.nps.gov/cebe/learn/news/join-the-national-park-service-in-ringing-bells-across-the-land-a-nation-remembers-appomattox.htm.

39. Bouie, "Remembering History as Fable"; Beutler, "Make the Confederacy's Defeat a National Holiday."

40. "Durham's Bennett Place Seeks Place in Civil War Spotlight," *News & Observer*, April 14, 2016; "Civil War History 101."

CONCLUSION

1. On the Civil War as a total war, see Royster, *Destructive War*; Grimsley, *Hard Hand of War*; Stout, *Upon the Altar of the Nation*; Neely, *Civil War and the Limits of Destruction*; Neely, "Was the Civil War a Total War?"; and Hsieh, "Total War and the American Civil War Reconsidered."

On the "dark turn," see Downs, *Sick from Freedom*; Miller, *Empty Sleeves*; Nelson, *Ruin Nation*; Berry, *Weirding the War*; Berry, "Afterword: Civil War at 150"; Gallagher and Meier, "Coming to Terms with Civil War Military History"; and Gallagher, "Dark Turn."

On savage and civilized warfare, see Foote, "Civilization and Savagery in the American Civil War"; Lee, *Barbarians and Brothers*; and Dilbeck, *More Civil War*.

2. September 4, 1864, Alexander Diary, Rare Books & Special Collections, Notre Dame University, Notre Dame, Ind.; "Thomas B. Alexander."

Bibliography

MANUSCRIPTS

Alabama
  W. S. Hoole Special Collections Library, University of Alabama, Tuscaloosa
      S. R. Norton Letters
Connecticut
  Manuscripts and Archives, Yale University, New Haven
      Goodyear Collection
Georgia
  Atlanta History Center, Atlanta
      John Malachi Bowden Papers
  Stuart A. Rose Manuscript, Archives, and Rare Book
      Library, Emory University, Emory
      James Robert McMichael Diary
Indiana
  Rare Books & Special Collections, Notre Dame University, Notre Dame
      Thomas B. Alexander Diary
      William Cline Diary
Massachusetts
  Boston Public Library, Boston
      Anti-Slavery Collection
Minnesota
  Minnesota Historical Society, St. Paul
      Hubert H. Humphrey Papers
Missouri
  State Historical Society of Missouri, Columbia
      Watson-Westlake Papers
New York
  New-York Historical Society, New York
      Alexander Robert Chisolm Papers
      William B. Gore Papers
      M. Jefferson Thompson Correspondence

New York Public Library, New York
 Diary of a Union Soldier of the 3rd Pennsylvania Cavalry
Special Collections, Hamilton College, Clinton
 Morris Brown Papers
North Carolina
 North Carolina Department of Archives and History, Raleigh
  Oscar Blacknall Papers
 Southern Historical Collection, Wilson Library,
  University of North Carolina, Chapel Hill
   Henry T. Bahnson Papers
   Henry A. Birdsall Diary
   Munson Monroe Buford Papers
   Julian Shakespeare Carr Papers
   Kena King Chapman Diary
   Henderson Dean Reminiscences
   Thomas Pollock Devereux Papers
   John Cheves Haskell Papers
   Stephen R. Mallory Diary and Reminiscences
   John Paris Papers
   Avington Wayne Simpson Papers
   Kirby Smith Papers
   Meriwether Jeff Thompson Papers
   Sarah Lois Wadley Papers
   J. E. Whitehorne Diary
 Special Collections, Perkins Library, Duke University, Durham
  Joseph Asbury Edwards Papers
  Raphael Semmes Papers
 Special Collections, Randall Library, University of North Carolina, Wilmington
  Nicholas W. Schenck Diary
 St. Mary's School, Raleigh
  Undated scrapbook
Ohio
 Ohio Historical Society, Columbus
  Lewis Hull Diary
Pennsylvania
 Gettysburg National Military Park, Gettysburg
  Samuel G. Boone Memoirs
South Carolina
 South Caroliniana Library, University of South Carolina, Columbia
  James R. Hagood, "Memoirs of the First South Carolina Regiment"
Virginia
 Appomattox Courthouse National Historical Park,
  Appomattox Courthouse
   John Wilson Warr Diary
 Library of Virginia, Richmond
  Marcellus French Papers

Records of the Virginia Civil War Commission
Virginia Historical Society, Richmond
Cullen Andrews Battle, *The Third Alabama Regiment*
Camp Chase Papers
Charles Bickem Fields Diary
Andrew Alexander Kean, "In a Uniform of Grey"
David McIntosh Diary
Pegram-Johnson-McIntosh Papers
VMI Archives, Virginia Military Institute, Lexington
Henkel Family Papers
Washington
Special Collections, University of Washington, Seattle
M. Adelaide Smith Papers
Washington, D.C.
Library of Congress
Robert Anderson Papers
Samuel Wylie Crawford Papers
"The U.S. Fighting Man's Code"
Alfred R. Waud Papers
Wisconsin
Wisconsin Historical Society, Madison
Newell Burch Diary

PERIODICALS

Appeal-Advance (Memphis)
Baltimore Daily Exchange
Boston Evening Transcript
Boston Herald
Burlington Weekly Hawk-Eye
California Farmer and Journal
of Useful Sciences
Charleston Courier
Charleston Mercury
Charlotte Daily Bulletin
Chicago Tribune
Congressional Globe
DeBow's Review
Delaware County American
Fayetteville Observer (Tennessee)
Frank Leslie's Illustrated Weekly
Freedom's Champion (Atchison, Kans.)
Harper's Weekly
The Independent
Journal of the House of Representatives
of the United States

Liberator
Louisiana Democrat
National Tribune (Washington, D.C.)
New Orleans Times
New York Evangelist
New York Herald
New York Illustrated News
New York Times
New York Tribune
News & Advance (Lynchburg, Va.)
News & Observer (Raleigh, N.C.)
Philadelphia Inquirer
Richmond Daily Examiner
Richmond Enquirer
Richmond Times-Dispatch
Roanoke Times
Spirit of Jefferson (Charlestown, W.Va.)
Times-Union (Henderson, N.C.)
Tri-Weekly Alamo Express
Washington Times
Weekly Vincennes Western Sun

Acts and Resolves Passed by the General Assembly of the State of Vermont, at the Annual Session, 1863. Montpelier: Freedmen, 1863.

The Addresses and Messages of the Presidents of the United States. New York: Edwin Williams, 1847.

Alexander, Edward Porter. *Fighting for the Confederacy: The Personal Recollections of General Edward Porter Alexander.* Edited by Gary W. Gallagher. Chapel Hill: University of North Carolina Press, 1989.

————. "Lee at Appomattox." *Century Magazine* 63 (April 1902): 921–31.

Allen, Henry W. *Recollections of Henry Watkins Allen.* New York: M. Doolady, 1866.

Anderson, Charles. *Texas, before and on the Eve of the Rebellion.* Cincinnati: Peter G. Thomson, 1884.

Anderson, Kitty. "Soldiers' Retreat." *Register of the Kentucky State Historical Society* 17 (1919): 67–77

Anderson, Robert. *An Artillery Officer in the Mexican War.* New York: Putnam, 1911.

Andrews, C. C. *History of the Campaign of Mobile.* New York: Van Nostrand, 1867.

Appomattox Court House National Historical Park, National Register of Historic Places Registration Form (1989).

Avary, Myrta Lockett. "A Lincoln Souvenir in the South." *Century Magazine* 73 (1907): 506–8.

Bacon, Georgeanna M. W. *Letters of a Family during the War for the Union, 1861–1865.* Np, 1899.

Barber, John Warner, and Henry Howe. *The Loyal West in the Times of the Rebellion.* Cincinnati: F. A. Howe, 1865.

Barrett, John G. *Yankee Rebel: The Civil War Journal of Edmund DeWitt Patterson.* Chapel Hill: University of North Carolina Press, 1966.

Barziza, Decimus et Ultimus. *The Adventures of a Prisoner of War, 1863–1864.* Edited by R. Henderson Shuffler. Austin: University of Texas Press, 1964.

Bates, James C. *A Texas Cavalry Officer's Civil War.* Edited by Richard G. Lowe. Baton Rouge: Louisiana State University Press, 1999.

Bates, William C. *Stars and Stripes in Rebeldom.* Boston: Burnham, 1862.

Battles and Leaders of the Civil War. 4 vols. New York: Century, 1887–88.

Beecham, Robert K. *Gettysburg.* Chicago: A. C. McClurg, 1911.

Berlin, Ira, Barbara J. Fields, Thavolia Glymph, Joseph P. Reidy, Leslie Rowland, Steven F. Miller, Julie Saville, Steven Hahn, Susan E. O'Donovan, John C. Rodrigue, René Hayden, Anthony E. Kaye, Kate Masur, and Stephen A. West. *Freedom: A Documentary History of Emancipation, 1861–1867.* 6 vols. New York: Cambridge University Press; Chapel Hill: University of North Carolina Press, 1995–2013.

Bird, W. H. *Stories of the Civil War.* Columbiana, Ala.: Advocate Printers, n.d.

Blackburn, J. K. P. "Reminiscences of the Terry Rangers." *Southwestern Historical Quarterly* 22 (1918): 38–77, 143–79.

Blakeslee, B. F. *History of the Sixteenth Connecticut Volunteers.* Hartford, Conn.: Case, Lockwood, & Brainard, 1875.

Boggs, Samuel S. *Eighteen Months a Prisoner under the Rebel Flag.* Lovington, Ill.: Boggs, 1887.

Boykin, Edward M. *The Falling Flag: Evacuation of Richmond, Retreat and Surrender at Appomattox.* New York: E. T. Hale, 1874.

Brinton, John H. *Personal Memoirs*. New York: Neale, 1914.

Brown, Norman D. *One of Cleburne's Command: The Civil War Reminiscences and Diary of Capt. Samuel T. Foster, Granbury's Texas Brigade, C.S.A.* Austin: University of Texas Press, 1980.

Buford, M. M. "Surrender of Johnston's Army." *Confederate Veteran* 28 (1920): 170–72.

Bull, Rice C. *Soldiering: The Civil War Diary of Rice C. Bull, 123rd New York Volunteer Infantry*. Edited by K. Jack Bauer. San Rafael, Calif.: Presidio, 1977.

Bundy, J. M. "The Last Chapter in the History of the War." *Galaxy* 8 (1869): 113–22.

Byers, S. H. M. *What I Saw in Dixie; or Sixteen Months in Rebel Prisons*. Dansville, N.Y.: Robbins & Poore, 1868.

Cadwallader, Sylvanus. *Three Years with Grant*. New York: Knopf, 1955.

"Capt. M. M. Buford." *Confederate Veteran* 38 (1930): 353.

Carr, Julian S. *Peace with Honor*. Durham, N.C.: Seeman Printery, 1923.

Carroll, John W. *Autobiography and Reminiscences of John W. Carroll*. Henderson, Tenn.: n.p., 1898.

Carter, Robert G. *Four Brothers in Blue*. Washington, D.C.: Gibson Bros., 1913.

Cauble, Frank P. *Surrender Proceedings: April 9, 1865, Appomattox Courthouse*. Lynchburg, Va.: H. E. Howard, 1987.

Cavada, Federico F. *Libby Life: Experiences of a Prisoner of War in Richmond*. Lanham, Md.: University Press of America, 1985.

Chamberlain, Era Jane Pettijohn. *Something of the Pettijohn (Pettyjohn) Family*. Spokane, Wash.: Shaw & Borden, 1948.

Chamberlain, Joshua Lawrence. *The Passing of the Armies: An Account of the Final Campaign of the Army of the Potomac*. New York: Putnam, 1915.

Chamberlayne, C. G. *Ham Chamberlayne—Virginian*. Richmond, Va.: Dietz, 1932.

Chase, Salmon P. *Inside Lincoln's Cabinet: The Civil War Diaries of Salmon P. Chase*. Edited by David Herbert Donald. New York: Longmans, Green, 1954.

"Civil War History 101: The Largest Troop Surrender Happened in Durham." WUNC, http://wunc.org/post/civil-war-history-101-largest-troop-surrender-happened-durham.

Clark, George. "Alabamians in the Crater Battle." *Confederate Veteran* 3 (1895): 68–69.

Clark, Walter. *Histories of the Several Regiments and Battalions from North Carolina in the Great War*. 5 vols. Raleigh: E. M. Uzzell, 1901.

Clarke, Mary B. *Live Your Own Life: The Family Papers of Mary Bayard Clarke*. Edited by Terrell A. Crow and Mary M. Barden. Columbia: University of South Carolina Press, 2003.

Cockrell, Thomas, and Michael B. Ballard, eds. *A Mississippi Rebel in the Army of Northern Virginia: The Civil War Memoirs of Private David Holt*. Baton Rouge: Louisiana State University Press, 1995.

Coco, Gregory A. *From Ball's Bluff to Gettysburg and Beyond: The Civil War Letters of Private Roland E. Bowen, 15th Massachusetts Infantry, 1861–1864*. Gettysburg, Pa.: Thomas, 1994.

Collins, John L. "A Prisoner's March from Gettysburg to Staunton." In *Battles and Leaders of the Civil War*, 3:429–30. New York: Century, 1888.

Comstock, Daniel. *Ninth Cavalry: One Hundred and Twenty-First Regiment Indiana Volunteers*. Richmond, Ind.: J. M. Coe, 1890.

Connelly, Thomas Lawrence. "Did David Crockett Surrender at the Alamo? A Contemporary Letter." *Journal of Southern History* 26 (1960): 368–76.

Connolly, James A. *Three Years with the Army of the Cumberland*. Bloomington: Indiana University Press, 1959.

Cooke, Giles Buckner. *Just before and after Lee Surrendered to Grant*. Houston, Tex.: n.p., 1922.

Corcoran, Michael. *The Captivity of General Corcoran*. Philadelphia: Barclay, 1862.

Coulter, E. Merton. "From Spotsylvania Courthouse to Andersonville: A Diary of Darius Starr." *Georgia Historical Quarterly* 41 (1957): 176–90.

Crawford, Samuel W. *The Genesis of the Civil War: The Story of Sumter, 1860–1861*. New York: C. L. Webster, 1887.

————. *History of the Fall of Fort Sumter*. New York: F. P. Harper, 1896.

Crist, Lynda L., ed. *Papers of Jefferson Davis*. 14 vols. Baton Rouge: Louisiana State University Press, 1971–2015.

Crossley, William J. *Extracts from My Diary*. Providence, R.I.: The Society, 1903.

Crummer, Wilbur Fisk. *With Grant at Fort Donelson, Shiloh and Vicksburg*. Oak Park, Ill.: E. C. Crummer, 1915.

Cumming, Joseph B. "How I Knew That the War Was Over." *Confederate Veteran* 9 (1901): 18–19.

Curran, Robert E. *John Dooley's Civil War: An Irish American's Journey in the First Virginia Infantry Regiment*. Knoxville: University of Tennessee Press, 2012.

Dana, Charles A. *Recollections of the Civil War*. New York: Appleton, 1898.

Darby, George W. *Incidents and Adventures in Rebeldom*. Pittsburg: Rawsthorne, 1899.

Davis, Jefferson. *Rise and Fall of the Confederate Government*. 2 vols. New York: Appleton, 1881.

Dawes, Rufus R. *Service with the Sixth Wisconsin Volunteers*. Marietta, Ohio: E. R. Alderman, 1890.

Day, W. W. *Fifteen Months in Dixie*. Owatonna, Minn.: People's Print, 1889.

Dinkins, James. *Personal Recollections and Experiences in the Confederate Army*. Cincinnati: R. Clarke, 1897.

Dodge, David. "Home Scenes at the Fall of the Confederacy." *Atlantic Monthly* 69 (1892): 661–69.

Domschke, Bernhard. *Twenty Months in Captivity: Memoirs of a Union Officer in Confederate Prisons*. Edited and translated by Frederic Trautmann. Rutherford, N.J.: Fairleigh Dickinson University Press, 1987.

Donaghy, John. *Army Experience of Capt. John Donaghy*. DeLand, Fla.: E. O. Painter, 1926.

Doubleday, Abner. *Chancellorsville and Gettysburg*. New York: Scribner's, 1882.

————. *Reminiscences of Forts Sumter and Moultrie in 1860–'61*. New York: Harper & Bros., 1876.

Douglas, Henry Kyd. *I Rode with Stonewall*. Chapel Hill: University of North Carolina Press, 1940.

Dowdey, Clifford, ed. *Wartime Papers of R. E. Lee*. Boston: Little, Brown, 1961.

Drake, Samuel G. *Biography and History of the Indians of North America*. Boston: Antiquarian Bookstore, 1841.

Duke, Basil W. *Reminiscences of General Basil W. Duke*. Garden City, N.Y.: Doubleday, Page, 1911.

Duncan, Russell, ed. *Blue-Eyed Child of Fortune: The Civil War Letters of Colonel Robert Gould Shaw*. Athens: University of Georgia Press, 1992.

East, Charles. *Sarah Morgan: The Civil War Diary of a Southern Woman*. New York: Simon & Schuster, 1992.

Eby, Henry Harrison. *Observations of an Illinois Boy in Battle, Camp, and Prisons, 1861–1865*. Mendota, Ill.: Eby, 1910.

Edwards, John N. *Shelby and His Men; or, The War in the West*. Cincinnati: Miami Print, 1867.

———. *Shelby's Expedition to Mexico*. Kansas City, Mo.: Kansas City Times, 1872.

Eisenschiml, Otto, ed. *Vermont General: The Unusual War Experiences of Edward Hastings Ripley*. New York: Devin-Adair, 1960.

Elliott, Charles W. "Some Unpublished Letters of a Roving Soldier-Diplomat: General Winfield Scott's Reports to Secretary of State James Monroe, on Conditions in France and England in 1815–1816." *Journal of American Military Foundation* 1 (1937): 165–73.

Ely, Alfred. *Journal of Alfred Ely, a Prisoner of War in Richmond*. New York: Appleton, 1862.

Emerson, Ralph Waldo. "American Civilization." *Atlantic Monthly*, April 1862.

Finney, Charles G. *Memoirs of Charles G. Finney*. New York: A. S. Barnes, 1876.

Fry, J. Reese. *A Life of Gen. Zachary Taylor*. Philadelphia: Grigg, Elliot, 1848.

French, Samuel Gibbs. *Two Wars: An Autobiography of General Samuel G. French*. Nashville: Confederate Veteran, 1901.

Gallagher, Patrick C. "Through Battle, Prison, and Disease: The Civil War Diaries of George Richardson Crosby." *Vermont History* 76 (2008): 19–45.

Gantt, George. *The Gettysburg Prisoners: March from Gettysburg to Staunton*. Broadside. Annapolis, Md.: n.p., 1863.

Garrison, William Lloyd. *No Compromise on Slavery*. New York: American Anti-Slavery Society, 1854.

Gaskell, J. E. "Surrendered at Vicksburg." *Confederate Veteran* 33 (1925): 286

Gautier, George R. *Harder Than Death*. Austin: n.p., 1902.

Geer, J. J. *Beyond the Lines*. Philadelphia: Daughaday, 1863.

General Regulations for the Army. Philadelphia: M. Carey and Sons, 1821.

General Report of the National Memorial Celebration and Peace Jubilee. Washington, D.C.: Government Printing Office, 1917.

Gibbon, John. *Personal Recollections of the Civil War*. New York: Putnam, 1928.

Goodman, Thomas M. *A Thrilling Record, Founded on Facts and Observations Obtained during Ten Days' Experience with Colonel William T. Anderson*. Des Moines: Mills, 1868.

Gordon, John B. *Reminiscences of the Civil War*. New York: Scribner's, 1903.

Gorman, John C. *Lee's Last Campaign*. Raleigh: W. B. Smith, 1866.

Goss, Warren Lee. *The Soldier's Story of His Captivity at Andersonville, Belle Isle, and Other Rebel Prisons*. Boston: Lee & Shepard, 1866.

Gould, John Mead. *History of the First—Tenth—Twenty-Ninth Maine Regiment*. Portland, Maine: S. Berry, 1871.

Grant, Ulysses S. *Papers of Ulysses S. Grant*. 31 vols. Carbondale: Southern Illinois University Press, 1967–2012.

———. *Personal Memoirs of U. S. Grant*. 2 vols. New York: Charles L. Webster, 1885.

Grigsby, Melvin. *The Smoked Yank*. Sioux Falls: Dakota Bell, 1888.

Hadley, J. V. *Seven Months a Prisoner*. Indianapolis: J. J. & F. J. Meikel, 1868.

Hagood, Johnson. *Memoirs of the War of Secession*. Columbia, S.C.: State, 1910.

Hale, Edward Everett. "The Man without a Country." *Atlantic Monthly* 12 (December 1863): 665–79.

Hall, Norman J. "From the Official Report of Norman J. Hall." In *Battles and Leaders of the Civil War*, 3:390–91. New York: Century, 1888.

Hancock, R. R. *Hancock's Diary*. Nashville: Brandon Print Co., 1887.

Hardee's Rifle and Light Infantry Tactics. Richmond, Va.: West & Johnston, 1861.

Hardman, Asa. "As a Union Prisoner Saw the Battle of Gettysburg." *Civil War Times* 51 (2012): 36–42.

Harries, William H. "The Iron Brigade in the First Day's Battle at Gettysburg." In *Glimpses of the Nation's Struggle*, 4:337–50. Military Order of the Loyal Legion of the United States, Wisconsin Commandery. St. Paul, Minn.: Collins, 1898.

———. "The Sword of General James J. Archer." *Confederate Veteran* 19 (1911): 419–20.

Harris, F. S. "Gen. Jas. J. Archer." *Confederate Veteran* 3 (January 1895): 18.

Hawkins, Norma Fuller. "Sergeant-Major Blanchard at Gettysburg." *Indiana Magazine of History* 34 (1938): 212–16.

Hawthorne, Nathaniel. "Chiefly about War Matters." *Atlantic Monthly* 10 (July 1862): 43–61.

Heaton, Lynda Rees. "War Experiences of Samuel Wheeler, Private in the First West Virginia Cavalry." *West Virginia History* 6 (2012): 45–69.

Hereford, Robert A. *Old Man River: The Memories of Captain Louis Rosche, Pioneer Steamboatman*. Caldwell, Idaho: Caxton, 1943.

Hitchcock, Henry. *Marching with Sherman*. New Haven: Yale University Press, 1927.

Hogane, J. T. "Reminiscences of the Siege of Vicksburg." *Southern Historical Society Papers* 11 (1883): 484–89.

Holt, Joseph. *Remarks of Hon. J. Holt at a Dinner in Charleston*. Washington, D.C.: Gibson Brothers, 1865.

Home Letters of General Sherman. New York: Scribner's, 1909.

Hoopes, John. "The Confederate Memoir of William M. Abernathy." *Confederate Veteran* 2 (2003): 11–23, and 3 (2003): 10–19.

Hughes, Nathaniel Cheairs. *I'll Sting If I Can: The Life and Prison Letters of Major N. F. Cheairs, C.S.A.* Signal Mountain, Tenn.: Mountain Press, 1998.

Hunt, Gaillard. "Narrative and Letter of William Henry Trescot." *American Historical Review* 13 (1908): 528–56.

Hunter, Alexander. *Johnny Reb and Billy Yank*. New York: Neale, 1905.

Hunter, Robert M. T. "The Peace Commission—Hon. R. M. T. Hunter's Reply to President Davis' Letter." *Southern Historical Society Papers* 4 (1877): 303–18.

Jewett, Clayton E., ed. *Rise and Fall of the Confederacy: The Memoir of Senator Williamson S. Oldham, C.S.A.* Columbia: University of Missouri Press, 2006.

Johnson, Richard W. *A Soldier's Reminiscences in Peace and War*. Philadelphia: Lippincott, 1886.

Johnson, W. Gart. "Prison Life at Harpers' Ferry and on Johnson's Island." *Confederate Veteran* 2 (1894): 242–43.

Johnston, Isaac N. *Four Months in Libby and the Campaign against Atlanta*. Cincinnati: Methodist Book Concern, 1864.

Johnston, Joseph E. *Narrative of Military Operations*. New York: Appleton, 1874.

Jordan, Thomas, and J. P. Pryor, *The Campaigns of Lieut.-Gen. Forrest*. New Orleans: Blelock, 1868.

Keiley, A. M. *In Vinculis, or The Prisoner of War*. Petersburg, Va.: Daily Index Office, 1866.

Kellogg, Robert H. *Life and Death in Rebel Prisons*. Hartford, Conn.: L. Stebbins, 1865.

Kelsey, D. M. *Deeds of Daring by the American Soldier*. Chicago: Werner, 1898.

Keyes, Erasmus D. *Fifty Years' Observations of Men and Events, Civil and Military*. New York: Scribner's, 1884.

Lawson, Albert. *War Anecdotes and Incidents of Army Life*. Cincinnati: A. Lawson, 1888.

Lee, Susan Pendleton. *Memoirs of William Nelson Pendleton*. Philadelphia: Lippincott, 1893.

Leon, Louis. *Diary of a Tar Heel Confederate Soldier*. Charlotte, N.C.: Stone Publishing, 1913.

Life, Trial, and Execution of Captain John Brown. New York: DeWitt, 1859.

Lincoln, Abraham. *Collected Works of Abraham Lincoln*. Edited by Roy P. Basler. 9 vols. New Brunswick, N.J.: Rutgers University Press, 1953.

Longstreet, James. *From Manassas to Appomattox*. Philadelphia: Lippincott, 1895.

Magruder, John B. "Our Mexican Problem." *New York Times*, April 2, 1916.

Mahood, Wayne. *Charlie Mosher's Civil War*. Hightstown, N.J.: Longstreet House, 1994.

Maine at Gettysburg. Portland, Maine: Lakeside Press, 1898.

Mansfield, Edward Deering. *Life of General Winfield Scott*. New York: A. S. Barnes, 1846.

Marbaker, Thomas D. *History of the Eleventh New Jersey Volunteers*. Trenton, N.J.: MacCrellish & Quigley, 1898.

Marshall, Charles. "Appomattox Courthouse." *Southern Historical Society Papers* 21 (1893): 353–60.

Martin, James M. *History of the Fifty-Seventh Regiment, Pennsylvania Veteran Volunteer Infantry*. Meadville, Pa.: McCoy & Calvin, 1904.

Mason, J. M. *Report of the Select Committee of the Senate Appointed to Inquire into the Late Invasion and Seizure of Public Property at Harper's Ferry*. Washington, D.C.: Government Printing Office, 1859.

Mattson, Hans. *Reminiscences: The Story of an Emigrant*. St. Paul, Minn.: D. D. Merrill, 1891.

Maury, Dabney H. *Recollections of a Virginian in the Mexican, Indian, and Civil Wars*. New York: Scribner's, 1894.

Maynard, Douglas. "Vicksburg Diary: The Journal of Gabriel M. Killgore." *Civil War History* 10 (1964): 33–53.

McArthur, Judith N., and Orville Vernon Burton, eds. *"A Gentleman and an Officer": A Military and Social History of James B. Griffin's Civil War*. New York: Oxford University Press, 1996.

McElroy, John. *Andersonville*. Toledo: D. R. Locke, 1879.

McFarland, Baxter. "The Eleventh Mississippi Regiment at Gettysburg." *Publications of the Mississippi Historical Society* 2 (1918): 549–68.

McKee, James Cooper. *Narrative of the Surrender of a Command of U.S. Forces at Fort Fillmore*. Boston: Lowell, 1886.

McLaws, Lafayette. "Gettysburg." *Southern Historical Society Papers* 7 (1879): 64–85.

Meredith, Jaquelin Marshall. "The First Day at Gettysburg." *Southern Historical Society Papers* 24 (1896): 182–87.

Minnich, J. W. "Famous Rifles." *Confederate Veteran* 30 (1922): 247–48

Minor, H. A. "Surrender of Mahone's Division." *Confederate Veteran* 22 (1914): 312–13.

Moore, Frank. *The Rebellion Record: A Diary of American Events*. 12 vols. New York: Putnam, 1861–68.

Moore, Frank, F. Milton Willis, and Edward S. Cornell. *Fort Sumter Memorial*. New York: E. C. Hill, 1915.

Morey, E. W. "Prison Life." In *Itinerary of the Seventh Ohio Volunteer Infantry*, edited by Lawrence Wilson, 330–43. New York: Neale, 1907.

Morgan, Thomas J. "Reminiscences of Service with Colored Troops in the Army of the Cumberland." In *Personal Narratives of Events of the War of the Rebellion, Being Papers Read before the Rhode Island Soldiers and Sailors Historical Society*, third ser., 13:5–52. Providence, R.I.: The Society, 1885.

Morton, John Watson. *The Artillery of Nathan Bedford Forrest's Cavalry*. Nashville: M. E. Church, South, 1909.

Mulholland, St. Clair A. *The Story of the 116th Regiment, Pennsylvania Volunteers*. Philadelphia: McManus, 1903.

Mullen, James M. "Last Days of Johnston's Army," *Southern Historical Society Papers* 18 (1890): 97–113.

Nelson, A. H. *The Battles of Chancellorsville and Gettysburg*. Minneapolis: n.p. 1899.

New York Monuments Commission. *Final Report on the Battlefield of Gettysburg*. 3 vols. Albany, N.Y.: J. B. Lyon, 1900.

Nisbet, James Cooper. *Four Years on the Firing Line*. Chattanooga: Imperial Press, 1914.

Northrop, John Worrell. *Chronicles from the Diary of a War Prisoner*. Wichita, Kans.: Northrop, 1904.

Oates, William C. *The War between the Union and the Confederacy*. New York: Neale, 1905.

Oeffinger, John C., ed. *A Soldier's General: The Civil War Letters of Major General Lafayette McLaws*. Chapel Hill: University of North Carolina Press, 2002.

Official Records of the Union and Confederate Navies in the War of the Rebellion. 30 vols. Washington, D.C.: Government Printing Office, 1894–1922.

"On 150th Anniversary of the End of the Civil War, the South Surrenders Again," WAMU, http://wamu.org/news/15/04/09/on_150th_anniversary_of_the_end_of_the_civil_war_the_south_surrenders_again.

Page, Charles D. *History of the Fourteenth Regiment, Connecticut Vol. Infantry*. Meriden, Conn.: Horton, 1906.

Peacock, G. J. "The Surrender at Appomattox Courthouse." *Southern Historical Society Papers* 19 (1891): 268–70.

Pemberton, John C. "Terms of Surrender at Vicksburg." *Southern Historical Society Papers* 10 (1882): 406–10.

Perry, Herman H. "Appomattox Courthouse: Account of the Surrender of the Confederate States Army, April 9, 1865." *Southern Historical Society Papers* 20 (1892): 56–61.

Pollard, Edward A. *Lee and His Lieutenants*. New York: E. B. Treat, 1867.

———. *The Lost Cause*. New York: E. B. Treat, 1866.

Poriss, Gerry, and Ralph Poriss, eds. *While My Country Is in Danger: The Life and Letters of Lieutenant Colonel Richard S. Thompson, Twelfth New Jersey Volunteers*. Hamilton, N.Y.: Edmonston, 1994.

Porter, David Dixon. *The Naval History of the Civil War*. New York: Sherman, 1886.

Porter, Horace. *Campaigning with Grant*. New York: Century, 1897.

———. "Lee's Surrender at Appomattox." *Outlook* 84 (1906): 970–76.

Proceedings of the Court of Inquiry, Relative to the Fall of New Orleans. Richmond, Va.: R. M. Smith, 1864.

Public Papers of the Presidents of the United States: F. D. Roosevelt, 1943. Washington, D.C.: Government Printing Office, 1943.

Public Papers of the Presidents of the United States: Richard Nixon. Washington, D.C.: Government Printing Office, 1972.

Putnam, George Haven. *A Prisoner of War in Virginia, 1864–1865.* New York: Putnam, 1912.

Racine, Philip N. *Unspoiled Heart: The Journal of Charles Mattocks of the 17th Maine.* Knoxville: University of Tennessee Press, 1994.

Ramsay, David. *The Life of George Washington.* New York: Hopkins & Seymour, 1807.

Ransom, John L. *John Ransom's Andersonville Diary.* New York: Eriksson, 1963.

Reagan, John H. *Memoirs.* New York: Neale, 1906.

Redpath, James. *The Public Life of Capt. John Brown.* Boston: Thayer and Eldridge, 1860.

Reed, John A. *History of the 101st Regiment, Pennsylvania Veteran Volunteer Infantry, 1861–1865.* Chicago: L. S. Dickey, 1910.

Reed, Merl E. "The Gettysburg Campaign—A Louisiana Lieutenant's Eye-Witness Account." *Pennsylvania History* 30 (1963): 184–91.

Reinhart, Joseph. *August Willich's Gallant Dutchmen: Civil War Letters from the 32nd Indiana Infantry.* Kent, Ohio: Kent State University Press, 2006.

"Remarks by the President at the United States Naval Academy Commencement." May 24, 2013, https://www.whitehouse.gov/the-press-office/2013/05/24/remarks-president-united-states-naval-academy-commencement.

Reports of the Joint Committee on the Conduct of the War—Fort Pillow Massacre. Washington, D.C.: Government Printing Office, 1864.

Rice, Edmund. "Repelling Lee's Last Blow at Gettysburg." In *Battles and Leaders of the Civil War,* 3:387–90. New York: Century, 1888.

Richardson, Albert D. *A Personal History of Ulysses S. Grant.* Hartford, Conn.: American Publishing, 1868.

Ripple, Erza Hoyt. *Dancing along the Deadline: The Andersonville Memoir of a Prisoner of the Confederacy.* Novato, Calif.: Presidio, 1996.

Rowland, Dunbar. *Jefferson Davis, Constitutionalist.* 10 vols. Jackson: Mississippi Department of Archives and History, 1923.

Sabre, Gilbert. *Nineteen Months a Prisoner of War.* New York: American News, 1865.

Schofield, John M. *Forty-Six Years in the Army.* New York: Century, 1897.

Scott, Winfield. *Memoirs of Lieut.-Gen. Scott.* New York: Sheldon, 1864.

Sears, Stephen W., ed. *The Civil War Papers of George B. McClellan.* New York: Ticknor & Fields, 1989.

Semmes, Raphael. *Memoirs of Service Afloat during the War between the States.* Baltimore: Kelly, Piet, 1869.

Sheridan, Philip H. *Personal Memoirs of P. H. Sheridan.* 2 vols. New York: Charles L. Webster, 1888.

Sherman, George R. "The Negro as Soldier." In *Personal Narratives of Events in the War of the Rebellion, Being Papers Read before the Rhode Island Soldiers and Sailors Historical Society,* vol. 7, no. 7: 1–34. Providence, R.I.: The Society, 1913.

Sherman, William T. *Memoirs of General William T. Sherman.* New York: Appleton, 1875.

Simons, Ezra de Freest. *A Regimental History: The One Hundred and Twenty-fifth New York State Volunteers.* New York: E. D. Simons, 1888.

Smith, John L. *Antietam to Appomattox with 118th Penna. Vols.* Philadelphia: J. L. Smith, 1892.

Smith, William H. "The Siege and Capture of Plymouth." In *Personal Recollections of the War of the Rebellion. Addresses Delivered before the New York Commandery of the Loyal Legion of the United States,* 342–43. New York: Commandery, 1891.

Spencer, Cornelia Phillips. *The Last Ninety Days of the War in North Carolina*. New York: Watchman, 1866.

Sprague, J. T. *The Treachery in Texas*. New York: New-York Historical Society, 1862.

Stephens, Alexander H. *Constitutional View of the Late War between the States*. 2 vols. Philadelphia: National Publishing Company, 1868–70.

Stevens, John W. *Reminiscences of the Civil War*. Hillsboro, Tex.: Hillsboro Mirror Print, 1902.

Strong, George Templeton. *Diary of George Templeton Strong*. Edited by Allan Nevins and Morton Halsey Thomas. Abridged by Thomas J. Pressly. Seattle: University of Washington Press, 1988.

Strong, William E. "The Campaign against Vicksburg." In *Military Essay and Recollections: MOLLUS, Illinois Commandery*, 2:345–50. Chicago: McClure, 1894.

Styple, William B., ed. *With a Flash of His Sword: The Writings of Holman S. Melcher, 20th Maine Infantry*. Kearny, N.J.: Bell Grove, 1994.

Sutton, E. H. *Civil War Stories*. Demorest, Ga.: Banner Printing, 1910.

Tarrant, E. W. "Siege and Capture of Fort Blakely." *Confederate Veteran* 23 (1915): 457–58.

Taylor, Michael W., ed. *The Cry Is War, War, War: The Civil War Correspondence of Lts. Burwell Thomas Cotton and George Job Huntley, 34th Regiment North Carolina Troops*. Dayton, Ohio: Morningside, 1994.

Taylor, Richard. *Destruction and Reconstruction: Personal Experiences of the Late War*. New York: Appleton, 1879.

———. "The Last Confederate Surrender." *Southern Historical Society Papers* 3 (1877): 155–58.

"Terms of Capitulation." *Southern Historical Society Papers* 16 (1888): 215.

"This Hallowed Ground." *Time*, April 16, 1965.

"Thomas B. Alexander." *Confederate Veteran* 36 (1928): 388–89.

Thompson, Robert Means, and Richard Wainwright. *Confidential Correspondence of G. V. Fox, Assistant Secretary of the Navy*. 2 vols. New York: Naval History Society, 1918.

Todhunter, R. "Colonel Todhunter's Account of the Closing Events." *Confederate Veteran* 15 (1907): 398.

Tunnard, William H. *A Southern Record: The History of the Third Regiment, Louisiana Infantry*. Baton Rouge: n.p., 1866.

United States Sanitary Commission. *Narratives of Privations and Sufferings of United States Officers and Soldiers while Prisoners of War at the Hands of the Rebel Authorities*. Philadelphia: King & Baird, 1864.

Vautier, John D. *History of the 88th Pennsylvania Volunteers*. Philadelphia: Lippincott, 1894.

Vesey, M. L. "Why Fort Donelson Was Surrendered." *Confederate Veteran* 37 (1929): 369–70.

Wainwright, Charles Shiels. *A Diary of Battle: The Personal Journals of Colonel Charles S. Wainwright*. Edited by Allan Nevins. New York: Harcourt, Brace & World, 1962.

Wakelyn, Jon. L. *Southern Unionist Pamphlets and the Civil War*. Columbia: University of Missouri Press, 1999.

Wallace, Lew. "The Capture of Fort Donelson." In *Battles and Leaders of the Civil War*, 1:389–428. New York: Century, 1887.

Wallace, Robert C. *A Few Memories of a Long Life*. N.p.: R. C. Wallace, 1915.

Wallber, Albert. "From Gettysburg to Libby Prison." In *War Papers Read before the Commandery of the State of Wisconsin, Military Order of the Loyal Legion of the United States*, 4:191–200. Milwaukee, Wis.: Burdick and Allen, 1914.

The War of the Rebellion: A Compilation of the Official Records of the Union and Confederate Armies. 70 vols. Washington, D.C.: Government Printing Office, 1880–1901.

Weems, Mason Locke. *A History of the Life and Death, Virtues and Exploits of General George Washington*. Philadelphia: John Bioren, 1800.

White, W. S. "Stray Leaves from a Soldier's Journal." *Southern Historical Society Papers* 11 (1883): 552–59.

Wiatt, William E. *Confederate Chaplain William Edward Wiatt*. Lynchburg, Va.: H. E. Howard, 1994.

Wiley, William. *Civil War Diary of a Common Soldier: William Wiley of the 77th Illinois Infantry*. Edited by Terrence J. Winschel. Baton Rouge: Louisiana State University Press, 2001.

Willson, Arabella M. *Disaster, Struggle, Triumph*. Albany, N.Y.: Argus, 1870.

Wilson, Henry. "The Crittenden Compromise—A Surrender." N.p.: n.p., 1861.

Wilson, John P. *When the Texans Came: Missing Records from the Civil War in the Southwest, 1861–1862*. Albuquerque: University of New Mexico Press, 2001.

Wilson, Joseph T. *The Black Phalanx*. Hartford, Conn.: American Publishing, 1888.

Woodward, C. Vann, ed. *Mary Chesnut's Civil War*. New Haven: Yale University Press, 1981.

Wyeth, John A. *Life of General Nathan Bedford Forrest*. New York: Harper & Bros., 1899.

Young, John Preston. *The Seventh Tennessee Cavalry*. Nashville: M. E. Church, South, 1890.

Young, John Russell. *Around the World with General Grant*. New York: American News, 1879.

SECONDARY SOURCES

Ahrens, Kent. "Nineteenth Century Painting and the United States Capitol." *Records of the Columbia Historical Society* 50 (1980): 191–222.

Allen, Michael J. *Until the Last Man Comes Home: POWs, MIAs, and the Unending Vietnam War*. Chapel Hill: University of North Carolina Press, 2009.

Amis, Moses N. *The City of Raleigh: Historical Sketches from Its Foundation*. Raleigh: Edwards & Broughton, 1887.

Anders, Leslie. "The Blackwater Incident." *Missouri Historical Review* 88 (1994): 416–29.

Anderson, Jean Bradley. *Durham County*. Durham, N.C.: Duke University Press, 2011.

Andrew, Rod, Jr. *Wade Hampton: Confederate Warrior to Southern Redeemer*. Chapel Hill: University of North Carolina Press, 2008.

Armstrong, A. F. H. "The Case of Major Isaac Lynde." *New Mexico Review* 36 (1961): 1–35.

Arthur, Anthony. *General Jo Shelby's March*. New York: Random House, 2010.

Ayers, Edward L. "Not Forgotten: Remembering Appomattox." *Southern Cultures* 21 (2015): 7–12.

Baldwin, John, and Ron Powers. *Last Flag Down: The Epic Journey of the Last Confederate Warship*. New York: Crown, 2007.

Ballard, Michael B. *A Long Shadow: Jefferson Davis and the Final Days of the Confederacy*. Jackson: University Press of Mississippi, 1986.

——. *Vicksburg: The Campaign That Opened the Mississippi*. Chapel Hill: University of North Carolina Press, 2004.

Bardaglio, Peter W. *Reconstructing the Household: Families, Sex, and the Law in the Nineteenth-Century South.* Chapel Hill: University of North Carolina Press, 1995.

Barrett, John G. *The Civil War in North Carolina.* Chapel Hill: University of North Carolina Press, 1963.

Bauer, K. Jack. *Zachary Taylor: Soldier, Planter, Statesman of the Old Southwest.* Baton Rouge: Louisiana State University Press, 1985.

Bergeron, Arthur W. "The Battle of Olustee." In *Black Soldiers in Blue: African American Troops in the Civil War Era,* edited by John David Smith, 138–51. Chapel Hill: University of North Carolina Press, 2002.

Berlin, Ira, Barbara J. Fields, Steven F. Miller, Joseph P. Reidy, and Leslie F. Rowland. *Slaves No More: Three Essay on Emancipation and Civil War.* Cambridge: Cambridge University Press, 1992.

Berry, Stephen W. "Afterword: Civil War at 150." *Common-Place* 14 (2014), www.common-place-archives.org/vol-14/no-02/afterword/#.WGJgKhuLTIU.

———. *All That Makes a Man: Love and Ambition in the Civil War South.* New York: Oxford University Press, 2003.

———, ed. *Weirding the War: Stories from the Civil War's Ragged Edges.* Athens: University of Georgia Press, 2011.

Beutler, Brian. "Make the Confederacy's Defeat a National Holiday." *New Republic,* April 6, 2015, www.newrepublic.com/article/121406/civil-war-150th-anniversary-confederacy-defeat-should-be-holiday.

Blair, William A. *Cities of the Dead: Contesting the Memory of the Civil War in the South, 1865–1914.* Chapel Hill: University of North Carolina Press, 2004.

Blight, David W. *Race and Reunion: The Civil War in American Memory.* Cambridge, Mass.: Belknap Press, 2001.

Bodnar, John E. *Remaking America: Public Memory, Commemoration, and Patriotism in the Twentieth Century.* Princeton: Princeton University Press, 1994.

Bouie, Jamelle. "Remembering History as Fable." *Slate,* http://www.slate.com/articles/news_and_politics/history/2015/04/appomattox_150th_anniversary_neglects_emancipation_our_commemoration_of.html.

Bowman, Shearer Davis. *At the Precipice: Americans North and South during the Secession Crisis.* Chapel Hill: University of North Carolina Press, 2010.

Bradley, Mark L. *This Astounding Close: The Road to Bennett Place.* Chapel Hill: University of North Carolina Press, 2000.

Brands, H. W. *Lone Star Nation.* New York: Doubleday, 2004.

Broers, Michael. "'Civilized, Rationale Behaviour'? The Concept and Practice of Surrender in the Revolutionary and Napoleonic Wars, 1792–1815." In *How Fighting Ends: A History of Surrender,* edited by Holger Afflerbach and Hew Strachan, 229–38. Oxford: Oxford University Press, 2012.

Brown, Kent Masterson. *Retreat from Gettysburg: Lee, Logistics, and the Pennsylvania Campaign.* Chapel Hill: University of North Carolina Press, 2005.

Brown, Russell K. "An Old Woman with a Broomstick: General David E. Twiggs and the U.S. Surrender in Texas, 1861." *Military Affairs* 48 (1984): 57–61.

Brown, Thomas J. *Civil War Canon: Sites of Confederate Memory in South Carolina.* Chapel Hill: University of North Carolina Press, 2015.

———. *The Public Art of Civil War Commemoration.* Boston: Bedford St. Martins, 2004.

Brundage, W. Fitzhugh. *The Southern Past: A Clash of Race and Memory*. Cambridge, Mass.: Belknap Press, 2005.

Burkhardt, George S. *Confederate Rage, Yankee Wrath: No Quarter in the Civil War*. Carbondale: Southern Illinois University Press, 2007.

Busey John W., and David G. Martin. *Regimental Strengths and Losses at Gettysburg*. 4th ed. Hightstown, N.J.: Longstreet House, 2005.

Calkins, Chris. *The Final Bivouac: The Surrender Parade at Appomattox and the Disbanding of the Armies*. Lynchburg, Va.: H. E. Howard, 1988.

Campbell, Eric A. "The Key to the Entire Situation: The Peach Orchard, July 2, 1863." In *The Most Shocking Battle I Have Ever Witnessed: The Second Day at Gettysburg*, 147–210. Gettysburg, Pa.: Gettysburg National Military Park, 2008.

Campbell, William J. "Surrender in the Northeastern Borderlands of Native America." In *How Fighting Ends: A History of Surrender*, edited by Holger Afflerbach and Hew Strachan, 125–40. Oxford: Oxford University Press, 2012.

Carnahan, Burrus M. *Act of Justice: Lincoln's Emancipation Proclamation and the Law of War*. Lexington: University Press of Kentucky, 2007.

Carter, Dan. T. *When the War Was Over: The Failure of Self-Reconstruction in the South, 1865–1867*. Baton Rouge: Louisiana State University Press, 1985.

Carwardine, Richard. *Lincoln: A Life of Purpose and Power*. New York: Knopf, 2006.

Castel, Albert. *General Sterling Price and the Civil War in the West*. Baton Rouge: Louisiana State University Press, 1968.

Castel, Albert, and Thomas Goodrich. *Bloody Bill Anderson: The Short, Savage Life of a Civil War Guerrilla*. Mechanicsburg, Pa.: Stackpole, 1998.

Catton, Bruce. *A Stillness at Appomattox*. Garden City, N.Y.: Doubleday, 1953.

Chaffin, Tom. *Sea of Gray: The Around-the-World Odyssey of the Confederate Raider Shenandoah*. New York: Hill and Wang, 2006.

Childs, John. "Surrender and the Laws of War in Western Europe, 1660–1783." In *How Fighting Ends: A History of Surrender*, edited by Holger Afflerbach and Hew Strachan, 153–68. Oxford: Oxford University Press, 2012.

Cimprich, John. *Fort Pillow: A Civil War Massacre and Public Memory*. Baton Rouge: Louisiana State University Press, 2011.

Cimprich, John, and Robert C. Mainfort. "Dr. Fitch's Report on the Fort Pillow Massacre." *Tennessee Historical Quarterly* 44 (1985): 31–36.

———. "The Fort Pillow Massacre: A Statistical Note." *Journal of American History* 76 (1989): 830–37.

———. "Fort Pillow Revisited: New Evidence about an Old Controversy." *Civil War History* 28 (1982): 293–306.

Clampitt, Brad R. "The Breakup: The Collapse of the Confederate Trans-Mississippi Army in Texas, 1865." *Southwestern Historical Quarterly* 108 (2005): 498–534.

Clark, James H. *Iron Hearted Regiment*. Albany, N.Y.: J. Munsell, 1865.

Coddington, Edwin B. *The Gettysburg Campaign: A Study in Command*. New York: Scribner's, 1968.

Comstock, Rock L. *Short History, Fort Sumter*. Charleston: National Parks Service, 1956.

Conroy, James B. *Our One Common Country: Abraham Lincoln and the Hampton Roads Peace Conference of 1865*. Guilford, Conn.: Lyons Press, 2014.

Cook, Robert J. *Troubled Commemoration: The American Civil War Centennial, 1961–1965.* Baton Rouge: Louisiana State University Press, 2007.

Cook, Robert J., Kenneth Noe, Dana Shoef, Jennifer Weber, and Daniel E. Sutherland. "Historians' Forum: The American Civil War's Centennial vs. the Sesquicentennial." *Civil War History* 57 (December 2011): 380–402.

Cooling, Benjamin Franklin. *Fort Donelson's Legacy: War and Society in Kentucky and Tennessee, 1862–1863.* Knoxville: University of Tennessee Press, 1997.

Cooper, William J. *We Have the War upon Us: The Onset of the Civil War.* New York: Knopf, 2012.

Cornish, Dudley Taylor. *The Sable Arm: Negro Troops in the Union Army, 1861–1865.* New York: Norton, 1966.

Cox, Karen L. *Dixie's Daughters: The United Daughters of the Confederacy and the Preservation of Confederate Culture.* Gainesville: University of Florida Press, 2003.

Craig, Berry. *Kentucky Confederates: Secession, Civil War, and the Jackson Purchase.* Lexington: University Press of Kentucky, 2014.

Cutrer, Thomas W. *Ben McCulloch and the Frontier Military Tradition.* Chapel Hill: University of North Carolina Press, 1993.

Davis, Edwin A. *Fallen Guidon: The Forgotten Saga of General Jo Shelby's Confederal Command.* Santa Fe: Stagecoach Press, 1962.

Davis, William C. *An Honorable Defeat: The Last Days of the Confederate Government.* New York: Harcourt, 2001.

———. *Three Roads to the Alamo.* New York: HarperCollins, 1998.

De Bruhl, Marshall. *Sword of San Jacinto: A Life of Sam Houston.* New York: Random House, 1993.

Desjardin, Thomas A. *Stand Firm Ye Boys of Maine: The 20th Maine and the Gettysburg Campaign.* New York: Oxford University Press, 2009.

Dilbeck, D. H. "'The Genesis of This Little Tablet with My Name': Francis Lieber and the Wartime Origins of General Orders No. 100." *Journal of the Civil War Era* 5 (2015): 231–53.

———. *A More Civil War: How the Union Waged a Just War.* Chapel Hill: University of North Carolina Press, 2016.

Donald, David Herbert. *Lincoln.* New York: Simon & Schuster, 1995.

Donovan, James. *Blood of Heroes: The 13-Day Struggle for the Alamo and the Sacrifice That Forged a Nation.* New York: Little, Brown, 2012.

Dowd, Clement. *Life of Zebulon B. Vance.* Charlotte, N.C.: Observer, 1897.

Downs, Gregory P. *After Appomattox: Military Occupation and the Ends of War.* Cambridge, Mass.: Harvard University Press, 2015.

Downs, Jim. *Sick from Freedom: African American Illness and Suffering during the Civil War and Reconstruction.* New York: Oxford University Press, 2012.

Duberman, Martin. *Charles Francis Adams.* Boston: Houghton Mifflin, 1960.

Dugard, Martin. *The Training Ground: Grant, Lee, Sherman, and Davis in the Mexican War, 1846–1848.* New York: Little, Brown, 2008.

Dunkelman, Mark H. *Brothers One and All: Esprit de Corps in a Civil War Regiment.* Baton Rouge: Louisiana State University Press, 2004.

Dunkerly, Robert M. *The Confederate Surrender at Greensboro.* Jefferson, N.C.: McFarland, 2013.

———. *To the Bitter End: Appomattox, Bennett Place, and the Surrenders of the Confederacy.* El Dorado Hills, Calif.: Savas Beatie, 2015.

Eisenhower, John S. D. *So Far from God: The U.S. War with Mexico, 1846–1848*. New York: Random House, 1989.

Ernsberger, Don. *Also for the Glory Muster: The Story of the Pettigrew-Trimble Charge at Gettysburg*. Bloomington, Ind.: Xlibris, 2008.

Escott, Paul D. *After Secession: Jefferson Davis and the Failure of Confederate Nationalism*. Baton Rouge: Louisiana State University Press, 1978.

Eustace, Nicole. *War of 1812: War and the Passions of Patriotism*. Philadelphia: University of Pennsylvania Press, 2012.

Farber, Daniel A. *Lincoln's Constitution*. Chicago: University of Chicago Press, 2003.

Faust, Drew Gilpin. *The Creation of Confederate Nationalism: Ideology and Identity in the Civil War South*. Baton Rouge: Louisiana State University Press, 1988.

———. *This Republic of Suffering: Death and the American Civil War*. New York: Knopf, 2008.

Feis, William B. "Jefferson Davis and the 'Guerrilla Option': A Reexamination." In *The Collapse of the Confederacy*, edited by Mark Grimsley and Brooks D. Simpson, 104–28. Lincoln: University of Nebraska Press, 2002.

Fellman, Michael. *Inside War: The Guerrilla Conflict in Missouri during the American Civil War*. New York: Oxford University Press, 1989.

Ferguson, James N. *An Overview of the Events at Fort Sumter, 1842–1991*. Charleston: National Parks Service, 1991.

Ferguson, Niall. *The Pity of War*. New York: Basic Books, 1999.

Fishel, Edwin C. *Secret War for the Union: The Untold Story of Military Intelligence*. Boston: Houghton Mifflin, 1996.

Foner, Eric. *The Fiery Trial: Abraham Lincoln and American Slavery*. New York: Norton, 2010.

———. *Free Soil, Free Labor, Free Men: The Ideology of the Republican Party before the Civil War*. New York: Oxford University Press, 1970.

Foote, Lorien. "Civilization and Savagery in the American Civil War." *South Central Review* 33 (2016): 21–36.

———. *The Yankee Plague: Escaped Union Prisoners and the Collapse of the Confederacy*. Chapel Hill: University of North Carolina Press, 2016.

Foster, Gaines M. *Ghosts of the Confederacy: Defeat, the Lost Cause, and the Emergence of the New South, 1865 to 1913*. New York: Oxford University Press, 1987.

Franks, Kenny Arthur. *Stand Watie and the Agony of the Cherokee Nation*. Memphis: Memphis State University Press, 1979.

Frazier, Donald S. *Blood and Treasure: Confederate Empire in the Southwest*. College Station: Texas A&M University Press, 1995.

Freehling, William W., and Craig M. Simpson. *Secession Debated: Georgia's Showdown in 1860*. New York: Oxford University Press, 1992.

Freeman, Douglas Southall. *R. E. Lee*. 4 vols. New York: Scribner's, 1934–35.

Gallagher, Gary W. "The Dark Turn." *Civil War Times* 55 (2016): 14–16.

Gallagher, Gary W., and Kathryn Shively Meier. "Coming to Terms with Civil War Military History." *Journal of the Civil War Era* 4 (2014): 487–508.

Gannon, Barbara A. *The Won Cause: Black and White Comradeship in the Grand Army of the Republic*. Chapel Hill: University of North Carolina Press, 2011.

Gardner, Sarah E. *Blood and Irony: Southern White Women's Narrative of the Civil War, 1861–1937*. Chapel Hill: University of North Carolina Press, 2004.

Glatthaar, Joseph T. *General Lee's Army: From Victory to Collapse*. New York: Free Press, 2008.

Goodheart, Adam. *1861: The Civil War Awakening*. New York: Knopf, 2011.

Gordon, Lesley J. *A Broken Regiment: The 16th Connecticut's Civil War*. Baton Rouge: Louisiana State University Press, 2015.

———. "'Surely They Remember Me': The 16th Connecticut in War, Captivity, and Public Memory." In *Union Soldiers and the Northern Homefront: Wartime Experiences, Postwar Adjustments*, edited by Paul A. Cimbala and Randall Miller, 327–60. Bronx, N.Y.: Fordham University Press, 2002.

Greenberg, Amy S. *A Wicked War: Polk, Clay, Lincoln, and the 1846 U.S. Invasion of Mexico*. New York: Knopf, 2012.

Greenberg, Kenneth S. *Honor and Slavery*. Princeton: Princeton University Press, 1996.

Grimsley, Mark. *The Hard Hand of War: Union Military Policy toward Southern Civilians, 1861–1865*. New York: Cambridge University Press, 1995.

———. "Learning to Say 'Enough': Southern Generals and the Final Weeks of the Confederacy." In *The Collapse of the Confederacy*, edited by Mark Grimsley and Brooks D. Simpson, 40–79. Lincoln: University of Nebraska Press, 2002.

Gruber, Ira. "Yorktown: The Final Campaign of the War for American Independence." In *Between War and Peace: How America Ends Its Wars*, edited by Matthew Moten, 21–42. New York: Free Press, 2011.

Guelzo, Allen C. *Gettysburg: The Last Invasion*. New York: Vintage, 2013.

Hacker, J. David. "A Census-Based Count of the Civil War Dead." *Civil War History* 57 (2011): 307–48.

Hamilton, James J. *The Battle of Fort Donelson*. South Brunswick, N.J.: Yoseloff, 1968.

Hardin, Stephen L. *Texian Iliad: A Military History of the Texas Revolution, 1835–1836*. Austin: University of Texas Press, 1994.

Harris, William C. "The Hampton Roads Peace Conference." *Journal of the Abraham Lincoln Association* 21 (2000): 30–61.

Hartwig, D. Scott. "Guts and Good Leadership: The Action at the Railroad Cut, July 1, 1863." *Gettysburg Magazine* 1 (1989): 5–14.

———. "I Have Never Seen the Like Before: Herbst's Woods, July 1, 1863." In *This Has Been a Terrible Ordeal: The Gettysburg Campaign and First Day of Battle*, 155–96. Gettysburg, Pa.: Gettysburg National Military Park, 2005.

———. "It Struck Horror to Us All." *Gettysburg Magazine* 4 (1991): 89–100.

———. *To Antietam Creek: The Maryland Campaign of September 1862*. Baltimore: Johns Hopkins University Press, 2012.

———. "Unwilling Witness to the Rage of Gettysburg." In *The Most Shocking Battle I Have Ever Witnessed: The Second Day at Gettysburg*, 39–74. Gettysburg, Pa.: Gettysburg National Military Park, 2008.

Hattaway, Herman, and Archer Jones. *How the North Won: A Military History of the Civil War*. Urbana: University of Illinois Press, 1983.

Hauptman, Laurence M. *Between Two Fires: American Indians in the Civil War*. New York: Free Press, 1995.

Hearn, Chester G. *Mobile Bay and the Mobile Campaign: The Last Great Battles of the Civil War*. Jefferson, N.C.: McFarland, 1993.

———. *Six Years of Hell: Harpers Ferry during the Civil War*. Baton Rouge: Louisiana State University Press, 1996.

Heidler, Jeanne T. "'Embarrassing Situation': David E. Twiggs and the Surrender of United States Forces in Texas, 1861." *Military History of the Southwest* 21 (1991): 157–72.

Hess, Earl J. *Civil War Infantry Tactics: Training, Combat, and Small-Unit Effectiveness.* Baton Rouge: Louisiana State University Press, 2015.

———. *Into the Crater: The Mine Attack at Petersburg.* Columbia: University of South Carolina Press, 2010.

———. *Pickett's Charge: The Last Attack at Gettysburg.* Chapel Hill: University of North Carolina Press, 2001.

———. *The Rifle Musket in Civil War Combat: Reality and Myth.* Lawrence: University Press of Kansas, 2008.

———. *The Union Soldier in Battle: Enduring the Ordeal of Combat.* Lawrence: University Press of Kansas, 1997.

Hesseltine, William B. *Civil War Prisons: A Study in War Psychology.* Columbus: Ohio State University Press, 1930.

Heyman, Max L. *Prudent Soldier: A Biography of Major General E. R. S. Canby, 1817–1873.* Glendale, Calif.: Arthur H. Clark, 1959.

Holley, Peggy Scott. "The Seventh Tennessee Volunteer Cavalry: West Tennessee Unionists in Andersonville Prison." *West Tennessee Historical Society Papers* 42 (1988): 39–58.

Holmes, Richard. *Firing Line.* London: J. Cape, 1985.

Holzer, Howard. *Lincoln, President-Elect: Abraham Lincoln and the Great Secession Winter, 1860–1861.* New York: Simon & Schuster, 2008.

———. *Lincoln and the Power of the Press.* New York: Simon & Schuster, 2014.

Horwitz, Tony. *Midnight Rising: John Brown and the Raid That Sparked the Civil War.* New York: Henry Holt, 2011.

Hsieh, Wayne W. "Total War and the American Civil War Reconsidered: The End of an Outdated 'Master Narrative.'" *Journal of the Civil War Era* 1 (2011): 394–408.

———. *West Pointers and the Civil War: The Old Army in War and Peace.* Chapel Hill: University of North Carolina Press, 2009.

Huch, Ronald K. "Fort Pillow Massacre: The Aftermath of Paducah." *Journal of the Illinois State Historical Society* 66 (1973): 62–70.

Hurst, Jack. *Nathan Bedford Forrest: A Biography.* New York: Knopf, 1993.

Isenberg, Nancy. *Sex and Citizenship in Antebellum America.* Chapel Hill: University of North Carolina Press, 1998.

Jabour, Anya. *Scarlett's Sisters: Young Women in the Old South.* Chapel Hill: University of North Carolina Press, 2007.

Janney, Caroline E. *Burying the Dead but Not the Past: Ladies' Memorial Associations and the Lost Cause.* Chapel Hill: University of North Carolina Press, 2008.

———. *Remembering the Civil War: Reunion and the Limits of Reconstruction.* Chapel Hill: University of North Carolina Press, 2013.

———. "War over a Shrine of Peace: The Appomattox Peace Monument and Retreat from Reconciliation." *Journal of Southern History* 77 (2011): 91–118.

Johnson, Clint. *Pursuit: The Chase, Capture, Persecution, and Surprising Release of Confederate President Jefferson Davis.* New York: Citadel Press, 2008.

Johnson, Timothy D. *Winfield Scott: The Quest for Military Glory.* Lawrence: University Press of Kansas, 1998.

Johnson, Walter. "On Agency." *Journal of Social History* 37 (2003): 113–24.

Jones, James Pickett. *Yankee Blitzkrieg: Wilson's Raid through Alabama and Georgia.* Athens: University of Georgia Press, 1976.

Jordan, Weymouth T., and Gerald W. Thomas. "Massacre at Plymouth: April 20, 1864." *North Carolina Historical Review* 72 (1995): 125–97.

Josephy, Alvin M. *The Civil War in the American West.* New York: Knopf, 1991.

Jung, Patrick J. *Black Hawk War of 1832.* Norman: University of Oklahoma Press, 2008.

Kachun, Mitchell A. *Festivals of Freedom: Memory and Meaning in African American Emancipation Celebrations, 1808–1915.* Amherst: University of Massachusetts Press, 2003.

Kammen, Michael G. *Mystic Chords of Memory: The Transformation of Tradition in American Culture.* New York: Knopf, 1991.

Kerby, Robert L. *Kirby Smith's Confederacy: The Trans-Mississippi South, 1863–1865.* New York: Columbia University Press, 1972.

Klein, Maury. *Days of Defiance: Sumter, Secession, and the Coming of the Civil War.* New York: Knopf, 1997.

Knight, Wilfred. *Red Fox: Stand Watie and the Confederate Indian Nations during the Civil War Years in Indian Territory.* Glendale Calif.: A. H. Clark, 1988.

Krebs, Daniel. "Ritual Performance: Surrender during the American War of Independence." In *How Fighting Ends: A History of Surrender,* edited by Holger Afflerbach and Hew Strachan, 169–85. Oxford: Oxford University Press, 2012.

Krick, Robert. "Confederate Disaster on Oak Ridge: Failures of Brigade Leadership on the First Day at Gettysburg." In *Three Days at Gettysburg,* edited by Gary W. Gallagher, 72–108. Kent, Ohio: Kent State University Press, 1999.

Kytle, Ethan J. "Fort Sumter Sesquicentennial: Charleston Changes Her Tune." *History News Network,* April 18, 2011, http://historynewsnetwork.org/article/138511.

LeBeau, Bryan F. *Currier & Ives: America Imagined.* Washington, D.C.: Smithsonian Institution, 2001.

Lee, Wayne E. *Barbarians and Brothers: Anglo-American Warfare, 1500–1865.* New York: Oxford University Press, 2011.

Levin, Kevin M. *Remembering the Battle of the Crater: War as Murder.* Lexington: University Press of Kentucky, 2012.

Levine, Bruce C. *Confederate Emancipation: Southern Plans to Free and Arm Slaves during the Civil War.* New York: Oxford University Press, 2006.

Livermore, Thomas L. *Numbers and Losses in the Civil War in America, 1861–1865.* Bloomington: Indiana University Press, 1957.

Loewen, James W. *Lies across America: What Our Historic Sites Get Wrong.* New York: New Press, 1999.

Lowe, Richard G. "Battle on the Levee: The Fight at Milliken's Bend." In *Black Soldiers in Blue: African American Troops in the Civil War Era,* edited by John David Smith, 107–35. Chapel Hill: University of North Carolina Press, 2002.

Lowry, Thomas P. *Curmudgeons, Drunkards, and Outright Fools.* Lincoln: University of Nebraska Press, 2003.

Mackey, Robert R. *The Uncivil War: Irregular Warfare in the Upper South, 1861–1865.* Norman: University of Oklahoma Press, 2004.

Mahon, John K. *History of the Second Seminole War, 1835–1842.* Gainesville: University Presses of Florida, 1985.

Maness, Lonnie E. "A Ruse That Worked: The Capture of Union City in 1864." *West Tennessee Historical Society Papers* 30 (1976): 91–102.

Marszalek, John F. "Where Did Winfield Scott Find His Anaconda?" *Lincoln Herald* 89 (1987): 77–81.

Marvel, William. *Andersonville: The Last Depot*. Chapel Hill: University of North Carolina Press, 1994.

———. *Lee's Last Retreat: The Flight to Appomattox*. Chapel Hill: University of North Carolina Press, 2002.

———. *Mr. Lincoln Goes to War*. Boston: Houghton Mifflin, 2006.

———. *A Place Called Appomattox*. Chapel Hill: University of North Carolina Press, 2000.

Mays, Thomas D. "The Battle of Saltville." In *Black Soldiers in Blue: African American Troops in the Civil War Era*, edited by John David Smith, 200–226. Chapel Hill: University of North Carolina Press, 2002.

———. *Cumberland Blood: Champ Ferguson's Civil War*. Carbondale: Southern Illinois University Press, 2008.

McClintock, Russell. *Lincoln and the Decision for War: The Northern Response to Secession*. Chapel Hill: University of North Carolina Press, 2008.

McCullough, Gary L. *North Carolina's State Historic Sites*. Winston-Salem, N.C.: John F. Blair, 2001.

McCurry, Stephanie. *Masters of Small Worlds: Yeoman Households, Gender Relations, and the Political Culture of the Antebellum South Carolina Low Country*. New York: Oxford University Press, 1995.

McGlone, Robert E. "Forgotten Surrender: John Brown's Raid and the Cult of Martial Virtues." *Civil War History* 40 (1994): 185–201.

McKay, Gary. *Sea King: The Life of James Iredell Waddell*. Edinburgh: Birlinn, 2009.

McKnight, Brian Dallas. *Confederate Outlaw: Champ Ferguson and the Civil War in Appalachia*. Baton Rouge: Louisiana State University Press, 2011.

McPherson, James M. *Battle Cry of Freedom: The Civil War Era*. New York: Oxford University Press, 1988.

———. *For Cause and Comrades: Why Men Fought in the Civil War*. New York: Oxford University Press, 1997.

———. *Tried by War: Abraham Lincoln as Commander in Chief*. New York: Penguin Press, 2008.

Menius, Arthur C. "James Bennitt: Portrait of an Antebellum Yeoman." *North Carolina Historical Review* 58 (1981): 305–26.

Miller, Brian Craig. *Empty Sleeves: Amputation in the Civil War South*. Athens: University of Georgia Press, 2015.

———. *John Bell Hood and the Fight for Civil War Memory*. Knoxville: University of Tennessee Press, 2010.

Minton, Amy R. "Defining Confederate Respectability: Morality, Patriotism, and Confederate Identity in Richmond's Civil War Public Press." In *Crucible of the Civil War: Virginia from Secession to Commemoration*, edited by Edward L. Ayers, Gary W. Gallagher, and Andrew J. Torget, 80–105. Charlottesville: University of Virginia Press, 2006.

Missall, John, and Mary Lou Missall. *The Seminole Wars: America's Longest Indian Conflict*. Gainesville: University Press of Florida, 2004.

Mitchell, Reid. *Civil War Soldiers*. New York: Viking, 1988.

Mobley, Joe A. "Zebulon B. Vance: A Confederate Nationalist in the North Carolina Gubernatorial Election of 1864." *North Carolina Historical Review* 77 (2000): 434–54.

Moneyhon, Carl. "1865: A State of Perfect Anarchy." In *Rugged and Sublime: The Civil War in Arkansas*, edited by Mark K. Christ, 145–62. Fayetteville: University of Arkansas Press, 1994.

Moore, Kenneth Bancroft. "Fort Pillow, Forrest, and the United States Colored Troops in 1864." *Tennessee Historical Quarterly* 54 (1995): 112–23.

Mountcastle, Clay. *Punitive War: Confederate Guerrillas and Union Reprisals*. Lawrence: University Press of Kansas, 2009.

Mueller, Doris Land. *M. Jeff Thompson: Missouri's Swamp Fox of the Confederacy*. Columbia: University of Missouri Press, 2007.

Murray, R. L. *The Redemption of the "Harper's Ferry Cowards": The Story of the 111th and 126th New York Volunteers at Gettysburg*. Wolcott, N.Y.: Benedum Books, 1994.

Neal, James R. "Surrendered: The Prisoner-of-War Condition in the American Civil War." Ph.D. diss., University of Nevada-Reno, 2015.

Neely, Mark E. *The Civil War and the Limits of Destruction*. Cambridge, Mass.: Harvard University Press, 2007.

———. *The Fate of Liberty: Abraham Lincoln and Civil Liberties*. New York: Oxford University Press, 1991.

———. "Was the Civil War a Total War?" *Civil War History* 37 (1991): 5–28.

Neely, Mark E., Harold Holzer, and Gabor S. Boritt. *The Confederate Image: Prints of the Lost Cause*. Chapel Hill: University of North Carolina Press, 1987.

Nelson, Megan Kate. "'The Difficulties and Seductions of the Desert': Landscapes of War in 1861 New Mexico." In *The Blue, the Gray, and the Green*, edited by Brian Allen Drake, 34–51. Athens: University of Georgia Press, 2014.

———. *Ruin Nation: Destruction and the American Civil War*. Athens: University of Georgia Pres, 2012.

Noe, Kenneth W. *Reluctant Rebels*. Chapel Hill: University of North Carolina Press, 2010.

Nolan, Alan T. "The Anatomy of the Myth." In *The Myth of the Lost Cause and Civil War History*, edited by Gary W. Gallagher and Alan T. Nolan, 11–34. Bloomington: Indiana University Press, 2000.

———. "The Price of Honor: R. E. Lee and the Question of Confederate Surrender." *Virginia Cavalcade* 41 (1992): 124–31.

Noles, Jim. "Confederate Twilight: The Fall of Fort Blakely." *Alabama Heritage* 91 (Winter 2009): 28–37.

North Carolina Troops. 18 vols. Raleigh: North Carolina Department of Archives and History, 1966–2011.

Oakes, James. *Freedom National: The Destruction of Slavery in the United States, 1861–1865*. New York: Norton, 2013.

———. *Scorpion Sting: Antislavery and the Coming of the Civil War*. New York: Norton, 2014.

O'Connell, Edward T. "Public Commemoration of the Civil War and Monuments to Memory." Ph.D. diss., Stony Brook University, 2008.

O'Flaherty, Daniel. *General Jo Shelby: Undefeated Rebel*. Chapel Hill: University of North Carolina Press, 1954.

Parrish, T. Michael. *Richard Taylor: Soldier Prince of Dixie*. Chapel Hill: University of North Carolina Press, 1992.

Paulus, Sarah Bischoff. "America's Long Eulogy for Compromise: Henry Clay and American Politics, 1854–1858." *Journal of the Civil War Era* 4 (2014): 28–52.

Perdue, Theda. "Stand Watie's War." *American History* 50 (2015): 32–41.

Peskin, Allan. *Winfield Scott and the Profession of Arms*. Kent, Ohio: Kent State University Press, 2003.

Pfanz, Harry W. *Gettysburg: The First Day*. Chapel Hill: University of North Carolina Press, 2001.

———. *Gettysburg: The Second Day*. Chapel Hill: University of North Carolina Press, 1987.

Phillips, Jason. *Diehard Rebels: The Confederate Culture of Invincibility*. Athens: University of Georgia Press, 2007.

Phipps, Michael. "Mahan at West Point, 'Gallic Bias,' and the 'Old Army.'" In *I Ordered No Man to Go When I Would Not Go Myself: Leadership in the Campaign and Battle of Gettysburg*, 1–43. Gettysburg, Pa.: Gettysburg National Military Park, 2002.

Pickenpaugh, Roger. *Captives in Gray: The Civil War Prisons of the Union*. Tuscaloosa: University of Alabama Press, 2009.

Pierson, Michael D. *Mutiny at Fort Jackson*. Chapel Hill: University of North Carolina Press, 2008.

Pitcaithley, Dwight T. "Public Education and the National Park Service." *Perspectives on History*, November 2007, 44–45.

Potter, David M. *Lincoln and His Party in the Secession Crisis*. New Haven: Yale University Press, 1942.

Prokopowicz, Gerald J. "Word of Honor: Abraham Lincoln and the Parole System in the Civil War." In *Lincoln Reshapes the Presidency*, edited by Charles M. Hubbard, 30–51. Macon, Ga.: Mercer University Press, 2003.

Prushankin, Jeffery S. *A Crisis in Confederate Command: Edmund Kirby Smith, Richard Taylor, and the Army of the Trans-Mississippi*. Baton Rouge: Louisiana State University Press, 2005.

Quigley, Paul. *Shifting Grounds: Nationalism and the American South, 1848–1865*. New York: Oxford University Press, 2012.

Rable, George C. *The Confederate Republic: A Revolution against Politics*. Chapel Hill: University of North Carolina Press, 1994.

———. *Damn Yankees! Demonization and Defiance in the Confederate South*. Baton Rouge: Louisiana State University Press, 2015.

Rafuse, Ethan S. *Robert E. Lee and the Fall of the Confederacy, 1863–1865*. Lanham, Md.: Rowman & Littlefield, 2008.

Ramsdell, Charles W. *Reconstruction in Texas*. New York: Columbia University Press, 1910.

Reardon, Carol. "Pickett's Charge: The Convergence of History and Myth in the Southern Past." In *The Third Day at Gettysburg and Beyond*, edited by Gary Gallagher, 56–92. Chapel Hill: University of North Carolina Press, 1994.

———. *Pickett's Charge in History and Memory*. Chapel Hill: University of North Carolina Press, 1997.

———. *With a Sword in One Hand and Jomini in the Other: The Problem of Military Thought in the Civil War North*. Chapel Hill: University of North Carolina Press, 2012.

Rhodes, James F. *History of the United States*. New York: Macmillan, 1928.

Ringold, May Spencer. "William Gourdin Young and the Wigfall Mission—Fort Sumter, April 13, 1861." *South Carolina Historical Magazine* 73 (1972): 27–36.

Rister, Carl Coke. *Robert E. Lee in Texas*. Norman: University of Oklahoma Press, 1942.

Robertson, James I. *Stonewall Jackson: The Man, the Soldier, the Legend*. New York: Macmillan, 1997.

Royster, Charles. *The Destructive War: William Tecumseh Sherman, Stonewall Jackson, and the Americans*. New York: Knopf, 1991.

Rubin, Anne Sarah. *A Shattered Nation: The Rise and Fall of the Confederacy, 1861–1868*. Chapel Hill: University of North Carolina Press, 2005.

Sanders, Charles W. *While in the Hands of the Enemy: Military Prison of the Civil War*. Baton Rouge: Louisiana State University Press, 2005.

Sauers, Richard A. *The Gettysburg Campaign, June 3–August 1, 1863: A Comprehensive Bibliography*. 2nd ed. Baltimore: Butternut and Blue, 2004.

Savage, Kirk. *Standing Soldiers, Kneeling Slaves: Race, War, and Monument in Nineteenth-Century America*. Princeton: Princeton University Press, 1999.

Schivelbusch, Wolfgang. *The Culture of Defeat: On National Trauma, Mourning, and Recovery*. New York: Metropolitan Books, 2003.

Seager, Robert, II. "Henry Clay and the Politics of Compromise and Non-Compromise." *Register of the Kentucky Historical Society* 85 (1987): 1–28.

Sears, Stephen W. *Gettysburg*. Boston: Houghton-Mifflin, 2003.

———. *Landscape Turned Red: The Battle of Antietam*. New Haven: Ticknor & Fields, 1983.

Settles, Thomas Michael. *John Bankhead Magruder: A Military Reappraisal*. Baton Rouge: Louisiana State University Press, 2009.

Shackel, Paul A. *Memory in Black and White: Race, Commemoration, and the Post-Bellum Landscape*. Walnut Creek, Calif.: Altamira Press, 2003.

Shapiro, Michael. "Becoming Union Square: Struggles for Legitimacy in Nineteenth-Century New York." Ph.D. diss., University of Massachusetts-Amherst, 2010.

Sheehan-Dean, Aaron. *Why Confederates Fought: Family and Nation in Civil War Virginia*. Chapel Hill: University of North Carolina Press, 2007.

Silber, Nina. *The Romance of Reunion: Northerners and the South, 1865–1900*. Chapel Hill: University of North Carolina Press, 1993.

Silkenat, David. *Driven from Home: North Carolina's Civil War Refugee Crisis*. Athens: University of Georgia Press, 2016.

———. *Moments of Despair: Suicide, Divorce, and Debt in Civil War Era North Carolina*. Chapel Hill: University of North Carolina Press, 2011.

Simpson, Brooks D. "Continuous Hammering and Mere Attrition: Lost Cause Critics and the Military Reputation of Ulysses S. Grant." In *The Myth of the Lost Cause and Civil War History*, edited by Gary W. Gallagher and Alan T. Nolan, 147–69. Bloomington: Indiana University Press, 2000.

———. "Facilitating Defeat: The Union High Command and the Collapse of the Confederacy." In *The Collapse of the Confederacy*, edited by Mark Grimsley and Brooks D. Simpson, 80–103. Lincoln: University of Nebraska Press, 2002.

———. *Let Us Have Peace: Ulysses S. Grant and the Politics of War and Reconstruction, 1861–1868*. Chapel Hill: University of North Carolina Press, 1991.

———. *Ulysses S. Grant: Triumph over Adversity, 1822–1865*. Boston: Houghton Mifflin, 2000.

Smith, John David. "Let Us All Be Grateful." In *Black Soldiers in Blue: African American Troops in the Civil War Era*, edited by John David Smith, 1–79. Chapel Hill: University of North Carolina Press, 2002.

Smith, Mark M. *The Smell of Battle, the Taste of Siege: A Sensory History of the Civil War*. New York: Oxford University Press, 2015.

Smith, Timothy. *The Golden Age of Battlefield Preservation*. Knoxville: University of Tennessee Press, 2008.

Snyder, Charles M., ed. *Oswego County in the Civil War*. Oswego, N.Y.: Oswego County
Historical Society, 1962.

Speer, Lonnie R. *War of Vengeance: Acts of Retaliation against Civil War POWs*.
Mechanicsburg, Pa.: Stackpole Books, 2002.

Springer, Paul J., and Glenn Robins. *Transforming Civil War Prisons: Lincoln, Lieber, and the
Politics of Captivity*. New York: Routledge, 2014.

Sternhell, Yael A. *Routes of War: The World of Movement in the Confederate South*.
Cambridge, Mass.: Harvard University Press, 2012.

Stickles, Arndt M. *Simon Bolivar Buckner: Borderland Knight*. Chapel Hill: University of
North Carolina Press, 1940.

Storey, Margaret M. *Loyalty and Loss: Alabama's Unionists in the Civil War and
Reconstruction*. Baton Rouge: Louisiana State University Press, 2004.

Stout, Harry S. *Upon the Altar of the Nation: A Moral History of the American Civil War*.
New York: Viking, 2006.

Striner, Richard. "Lincoln and the Hampton Roads Conference." In *1865: America
Makes War and Peace in Lincoln's Final Year*, edited by Harold Holzer and Sara Vaughn
Gabbard, 40–51. Carbondale: Southern Illinois University Press, 2015.

Strozier, Charles. "The Tragedy of Unconditional Surrender." *MHQ* 2 (1990): 8–15.

Sutherland, Daniel E. *American Civil War Guerrillas: Changing the Rules of Warfare*. Santa
Barbara, Calif.: Praeger, 2013.

———. "Guerrillas: The Real Civil War in Arkansas." *Arkansas Historical Quarterly* 52
(1993): 257–85.

———. *A Savage Conflict: The Decisive Role of Guerrillas in the American Civil War*. Chapel
Hill: University of North Carolina Press, 2009.

Symonds, Craig L. *Lincoln and His Admirals*. New York: Oxford University Press, 2008.

Tap, Bruce. "'These Devils Are Not Fit to Live on God's Earth': War Crimes and the
Committee on the Conduct of the War, 1864–1865." *Civil War History* 42 (1996): 116–25.

Teetor, Paul R. *A Matter of Hours: Treason at Harper's Ferry*. Rutherford, N.J.: Fairleigh
Dickinson University Press, 1982.

Tetlock, Philp E., David Armor, and Randall S. Peterson. "The Slavery Debate in
Antebellum America: Cognitive Style, Value Conflict, and the Limits of Compromise."
Journal of Personality and Social Psychology 66 (1994): 115–26.

Thomas, Emory M. *The Confederate Nation, 1861–1865*. New York: Harper & Row, 1979.

Trask, Kerry A. *Black Hawk: The Battle for the Heart of America*. New York: Henry Holt,
2006.

Trefousse, Hans L. *Ben Butler: The South Called Him Beast!* New York: Twayne, 1957.

Trenerry, Walter N. "Lester's Surrender at Murfreesboro." *Minnesota History* 39 (1965):
191–97.

Tucker, Spencer. *Unconditional Surrender: The Capture of Forts Henry and Donelson*.
Abilene, Tex.: McWhiney Foundation Press, 2001.

Tunnell, Ted. "A 'Patriotic Press': Virginia's Confederate Newspapers, 1861–1865." In
Virginia at War: 1864, edited by William C. Davis and James I. Robertson Jr., 35–50.
Lexington: University Press of Kentucky, 2009.

Varon, Elizabeth R. *Appomattox: Victory, Defeat, and Freedom at the End of the Civil War*.
New York: Oxford University Press, 2014.

———. *Disunion! The Coming of the American Civil War, 1789–1859*. Chapel Hill: University
of North Carolina Press, 2008.

Vatavuk, William M. *Dawn of Peace: The Bennett Place State Historic Site*. Durham, N.C.: Bennett Place Support Fund, 1989.

Wadsworth, Richard. *Incident at San Augustine Springs: A Hearing for Major Isaac Lynde*. Las Cruces, N.Mex.: Yucca Tree Press, 2002.

Wagner-Pacifici, Robin. *The Art of Surrender: Decomposing Sovereignty at Conflict's End*. Chicago: University of Chicago Press, 2005.

Wahlstrom, Todd W. *The Southern Exodus to Mexico: Migration across the Borderlands after the American Civil War*. Lincoln: University of Nebraska Press, 2015.

Ward, Andrew. *River Run Red: The Fort Pillow Massacre in the American Civil War*. New York: Viking, 2005.

Waugh, Joan. "'I Only Knew What Was in My Mind': Ulysses S. Grant and the Meaning of Appomattox." *Journal of the Civil War Era* 2 (2012): 307–36.

———. "Ulysses S. Grant, Historian." In *The Memory of the Civil War in American Culture*, edited by Alice Fahs and Joan Waugh, 5–38. Chapel Hill: University of North Carolina Press, 2004.

Waugh, John C. *Class of 1846: From West Point to Appomattox*. New York: Warner Books, 1994.

Wert, Jeffry D. *The Sword of Lincoln: The Army of the Potomac*. New York: Simon & Schuster, 2005.

Whittington, Terry. "In the Shadow of Defeat: Tracking the Vicksburg Parolees." *Journal of Mississippi History* 4 (2002): 307–30.

Wiley, Bell Irvin. *The Life of Johnny Reb: The Common Soldier of the Confederacy*. Baton Rouge: Louisiana State University Press, 1943.

Williams, T. Harry. *P. G. T. Beauregard: Napoleon in Gray*. Baton Rouge: Louisiana State University Press, 1954.

Wills, Brian Steel. "Confederate Sun Sets on Selma." In *Yellowhammer War*, edited by Kenneth W. Noe, 71–89. Tuscaloosa: University of Alabama Press, 2013.

———. *The River Was Dyed with Blood: Nathan Bedford Forrest and Fort Pillow*. Norman: University of Oklahoma Press, 2014.

Wilson, Charles Reagan. *Baptized in Blood: The Religion of the Lost Cause, 1865–1920*. Athens: University of Georgia Press, 1980.

Wineapple, Brenda. *Ecstatic Nation: Confidence, Crisis, and Compromise, 1848–1877*. New York: HarperCollins, 2013.

Witt, John Fabian. *Lincoln's Code: The Laws of War in American History*. New York: Free Press, 2012.

Woodworth, Steven E. *Nothing but Victory: The Army of Tennessee, 1861–1865*. New York: Knopf, 2005.

Wyatt-Brown, Bertram. *The Shaping of Southern Culture: Honor, Grace, and War, 1760s–1890s*. Chapel Hill: University of North Carolina Press, 2001.

———. *Southern Honor: Ethics and Behavior in the Old South*. New York: Oxford University Press, 1982.

———. *Yankee Saints and Southern Sinners*. Baton Rouge: Louisiana State University Press, 1985.

Wynstra, Robert J. *Rashness of That Hour: Politics, Gettysburg, and the Downfall of Confederate Brigadier General Alfred Iverson*. New York: Savas Beatie, 2010.

Yuhl, Stephanie E. *A Golden Haze of Memory: The Making of Historic Charleston*. Chapel Hill: University of North Carolina Press, 2005.

Index

Hampton, Va., 278
Hampton, Wade, 229–30, 232–34, 238
Hampton Roads Peace Conference, 185–88, 192
Hancock, Winfield Scott, 125
Hardee, William J., 225
Hardman, Asa, 116–17
hard war, 161, 168–69, 180, 185, 312n1
Harpers Ferry, Va., 2, 16, 37, 55–61, 78, 94, 99, 128, 190
Harper's Ferry Cowards, 100, 124–25
Harpeth River, battle of, 144
Harris, Isham, 159, 248
Harrison, Albertis S., 289
Hart, Peter, 32
Hawkins, Isaac, 153–54, 157
Hawthorne, Nathaniel, 55
Hayden, Anson R., 130
Hays, Alexander, 125, 128–29
Henkel, David, 85
Henry, Patrick, 71
Hess, Earl, 79
Heth, Henry, 110, 114, 201
Hicks, Stephen, 154–56
Higgins, Edward, 69
Higley, Lewis, 176
Hill, A. P., 58
Hill, B. J., 240
Hitchcock, Ethan Allen, 170
Hitchcock, Henry, 232, 234
Hoffman, William, 94
Hoke, Robert F., 175–76
Holden, William Woods, 185
Holt, Joseph, 275
Home Guard, 68, 102
honor, 3–4, 6–7, 9–11, 16, 30, 34, 37, 40–42, 47, 49, 52, 55, 61, 63, 69–72, 86, 93–95, 104, 122, 125, 128, 140, 142–45, 147, 151, 157, 164–66, 169, 175, 185, 187, 193, 196–97, 209–10, 213–15, 219–21, 225–26, 228, 238, 246–47, 249–50, 252, 257, 259, 262–63, 265, 270, 274–76, 282–85, 287, 290
Hood, John Bell, 120–21, 246
Hooker, Joseph, 119
Hough, Daniel, 34–35
Houston, Sam, 13, 44

Howard, Joseph, 165
Howard, O. O., 114–15, 117
Huger, Benjamin, 91
Hull, William, 6
Humphrey, Hubert, 290
Hunter, Alexander, 97–99, 106–7
Hunter, David, 59
Hunter, Robert M. T., 185–86, 191–92
Hurst, Fielding, 152
Hurst, Samuel, 97

Iraq War, 294
Irsch, Francis, 119
Irwinville, Ga., 195, 251
Island No. 10, 91, 93, 156
Iverson, Alfred, 115, 224

Jackson, Andrew, 10–11, 43
Jackson, George, 166
Jackson, J. Warren, 118
Jackson, Miss., 145
Jackson, Tenn., 153, 159
Jackson, Thomas (Stonewall), 14, 55–60, 93, 276
Jacksonport, Ark., 2, 255–57, 263–64
James, Frank, 182
James, Jesse, 182
Janney, Caroline, 211, 270
Jefferson, Thomas, 5, 10
Jerusalem Plank Road, battle of, 180
Jesup, Thomas, 11–12
Johnson, Andrew, 230–32, 234
Johnson, Gart, 78, 216–17
Johnson, Lyndon B., 289–90
Johnson, Samuel, 178
Johnson's Island Prison, 94, 136–37, 174, 186, 216, 253, 257
Johnston, Isaac, 85
Johnston, Joseph, 55, 75, 146, 187, 193, 195, 198–99, 201, 217–18, 222–41, 245, 247, 249, 255, 257–61, 264, 279, 285, 290, 293–94
Joint Committee on the Conduct of the War, 154
Jones, Sam (Seminole), 12
Jones, Samuel (Confederate), 222, 239
Judah, Henry, 239

Printed in the USA
CPSIA information can be obtained
at www.ICGtesting.com
LVHW051653100823
754831LV00004B/373